The *Plane & Pilot* International Aircraft Directory

The *Plane & Pilot* International Aircraft Directory

Editors of Plane & Pilot *Magazine*
and Steve Werner

TAB Books
Imprint of McGraw-Hill

New York San Francisco Washington, D.C. Auckland Bogotá
Caracas Lisbon London Madrid Mexico City Milan
Montreal New Delhi San Juan Singapore
Sydney Tokyo Toronto

© 1995 by **the Editors of *Plane & Pilot* magazine and Steve Werner**.
Published by TAB Books, a division of McGraw-Hill, Inc.

pbk   5 6 7 8 9 10 FGR/FGR 9 9 8
hc   1 2 3 4 5 6 7 8 9 FGR/FGR 9 9 8 7 6 5

Library of Congress Cataloging-in-Publication Data
The Plane & pilot international aircraft directory / by the editors of
  Plane & pilot magazine and Steve Werner.
     p.   cm.
   Includes index.
   ISBN 0-07-050304-4.—ISBN 0-07-050305-2 (pbk.)
   1. Airplanes—Catalogs. 2. Airplanes—History. I. Werner,
Steve, 1950–   . II. Plane & pilot.
TL509.P56 1995
629.133'34'0296—dc20   95-8613
                                                        CIP

Acquisitions Editor: Jeff Worsinger
Editorial Team: Robert E. Ostrander, Executive Editor
                Jodi L. Tyler, Indexer
Production Team: Katherine G. Brown, Director
                 Toya Warner, Computer Artist
                 Janice Stottlemeyer, Computer Artist
                 Wanda S. Ditch, Desktop Operator
Design Team: Jaclyn J. Boone, Designer
             Katherine Stefanski, Associate Book Designer   0503052

Contents

Preface

The aircraft directory

IT HAS BEEN 14 YEARS since the editors of *Plane & Pilot* magazine have brought you an updated version of the *Aircraft Directory*. This latest edition of the *Aircraft Directory* is revised to include the up-to-date specification figures, performance data, design changes, and new models of current production aircraft. Also of special note are the greatly expanded homebuilt/kitbuilt section and sailplane/motorglider section that provide specifications, performance data, and, in many cases, pricing for aircraft in these highly expanding areas of general aviation. As with each year, more significantly interesting airplanes from the years past, as well as current aircraft developments, are added to this collection. New information on those aircraft included in this and past editions is updated when new information becomes available.

The 1995 edition of the *Aircraft Directory* includes many of the private and commercial airplanes, whether of domestic or foreign manufacture, that are in active service or currently found on the United States FAA registry. This broad category includes new and late production models, current and discontinued homebuilts, military surplus, antiques, and some foreign makes. The directory also includes a select number of classics, war birds, and prototypes that are no longer in active service in an effort to better acquaint pilots with the past so that they can appreciate the present and to pay tribute to those planes that have played such an important role in our aviation heritage.

Aviation enthusiasts will find the *Aircraft Directory* to be a portable, easy-to-use reference tool for spot-checking facts about a particular model, identifying unusual aircraft, and recognizing trends in airplane design. The directory is a thorough collection of performance data, airframe and powerplant information, historical facts, and prices to help answer the questions most commonly asked by pilots.

While the aircraft found on the following pages are mostly produced or designed in the United States, they nevertheless represent the majority of civilian aircraft in service throughout the world. This is not to say that foreign aircraft abroad do not abound, but rather that the aircraft wholly designed and produced by them amount to a relatively small number.

How to use the directory

The standard data and performance figures given for each airplane are in the following terms:

All weights are given in pounds with the gross weight representing the maximum takeoff weight and the empty weight representing the standard equipped weight. Fuel capacity is in total, not usable, U.S. gallons, and where two figures are given, they represent the standard and the standard plus optional capacities. Engines are rated in horsepower or maximum continuous horsepower (hp) for normally aspirated piston and turbocharged piston models or shaft horsepower (shp) for turboprops and pounds of thrust (lbs s.t.) in the case of jets and fanjets. Speeds are in miles per hour (mph) with cruise speeds generally computed at 75 percent power at whatever that particular aircraft's optimum operational altitude is.

The initial climb rate is in feet per minute (fpm), usually computed at sea level. The range is given in statute miles (sm), and where two figures are given, they apply to the standard and optional fuel loads. Wherever possible, range is quoted for 65- or 75-percent power at optimum altitude with reserves allowed for. Ceiling loosely refers to maximum service ceiling (all engines operating for multi-engine airplanes). Takeoff and landing distance refer to the total distance in feet needed to clear a 50-foot obstacle, unless otherwise specified as takeoff run or landing roll when only the runway length is measured (older airplanes were often rated this way).

Aircraft pricing and informational resources

Pricing information for the most popular aircraft of interest to a pilot is represented by propellers to indicate a price range. A price range has not been indicated when an aircraft is not normally privately owned (airliners), historical (too few to determine a price range), a warbird, or when no pricing information was available. Additionally, the aircraft have been grouped in appendix A according to the price range.

= under $25,000

= $25,000–$75,000

= $75,000–$150,000

= $150,000–$300,000

= over $300,000

Readers may obtain additional information about a specific aircraft by referring to appendix B, which provides the addresses for companies and individuals supplying production aircraft, homebuilt/kitbuilt aircraft, and sailplanes. In those instances where an address is not listed, the manufacturer might no longer exist or kits and plans might no longer be available. Monthly editions of *Plane & Pilot* provide updated information regarding companies and individuals mentioned in the appendix.

It is our intention that the information in this publication will provide quick answers to basic questions about the multitude of active aircraft. It is our purpose to give aviation enthusiasts an easy reference tool that is more complete than other books published on the subject and more convenient than those cumbersome volumes of aircraft data generally limited to libraries.

Introduction

ON DECEMBER 17, 1903, THE WORLD WAS CHANGED FOREVER. The events of that day on a sandy beach in Kitty Hawk, North Carolina, brought forth by two brothers from Dayton, Ohio, ushered in a new era in technology, a technology that would change the course of history, the technology of the flying machine. In 1903, the idea and experimentation of man flying was nothing new. In fact, man had been enamored with flight ever since he first saw a bird take to the skies. The trick, of course, was to devise how man could emulate the bird and take leave of the earth's surface and soar on the winds and currents of air.

In the fifteenth century, Leonardo DaVinci built models and drew working drawings for manned flying machines and helicopters. The models proved that a heavier-than-air craft could indeed ride on currents of air. In 1783, the first successfully manned hot-air balloons were brought into vogue by Jacques and Joseph Montgolfier. These two French aeronaut brothers showed the world that man could indeed rise above the Earth and travel great distances in a relatively short time. The only drawback with balloon flight soon proved to be the lack of directional controllability. Nonetheless, man could fly.

Otto Lilienthal, in nineteenth-century Germany, constructed man-controlled gliders that greatly resembled our modern hanggliders. Through his experimentation, Lilienthal proved that aircraft direction could be altered by the shifting of weight—in this case, the weight of the pilot. Gliders proved that man could indeed fly, but the real puzzle was how to get man to fly under his own controlled power. Also, to make manned flight really practical, he would have to be able to get airborne from level ground, fly to a destination, and land safely again on level ground.

Many different power supplies were tried, and many failed for one reason or another. At this point in the late nineteenth century, technological advancement in aviation began to take off, so to speak. Through their extensive experimentation, Orville and Wilbur Wright—the two brothers from Dayton who were proprietors of a bicycle shop—invented the first practical engine to power the first aeroplane. Centuries of the combined efforts of hundreds of inventors, scientists, mechanics, and dreamers finally became a reality on that windy and chilly day in December 1903.

Never in the history of man has a technology and its related sciences evolved so rapidly and in so many directions. In just 92 years, man has pushed the aviation envelope from a scant 100-yard straightline flight to putting man and machinery into space, on the Moon, and beyond. We have seen aviation and the airplane shrink our planet by closing man's travel time from place to far-off place. We have seen the airplane become an instrument of leisurely joy, of hard-fought competition, and of terrifying war and destruction. Through every one of these avenues, the airplane and its form has progressed and in some cases regressed, but it has always evolved.

Advancements have made their way through by way of necessity and by way of luck through mistake. In peacetime, aircraft design and evolution progressed as a result of competitions and sport. The will of man to go farther and faster lead aircraft development through racing and record-setting. In the early years of aviation, there was a record to be set at every turn and a world of never-ending turns. When peacetime turned to wartime, worldwide government intervention accelerated aviation technology to a head-spinning pace as the need to gain the technological upper hand was always the difference between winning and losing in a given conflict. In times of postwar peacetime, technology took the form of creative checks and balances between nations and superpowers with surveillance and intelligence becoming the thrust of direction for aviation to take. Peeking into our neighbor's backyard became a dangerous game of cat and mouse.

Through all the different avenues of advancement, the effects have ultimately trickled down to the general-aviation level where the improvements reaped have made flying available to virtually any individual with a mind to do so. Although general aviation had some rough and unsteady times from the early 1980s to the middle 1990s, its growth was stronger than ever. The homebuilt aircraft movement continued to show that even when things get tough in general aviation, pilots do almost anything to devise a way to fly within their means.

Throughout the good times and the bad times, every aspect of the airplane has advanced in leaps and bounds. Engines and power systems have evolved. Redundant systems have improved; building a better, stronger, lighter, more efficient, and safer system has become the norm. Navigational systems and avionics have become so advanced as to actually fly the aircraft themselves in order to reduce the in-cockpit workload for the pilot so that his or her attentions can be more efficiently utilized.

With the skies becoming steadily crowded, the military technology of global positioning system (GPS) was made available to all general aviators to make navigating the skies more precise, less arduous, and safer in congested airspace. To this day, the technology shows no sign of slowing and continues to move in directions never thought of before.

We editors of *Plane & Pilot* magazine have compiled the *International Aircraft Directory* to celebrate the technology of the airplane and aviation and to provide for readers an overview of aircraft history and its evolution. We say "overview" because it is not a definitive work. Of the tens of thousands of flying machines throughout history, we have only scratched the surface. We have indeed compiled the most popular and recognizable as well as the most influential designs of the twentieth century from around the world to provide a reference tool for the aviation enthusiast.

We at *Plane & Pilot* magazine hope that *The International Aircraft Directory* will become a well-read, useful, and enjoyable addition to your aviation library.

Steven E. Higginson
Features Editor

Section 1

Single-engine aircraft

The single-engine aircraft has remained throughout the history of aviation as the preeminent platform for airframe design. In the beginning, one engine was the logical choice for weight considerations. Also, engine technology was not advanced to the point of providing decent power-to-weight ratios that were attractive for the flying machines of that time. As engine power technology continued to develop, manned, powered flight and the single-engine aircraft were a natural combination as an economical and practical mode of personal transportation. For the sportsman aviator in today's world, it has remained the logical choice.

For the past decade, the economic tides of the world have fought hard against the single-engine lightplane manufacturers, and in its wake, there have been many casualties. Few have survived the wrath of regulations and recent product liability litigation. Many of the giants in the single-engine aircraft industry have been forced to cut back or even discontinue their once flourishing model lines in order to survive. Many have struggled in order to keep the industry alive and through persistence have been successful in bringing the single-engine industry back from the brink of extinction. This section is a testimonial to those who have persevered to make sure that general aviation and the single-engine industry would survive and continue the path of technological history.

AEROCAR
1949

STANDARD DATA: Seats 2. Gross wt. 2,050. Empty wt. 1,400. Fuel capacity 24. Engine 135-hp Lycoming. **PERFORMANCE:** Top mph 110. Cruise mph 100. Range 300. Ceiling 12,000. Initial climb rate 500. Takeoff run 655. Landing roll 300.

This convertible airplane/automobile was not the only attempt in the late 1940s to create a roadable aircraft, but it is probably the most familiar. It was first flown in 1949 and was originally powered by a 135-hp Lycoming that could produce 140 hp for takeoff. A Hartzell ground-adjustable prop was standard equipment. Later models utilized the 143-hp Lycoming. The first six Aerocars produced were used for demonstration purposes. The aircraft is made up of an automobile section and a flight section that includes a pair of rigidly braced wings and a tail assembly. The engine, located behind the seats, provides frontwheel drive for the automobile and powers the pusher propeller aft of the tail unit. When the flight section is detached, it can be towed by means of wheels inset in the wings. The Model I was replaced by a Model III that incorporated an improved fiberglass body and retractable wheels. The Model II was a nonroadable version that made use of the same wing and tail assembly as the Model I.

AERO COMMANDER "LARK"
1968–71

STANDARD DATA: Seats 4. Gross wt. 2,475. Empty wt. 1,532. Fuel capacity 44. Engine 180-hp Lycoming. **PERFORMANCE:** Top mph 138. Cruise mph 132. Stall mph 59. Initial climb rate 718. Range 525. Ceiling 11,000. Takeoff distance (50') 1,250. Landing distance (50') 1,280.
STANDARD DATA: Seats 4. Gross wt. 2,250. Empty wt. 1,280. Fuel capacity 44. Engine 150-hp Lycoming. **PERFORMANCE:** Top mph 142. Cruise mph 128. Stall mph 48. Range 560. Ceiling 13,000. Initial climb rate 850. Takeoff run 750. Landing roll 390.

Aero Commander, a division of North American Rockwell, introduced the Lark in April 1968. It was intended to meet the needs of both the business and the pleasure pilot for a reasonable price. Equipped with a Lycoming 180-hp engine and a fixed-pitch prop, this airplane provides rather unspectacular cruise performance and short field capability for its class. The history of the basic airframe began in 1961 when Volaircraft Incorporated received type approval for the Volaire Model 10, a three-prototype version. The production version, the Model 1050, received type certification in 1965 with four seats and 150-hp. This design was acquired by Aero Commander 100. With the merger of Aero Commander and North American Rockwell the name changed again, this time to "Darter." The Lark represents the final evolution of the line featuring a swept tail fin and rudder, a more powerful engine, detail refinements to reduce drag, and deluxe furnishing of the cabin. With the introduction of the Aero Commander 112 (subsequently Rockwell Commander 112), the Lark and Darter both went out of production in the early part of 1971.

AERO COMMANDER 200
1958–67

STANDARD DATA: Seats 4. Gross wt. 3,000. Empty wt. 1,940. Fuel capacity 80. Engine 285-hp Lycoming. **PERFORMANCE:** Top mph 235. Cruise mph 215. Stall mph 54. Range 1,060. Ceiling 18,500. Initial climb rate 1,450. Takeoff run (50') 1,200. Landing distance (50') 1,150.
STANDARD DATA: Seats 4. Gross wt. 3,000. Empty wt. 1,870. Fuel capacity 80. Engine 260-hp Continental. **PERFORMANCE:** Top mph 208. Cruise mph 204. Stall mph 55. Range 1,300. Initial climb rate 1,350. Ceiling 21,000.

The Aero Commander 200 began as a product of the Meyers Aircraft Co. In its hands, the airplane evolved from the two-place Meyers 145 to the Meyers 200 that was initially produced with a 240-hp engine. Small numbers of this model were produced until the design was acquired by Aero Commander in 1965. On the part of Aero Commander, it was an apparent move to acquire a foothold in the single-engine retractable field with a design that had already established a reputation for high performance for its size and power. During its nine years of production, the Aero Commander 200 was upgraded in horsepower from 260 hp to 285 hp. With the larger engine, the airplane had a top speed of 235 mph and a cruise speed of 215 mph. Fuel consumption was only 12 gph. Takeoff and landing distances were also minimal, and the gear was sturdy enough to extend up to speeds of 210 mph. Though the airplane was high-spirited and somewhat temperamental, it achieved a strong following for its speed and outstanding flight characteristics. An interesting modification of this design, called the Interceptor 400, was tested by the Interceptor Corp. Equipped with an AiResearch turboprop powerplant flat-rated at 400 shp, cruising speeds in excess of 280 mph were reported.

AERONCA C-2
1929

STANDARD DATA: Seats 1. Gross wt. 700. Empty wt. 426. Engine 26-hp Aeronca two-cylinder. **PERFORMANCE:** Top mph 75. Cruise mph 60. Range 200. Initial climb rate 450.

Cincinnati's Aeronautical Corp. of America debuted the Aeronca C-2 at the Los Angeles Air Races of 1929. It was the first truly lightplane to be manufactured in quantity. Despite the obvious limitations of its 26-hp engine, specifically designed for use in the company's light aircraft, performance was said to be good. Construction of the C-2 was conventional, utilizing a high-braced wing with two spruce spars and a welded steel-tube fuselage covered with fabric. Production totaled 112, including the C-2 Deluxe version, which featured a 36-hp Aeronca powerplant. The increased horsepower added about 20 mph to the C-2's top speed and cruise speed but limited its range to 175 miles.

AERONCA C-3
1934

STANDARD DATA: Seats 2. Gross wt. 1,005. Empty wt. 569. Engine 40-hp Aeronca two-cylinder. **PERFORMANCE:** Top mph 95. Cruise mph 87. Range 200. Ceiling 12,000. Initial climb rate 450.

The Aeronca C-3 was an offshoot of the C-2 Deluxe. Introduced in 1934, it was similar to the C-2 in structure but was expanded to accommodate side-by-side seating for two. The C-3 was produced in two versions. The Master was changed to

an enclosed cabin design. The Collegian retained the open cockpit styling and is easily confused with its C-2 predecessor. By this time, the production of both the engine and airframe of the Aeronca took place in Britain where several are still active. In this country, roughly 17 are still flying with the original Aeronca engine. Others in use have Lycomings and Continentals installed.

AERONCA L
1935

STANDARD DATA: Seats 2. Gross wt. 1,680. Empty wt. 1,036. Engine 70-hp Le Blond radial. **PERFORMANCE:** Top mph 115. Cruise mph 100. Initial climb rate 500.

The Aeronca L cabin monoplane was the Aeronautical Corporation of America's first attempt at constructing a low-wing side-by-side cabin airplane. It was produced in four versions: the LA with a 70-hp Le Blond, the LB using an 85-hp LeBlond, the LC using a 90-hp Warner Scarab Junior, and the LD powered by a 90-hp Lambert. The airframe of the Model L is of conventional mixed construction. The wings were built around a structure of spruce spars and ribs. The fuselage was a framework of welded steel tubing. Both the fuselage and the wings were covered with fabric. Although several Model Ls are still registered in this country, only one remains active.

AERONCA 65TC & L-3
1939

STANDARD DATA: Seats 2. Gross wt. 1,260. Empty wt. 793. Fuel capacity 12. Engine 65-hp Continental. **PERFORMANCE:** Top mph 95. Cruise mph 87. Landing mph 42. Range 225. Initial climb rate 450. Ceiling 10,000.
STANDARD DATA: (Model K) Seats 2. Gross wt. 1,040. Empty wt. 590. Fuel capacity 10. Engine 36-hp Aeronca E-113C. **PERFORMANCE:** Top mph 80. Cruise mph 70. Stall mph 35. Initial climb rate 400. Ceiling 12,500. Range 175.

The Aeronca C-3 evolved into the Aeronca K Scout in 1937. In turn, the K evolved into the SOC Chief in 1938. The latter was propelled by 50-hp Franklin or Lycoming engine options. In 1939, the 65-series appeared and featured the 65-hp Continental option. The 65-series is currently the most abundant version. The 65TC Defender, a tandem two-seat trainer, was widely used throughout the war, particularly in the Civilian Pilot Training Program. The Model L-3, the military version of the same airplane, featured a wider fuselage and larger window area to facilitate its role as an observation plane. Although provided with dual controls, the L-3 was designed to be flown from the front seat. The observer's seat might face forward or aft. Many of the planes reached civilian hands after World War II, and approximately 100 of both types are presently active.

AERONCA 7AC
CHAMPION
1945–48

STANDARD DATA: (7AC) Seats 2. Gross wt. 1,220. Empty wt. 740. Fuel capacity 13. Engine 65-hp Continental. PERFORMANCE: Top mph 95. Cruise mph 85. Stall mph 38. Initial climb rate 370. Range 270. Ceiling 12,500. Takeoff distance (50') 632. Landing distance (50') 885.
STANDARD DATA: (7AC) Seats 2. Gross wt. 1,300. Empty wt. 810. Fuel capacity 18.5. Engine 85-hp Continental. PERFORMANCE: Top mph 102. Cruise mph 92. Stall mph 44. Initial climb rate 750. Range 315.
STANDARD DATA: (7EC) Seats 2. Gross wt. 1,450. Empty wt. 820. Fuel capacity 18.5–24. Engine 90-hp Continental. PERFORMANCE: Top mph 135. Cruise mph 100. Stall mph 40. Initial climb rate 315.

Though similar to the prewar L-3, the Champion is in reality a tandem version of the Chief series. The original Champ, which first flew in 1944, was powered by a 65-hp Continental engine and was designated the 7AC. The design proved to be popular, and Aeronca increased the plane's power rating to 85 hp before the Champion Aircraft Corp. acquired the tooling and rights to the design in 1951. Over 10,000 Model 7s were turned out by Aeronca between 1946 and 1951. In 1955, the Champion firm reinstituted production of the 90-hp version, the Model 7EC Traveller. Production continued with minor refinements until 1964 when production tapered off in favor of the 7ECA, a further improved version of the original airframe. Over 3,500 of the original Model 7s are still active.

AERONCA 11AC/11CC
1938–46

STANDARD DATA: (Chief) Seats 2. Gross wt. 1,155. Empty wt. 675. Fuel capacity 12. Engine 65-hp Lycoming. PERFORMANCE: Top mph 105. Cruise mph 95. Stall mph 37. Initial climb rate 600. Ceiling 14,000. Range 240.
STANDARD DATA: (Super Chief) Seats 2. Gross wt. 1,350. Empty wt. 820. Fuel capacity 23. Engine 85-hp Continental. PERFORMANCE: Top mph 110. Cruise mph 97. Stall mph 43. Initial climb rate 650. Ceiling 14,500. Range 370. Takeoff (50') 620. Landing (50') 860.

After World War II, the Chief was introduced as the Model 11 AC. It was a variation of the Model 7 Champion and differed primarily by having increased fuselage width to permit side-by-side seating and a lowered cowling line to permit better visibility. The wings and engine are identical to and interchangeable with those of the Champion. The 11AC was powered by a 65-hp Continental. A further improvement on the Chief was designated the 11CC Super Chief and was powered by an 85-hp Continental. It featured new balanced elevator surfaces to meet new trim requirements called for in the Civil Air Regulations. Its cruise speed was 95 mph, and its climb rate was 600 fpm. The Chief is the version that is still present in the greatest numbers. The plane is quite popular, with over 1,000 of the various designations currently active.

AERONCA 15AC
"SEDAN"
1948–50

STANDARD DATA: Seats 4. Gross wt. 2,050. Empty wt. 1,150. Fuel capacity 40. Engine 145-hp Continental. PERFORMANCE: Top mph 120. Cruise mph 105. Stall mph 53. Initial climb rate 650. Range 430. Ceiling 12,400.
The last civilian airplane to be produced by the Aeronca Manufacturing Corp., the 15AC Sedan, was also Aeronca's first four-seater airplane. A prototype appeared in 1947, and production began in 1948. The Sedan soon became a familiar sight at civilian fields. A large number of Sedans were built, and over 200 of them are still active today. It featured an all-metal construction with a metal-skinned single-spar wing and fabric-covered, welded, steel-tube fuselage. Optional Franklin

AERONCA 15AC "SEDAN"

165-hp engines were fitted into a few 15AC Sedans. Another option put the Aeronca on floats, and that version was called the S15AC.

AEROSPATIALE "TAMPICO"

STANDARD DATA: Seats 4. Gross wt. 2,332. Empty wt. 1,428. Fuel capacity 40. Engine 160-hp Lycoming O-320-D2A. **PERFORMANCE:** Top mph 127. Cruise mph 122. Initial climb rate 738. Ceiling 11,000. Range 505. Takeoff distance (50') 1,706. Landing distance (50') 1,378.

One of the most prolific general aircraft manufacturers in recent years has been Aerospatiale General Aviation. Its "Caribbean Series" of private and training aircraft has sold in tremendous numbers in recent years and has shown good and reliable performance. The Tampico Club is Aerospatiale's entry or training level airplane and has been widely accepted as a viable training platform here in the United States. With 160 hp, the Tampico doesn't exactly burn up the skies, but it does supply plenty of power to haul around two average couples and 70 pounds of baggage on full fuel. Because of the Aerospatiale's exclusive forward positioning of the vertical stabilizer and the rear-mount horizontal stabilizer, the Tampico can handle up to 25-mph crosswinds without a problem.

AEROSPATIALE "TBM 700"
1992–95

STANDARD DATA: Seats 6. Gross wt. 5,911. Empty wt. 3,282. Fuel capacity 298 Jet A1-JP4-JP5. Engine 700-shp Pratt & Whitney PT6 A 40/1 turboprop. **PERFORMANCE:** Top mph 345. Cruise mph 288. Initial climb rate 2,300. Ceiling 30,000. Range 2,000.

The TBM 700 is an international joint venture development by two of general aviation's aircraft manufacturing leaders. Mooney Aircraft Corporation and Aerospatiale General Aviation combined their resources to bring the most versatile and most advanced single-engine aircraft into the business aviation marketplace. The TBM 700 is a pressurized cabin-class turboprop that is capable of a 300-knot cruise at 25,000 ft. With a cabin pressure differential of 6.2 psi, which translates to a cabin altitude of only 6,400 ft., the TBM 700 has one of the most efficient pressurization systems available in general aviation. To date, ground speeds in excess of 440 knots have been recorded, which makes the TBM 700 the fastest single-engine, turboprop available today.

AEROSPATIALE "TOBAGO"/ "TOBAGO XL"

STANDARD DATA: Seats 4. Gross wt. 2,535. Empty wt. 1,532; (XL) 1,576. Fuel capacity 55.5. Engine (std.) 180-hp Lycoming O-360-A1AD; (XL) 200-hp Lycoming IO-360-A1B6. **PERFORMANCE:** Top mph 147; (XL) 161. Cruise mph 143; (XL) 150. Initial climb rate 787; (XL) 940. Ceiling 13,000. Range 580; (XL) 648. Takeoff distance (50') 1,657; (XL) 1,558. Landing distance (50') 1,509; (XL) 1,475.

The fixed-gear 180-hp Tobago and 200-hp Tobago XL are in the middle of the Aerospatiale line. Designed as medium-performance cross-country cruisers, both Tobagos possess a good combination of speed, simplicity, luxury, and efficiency. All of the "Caribbean series" aircraft are noted for having extremely spacious and comfortable cabins, and the attention to ergonomic design is well thought out. Access to the cockpit is gained through two gull-wing doors on either side of the fuselage. Both aircraft perform reasonably in and out of short-field situations.

AEROSPATIALE "TRINIDAD/ TRINIDAD TC"

STANDARD DATA: Seats 4. Gross wt. 3,086. Empty wt. 1,763; (TC) 1,850. Fuel capacity 86. Engine 250-hp Lycoming IO-540 (TC) 250-hp Lycoming TIO-540. **PERFORMANCE:** Top mph 192; (TC) 230. Cruise mph 189; (TC) 215. Initial climb rate 1,200; (TC) 1,126. Ceiling 20,000; (TC) 25,000. Range 966; (TC) 962. Takeoff distance (50') 2,099; (TC) 1,953. Landing distance (50') 1,772; (TC) 1,750.

At the top of the Aerospatiale TD line is the Trinidad and Trinidad TC (turbocharged), which combine many of the features found in the lesser-appointed "Caribbean series" aircraft. The biggest differences are retractable landing gear and horsepower plus creature comforts such as avionics, soundproofing, and trim packages. Of course, with the higher horsepower and the addition of retracts comes an increase in gross weight, useful load, and climb rate. Comfort and luxury levels are elevated, and cruise and max speed are substantially increased. The Trinidad can handle four full-sized adults and carry 143 pounds of luggage to boot. The combination of speed, comfort, roominess, great visibility, and sleek design make the Trinidad an exceptional cross-country machine.

ALL AMERICAN "ENSIGN"
1945

STANDARD DATA: Seats 2. Gross wt. 1,150. Empty wt. 900. Engine 85-hp Continental. **PERFORMANCE:** Top mph 125. Cruise mph 112. Initial climb rate 700. Ceiling 14,000. Range 400.

All American Aircraft, Inc., originally specialized in subcontract work but eventually designed and built the two-place Ensign. The plane subsequently took to the air for the first time in 1945. The original plans called for engines ranging from 85 to 125 hp. Seating was side-by-side fashion under an unusually large, blown plexiglass canopy on the prototype. Full dual controls were optional. The Ensign was of all-metal construction with a semimonocoque fuselage with low wings and fixed landing gear. Few models are still active.

AMERICAN CHAMPION "SCOUT"
1993–95

STANDARD DATA: Seats 2. Gross wt. 2,150. Empty wt. 1,315. Fuel capacity 35–70. Engine 180-hp Lycoming O-360. **PERFORMANCE:** Top mph 141. Cruise mph 135. Initial climb rate 1,420. Ceiling 16,500. Range 465–940. Takeoff distance (50') 650. Landing distance (50') 1,245. WRITE TO: American Champion Aircraft, P.O. Box 37, Rochester, WI 53167.

American Champion became somewhat of a legend when it rescued the Bellanca Super Decathlon from extinction. To follow suit, American Champion has reintroduced the Scout with some major improvements over the older Bellanca 8GCBC model. At the top of the improvement list is an all-new aluminum spar-and-rib wing. This has done away with

the rot and moisture-damage-prone wood-structure version and has also reduced overall wing deflection under load. Also upgraded are the crack-prone landing gear U-bolts and the addition of 30 more horsepower. These improvements have turned an already good workhorse into a high-versatility utilitarian. With the addition of 14 inches of flap surface-length and nine-inch tundra tires, the Scout has exceptional short-field capability in or out of the rough.

AMERICAN CHAMPION "CITABRIA EXPLORER"
1994–95

STANDARD DATA: Seats 2. Gross wt. 1,650/1,800. Empty wt. 1,200. Fuel capacity 35. Engine 160-hp Lycoming O-320-D2A. **PERFORMANCE:** Top mph 135. Cruise mph 120. Initial climb rate 1,345. Ceiling 18,000. Range 570. Takeoff distance (50') 457. Landing distance (50') 690. WRITE TO: American Champion Aircraft, P.O. Box 37, Rochester, WI 53167.

After rescuing the Bellanca Super Decathlon from extinction, American Champion resurrected a new and improved Scout. The natural progression was then to bring back the Citabria in order to make the entire aircraft line complete. American Champion has incorporated major improvements into the old Bellanca 7GCBC model. These new additions include 10 extra horsepower and an all-new aluminum-spar-and-rib wing. This new structural wing design has done away with the rot and moisture-damage-prone wood structure version and has reduced overall twist and deflection under load. This makes for a much more solid and precise flying craft.

AMERICAN EAGLE
1925

STANDARD DATA: Seats 3. Gross wt. 2,057. Empty wt. 1,227. Engine 90-hp Curtiss eight-cylinder, water-cooled. **PERFORMANCE:** Top mph 101. Cruise mph 85. Landing mph 30. Initial climb rate 575. Range 425. Ceiling 12,000.

The American Eagle Aircraft Corporation was established in 1925. Its president was E.E. Porterfield, who later founded the Porterfield Aircraft Corp. The American Eagle open-cockpit, three-seat biplane was powered by a 90-hp, water-cooled Curtiss engine; its radiator was fitted under the fuselage and featured adjustable shutters. A later model of the biplane was powered by a 100-hp Kinner five-cylinder air-cooled radial engine. The three occupants are seated with one in the rear seat and two side-by-side in the front seat. Its construction made use of wooden wings and a steel-tube fuselage. It originally sold for $2,995.

AMERICAN EAGLECRAFT "EAGLET"
1929–66

STANDARD DATA: (1930) Seats 2. Gross wt. 922. Empty wt. 509. Engine 45-hp Szekely, three-cylinder radial. **PERFORMANCE:** Top mph 90. Cruise mph 75. Landing mph 25. Initial climb rate 700. Ceiling 14,500.
STANDARD DATA: (1965) Seats 2. Gross wt. 1,050. Empty wt. 638. Engine 50-hp Continental. **PERFORMANCE:** Top mph 92. Cruise mph 75. Landing mph 28. Initial climb rate 700. Range 225. Ceiling 14,500.

The Eaglet, a light two-seat monoplane, endured several changes in ownership during its lifetime. It was originally built by the American Eagle Aircraft Corp. In 1931, its production was taken over by the American Eagle-Lincoln Aircraft Company when its parent company merged with the Lincoln Aircraft Company. In the same year, the company changed its name to the Victor H. Roose Aircraft Co. The Roose company continued the production of the Eaglet powered by a Szekely radial engine. Its braced high-wing structure was of the conventional wooden two-spar type with fabric covering. The fuselage utilized a rectangular structure of welded steel tubes and was also covered with fabric. Its single large cockpit had room for two to sit in tandem fashion with dual controls. The Eaglet's production was taken over by the American Eaglecraft Co. in the 1960s. The company built an aircraft that was basically a modernized version of the famous Eaglet of the 1930s.

ANDERSON GREENWOOD
1950

STANDARD DATA: Seats 2. Gross wt. 1,400. Empty wt. 850. Fuel capacity 23. Engine 90-hp Continental. **PERFOR-**

MANCE: Top mph 120. Cruise mph 110. Ceiling 19,000. Initial climb rate 750. Landing speed 49.

The Anderson Greenwood enjoyed an extremely short production life. First produced in 1950, only four aircraft were completed before production was terminated. Today, only two are active. The twin-boom tail assembly and pusher design of the Anderson Greenwood made for easy cabin entry (like that of an automobile), propeller safety, and excellent visibility. The aircraft was designed in the late 1940s by three engineers, Anderson, Greenwood, and Slaughter, the latter being left out of the plane's name for obvious reasons. Cessna later imitated the Anderson Greenwood's design with the one-time experimental XMC. Occupants are seated in side-by-side fashion, and the cockpit has dual controls. There is a door on each side of the cabin.

ARROW SPORT F
1936

STANDARD DATA: Seats 2. Gross wt. 1,675. Empty wt. 1,172. Fuel capacity 20. Engine 82-hp Ford V-8. **PERFORMANCE:** Top mph 100. Cruise mph 95. Stall mph 38. Initial climb rate 700. Ceiling 12,000. Range 300.

The Arrow Sport F came about when the Bureau of Air Commerce awarded the Arrow Aircraft and Motor Corp. a contract to design and build a lightplane that could be powered by a modified eight-cylinder automobile engine. It was the fourth such airplane to be ordered by the Development Section to investigate the possibilities of using cheap, mass-produced automobile engines. The resulting Arrow Sport F (or V-8) was a side-by-side monoplane of mixed construction with a two-spar fabric-covered wing and a fabric-covered steel-tube fuselage. It was available in three models: "The Master," which was a standard open-cockpit type; "The Master Coupe," which was fitted with a coupe top; and the "De Luxe Coupe," which had a deluxe finish and was fitted with blind-flying instruments, wheel pants, and other accessories. The engine chosen was a converted Ford V-8 air-cooled powerplant. Several Arrow Sport Fs are still registered.

AUSTER
1942–68

STANDARD DATA: Seats 2. Gross wt. 2,200. Empty wt. 1,480. Fuel capacity 19. Engine 145-hp de Havilland Gipsy Major. **PERFORMANCE:** Top mph 122. Cruise mph 107. Stall mph 34. Initial climb rate 660. Range 315. Ceiling 12,000. Takeoff run 375. Landing roll 270.

The Auster was a continuation of the British Taylorcraft Model D, which was in turn produced under license from Taylorcraft in the United States. The first Austers were produced in 1942 as air observation-post monoplanes powered by 130-hp Gipsy Major engines. Later versions were fitted with various powerplants including: 130-, 160-, and 180-hp Lycomings; 75-hp Continental; 145-hp Gipsy Major; and 100-hp Blackburn Cirrus Minor. Most had accommodations for two seated in tandem fashion, but some were converted to three- and four-seaters. In 1962, Auster Aircraft, Ltd. was absorbed into Beagle Aircraft, Ltd. and became Beagle Auster. The Husky was introduced in 1960 with a 160-hp Lycoming and then in 1962 with a 180-hp Lycoming. The Terrior, a redesigned version of the early MK 6, was produced in 1961 with the same 145-hp de Havilland powerplant.

BEAGLE "PUP"
1968–71

STANDARD DATA: Seats 2–4. Gross wt. 1,900. Empty wt. 1,090. Fuel capacity 29–41. Engine 150-hp Lycoming. **PERFORMANCE:** Top mph 139. Cruise mph 129. Stall mph 56. Initial climb rate 840. Range 417–605. Ceiling 14,000. Takeoff distance (50') 1,350. Landing distance (50') 1,430.

An aerobatic lightplane, the Pup was built by Beagle Aircraft in England. The Pup was sold in three models: the Pup-100, -150, and -180. The Pup-100 model carries two seats and two optional children's seats. It is powered by a 100-hp Rolls-Royce/Continental four-cylinder engine. Production of the Pup-100 began in February 1968. The Pup-150 is quite similar to the Pup-100. The fuselage is only three inches longer while wingspan dimensions of the low-wing tricycle-gear airplane remain the same. A 150-hp Lycoming engine allows optional seating for four. The Pup-150 also offered a larger 34-Imperial-gallon fuel tank as opposed to the standard 24-Imperial-gallon tank installed as standard equipment in the -100 and -150 models. A large rudder on the -150 allows full aerobatics including unlimited spinning. The Pup-180 is also very similar to the Pup-100 but has a full four seats and is fitted with a 180-hp four-cylinder Lycoming engine. Many of the Pup-180s produced were exported.

BEECHCRAFT "STAGGERWING"
1932–48

STANDARD DATA: (G-17S) Seats 4–5. Gross wt. 4,250. Empty wt. 2,800. Fuel capacity 170. Engine 450-hp Pratt & Whitney Wasp Junior. **PERFORMANCE:** Top mph 212. Cruise mph 201. Stall mph 60. Initial climb rate 1,500. Ceiling 20,000. Range 1,300. Takeoff distance (50') 1,130. Landing distance (50') 980.

One of the all-time classic airplanes produced in this country is the Beech Staggerwing. The original version of the Model 17 was first flown in 1932 and was powered by a 420-hp Wright Whirlwind. The next preproduction model was fitted with a 690-hp Wright Cyclone, but although the basic design would appear to give stable flight characteristics, the horsepower was excessive, resulting in "porpoising" due to the short fuselage. The first production model, built from 1934 to 1936, was the B17 powered by a 285-hp Jacobs (B17B), a 285-hp Wright (B17E), a 225-hp Jacobs (B17L), or a 420-hp Wright (B17R). In fact, throughout the Staggerwing's production, no less than eight different engines ranging from 225 hp to 690 hp were used. The most popular model was the D17S with a 420-hp Pratt & Whitney R-985 Wasp Junior nine-cylinder air-cooled radial engine built from 1937 to 1945. The C17 was produced from 1936 to 1937; the E17 was built from 1937 to 1944; the F17 was built for the military from 1938 to 1944; and the last in the series was the G17 built from 1946 to 1948.

An early refinement of this classic five-seater was the installation of the retractable landing gear system, but the most significant feature was the negative stagger of the wings. There are many reasons for this design, beginning with the fact that automatic stability in a stall is achieved because the lower wing stalls first, since it's in a forward position, lowers the nose of the airplane before the upper wing has a chance to stall. The upper wing retains its lift, and that wing's position above the center of gravity provides pendulous stability at stall speeds. Additionally, the negative stagger permits good pilot visibility to the side and back and allows for a flat bottom on the fuselage, which enables belly landings to be made without any possibility of nosing over. Cabin doors can be entered without interference from the lower wing, and servicemen can stand on the lower leading wing to reach the fuel ports in the upper wing.

After World War II, approximately 20 G17 models were built and sold new for $29,000. They were fitted with enclosed gear fairings, cowl flaps, a longer windshield, larger vertical fin, and the engine was moved forward 12 inches. At 9,700 feet, pulling 65 percent power, the G17 exceeds 200 mph. Most of the time it cruises at 53 percent power at 185 mph, burning around 22 gph with its 450-hp radial. Six fuel tanks (two in the upper wing, two in the lower wing, one forward fuselage tank, and one rear fuselage tank) carry 179 gallons to yield a 7-hour endurance or 1,300-mile range. A total of 781 Staggerwings were built, of which 353 were commercial and 428 were for the military. About 250 exist today with 150 flying. More than 50 percent are owned by airline pilots.

BEECHCRAFT "SKIPPER" 1979–81

STANDARD DATA: Seats 2. Gross wt. 1,675. Empty wt. 1,100. Fuel capacity 30. Engine 115-hp Lycoming. **PERFORMANCE:** Top mph 122. Cruise mph 121. Stall mph 54. Initial climb rate 720. Ceiling 12,900. Takeoff distance (50') 1,280. Landing distance (50') 1,313. Range 447.

Originally designated the PD 28'S, this single-engine trainer was first delivered in early 1979. A low-wing T-tail model, it was powered by a four-cylinder Lycoming engine rated at 115 hp at 2,700 RPM. The Skipper's canopy-type cabin gives the instructor and student pilot optimum, all-around visibility, while both left and right doors provide for convenient entry. An external tunnel on the bottom of the fuse-lage houses primary controls and makes for additional cabin room, as well as allowing for easy maintenance.

A new concept in airfoil design was utilized by the Skipper. Its airfoil section is an outgrowth of NASA's high-speed, super-critical airfoil technology and provides a lower drag, higher lift capability. The T-tail configuration places the horizontal stabilizer above the slipstream in undisturbed air to give smoother flight and more positive control during landing maneuvers. The Skipper is the third Beechcraft T-tail model, following the Super King Air and Duchess. A substantial portion of its construction is bonded metal, including the lower cabin section of the fuselage, the entire wing, the leading edge of the vertical stabilizer, the trim tabs, and the rudder.

The landing gear is a low-maintenance, spring system designed for sturdiness and utility. Control response is su-

perbly balanced, and the ailerons are quite frisky in all speed ranges right down to the stall. Stalling the Skipper is almost fun. The wings give lots of prestall buffet to let you know that it is about to quit flying. For cross-country flights, the 29 gallons of usable fuel combine with a 65-percent power setting to yield a 4.6-hour endurance. Only 312 of these two-place trainers were built before production was halted abruptly in 1981.

BEECHCRAFT SPORT 150 1966–78

STANDARD DATA: (Sport) Seats 2–4. Gross wt. 2,150. Empty wt. 1,423. Fuel capacity 57. Engine 150-hp Lycoming. **PERFORMANCE:** Top mph 127. Cruise mph 123. Stall mph 57. Initial climb rate 680. Ceiling 11,650. Range 622. Takeoff distance (50') 1,635. Landing distance (50') 1,693.
STANDARD DATA: (Sport III) Seats 2–4. Gross wt. 2,350. Empty wt. 1,365. Fuel capacity 60. Engine 150-hp Lycoming. **PERFORMANCE:** Top mph 140. Cruise mph 131. Stall mph 55. Initial climb rate 740. Ceiling 11,900. Range 883. Takeoff distance (50') 1,255. Landing distance (50') 1,220.

Primarily designed as a two-place trainer, the Sport III was introduced in 1965 along with the Super III as a complement to the existing Musketeer A23/Custom III. It was powered by a 150-hp Lycoming engine turning a fixed-pitch prop and could be outfitted with an optional rear seat for two additional passengers but not without a loss in maximum range. With four adults (and no baggage aboard) the range was reduced by more than half due to fuel weight limitations. The Sport III was also available in an aerobatic version.

Like all Musketeers, the Sport made use of a honeycomb wing structure and bonded skins that reduce rivet-head drag and add to the plane's sleek appearance. In 1972, Beech changed the names of its other Musketeers but retained the Sport. The term Musketeer was dropped and the line of light Beechcrafts was known as the Aero Center line. Later, fuel capacity in all models was increased by five gallons and for the first time all three Aero Center models could be equipped with EdoAire Mitchell Century III autopilots. In 1979, this 150-hp version of the original Musketeer design was replaced by the Skipper 77 as Beechcraft's trainer model in its Aero Center line.

BEECHCRAFT CUSTOM 180 "SUNDOWNER" 1962–83

STANDARD DATA: (Sundowner) Seats 4. Gross wt. 2,450. Empty wt. 1,505. Fuel capacity 57. Engine 180-hp Lycoming.

PERFORMANCE: Top mph 141. Cruise mph 127. Stall mph 59. Initial climb rate 792. Ceiling 12,600. Range 670. Takeoff distance (50') 1,955. Landing distance (50') 1,484.
STANDARD DATA: (Musketeer Custom III) Seats 4. Gross wt. 2,450. Empty wt. 1,365. Fuel capacity 60. Engine 165-hp Lycoming. **PERFORMANCE:** Top mph 146. Cruise mph 138. Stall mph 58. Initial climb rate 728. Ceiling 11,870. Range 906. Takeoff distance (50') 1,460. Landing distance (50') 1,260.

The first of Beech's "Three Musketeers" was introduced to the flying public in 1962 as a four-place, 160-hp Model 23. More than 500 of these 23s had been sold when a redesigned model, the A-23, went into production in 1964. The A-23, powered by a 165-hp fuel-injected Continental engine, had an increased landing flap angle and a restyled interior. This Musketeer became the Custom III in 1966 when it was joined by the Super III and the Sport III. An aerobatic version of the Musketeer Sport III joined the fleet in 1968, and an aerobatic version of the Custom made its debut in 1969. Beech redesigned the Musketeer fuselage in 1970, giving it rounded sides and more cabin room. The panel was improved extensively and a third side window was added. When names were changed in 1972, the Custom became the Sundowner. Like other models, the Sundowner is also available with an autopilot, and its useful fuel has been boosted to 57 gallons. This extra gasoline translates into greater range and 30 pounds of additional useful load. The Sundowner is equipped with a fixed-pitch propeller and nonretractable landing gear. An Aerobatic version was available and approved for rolls, Immelmann turns, loops, spins, chandelles, and the like.

BEECHCRAFT "SIERRA"/"SUPER"/ "SUPER 200" 1966–83

STANDARD DATA: (Sierra) Seats 6. Gross wt. 2,750. Empty wt. 1,701. Fuel capacity 57. Engine 200-hp fuel-injected Lycoming. **PERFORMANCE:** Top mph 163. Cruise mph 158. Stall mph 69. Initial climb rate 927. Ceiling 15,385. Range 744. Takeoff distance (50') 1,561. Landing distance (50') 1,462.
STANDARD DATA: (Super III) Seats 4. Gross wt. 2,450. Empty wt. 1,365. Fuel capacity 60. Engine 200-hp Lycoming. **PERFORMANCE:** Top mph 158. Cruise mph 150. Stall mph 61. Initial climb rate 880. Ceiling 14,850. Range 823. Takeoff distance (50') 1,380. Landing distance (50') 1,300.
The classiest of the Musketeers in 1966 was the Super III with 200 hp, six seats optional, a constant-speed prop, and nonretractable landing gear. In 1970, a retractable version was added to the Musketeer line, the Super R. Both models were continued through the next year, when the fixed-gear model

was dropped. As part of the Aero Center line, the 200-hp retractable version became known as the Sundowner. The name changes and the "cleaning up" of the Musketeer line was all part of a major corporate redirection by Beech management to devote more attention to the small airplanes. Beech Aero Centers were set up around the country, franchised just to sell the Sport, Sundowner and Sierra. More recent Sierras benefit from increased useful fuel, an optional autopilot, a larger diameter propeller, and wheel well fairings. The result is increased range, a greater rate of climb, and a higher cruise speed and service ceiling.

BEECHCRAFT T-34 MENTOR 1953–58

STANDARD DATA: Seats 2. Gross wt. 2,950. Empty wt. 2,156. Fuel capacity 50. Engine 225-hp Continental. **PERFORMANCE:** Top mph 189. Cruise mph 173. Stall mph 53. Initial climb rate 1,120. Range 975. Ceiling 20,000. Takeoff distance (50') 1,200. Landing distance (50') 960.

An outstanding buy in a military surplus aircraft, when you can find one, is the Beech T-34 Mentor. Built originally for the U.S. Air Force and Navy pilot training programs, a few are found now in civilian life. In Japan, the Fuji Company built 176 T-34s for Japanese and Philippine military forces. The Canadian Car and Foundry produced 125 Mentors, and an additional 75 were assembled in Argentina. The tandem twoseaters are today highly prized for civilian use since they are fully aerobatic if all FAA maintenance advisory bulletins have been followed.

The Mentor makes wide use of standard parts from the Beech Bonanza. The landing gear was designed to survive the hard simulated carrier landings practiced by student pilots. Mentors are often found in military flying clubs and, due to top military maintenance, are usually in top condition. If you can find a T-34 with all airplane logs complete, you're no doubt getting an excellent plane for your money. Under a U.S. Navy development program, Beech has upgraded T-34 Mentors to turbine-powered YT-34s. Using only 400-hp from the 715-hp turbine engine, the modified aircraft have exceeded 275 mph. The ultimate objective was to provide all-new turbine-powered aircraft in the Navy pilot training program.

BEECHCRAFT MODEL 33 "BONANZA"/ "DEBONAIR" 1960–94

STANDARD DATA: (F-33A) Seats 6. Gross wt. 3,400. Empty wt. 2,125. Fuel capacity 74. Engine 285-hp fuel-injected Continental. PERFORMANCE: Top mph 209. Cruise mph 198. Stall mph 59. Initial climb rate 1,167. Ceiling 17,858. Range 824. Takeoff distance (50') 1,769. Landing distance (50') 1,324.
STANDARD DATA: (Debonair) Seats 4–5. Gross wt. 2,900. Empty wt. 1,730. Fuel capacity 64. Engine 225-hp Continental. PERFORMANCE: Top mph 195. Cruise mph 185. Stall mph 60. Initial climb rate 930. Range 650. Ceiling 17,800. Takeoff distance (50') 1,288. Landing distance (50') 1,298.

The Model 33 Debonair flew for the first time in September 1959. It was basically similar to the Model 35 Bonanza, but had a conventional tail assembly in place of the "V"-type tail. The Debonair was produced in four-seat versions with a 225-hp Continental, six-cylinder engine. It had a simplified interior and less elaborate equipment than the Model 35. In 1961, the aileron and elevator trim tabs were improved, and larger rear windows and a restyled cabin interior with bucket-seats were featured. In 1966, the option of a 285-hp powerplant was added.

The Debonair name was dropped in 1967 and the subsequent aircraft, now a part of the Bonanza family, were simply designated E33, F33 and G33. During these years all model numbers ending in "A" featured the 285-hp Continental. All others retained the 225-hp engine. In 1972, the G33 was introduced with a 260-hp Continental. Currently, only the F-33A remains in production. Since its introduction as the Beechcraft Debonair, approximately 3,100 Model 33s have been produced.

Recent standard features for all Bonanza models are a 15-degree approach flap setting and a 28-volt electrical sys-

tem. The approach flaps are identical to the Baron models and will allow for a maximum extension speed of 175 mph. An improved electrical system speeds up the landing gear cycle and allows Bonanzas to be equipped with propeller deicing. Also, all late model Bonanzas offer increased oxygen capacity. Single-piece headliners and redesigned cabin sidewalls make for a clean appearance and reduced cabin sound levels. As of 1981 airspeed indicators read in knots only, and an electronic fuel-flow sensor has replaced the mechanical sensor to ensure greater gauge accuracy.

BEECHCRAFT MODEL 35 "BONANZA" 1947–81

STANDARD DATA: (V-35B) Seats 4. Gross wt. 3,400. Empty wt. 2,106. Fuel capacity 74. Engine 285-hp Continental. PERFORMANCE: Top mph 209. Cruise mph 198. Stall mph 59. Initial climb rate 1,167. Ceiling 17,858. Range 824. Takeoff distance (50') 1,769. Landing distance (50') 1,324.
STANDARD DATA: (C-D35) Seats 4. Gross wt. 2,725. Empty wt. 1,675. Fuel capacity 359. Engine 205-hp Continental. PERFORMANCE: Top mph 190. Cruise mph 180. Stall mph 55. Initial climb rate 1,100. Ceiling 18,000. Range 775. Takeoff distance (50') 1,375. Landing distance (50') 970.
STANDARD DATA: (E-35) Seats 4. Gross wt. 2,775. Empty wt. 1,722. Fuel capacity 39. Engine 225-hp Continental. PERFORMANCE: Top mph 194. Cruise mph 184. Stall mph 55. Initial climb rate 1,300. Range 775. Ceiling 19,000. Takeoff distance (50') 1,300. Landing distance (50') 970.
STANDARD DATA: (N-P35) Seats 4–5. Gross wt. 3,125. Empty wt. 1,855. Fuel capacity 49–78. Engine 260-hp Continental. PERFORMANCE: Top mph 205. Cruise mph 195. Stall mph 60. Initial climb rate 1,150. Ceiling 19,200. Range 690–1,215. Takeoff distance (50') 1,050. Landing distance (50') 840.

The Beechcraft Bonanza is one of the most outstanding aircraft in its class. It has been described as the best aerodynamically designed airplane ever offered to general aviation. The Bonanza was introduced as a production model in 1947 and was labeled the Model 35. Subsequent aircraft were designated A35, B35, C35, and the like until the S35, after which the letter V was placed in front of the model number and the lettering process began all over again. Early models were fitted with 185-hp powerplants and seated four persons. In 1952, the C-model appeared with enlarged tail surfaces and a 205-hp engine. The 225-hp Continental was first used in 1954 with the

E35. The H35 utilized a 240-hp engine and the J through M models were fitted with 250-hp Continentals. The 260-hp engine was introduced in the N35, and the 285-hp engine first appeared in 1964 in the S35.

Early model Bonanzas are still highly competitive on the used-plane market and are highly prized as personal transportation aircraft. All were four-seaters until the S35, after which all have accommodations for up to six. Like other Bonanzas, the V35B model benefits from the new 15-degree flap setting and the 28-volt electrical system to support optional propeller deicing equipment. For improved soundproofing and a neat appearance, the interior sidewalls and the one-piece headliner are constructed of sound-absorbing foam.

BEECHCRAFT A36/A36TC "BONANZA" 1968–94

STANDARD DATA: (A36) Seats 6. Gross wt. 3,600. Empty wt. 2,195. Fuel capacity 74. Engine 285-hp Continental. **PERFORMANCE:** Top mph 206. Cruise mph 193. Stall mph 60. Initial climb rate 1,030. Ceiling 16,600. Range 802. Takeoff distance (50') 2,040. Landing distance (50') 1,450.
STANDARD DATA: (A36TC) Seats 6. Gross wt. 3,650. Empty wt. 2,278. Fuel capacity 74. Engine 300-hp Turbocharged Continental. **PERFORMANCE:** Top mph 246. Cruise mph 223. Stall mph 66. Initial climb rate 1,165. Ceiling 25,000. Range 774. Takeoff distance (50') 2,012. Landing distance (50') 1,449.

The biggest single-engine Bonanza, the A36, was introduced in 1968 to compete with Piper's Cherokee Six and the 200-series haulers from Cessna. It remains the only retractable in the single-engine, six-seater utility class. The A36 was developed by lengthening the fuselage of the Model 33 and using the same durable wing, landing gear and Continental engine of the Bonanza family. Six seats are available, and with club seating arrangements and a foldout table, it becomes a flying office. In 1975, the A36 outsold all other Bonanza models for the first time.

With a longer cabin and wide double doors, the Bonanza A36 offers greater utility and convenience without sacrificing performance and economy. In 1977, for the first time, the A36 was offered with factory-installed electric trim, formerly available only on aircraft equipped with an autopilot. The A36 accounted for 50 percent of the total Bonanza production in 1977, and that percentage increased in 1978. Beech added a turbocharged version of its Bonanza A36 in mid-1979. The aircraft is certified to a maximum operational altitude of 25,000 feet and has approximately the same takeoff distance as the A36. Power is supplied by a 300-hp Continental engine, which conforms to the minimum horsepower concept introduced on the Baron 58P and 58TC in 1977. The A36TC has a gross weight of 3,650 pounds, which is 50 pounds more than the standard A36. A shortened three-blade propeller reduces tip speed, increases ground clearance, and reduces noise.

Standard features on late models of both the normally aspirated and turbocharged versions are an extended rear compartment for up to 70 pounds of baggage, bringing the baggage total to 470 pounds with four seats occupied, 15-degree approach-flap setting, and optional propeller anti-icing. The Model 36 continues to be the biggest seller of the Bonanza family. Along with other Bonanza models, the A36 recently has benefited from improved soundproofing, thanks to a foam, one-piece headliner and redesigned cabin sidewalls.

BELL P-63 "KING COBRA" 1942–45

STANDARD DATA: Seats 1. Gross wt. 8,800. Empty wt. 6,375. Fuel capacity 136. Engine 1,325-hp Allison. **PERFORMANCE:** Top mph 410. Cruise mph 378. Initial climb rate 3,500. Ceiling 43,000.

Bell began development of the P-39 Aircobra in 1937 to meet the need for a fighter with great firepower. The design was quite radical for its time, featuring tricycle gear and an engine that was mounted behind the pilot. The propeller was driven by a drive shaft that ran between the pilot's legs. Mounted in the nose was a 37mm cannon. Though nearly 10,000 of this type were built, it was unspectacular as a fighter and eventually found a role as a tank-buster on the Russian front. A greatly modified development of the P-39, the P-63 King Cobra, was designed in 1942. Easily recognized by its larger tail surface and more prominent airscoop, the King Cobra also met with an unenthusiastic reception. Of those that weren't lend-leased to Russia, many were converted into target planes for use with dummy bullets. A few King Cobras have been altered for racing. Several exist in flying condition.

BELLANCA "AIRCRUISER" 1932–38

STANDARD DATA: Seats 11–17. Gross wt. 11,400. Empty wt. 6,300. Fuel capacity 300. Engine 875-hp Wright Cyclone. **PERFORMANCE:** Top mph 165. Cruise mph 137. Initial climb rate 620. Range 610–1,100. Ceiling 17,500.

BELLANCA "AIRCRUISER"

The Aircruiser single-engine commercial sesquiplane entered production in 1932 as a refinement of the Airbus and was designed to carry 11 to 17 passengers. It could be fitted with either wheel or float undercarriage and was powered by either a Wright Cyclone or Pratt & Whitney Hornet engine. The Cyclone produced 760 hp with 875 hp available for takeoff. The Hornet was rated at 750 hp. The Aircruiser made use of an unusual wing configuration. The top plane was of conventional design; however, the lower airfoils consisted of inner sections with a coarse anhedral and outer sections that sloped up from the extremities of the inner sections to the top wing to form airfoil-sectioned bracing struts. While the top wings had solid spruce spars, the lower wings were built from welded steel-tube spars and ribs. The Aircruiser also featured electrical wing flaps. In 1935, an Aircruiser was purchased by the Mackenzie Air Service of Edmonton, Alberta. In three weeks the plane carried 30,537 pounds of radium and silver ore over the 900-mile route from the Eldorado Mining Co. to the railhead at Fort McMurray.

BELLANCA "PACEMAKER"/ "SKYROCKET" 1928–47

STANDARD DATA: (Senior Pacemaker) Seats 6–8. Gross wt. 5,600. Empty wt. 2,900. Fuel capacity 100. Engine 420-hp Wright Whirlwind radial. **PERFORMANCE:** Top mph 170. Cruise mph 145. Initial climb rate 900. Ceiling 18,000. Range 1,180.
STANDARD DATA: (Senior Skyrocket) Seats 6–8. Gross wt. 5,600. Empty wt. 3,520. Engine 550-hp Pratt & Whitney Wasp. **PERFORMANCE:** Top mph 190. Cruise mph 175. Initial climb rate 1,240. Ceiling 25,000. Range 1,280.

The Model 300 Pacemaker was first produced in 1928 and versions of this basic design were built until 1936. The first derivative was the Model 400 whose major difference was the swapping of a 420-hp Wright Whirlwind for the original 300-hp Wright Whirlwind nine-cylinder radial engine. Production of the Pacemaker continued throughout the 1930s. The Skyrocket was evolved from the Pacemaker and first flew in 1930. Aside from minor changes, the Skyrocket differed by

its 550-hp Pratt and Whitney Wasp nine-cylinder radial engine and an increased seating capacity from the Pacemaker's six to eight persons. Production of the Skyrocket continued until 1936. In 1946, license for production of the airplane was taken over by a Canadian firm, Northwest Industries, and the aircraft's designation was changed from the Bellanca 31-42 to the Bellanca 31-55A. Under the new license, the Skyrocket remained substantially the same as the prewar model. All currently active planes are registered in Canada.

BELLANCA 7AC "CHAMP" 1970–72

STANDARD DATA: Seats 2. Gross wt. 1,220. Empty wt. 750. Engine 60-hp Franklin. **PERFORMANCE:** Top mph 91. Cruise mph 86. Stall mph 28. Range 310. Initial climb rate 460. Takeoff run 450. Landing roll 300.

During the period between 1946 and 1948, Aeronca built some 7,200 Model 7AC Champs, but the 7AC was dropped from the line when Champion Aircraft Corp. acquired manufacturing rights to the airframe in 1951; however, when Champion merged with Bellanca in 1970, it was decided to reinstate the design in an improved version. Production began sporadically due to the loss of the main production facility in a fire, but soon the Champ was coming off the assembly in increasing numbers. The primary difference in the new 7AC is the use of a 65-hp Continental four-cylinder engine as a replacement for the original 60-hp Franklin two-cylinder, which is no longer in production. Use of the new engine allowed for a redesigned cowling and air scoop that substantially improved forward visibility. Other new features included a lightweight cantilever spring-steel main landing gear and modern materials in interior design.

BELLANCA 8GCBC "SCOUT" 1970–80

STANDARD DATA: (8GCBC) Seats 2. Gross wt. 2,150. Empty wt. 1,315. Fuel capacity 35. Engine 180-hp Lycoming. **PERFORMANCE:** Top mph 128. Cruise mph 123. Stall mph 52. Initial climb rate 1,080. Takeoff distance (50') 525. Landing distance (50') 690.
STANDARD DATA: (7GC8C) Seats 2. Gross wt. 1,650. Empty wt. 1,037. Fuel capacity 35. Engine 150-hp Lycoming. **PERFORMANCE:** Top mph 128. Cruise mph 125. Stall

mph 45. Initial climb rate 1,145. Ceiling 17,000. Range 537. Takeoff distance (50') 525. Landing distance (50') 690.

The basic utility version of the Citabria is known as the 8GCBC Scout. Its predecessor was the 7GCBC Scout that was powered by the smaller 150-hp Lycoming. The new multipurpose 180-hp Scout was introduced early in 1974 and enjoyed a high demand for the first production models. The Scout can be used for power line patrol, forestry work, cargo hauling, and training. When fitted with Sorensen spray equipment, it becomes a highly efficient and economical agricultural plane. The Scout can also be equipped with Edo 2000 floats and with skis for north-country flying. Its 180-hp engine provides good short-field performance.

BELLANCA "CITABRIA"
1964–80

STANDARD DATA: (Bellanca) Seats 2. Gross wt. 1,650. Empty wt. 1,110. Fuel capacity 35. Engine 150-hp Lycoming. PERFORMANCE: Top mph 130. Cruise mph 129. Stall mph 51. Initial climb rate 1,120. Range 560. Ceiling 17,000. Takeoff distance (50') 630. Landing distance (50') 755.
STANDARD DATA: (Champion) Seats 2. Gross wt. 1,650. Empty wt. 980. Fuel capacity 26. Engine 100-hp Lycoming. PERFORMANCE: Top mph 117. Cruise mph 112. Stall mph 50. Initial climb rate 725. Ceiling 12,000. Range 728. Takeoff distance (50') 890. Landing distance (50') 755.

The name "Citabria" is actually "airbatic" spelled backward. The Champion 7ECA Citabria was a modernized version of the Champion Model 7EC Traveler. Champion's first Citabria flew as a prototype in May 1964. Its production as a replacement for the Traveler began in August of the same year. The Champion two-seat aircraft was powered by a 108-hp Continental four-cylinder engine. When Bellanca introduced its version of the 7ECA, the airplane was fitted with a 115-hp Lycoming. The Citabria's basic wing, fuselage, and undercarriage are similar to previous tandem two-seaters. Major changes to the aerobatic, high-winger include the enlarged rear cabin windows, the square-cut vertical tail surfaces, and low-drag wheel spats similar to those on the Champion 7KC Olympia. Models 7GCAA, 7KCAB, and 7GCBA are generally similar to the Citabria 7ECA, with the exception that they are all powered by a 150-hp Lycoming engine. In addition, the 7KCAB has special fuel and oil systems for inverted flying, and the 7GCBC is fitted with flaps. The Citabria was the country's first aircraft certified for aerobatic flight by the FAA and is still the lowest priced production aircraft with these capabilities. Production of the Citabria was discontinued in 1980 when Bellanca Aircraft Corp. declared bankruptcy.

BELLANCA 8KCAB "DECATHLON"
1964–80

STANDARD DATA: Seats 2. Gross wt. 1,800. Empty wt. 1,275. Fuel capacity 40. Engine 150-hp Lycoming. PERFORMANCE: Top mph 145. Cruise mph 135. Stall mph 53. Initial climb rate 1,025. Range 550. Ceiling 16,000. Takeoff distance (50') 650. Landing distance (50') 755.

Following the acquisition of the Champion Aircraft Corp. in September 1970, Bellanca Aircraft continued the production of the Citabria. The fully aerobatic Citabria, model 8KCAB, is now named the Decathlon. Designed for loads of +6G and –5G, it can be flown in inverted flight for periods up to four minutes without loss of oil or oil pressure. Generally similar in all respects to the 150-hp Model 7 Citabria, the high-wing aerobat was, for a time, the only unlimited aerobatic competition aircraft produced in the United States. Although maximum speed is limited to 138 mph, a retrofit of the windshield will increase top speed. Some claim that with the Decathlon's standard top speed, it could not achieve the necessary vertical speed to complete the AC or AAC compulsory unlimited sequence, which requires flying off the top of the vertical snaps and vertical rolls. When Bellanca Aircraft Corp. declared bankruptcy in 1980, production of the Decathlon ceased.

BELLANCA "JUNIOR"/ "CRUISAIR"/ "CRUISEMASTER" 1937–59

STANDARD DATA: (1413) Seats 4. Gross wt. 3,000. Empty wt. 1,850. Fuel capacity 60. Engine 260-hp Continental. **PERFORMANCE:** Top mph 208. Cruise mph 203. Stall mph 62. Initial climb rate 1,500. Ceiling 22,500. Range 1,000. Takeoff distance (50') 1,000. Landing distance (50') 800.
STANDARD DATA: (1419-2) Seats 4. Gross wt. 2,700. Empty wt. 1,640. Fuel capacity 40. Engine 230-hp Continental. **PERFORMANCE:** Top mph 206. Cruise mph 196. Stall mph 48. Initial climb rate 1,500. Range 624. Ceiling 20,000. Takeoff distance (50') 1,060. Landing distance (50') 935.
STANDARD DATA: (Cruisemaster 1419) Seats 4. Gross wt. 2,600. Empty wt. 1,525. Fuel capacity 20. Engine 190-hp Lycoming. **PERFORMANCE:** Cruise mph 180. Stall mph 43. Initial climb rate 1,400. Ceiling 22,500. Range 680.
STANDARD DATA: (Cruisair 149) Seats 3. Gross wt. 1,750. Empty wt. 1,050. Fuel capacity 20. Engine 90-hp Ken Royce radial. **PERFORMANCE:** Top mph 133. Cruise mph 120. Stall mph 43. Initial climb rate 750. Ceiling 12,500. Range 410.
STANDARD DATA: (Junior 149) Seats 3. Gross wt. 1,650. Empty wt. 943. Fuel capacity 22. Engine 90-hp LeBlond radial. **PERFORMANCE:** Top mph 137. Cruise mph 120. Stall mph 45. Initial climb rate 800. Ceiling 14,760. Range 500.
STANDARD DATA: (Junior 147) Seats 3. Gross wt. 1,650. Empty wt. 912. Fuel capacity 22. Engine 75-hp LeBlond radial. **PERFORMANCE:** Top mph 115. Cruise mph 105. Stall mph 45. Initial climb rate 600. Ceiling 12,000. Range 500.

BELLANCA "JUNIOR CRUISAIR"

BELLANCA 14-13 "CRUISAIR"

BELLANCA 14-19 "CRUISMASTER"

The earlier versions of the Bellanca, produced from shortly after the end of World War II until 1962, are sometimes humorously referred to as the "Cardboard Constellations." This friendly remark refers to the tail surfaces that in earlier versions featured twin vertical fins outboard from the central vertical stabilizer and rudder. The first Bellancas of this series were produced between 1937 and 1940 and were known as the Junior. The 147 had a 75-hp LeBlond engine and fixed landing gear; the 149 was fitted with a 90-hp of the same make and retractable gear. Cruisair became the name applied to the 147 and 149 when they received 75-hp and 90-hp Ken Royce engines, respectively.

In 1946, the first 1413 Cruisairs were introduced with 150-hp Franklin engines, and in the following years updated versions, the 1413-2 and 1413-3, were built. This latter plane stayed in production, along with the first 190-hp Cruisemaster 1419 introduced in 1948 until 1956. In 1958, Northern Aircraft Inc. took over production and built the Cruisemaster 1419-2 with its 230-hp Continental engine. Northern Aircraft became the Downer Aircraft Company in 1959, and introduced the 1419-3 "260," a considerably more powerful Cruisemaster with a 260-hp Continental, tricycle landing gear, and other refinements. Inter-Air acquired production rights in 1962, and the 260A received its first conventional tail section. Shortly afterwards, Inter-Air became known as the Bellanca Sales Company, a subsidiary of Miller Flying Service.

BELLANCA 300 "VIKING" 1971–80

STANDARD DATA: Seats 4. Gross wt. 3,325. Empty wt. 2,217. Fuel capacity 60–75. Engine 300-hp Continental. **PERFORMANCE:** Top mph 226. Cruise mph 188. Stall mph 70. Initial climb rate 1,170. Range 734. Ceiling 17,000. Takeoff distance (50') 850. Landing distance (50') 1,100.

The modern Bellanca first flew in 1962. At that time, under the name of Inter-Air, the design was revised to eliminate the triple tail and replace it with a large, single, vertical fin. There were several other new design features, but many of the earlier features of the Cruisemaster were retained, including the laminated wood wing of spruce and mahogany, which is pressure sealed in plastic. The fuselage and tail surfaces, however, are constructed of metal tubing covered with Dacron. In addition to changing the tail surfaces, the cabin was extensively redesigned and enlarged, along with the cowling and landing gear. This radically revised Bellanca entered quantity production in 1964 and was produced in increasing numbers until 1980. A 260-hp engine powered the Bellanca 260C Viking; however, the standard engine in the 300 series was rated at 300-hp. The buyer can choose between a Continental IO-520D six-cylinder engine or the Lycoming IO-540.

The standard fuel tanks hold 58 gallons or 72 gallons in the Super 300 Viking, although optional long-range tanks provide a total fuel capacity of 92 gallons. The Super 300 Viking is the same airplane, only equipped with a more luxurious cabin and the larger fuel tanks. Bellanca also produced the Turbo Viking 300, similar to the Standard Viking 300, but fitted with a 310-hp Lycoming turbocharged engine. All Vikings have retractable tricycle gear. The main gear retracts forward into the wing, and the nosewheel retracts rearward. When retracted, the wheels protrude slightly to reduce danger in a gear-up landing. Bellanca made it a practice to offer many extra features normally considered as standard equipment. A good example is the standard installation of an autopilot. After about 43 years of production, Bellanca's family of single-engine wooden-winged retractables was laid to rest when the company declared bankruptcy in 1980.

BELLANCA
T-250 "ARIES"
1978–80

STANDARD DATA: Seats 4. Gross wt. 3,150. Empty wt. 1,888. Fuel capacity 76. Engine 250-hp Lycoming. **PERFORMANCE:** Cruise mph 208. Stall mph 64. Initial climb rate 1,240. Ceiling 18,100. Range 1,170.

The title of fastest normally aspirated single has been bandied back and forth for years. Throughout the late 1950s and early 1960s, the V-tail Bonanza was the often challenged but undefeated champ. Then there was the exercise in horsepower overkill known as the Comanche 400, followed by the Aero Commander 200 and the Waco Meteor. The trouble was that all except the Bonanza were economic failures. The Bellanca Aries T-250 was initiated by Anderson, Greenwood and Company when it assumed financial control of Bellanca. Unfortunately, the Aries did not get into production before Bellanca declared bankruptcy in 1980.

For lower-cost production, the Aries utilized flat skins wherever possible and simple rather than compound curves. The wings and T-tail are laminar-flow constant-chord airfoils. Power is supplied by a carbureted six-cylinder Lycoming that is roughly the same engine that powered the old 250 Co-

manche, delivering 250 hp at 2,575 RPM. Other hints that the T-250 is fast are the use of flush riveting, sealed nosegear doors, butt skin joints and flush vents, drains, and engine breather. The cabin accommodates four, but there is enough room so the Aries could be configured to handle one more.

BOEING/STEARMAN
"KAYDET" SERIES
(PT-13,17-1827 and N2S)
1934–45

STANDARD DATA: Seats 2. Gross wt. 2,717. Empty wt. 1,936. Fuel capacity 43. Engine 220-hp Lycoming R-680 or 220-hp Continental R-670. **PERFORMANCE:** Top mph 124. Cruise mph 106. Landing mph 52. Initial climb rate 840. Range 505. Ceiling 11,200.

In 1934, the Stearman Aircraft Co. became a Boeing subsidiary and placed in production its Model 73. It was a variation of both the Stearman Model C series that was produced between 1926 and 1930 and the Model 70 prototype that was completed in 1933. Out of this biplane grew a family of primary trainers, of which over 2,000 were produced by 1945. The Model 76 was simply a larger version of the Model 75, which was the most prominent member of the family.

The Model 75 was powered by a 215-hp Lycoming and was designated by the military as the PT-13. The series that was produced in the largest numbers was the Model A75N1. It was similar to the PT-13 but was powered by a 220-hp Continental radial engine; its military designation was PT-17. The Royal Canadian Air Force ordered 300 winterized versions of the PT-17 and unofficially changed the name to Kaydet, a name that has come to apply to the entire family of Stearmans.

The last of the 75 series to be produced was the Model E-75 powered by a 220-hp Lycoming engine. When production was terminated on VJ-Day, its production totaled over 1,700 as both the PT-13D and the N2S-5. Thousands of Model 75s have become available for civilian use and are widely employed as private and agricultural aircraft. In some cases, their original engines have been replaced by the Pratt & Whitney Wasp juniors providing twice the power.

BUCKER BU131
"JUNGMANN"
1939–56

STANDARD DATA: Seats 2. Gross wt. 1,474. Empty wt. 836. Engine 105-hp Hirth. **PERFORMANCE:** Top mph 115.

Cruise mph 106. Stall mph 51. Initial climb rate 650. Range 400. Ceiling 14,000.

The Bucker Jungmann, which first appeared in Germany in 1934, has proved to be one of the most popular two-seat, tandem aerobatic biplanes in the world. Several thousand were produced at the Bucker factory near Berlin during the 1930s and 1940s and many others were constructed under license in Spain, Switzerland, and Czechoslovakia. Originally, the Jungmann was powered by an 80-hp Hirth engine. Later in 1936, the 105-hp Hirth became the standard engine. Several Jungmanns have found their way into the United States, and some have been adapted to larger American engines. The biplane is capable of performing remarkably graceful and precise aerobatics and is in great demand.

BUCKER "JUNGMEISTER"
1935, 1967–75

STANDARD DATA: Seats 1. Gross wt. 1,290. Empty wt. 925. Engine 160-hp Siemens. **PERFORMANCE:** Top mph 137. Cruise mph 125. Initial climb rate 1,150. Stall mph 54. Range 310. Ceiling 19,500.

The Jungmeister, first introduced in 1935, quickly developed an international reputation for its outstanding aerobatic capabilities. Until recently, Jungmeisters were heavily involved in world aerobatic competition and were widely used by exhibition pilots. Most of the 700 or so Jungmeisters built were constructed in Germany, but others of the type were built in Spain and Switzerland. Several examples are currently registered in the United States, at least three of which have been reengined with Warner radials. In 1968, the Aero Technik Canary in Munich, Germany, began production of the BU-133 D-1, also called the Jungmeister. Its engine is a remanufactured Siemens-Halske Sh-14A4; however, due to this engine's limited availability and demand for more power, a new version, the BU-133F, is being built by Wolf Hirth-GmbH with a 220-hp Franklin engine.

BUHL LA.1 "BULL-PUP"
1930

STANDARD DATA: Seats 1. Gross wt. 850. Empty wt. 550. Engine 40-hp Szekely. **PERFORMANCE:** Top mph 95. Cruise mph 76. Initial climb rate 800. Ceiling 14,000.

The LA Bull-Pup, produced by the Buhl Aircraft Company in 1930, was powered by a 45-hp A.H.C. (Szekely) SR-3 three-cylinder radial engine. The wire-braced wooden wing is fabric covered and has two spars. The fuselage is an oval metal monocoque. The wing is supported by a turnover pylon mounted in front of the single-seat cockpit. Some Bull-Pup owners have modified their planes with 65-hp Continental engines that help performance considerably.

CALLAIR
1941–57

STANDARD DATA: (A-1) Seats 2–3. Gross wt. 1,550. Empty wt. 1,000. Fuel capacity 25. Engine 100-hp Lycoming. **PERFORMANCE:** Top mph 115. Cruise mph 105. Stall mph 40. Initial climb rate 500. Ceiling 13,000. Range 260. **STANDARD DATA:** (A-2, A-3). Seats 2. Gross wt. 1,550. Empty wt. 975. Fuel capacity 30. Engine 125-hp Lycoming. **PERFORMANCE:** Top mph 120. Cruise mph 109. Stall mph 45. Initial climb rate 1,000. Ceiling 17,500. Range 456. Takeoff run 426. Landing roll 300.

The first CallAir flew in 1941 and was designated the Model A. The last version was introduced in 1957 and was named the A-6. Throughout the years of its existence, the basic difference between any of the models was the powerplant; otherwise, the Model A-4 differed little externally from the original Model A. The CallAir was built with mixed construction: fabric-covered wooden wings and a fabric-covered steel-tube fuselage. The Model A-2, with a 125-hp Lycoming, and the Model A-3, with a 125-hp Continental, were produced during the years between 1946 and 1948. The first production models of the A-4 appeared in 1955, and the major refinement was the addition of 25 more horsepower with the installation of a 150-hp Lycoming. All models shared the same two-to-three-seat cabin and low wing with exposed struts.

Another version of the CallAir was introduced in 1956 and was basically an agricultural development of the Model A-4. Designated the A-S, it was normally flown as a single-seater with the cockpit offset to the starboard side due to the inclusion of the dust hopper. The Model A-6 flown in 1957 was identical, apart from another jump in horsepower to a 180-hp Lycoming. The Intermountain Manufacturing Co. developed a series of low-priced agricultural aircraft from the CallAir, and the first airplane rolled off the production line in 1963. The A-9 featured a 235-hp Lycoming; its top speed was now 130 mph, and its climb rate was now 650 fpm. The dust hopper was moved to a position in front of the cockpit.

CESSNA "AIRMASTER"
1933–42

STANDARD DATA: Seats 4. Gross wt. 2,450. Empty wt. 1,380. Engine 145-hp Warner Scarab radial. **PERFORMANCE:** Top mph 162. Cruise mph 150. Stall mph 50. Initial climb rate 1,000. Range 472. Ceiling 18,000.

Clyde Cessna first entered the lightplane market on his own in 1927. Between the years of 1928 and 1930 he produced a series of airplanes that were remarkably clean and efficient. The final manifestation of this series was the Cessna AW, a four-seat cabin monoplane utilizing the 125-hp Warner Scarab engine followed by the BW. The Depression caught up with Cessna in 1930, forcing the factory to suspend production; however, in 1933, Cessna was back in business again, this time with a much improved version of the AW, featuring an improved landing gear and a 145-hp engine. This first model, designated the C-34, was possibly the most efficient airplane in its class, and nearly 100 were built. The C-145 Airmaster is basically a modified C-34 featuring revised flaps and a wider gear. In 1932, the Airmaster was made available with the 165-hp Super Scarab, and the line continued in production until 1942.

CESSNA 120/140
1946–50

STANDARD DATA: Seats 2. Gross wt. 1,450. Empty wt. 770. Fuel capacity 21. Engine 80- to 90-hp Continental. **PERFORMANCE:** Top mph 119. Cruise mph 103. Stall mph 53. Initial climb rate 680. Range 439. Ceiling 15,600. Takeoff run 650. Landing roll 460.

Cessna's 140 was a somewhat more deluxe version of the 120 model when both debuted in 1946. Along with a few cabin refinements, the 140 had a starter, generator, battery, and manually operated plain-hinge flaps. Both were powered by the Continental C85-12, which developed a lusty 85-hp at full RPM, but the 140 could accept the additional surge of a 90-hp Continental up front. A grand total of 2,164 120s were produced by Cessna before this model was phased out in 1948. The side-by-side two-seat 140 continued in production with a choice of the 85-hp or 90-hp engine.

Introduced in 1949 as the 140A, the 90-hp version had a metal skin in place of fabric covering on the wings. It featured single wing struts in place of the earlier "V" struts. More than 5,500 140s and 140As were built before the series was permanently discontinued in 1950. Although the 150 with its tricycle gear was later designed as a replacement for the 120/140 series, there are many pilots who continue to favor the lovable old tail-draggers. A Cessna 140 owned by a flying school in Canada logged more than 17,500 hours of flight time before being respectfully retired. Along with the Aeroncas, Cubs, and Luscombes, the Cessna 140 did its share in making general aviation what it is today.

CESSNA 150 "COMMUTER"/ "AEROBAT"
1959–77

STANDARD DATA: (150) Seats 2. Gross wt. 1,600. Empty wt. 1,111. Fuel capacity 26–38. Engine 100-hp Teledyne Continental. **PERFORMANCE:** Top mph 125. Cruise mph 123. Stall mph 48. Initial climb rate 670. Ceiling 14,000. Range 591–667. Takeoff distance (50') 1,385. Landing distance (50') 1,075.
STANDARD DATA: (Aerobat) Seats 2. Gross wt. 1,600. Empty wt. 1,093. Fuel capacity 26–38. Engine 100-hp Teledyne Continental. **PERFORMANCE:** Top mph 124. Cruise mph 121. Stall mph 48. Initial climb rate 670. Ceiling 14,000. Range 385–656. Takeoff distance (50') 1,385. Landing distance (50') 1,075.

The 150 Cessna is one of the leading examples of the light civilian pilot trainer and personal aircraft. It is basically unchanged since it was introduced in 1959, and the only differences in model years are in minor styling, equipment, and accessories. As a trainer, it is very easy to learn to fly in and can be used in all stages of instruction from solo through instrument and commercial ratings. As a personal plane, it is limited by two seats in the normal arrangement, although there is quite ample baggage space. The three versions (standard, trainer, and commuter) vary only in deluxe extras.

A pilot new to the Cessna 150 will find it as easy to handle as anything with wings. Its light weight makes it somewhat bouncy in rough air. There are no tricky characteristics, and recoveries from any attitude are gentle and steady. Operational costs are about the rock bottom of the price lists. As a new or used airplane, the Cessna is not topped in its class by another make or design as a good, general all-purpose light two-seater.

In 1970, Cessna introduced the Model A150K Aerobat, a 150 with structural changes to allow aerobatics. It is rated at +6G to –3G, which permits most standard aerobatic maneuvers such as snap rolls, barrel and aileron rolls, Cuban eights, loops, etc. Empty weight of the Aerobat is slightly higher than the standard 150, and speed is reduced by two mph.

CESSNA 152/152 "AEROBAT"
1978–81

STANDARD DATA: (152) Seats 2. Gross wt. 1,670. Empty wt. 1,107. Fuel capacity 26–39. Engine 110-hp Lycoming. **PERFORMANCE:** Top mph 126. Cruise mph 123. Stall mph 49. Initial climb rate 715. Ceiling 14,700. Range 368–794. Takeoff distance (50') 1,340. Landing distance (50') 1,200.
STANDARD DATA: (Aerobat) Seats 2. Gross wt. 1,670. Empty wt. 1,135. Fuel capacity 26–39. Engine 110-hp Lycoming. **PERFORMANCE:** Top mph 125. Cruise mph 122. Stall mph 49. Initial climb rate 715. Ceiling 14,700. Range 362–788. Takeoff distance (50') 1,340. Landing distance (50') 1,200.

In 1978, Cessna Aircraft introduced a new training airplane to "replace" the Model 150 after a 19-year production run that amounted to almost 24,000 airplanes. Though to most eyes the new Model 152 still looked like the original 150, it was introduced with the intention of providing an airplane that burns 100-octane fuel with lower sound levels, better fuel consumption, and an increased payload. The Lycoming "Blue Streak" engine produces 110-hp at a low 2,500 rpm. Possibly the most remarkable improvement is the increase of the trainer's maximum useful load by over 100 pounds to 589. With full fuel, the 152 has 433 pounds of payload for people, baggage, and/or accessories. Contributing to the impressive useful load is an unusable fuel quantity of only 1½ gallons. Cessna's 69-inch prop teams with the derated engine to produce more efficient climb and cruise performance at a reduced RPM.

The 152 Aerobat is also available. It meets requirements for aerobatic maneuvers of 6Gs positive and 3Gs negative load. The most recent improvements include a system that injects fuel evenly into all four cylinders for prompt ignition and even combustion. With the 152's optional fuel tanks, it can cover 794 miles while traveling at 122 mph at 7,000 feet and carrying a useful load of 1,101 pounds.

Cessna offered a training version for the first time in 1981; the Trainer included a package price for the most frequently ordered avionics and accessories for training purposes. Main gear tires are 15-6.00 × 6 to reduce frontal area and save weight.

CESSNA 170
1948–56

STANDARD DATA: Seats 4. Gross wt. 2,200. Empty wt. 1,205. Fuel capacity 42. Engine 145-hp Continental. **PERFORMANCE:** Top mph 140. Cruise mph 120. Stall mph 52. Initial climb rate 690. Range 540. Ceiling 15,500. Takeoff distance (50') 1,820. Landing distance (50') 1,145.

The conventional-gear Cessna 170 was the forerunner of the 172/Skyhawk series in production until 1986. Basically, the 170 was a four-place, 145-hp version of the 140 series. It remained unchanged until 1953 when the engine cowling was redesigned and lengthened. Final alterations, made in 1955, increased the size of the rear windows, revised the tailwheel, and added an additional flap position. Of the 5,171 Cessna 170s that were built, more than 3,000 are found on the active list in the United States today while many others are still flying in Canada, Europe, and Latin America. Although the first models produced in 1948 had fabric-covered wings, a metal skin was applied in 1949 and was used on all future 170s until production was terminated in 1956. Although not speedy, it is still a good buy on the used aircraft market. It represents one of the lowest-priced four-seaters available.

CESSNA 172 SKYHAWK
1956–86

STANDARD DATA: (1986) Seats 4. Gross wt. 2,400. Empty wt. 1,414. Fuel capacity 43–68. Engine 160-hp Lycoming. **PERFORMANCE:** Top mph 142. Cruise mph 138. Stall mph 53. Initial climb rate 700. Ceiling 13,000. Range 506–869. Takeoff distance (50') 1,825. Landing distance (50') 1,280.
STANDARD DATA: (1976) Seats 4. Gross wt. 2,300. Empty wt. 1,387. Fuel capacity 42–52. Engine 150-hp Lycoming. **PERFORMANCE:** Top mph 144. Cruise mph 138. Stall mph 41. Initial climb rate 645. Range 657. Ceiling 13,100. Takeoff distance (50') 1,525. Landing distance (50') 1,250.
STANDARD DATA: (1963) Seats 4. Gross wt. 2,300. Empty wt. 1,260. Fuel capacity 42. Engine 140-hp Continental. **PERFORMANCE:** Top mph 138. Cruise mph 130. Stall mph 49. Initial climb rate 645. Range 595. Ceiling 13,100. Takeoff distance (50') 1,525. Landing distance (50') 1,250.

The Cessna 172/Skyhawk has undoubtedly been the most popular four-place aircraft among general aviation pilots for close to three decades. First produced in 1956, the 172 was climb rate 800. Ceiling 16,800. Range 828. Takeoff distance (50') 1,775. Landing distance (50') 1,340.

initially a revision of the model 170 with a tricycle landing gear and redesigned tail surfaces. It didn't take long for the 172 to "catch on," and in 1960 a more deluxe version, the Skyhawk, was introduced. The 1960 models incorporated the swept vertical fin, an external baggage door, and a shorter undercarriage for easier cabin entry. The large wrap-around rear window was installed in 1963, providing a full 360-degree field of vision.

Other than a few wingtip and cabin refinements, the 172/Skyhawk series remained unchanged until 1968 when a 150-hp four-cylinder Lycoming replaced the 145-hp Continental O-300-C engine. The 1970 models offered conical camber wingtips, a light gray instrument panel, and other small refinements. A wider, softer spring-steel gear called Land-O-Matic was fitted onto the 172 in 1971, similar to the main legs on the 150 and Cardinal. The 172/Skyhawk featured an increased vertical fin, which was now a standard item on all new Cessnas. More recent versions sport the redesigned camber-lift wing introduced on the 1972/182 model, as well as improved soundproofing and a new instrument panel arrangement.

The Skyhawk/100, introduced in 1977, had more horsepower and speed, greater climb performance, and a higher service ceiling—all this with less fuel consumption than previous models. Using a 160-hp Lycoming, the Skyhawk has at its disposal 10 additional horsepower to yield a 1½-mph increase in cruise speed and a 5-percent improvement in fuel consumption. It will clear a 50-foot obstacle in 1,440 feet, 85 feet less than earlier model Skyhawks. In addition, the modern engine is designed to use the readily available 100-octane fuel. Other refinements include improved instrument visibility, a flap control with infinite settings, a vernier mixture control and optional rudder trim.

Air conditioning was added as an option in 1978, and in 1979 the Skyhawk's flap extension speed was increased from 98 mph to 127 mph, permitting earlier use of the flaps. For 1981, the Skyhawk offered increased useful load, a new engine, improved handling, and a new avionics cooling system. The ramp weight was increased 100 pounds, allowing for 89 pounds of extra useful load after 11 pounds are subtracted as a result of a heavier engine. The new engine was a 160-hp Lycoming O-320-D2J with an oil cooler and full-flow oil filter as standard accessories. Also, a rounded leading edge on the elevator reduced elevator forces required during landing flare.

CESSNA CUTLASS RG
1979–86

STANDARD DATA: Seats 4. Gross wt. 2,650. Empty wt. 1,555. Fuel capacity 66. Engine 180-hp Lycoming. **PERFORMANCE:** Top mph 167. Cruise mph 161. Stall mph 58. Initial

A retractable version of Cessna's ever-popular Skyhawk was introduced in late 1979. Designated the Cutlass RG, it carries 180-hp in the nose, 20-hp more than its sister ship. Even with the addition of retractable gear mechanisms, the Cutlass achieves an impressive 14.7 pounds/hp power loading ratio, compared to 14.4 for the Skyhawk or the Piper Arrow IV and Beech Sierra at 13.75 pounds/hp. Everything from the firewall back and the belly upward is 172. The gear is the same used in the Skylane RG and can be operated at anytime under 161 mph, taking about five seconds to cycle.

The Cutlass fit into the airplane market as the lowest-priced four-place retractable and was economical to operate with a fuel consumption rate of 10 gph at 75 percent power. Cruise at 9,000 feet and 75 percent power is 161 mph. With a maximum usable fuel capacity of 62 gallons, range at that power setting is 829 miles. The useful load of 1,092 pounds and four seats allows the Cutlass to achieve 64 seat-miles per gallon. Because it was built from the time-tested Skyhawk airframe, proven Skylane RG landing gear, and the reliable Lycoming O-360 engine, people at Cessna liked to joke that it was "a new Cessna that already withstood the test of time."

CESSNA HAWK XP
1970–81

STANDARD DATA: Seats 4. Gross wt. 2,550. Empty wt. 1,538. Fuel capacity 52–68. Engine 195-hp Teledyne Continental. **PERFORMANCE:** Top mph 153. Cruise mph 149. Stall mph 54. Initial climb rate 870. Ceiling 17,000. Range 506–731. Takeoff distance (50') 1,360. Landing distance (50') 1,345.

The Hawk XP is a single-engine airplane introduced by Cessna in 1977. Utilizing a 195-hp fuel-injected powerplant turning a constant-speed propeller, it offers the pilot 1,000 pounds of useful load and a 150-mph cruising speed for cross-country transportation. It was Cessna's attempt to add another option to the four-place airplane market. The Hawk combines optimum payload, speed, and climb performance for the moderate price bracket. Its 76-inch propeller delivers takeoff thrust at a low 2,600 RPM, thus reducing internal and external noise levels. Even with full fuel (49 useful gallons), the plane has 707 pounds of useful load remaining. At gross weight it can clear a 50-foot obstacle in 80 feet less than the Skyhawk/100 and 40 feet less than the Cardinal.

Like most other single-engine Cessnas, the Hawk incorporates flap control with multiple settings, a vernier fuel mixture control and a reengineered instrument panel. Rudder trim was included as standard equipment. In 1979, optional integral fuel cells increased usable fuel to 66 gallons for a range of 938 miles with a 45-minute reserve. Flap extension is permitted at 127 mph (110 knots) compared to 98 mph (85 knots) on pre-1979 models. In addition to the standard four seats, an optional child's seat could be added for extra seating capacity. With the 1981 model year, handling characteristics of the XP were significantly improved by the addition of rounded leading edges on the elevators. The forces required during landing flare were reduced, balked-landing climb capability was enhanced, and trim requirements during flap-setting changes were reduced.

CESSNA 175 "SKYLARK" 1958–62

STANDARD DATA: Seats 4. Gross wt. 2,350. Empty wt. 1,312. Fuel capacity 52. Engine 170-hp Continental. **PERFORMANCE:** Top mph 147. Cruise mph 139. Stall mph 62. Initial climb rate 850. Ceiling 15,900. Range 595. Takeoff distance (50') 1,340. Landing distance (50') 1,155.

Originally introduced in 1958, the Skylark was intended to fill the gap between the 145-hp Skyhawk and the 230-hp Skylane. It featured numerous refinements on the basic 172 configuration. A 175-hp geared Continental boosted the maximum cruise speed from 124 mph for the Skyhawk to 139. The Skylark boasted a 210-fpm increase in initial climb rate over its sister ship. Other improvements included a free-blown windshield, electric fuel gauges, fiberglass speed-fairings, a new panel design, and a redesigned interior decor; otherwise, the Skylark handled and flew much like the Skyhawk. In fact, the only way to tell them apart was that the Skylark had a bump in the cowl to allow for the engine gearing mechanism. Cessna discontinued the 175 after about five years because it earned a reputation for engine problems. This was possibly due to the fact that near 3,000 RPMs for cruise and takeoff were required, but pilots were hesitant to follow the manual; they cut back and caused the engine to overheat. Even during runup, the tach needle slid easily down to 2,600 RPM, redline for most planes. Because pilots often failed to fly up to the Skylark's potential, they tended to be skeptical about its performance claims over the Skyhawk.

CESSNA 177 "CARDINAL CLASSIC" 1968–78

STANDARD DATA: Seats 4. Gross wt. 2,500. Empty wt. 1,533. Fuel capacity 50–61. Engine 180-hp Lycoming. **PERFORMANCE:** Top mph 160. Cruise mph 150. Stall mph 53. Initial climb rate 840. Ceiling 14,600. Range 636–776. Takeoff distance (50') 1,400. Landing distance (50') 1,220.

Don't confuse the 1968 and 1969 Cardinal with the 1970 through 1973 models. The original 1968 Cardinal was powered by a 150-hp Lycoming engine. It soon became obvious that the 150 hp just couldn't do the job, so a replacement 180-hp Lycoming was installed in 1969. Cessna made a major change on the Cardinal for 1970 with a revised airfoil that much improves low-speed handling. The airplane also has a constant-speed propeller and cowl flaps, moving it out of the Skyhawk class and into the realm of the Skylane. It could be fitted with optional children's jump seats and offered a range of more than 800 miles. The new wing allowed safe low-speed approaches, and the engine/prop combination yielded fine takeoff, climb, and go-around performance. The 1970 models replaced the earlier straight wingtips with drooping conical camber tips.

CESSNA "CARDINAL RG" 1970–78

STANDARD DATA: Seats 4. Gross wt. 2,800. Empty wt. 1,707. Fuel capacity 61. Engine 200-hp Lycoming. **PERFORMANCE:** Top mph 180. Cruise mph 170. Stall mph 57.5. Initial climb rate 925. Range 823–1,030. Ceiling 17,100. Takeoff distance (50') 1,585. Landing distance (50') 1,350.

First announced by Cessna on Dec. 3, 1970, the Cardinal RG (retractable gear) has become the choice for many who look for a single-engine plane with good cruising speed yet with a reasonable price tag. With no wing struts to create drag and a hydraulically retractable tricycle landing gear, the RG can reach a cruise speed of 171 mph while burning only eight gph at 9,500 feet. Since its introduction, the RG has been handed some important changes, such as an improved propeller that has increased the airspeed about six mph and the removal of the foot step under the cabin door. The sleek-looking high-winger is powered by a 200-hp four-cylinder fuel-injected Lycoming engine.

The landing gear is retracted by an electrically powered hydraulic pump in a self-contained hydraulic system. When the gear is retracted, the main gear is flush with the fuselage using no wheel doors; the nose gear is faired by wheel doors. On late models, the landing gear has improved hydraulics, wheel doors, wheels, brakes, and nose gear trunion. The instrument panel was completely redesigned to provide more space and better locations for key instruments and avionics.

CESSNA L-19 "BIRD DOG" 1950–63

STANDARD DATA: Seats 2. Gross wt. 2,400. Empty wt. 1,614. Fuel capacity 41. Engine 210-hp Continental. **PERFORMANCE:** Top mph 115. Cruise mph 104. Stall mph 54. Initial climb rate 1,150. Range 530. Ceiling 18,500. Takeoff distance (50') 560. Landing distance (50') 600.

The Cessna L-19 "Bird Dog" was adopted by the U.S. Army for liaison and observation work in 1950. The airplane was used extensively in Korea and later in Vietnam in these and other capacities. A total of 3,381 L-19 series aircraft were built by Cessna, the last in 1963. Some have reached civilian hands and are prized as short-field utility aircraft. Ector Aircraft Co. of Odessa, Texas, marketed an extensively rebuilt civilian version of the Bird Dog under the name of "Mountaineer." It is powered by a 213-hp engine turning a constant-speed prop. A "Super" version is also produced with a 240-hp Lycoming.

CESSNA 180 "SKYWAGON" 1953–81

STANDARD DATA: Seats 4–6. Gross wt. 2,800. Empty wt. 1,643. Fuel capacity 88. Engine 230-hp Teledyne Continental. **PERFORMANCE:** Top mph 170. Cruise mph 163. Stall mph 55. Initial climb rate 1,100. Range 903. Ceiling 17,700. Takeoff distance (50') 1,205. Landing distance (50') 1,365.

Cessna's 180 represents another well-designed airframe that has withstood the test of time. Production deliveries of the 180 started in 1953, and it was produced through 1981 with

several minor changes in design and increased engine power. Early models of this conventional-gear high-wing aircraft were powered by a 225-hp Continental engine but were otherwise similar to a Cessna 170. Although the dimensions of the 180 have been altered only a scant three inches, models since 1966 seat six persons. In 1956, a 230-hp powerplant was swapped for the original engine. The last 180s retain this engine as well as conventional gear for operation from short or rough landing strips. Also, the original vertical fin is still used in place of the swept-fin introduced on all other Cessnas (except the 185) in 1960.

The same high-compression powerplant used for the Skylane was also used for the Skywagon 180 in 1977. It achieves 230 hp at 200 RPMs less than before and adds over 50 miles to the airplane's range. In addition, takeoff performance is improved along with reduced sound levels. In 1979, wheel fairings were added as an option and were claimed to raise both maximum and cruise speeds by one knot. Both Skywagons can be converted quickly from six-place seating to provide more than 721 cu. ft. of cargo area. For agricultural uses, 1980 improvements included the option of a 151-gallon, fan-driven Sorenson spray system, deflector cable plus windshield, and landing-gear wire cutters. Also, the 20-degree flap speed was increased from 90 mph to 110 mph.

CESSNA 182 "SKYLANE" 1956–86

STANDARD DATA: Seats 4. Gross wt. 3,100. Empty wt. 1,720. Fuel capacity 92. Engine 230-hp Continental. **PERFORMANCE:** Top mph 168. Cruise mph 163. Stall mph 56. Initial climb rate 865. Ceiling 14,900. Range 945. Takeoff distance (50') 1,515. Landing distance (50') 1,350.

STANDARD DATA: (Turbo 182) Seats 4. Gross wt. 3,100. Empty wt. 1,725. Fuel capacity 92. Engine 235-hp turbocharged Lycoming. **PERFORMANCE:** Top mph 193. Cruise mph 181. Stall mph 56. Initial climb rate 965. Ceiling 20,000. Range 857. Takeoff (50') 1,475. Landing (50') 1,350.

The Cessna 182 Skylane is a popular, performing airplane. The only other fixed-gear four-place airplane that has chalked up more sales is its little brother, the 172 Skyhawk. Using the 180 series airframe, Cessna installed a tricycle landing gear, and the 182 came into being. The deluxe Skylane model appeared in 1958 and, along with most of the Cessna line, the swept vertical fin was added in 1960. The wrap-around rear window and electric flaps were new features in 1962.

With a constant-speed prop in front of a 230-hp Continental engine, the 182 Skylane carries four adults, their luggage, and a full load of fuel at 160 mph for more than 600 miles. A spacious panel provides ample room for installation of full IFR equipment for the instrument-rated owner. The 1969 features included a restyled panel with electro-luminescent lighting and a revised flap control indicator that retained the preselect feature. In 1972, a tubular spring-steel gear was installed on the 182 Skylane, bringing what was formerly a maximum landing weight of 2,800 pounds up to the gross weight of 2,950. Other changes included the addition of cuffed leading edges similar to the Robertson wing; restyled gear fairings, wing root fairings, fuel tank covers, fin tip, and rudder fairings to improve airflow and reduce drag; new stronger wheels and brakes; and optional electric elevator trim.

For 1977, the Skylane made use of a new powerplant that is capable of providing 230 hp at 200 RPMs less than the previous engine. Also, its higher compression ratio makes more efficient use of readily available 100-octane fuel. The Skylane will fly about 52 miles farther than its predecessors. A bonded wing added in 1979 provides an added standard fuel capacity of 12 gallons more than the previous year's optional long-range tanks, or 1,013 miles at 166 mph compared to 599 miles with the earlier standard tanks. There is also the added benefit of a decrease in unusable fuel.

For 1981, the Skylane was joined by a turbocharged stablemate powered by the same turbocharged 235-hp Lycoming engine found in the Turbo Skylane RG. Both the Skylane and Turbo Skylane now have a 3,100-pound maximum takeoff weight. That gives the normally aspirated Skylane 150 pounds of extra takeoff weight. The Turbo 182 has a top speed of 168 knots and cruises at 158 knots at 75 percent power and 20,000 feet and 145 knots (167 mph) at 75 percent power and 10,000 feet. When production of Piper's Turbo Dakota discontinued, the Turbo Skylane was the only player in its class.

CESSNA "SKYLANE RG" 1978–86

STANDARD DATA: (RG) Seats 4. Gross wt. 3,100. Empty wt. 1,750. Fuel capacity 92. Engine 235-hp Continental. **PERFORMANCE:** Top mph 184. Cruise mph 180. Stall mph 58. Initial climb rate 1,140. Ceiling 14,300. Range 972. Takeoff distance (50') 1,570. Landing distance (50') 1,320.
STANDARD DATA: (Turbo RG) Seats 4. Gross wt. 3,100. Empty wt. 1,797. Fuel capacity *2??*. Engine 235-hp turbocharged Lycoming. **PERFORMANCE:** Top mph 215. Cruise mph 199. Stall mph 58. Initial climb rate 1,040. Ceiling 20,000. Range 949. Takeoff distance (50') 1,570. Landing distance (50') 1,320.

The Skylane RG is the most recent addition to Cessna's high-performance retractable single-engine lineup. It retains all the features that have made the Skylane the most popular 200-hp plus single-engine airplane ever built. Without the drag of nonretractable gear, speed and climb performance have been greatly improved. The Skylane RG has a maximum speed of 184 mph and a climb speed of 1,140 fpm that puts the airplane at 7,500 feet in less than 10 minutes. Despite the addition of retractable gear, the useful load has actually been increased by 145 pounds. The retractable gear has been designed with simplicity in mind. Retraction time is seven seconds, with the main gear retracting into the wheel wells in the fuselage and the nose gear rotating forward.

In 1979, Cessna added a turbocharged version of the Skylane RG to its line. The turbocharged model provides sea-level performance at altitude. Its rate of climb at 10,000 feet is 890 fpm, while at 20,000 feet it's 660 fpm. Above 10,000 feet, the Turbo RG will climb twice as fast as the normally aspirated model. The only noticeable external difference between the two is the one exhaust pipe instead of the two pipes on the nonturbocharged version. In 1980, both Skylane RG models added air conditioning as an option. Although not certified for flight into known icing, an optional anti-ice system includes propeller anti-ice, windshield anti-ice, heated pitot and stall warning, plus an ice detection light. Also, 1981 and later models can be fitted with three-blade propellers and an autopilot as options.

CESSNA 185 "SKYWAGON" 1961–81

STANDARD DATA: (1961–65) Seats 5–6. Gross wt. 3,200. Empty wt. 1,520. Fuel capacity 84. Engine 260-hp Continental. **PERFORMANCE:** Top mph 176. Cruise mph 165. Stall mph 62. Initial climb rate 1,000. Ceiling 17,300. Range 885–1,005. Takeoff distance (50') 1,510. Landing distance (50') 1,267.
STANDARD DATA: (1966–80) Seats 6. Gross wt. 3,350. Empty wt. 1,688. Fuel capacity 88. Engine 280-hp Teledyne Continental (300-hp at takeoff). **PERFORMANCE:** Top mph 178. Cruise mph 169. Stall mph 56. Initial climb rate 1,075. Ceiling 17,900. Range 742. Takeoff distance (50') 1,430. Landing distance (50') 1,400.

Based upon the 180 airframe, the Skywagon 185 is famous for its size, speed, and ease of flying. For the first five years, it was powered by the 260-hp Continental. That engine was replaced the following year by the 520-cu. in., six-cylinder powerplant rated at 300 hp for takeoff at 2,850 RPM. The 185 will take off in 1,025 feet, climb out at better than 1,000 fpm, and cruise at 167 mph while carrying a 1,663-pound useful load. Fuel injection enhances its all-weather reliability and economical operation. Its high-lift wing with modified Frise all-metal ailerons and 28.8 sq. ft. of Para-Lift flaps afford easy handling over obstacles. A full six-place aircraft, its seats are easily removable to provide fast change to all-cargo configuration. Its rugged interior and reinforced floor allow it to handle heavy loads, and its double cargo doors facilitate loading. Like the 180, the 185 is easily transformed into a skiplane, floatplane, or amphibian. In 1979, optional wheel fairings were offered to increase speeds by one knot, and a McCauley three-blade propeller could be ordered for smoother, quieter flight and more ground clearance. In addition to the same spray system option offered for the 180, the 185 received a three-blade propeller for lower vibration and a quieter cabin in 1980. Also, the 20-degree flap speed was increased from 90 mph to 110 mph.

CESSNA AG "CARRYALL" 1972–79

STANDARD DATA: Seats 2. Gross wt. 3,350. Empty wt. 1,895. Fuel capacity 88. Engine 300-hp Teledyne Continental fuel injected. **PERFORMANCE:** Top mph 148. Cruise mph 140. Stall mph 56. Initial climb rate 845. Range 650. Ceiling 13,400. Takeoff distance (50') 1,450. Landing distance (50') 1,400.

Based on the Model 185, the AG Carryall was introduced in 1971 as a multipurpose aircraft capable of performing both agricultural and general purpose duties. It is perfect for farmers who require both spraying capabilities and transportation. The AG Carryall is fitted with dual seating but has optional arrangements for four to six. It also features spray booms and a 151-gallon chemical tank. The most recent models have been equipped with an improved electrical system and an increased flap-extension speed. In 1979, the fuel tanks were enlarged to carry up to 88 gallons for extended range. Removable spray booms allow conversion from sprayplane to transportation airplane. Its Camber-Lift wing Land-O-Matic gear and Para-Lift flap give the AG Carryall the stability, maneuverability, and performance required for agricultural flying.

CESSNA 190/195 1947–54

STANDARD DATA: (190) Seats 5. Gross wt. 3,350. Empty wt. 2,015. Fuel capacity 80. Engine 240-hp Continental. **PERFORMANCE:** Top mph 170. Cruise mph 160. Stall mph 63. Initial climb rate 1,050. Ceiling 16,000. Range 750. Takeoff distance (50') 1,670. Landing distance (50') 1,495.
STANDARD DATA: (195) Seats 5. Gross wt. 3,350. Empty wt. 2,030. Fuel capacity 80. Engine 300-hp Jacobs Radial. **PERFORMANCE:** Top mph 180. Cruise mph 165. Stall mph 63. Initial climb rate 1,210. Range 750. Ceiling 18,300. Takeoff distance (50') 1,670. Landing distance (50') 1,495.

The model 190 and 195 have become Cessna classics. Some 995 of the 195s were produced between 1947 and 1954, and more than half of this number are still rated airworthy. Easily identified by their gleaming spinners and large cowlings encasing the nine-cylinder radial engines, these high-wing five-place airplanes have seen many years of service since production was discontinued. Both the 190 and 195 entered production in 1947. The 190 was powered by a 240-hp Continental radial driving a Hamilton Standard constant-speed airscrew. The 195 was virtually the same, with the exception of a more powerful 300-hp Jacobs. Engine variations resulted in two other versions, the 195B and the 195A. The 195B was fitted with the 275-hp Jacobs; the 195A, the last to be built, was powered by a Jacobs 245-hp radial and had a 50-percent increase in flap area on the huge, strutless wings. With an oil capacity of five gallons (minimum recommended is three gallons) the stock 195s with steel-cylinder engines will gulp about two quarts per hour, but chrome barrels will decrease the radial's consumption.

CESSNA 205/206/ "STATIONAIR 6" 1963–86

STANDARD DATA: (Stationair 6) Seats 6. Gross wt. 3,600. Empty wt. 1,927. Fuel capacity 92. Engine 285-hp Continental (300 hp at takeoff). **PERFORMANCE:** Top mph 179. Cruise mph 169. Stall mph 62. Initial climb rate 920. Ceiling 14,800. Range 783. Takeoff distance (50') 1,780. Landing distance (50') 1,395.
STANDARD DATA: (Turbo Stationair 6) Seats 6. Gross wt. 3,600. Empty wt. 2,003. Fuel capacity *9??*. Engine 285-hp turbocharged Continental (310 hp at takeoff). **PERFORMANCE:** Top mph 200. Cruise mph 192. Stall mph 62. Initial climb rate 1,010. Ceiling 27,000. Range 737. Takeoff distance (50') 1,640. Landing distance (50') 1,395.
STANDARD DATA: (205) Seats 6. Gross wt. 3,300. Empty wt. 1,750. Fuel capacity 84. Engine 260-hp Continental

PERFORMANCE: Top mph 165. Cruise mph 158. Stall mph 57. Initial climb rate 965. Ceiling 16,100. Range 915. Takeoff distance (50') 1,465. Landing distance (50') 1,510.
STANDARD DATA: (U 206) Seats 4–6. Gross wt. 3,600. Empty wt. 1,710. Fuel capacity 65–84. Engine 300-hp Continental, **PERFORMANCE:** Top mph 174. Cruise mph 164. Stall mph 61. Initial climb rate 920. Ceiling 14,800. Range 650–830. Takeoff distance (50') 1,780. Landing distance (50') 1,395.
STANDARD DATA: (P-206) Seats 6. Gross wt. 3,600. Empty wt. 1,820. Fuel capacity **??6544??**. Engine 285-hp Continental. **PERFORMANCE:** Top mph 174. Cruise mph 164. Stall mph 61. Initial climb rate 920. Ceiling 14,800. Range 650–830. Takeoff distance (50') 1,780. Landing distance (50') 1,395.
STANDARD DATA: (TU206) Seats 4–6. Gross wt. 3,600. Empty wt. 1,795. Fuel capacity 65–84. Engine 285-hp turbocharged Continental. **PERFORMANCE:** Top mph 200. Cruise mph 182. Stall mph 61. Initial climb rate 1,030. Ceiling 26,300. Range 700–890. Takeoff distance (50') 1,810. Landing distance (50') 1,395.
STANDARD DATA: (TP206) Seats 6. Gross wt. 3,600. Empty wt. 1,915. Fuel capacity **??6544??**. Engine 285-hp turbocharged Continental. **PERFORMANCE:** Top mph 200. Cruise mph 182. Stall mph 61. Initial climb rate 1,030. Ceiling 26,300. Range 700–890. Takeoff distance (50') 1,810. Landing distance (50') 1,395.

The Cessna 205 was introduced in 1962 as an advanced version of the Skylane. It had an enlarged cabin to house six passengers and a 260-hp Continental engine. In 1964, this aircraft evolved into the Model 206, which was in turn available in three versions: U206 Super Skywagon, P206 Utility, and P206 Super Skylane. All three were powered by the 285-hp Continental engine. The Super Skywagon featured conical-camber wingtips, a tailplane of greater span, larger flaps, and double cargo doors for easy loading. The Utility version had only the usual passenger door, while the Super Skylane was the deluxe six-seat version with passenger doors on both sides in the front and a third on the rear portside. Starting in 1966, these versions also became available with turbocharging, and in 1968 the Super Skywagon's horsepower was boosted to 300. The 300-hp turbosystem Super Skywagon provided excellent over-the-weather capability with its 26,300-foot service ceiling. To permit full use of its high-altitude performance, a 76 cu. ft. oxygen system (three to four hours) included a pilot's mask with built-in microphone, five passenger oxygen masks, and other essentials.

By 1971, Cessna replaced the 206 series with the Stationair and Turbo Stationair in order to emphasize the difference between these streamlined cargo/utility aircraft and the conventional-geared 180/185 models. The Stationair and the Turbo Stationair retained the 285-hp Continental used in all previous models. All Stationairs were fitted with double cargo doors on the starboard side and could be converted easily from cargo to passenger configuration. The doors can accommodate a $4 \times 3 \times 3$-foot crate and can also be removed for photography missions or air drops. Though the basic Stationair engine is rated at 285 hp for maximum continuous operation, it delivers up to 300 hp for takeoff.

For 1977, the turbocharged Continental powerplant was refined to deliver the same continuous power at 100 RPMs less, while its available takeoff horsepower was increased from 300 to 310. Just as before, the normally aspirated engine in the Stationair provides 300 hp for takeoff. In 1978, the Stationair 6 and Turbo Stationair 6 introduced club seating in the Cessna single-engine line, replacing the 206 and Turbo Stationair. In 1979, the major change was the addition of 16 gallons of fuel, with the change to 92-gallon fuel tanks as standard equipment.

In 1980, anti-icing was added as an option. The same as used on the Skylane RG, it included propeller anti-ice, windshield anti-ice, heated pitot tube and stall warning, plus an ice detector light. Standard features for 1981 models included improved avionics cooling, a new muffler for the normally aspirated model, and an antiprecipitation static antenna when factory installed radios were ordered.

CESSNA "STATIONAIR 8"/7/"SKYWAGON" 207 1969–86

STANDARD DATA: (Stationair 8) Seats 8. Gross wt. 3,800. Empty wt. 2,110. Fuel capacity 61–80. Engine 285-hp fuel-injected Continental (300 hp at takeoff). **PERFORMANCE:** Top mph 173. Cruise mph 165. Stall mph 67. Initial climb rate 810. Ceiling 13,300. Range 403–604. Takeoff distance (50') 1,970. Landing distance (50') 1,500.
STANDARD DATA: (Turbo Stationair 8) Seats 8. Gross wt. 3,800. Empty wt. 2,183. Fuel capacity 61–80. Engine 285-hp turbocharged Continental (310 hp at takeoff). **PERFORMANCE:** Top mph 196. Cruise mph 185. Stall mph 67. Initial climb rate 885. Ceiling 26,000. Range 345–547. Takeoff distance (50') 1,860. Landing distance (50') 1,500.
STANDARD DATA: (Stationair 7) Seats 7. Gross wt. 3,800. Empty wt. 2,076. Fuel capacity 61–80. Engine 285-hp Continental (300 hp at takeoff). **PERFORMANCE:** Top mph 173. Cruise mph 165. Stall mph 67. Initial climb rate 810. Ceiling 13,300. Range 449–650. Takeoff distance (50') 1,970. Landing distance (50') 1,500.
STANDARD DATA: (Turbo Stationair 7) Seats 7. Gross wt. 3,800. Empty wt. 2,157. Fuel capacity 61–80. Engine 285-hp turbocharged Continental (310 hp at takeoff). **PERFORMANCE:** Top mph 196. Cruise mph 185. Stall mph 67. Initial climb rate 885. Ceiling 26,000. Range 403–604. Takeoff distance (50') 1,860. Landing distance (50') 1,500.

Cessna seemed willing to go to any length to sell airplanes. The company went to a length of 31 feet, 9 inches on the Model 207. The 165 cubic feet of fuselage can accommodate almost a ton of cargo or a starting basketball team and two substitutes. Power is the Continental IO-520F equipped with fuel injection to deliver 300 hp for takeoff and 285 hp max continuous. The Turbo model is outfitted with the TSIO-520G and delivers the same power for takeoff and continuous flight.

There is a separate baggage panel. The 14-foot-long cabin is entered by wide doors on each side forward and an optional double cargo door aft on the right. With full standard fuel and seven 170-pound adults aboard, the basic airplane is more than 4,000 below its maximum allowable gross weight.

In more recent models, aerodynamic improvements have resulted in an almost three percent increase in all airspeeds. Such improvements include redesigned wheel fairings, bonded fuel tank covers, and new fin and rudder tip fairings. For 1977, the 207 was fitted with a three-blade propeller as standard equipment on both the normally aspirated and Turbo models. Like the Turbo Stationair, the 207's engine is capable of delivering 310 hp for takeoff at 2,700 RPM instead of 2,850 RPM as before. The Continental powerplant also develops 285 hp at a slower engine speed so that maximum cruise speed is up six mph between 10,000 and 20,000 feet.

In 1978, the Stationair 7 and Turbo Stationair 7 replaced the Skywagon 207. While essentially the same aircraft, it cleared up the confusion of relating this airplane to the 180/185 Skywagons. The only change for 1979 was a 92-gallon fuel capacity, up 16 gallons from previous years. In 1980, the Stationair 7 became the Stationair 8, with the new designation reflecting the change to seating for eight. The intention was to lower the cost per seat-mile. In the utility configuration, useful load of the Stationair 8 is 1,745 pounds. In both normal and turbo models, a forward baggage compartment can hold 120 pounds. The turbo version can also be equipped with an easily attachable cargo pack with a 300-pound capacity. Standard features for 1981 and later models included an anti-precipitation-static navigation antenna, an improved avionics cooling system, and a more effective muffler for the normally aspirated model. Options included a high-capacity alternator and cabin intercom system.

CESSNA "AG WAGON"/ "AG TRUCK"/ "AG HUSKY" 1965–83

STANDARD DATA: (AG Husky) Seats 1. Gross wt. 4,400. Empty wt. 2,293. Fuel capacity 54. Engine 310-hp turbocharged Continental. **PERFORMANCE:** Top mph 126. Cruise mph 118. Stall mph 67. Initial climb rate 510. Ceiling 14,000. Range 245. Takeoff distance (50') 1,975. Landing distance (50') 1,265.
STANDARD DATA: (AG Wagon) Seats 1. Gross wt. 4,000. Empty wt. 2,164. Fuel capacity 54. Engine 285-hp fuel-injected Continental (300 hp at takeoff). **PERFORMANCE:** Top mph 151. Cruise mph 112. Stall mph 63. Initial climb rate 550. Ceiling 9,100. Range 260. Takeoff distance (50') 1,885. Landing distance (50') 1,265.
STANDARD DATA: (AG Truck) Seats 1. Gross wt. 4,200.

Empty wt. 2,222. Fuel capacity 54. Engine 285-hp fuel-injected Continental (300 hp at takeoff). **PERFORMANCE:** Top mph 120. Cruise mph 111. Stall mph 65. Initial climb rate 490. Ceiling 8,100. Range 250. Takeoff distance (50') 2,140. Landing distance (50') 1,265.

CESSNA AG WAGON

CESSNA AG TRUCK

CESSNA AG HUSKY

Especially designed or agricultural use, the AG Wagon incorporates a variety of features to improve both the effectiveness and safety of spraying and dusting operations. The AG Truck is basically similar to the AG Wagon except that it carries a 280-gallon hopper rather than the former's 200-gallon hopper. Both airplanes are equipped with extra-heavy spring-steel landing gear with oversized tires; camber-lift wings and wing fences for better slow-speed control and smooth airflow; ample cockpit safety padding, wire cutters, and cable deflector; and various chemical dispersal systems. The cockpit features 360-degree vision and an airscoop that develops slight pressurization to keep out dust and chemicals.

Both the AG Wagon and AG Truck are powered by a 300-hp Teledyne Continental turning a constant-speed propeller. The AG Pickup, which was discontinued in 1972, and previous AG models housed smaller 230-hp Continentals. Cessna introduced the turbocharged AG Husky to its agricultural line in 1979. The highly efficient turbocharged Husky has a 310-hp engine to provide extra performance at varying operating altitudes. Standard equipment on the AG Husky is a 280-gallon hopper, an exclusive dispersal system, special lighting package, and a three-blade wide-chord prop. A new high-volume dispersal system that was standard on 1981–83 models allowed capability for up to 25 percent more chemical flow. Also, a redesigned emergency dump control gives fast, more convenient operation. Standard equipment on the AG Truck was an 86-inch two-blade threadless retention propeller. An 80-inch three-blade prop was an option.

CESSNA 210 "CENTURION" 1960–86

STANDARD DATA: (Centurion) Seats 4–6. Gross wt. 3,800. Empty wt. 2,133. Fuel capacity 90. Engine 300-hp Teledyne Continental (at takeoff). PERFORMANCE: Top mph 201. Cruise mph 198. Stall mph 64. Initial climb rate 950. Ceiling 17,300. Range 926. Takeoff distance (50') 2,030. Landing distance (50') 1,500.

STANDARD DATA: (Turbo) Seats 4–6. Gross wt. 4,000. Empty wt. 2,221. Fuel capacity 90. Engine 310-hp turbocharged Teledyne Continental (at takeoff). PERFORMANCE: Top mph 235. Cruise mph 226. Stall mph 67. Initial climb rate 930. Ceiling 27,000. Range 869 (80%). Takeoff distance (50') 2,160. Landing distance (50') 1,500.

STANDARD DATA: (Pressurized) Seats 4–6. Gross wt. 4,000. Empty wt. 2,340. Fuel capacity 90. Engine 310-hp turbocharged Continental (at takeoff). PERFORMANCE: Top mph 237. Cruise mph 230. Stall mph 67. Initial climb rate 930. Ceiling 23,000. Range 926 (70%). Takeoff distance (50') 2,160. Landing distance (50') 1,500.

STANDARD DATA: (Early 210) Seats 4. Gross wt. 2,900. Empty wt. 1,735. Fuel capacity 84. Engine 260-hp Continental. PERFORMANCE: Top mph 199. Cruise mph 190. Stall mph 59. Initial climb rate 1,300. Ceiling 20,700. Range 985. Takeoff distance (50') 1,135. Landing distance (50') 1,190.

CESSNA TURBO CENTURION II

CESSNA PRESSURIZED CENTURION

Until the introduction of the Cardinal RG in 1971, the Cessna 210 Centurion was the only single-engine, high-wing, retractable gear airplane manufactured by the largest maker of light aircraft. The Centurion was introduced in 1960, and the early versions had a top speed of about 195 mph. A gain in horsepower to 185 increased the top speed by five mph, but it was not until 1966, when a turbocharged engine was made available, and 1967, when the strutless wing was installed, that the Centurion became a truly high-speed aircraft. Service ceiling with the turbocharged engine is high enough to get over most weather problems. The maximum takeoff and landing weight had been increased to 3,800 pounds, with almost half of

that in useful load. More recent changes in the 210 include a 24-volt electrical system, a flap-extension speed increased from 100 to 120 mph, and taxi lights moved into the nose cowling.

Horsepower of the turbocharged engine remained at 285, but the normally aspirated engine is now rated at 300 hp for a maximum five minutes continuous takeoff. Like other Cessna models employing the turbocharged version of the basic 285-hp Continental, the Turbo Centurion makes use of 310 hp on takeoff. Overall, the 1977 T210 climbs and cruises faster and more efficiently than its 1976 counterpart. Maximum cruise speed is up by approximately six mph at altitudes between 10,000 and 20,000 feet. Also, the reduction in takeoff distance is a significant 130 feet less than before. Other refinements included power switch/circuit breakers, simplified wiring, improved ventilation, and a redesigned vernier mixture control. In 1978, Cessna introduced the world's first pressurized single-engine aircraft, the Pressurized Centurion with standard seating for six, the economy of up to 77 seat-miles per gallon, and a payload of more than 1,100 pounds with full fuel. The pressurized differential provides a 12,000-foot cabin at 23,000 feet. A special high-capacity turbocharger on the Continental powerplant supports the pressurization system.

Improvements for 1979 included elimination of the main landing gear doors to decrease the empty weight of the aircraft by 25 pounds, dropping gear-retraction time to less than eight seconds, and simplifying maintenance. For the Turbo Centurion, takeoff weight was increased by 200 pounds to 4,000 pounds so that it now equaled the figures for the pressurized model. In 1980, air conditioning and deice became an option for all Centurion models. Newer standard features were an improved avionics cooling system and an antiprecipitation antenna.

CHAMPION "TRAVELLER"/ "CHALLENGER" 1955–65

STANDARD DATA: (Traveller) Seats 2. Gross wt. 1,450. Empty wt. 820. Fuel capacity 24. Engine 90-hp Continental. PERFORMANCE: Top mph 135. Cruise mph 112. Stall mph 40. Initial climb rate 700. Range 500. Ceiling 15,500. Takeoff run 890. Landing roll 755.

STANDARD DATA: (Challenger) Seats 2. Gross wt. 1,650. Empty wt. 1,050. Fuel capacity 39. Engine 150-hp Lycoming. PERFORMANCE: Top mph 162. Cruise mph 125. Stall mph 36. Initial climb rate 1,145. Range 510. Ceiling 17,500. Takeoff distance (50') 493. Landing distance (50') 580.

Champion Aircraft, formed in June 1954, acquired the manufacturing rights to Aeronca's Model 7 Champ and put the monoplane back into production as the 7EC Traveller. The Traveller was powered by a 90-hp Continental four-cylinder engine. The first Champion-built models were marketed in 1955, and several revised versions soon followed. The Tri-Traveller was introduced in 1957 with tricycle landing gear added to the Traveller airframe. In 1958, the 7GC entered production as the Sky-Trac with a 140-hp Lycoming. From this evolved the 7GCB Challenger powered by a 150-hp Lycoming. The 7ECA Citabria was a refinement of the Traveller Deluxe, which was in turn a further development of the 7EC Traveller. The Challenger was out of production by 1965, but the Citabria was continued until 1970, when it was bought by Bellanca.

CHAMPION 7FC "TRI-TRAVELLER" 1956–64

STANDARD DATA: Seats 2. Gross wt. 1,500. Empty wt. 910. Fuel capacity 26. Engine 90-hp Continental. PERFORMANCE: Top mph 135. Cruise mph 105. Stall mph 40. Initial climb rate 800. Range 500. Ceiling 12,000. Takeoff run 250.

The Champion 7FC Tri-Traveller is derived from the Model 7EC Traveller, and production began in 1956. The Tri-Traveller differed from its predecessors by employing a tricycle fixed undercarriage. This tandem two-seater is powered by a single 90-hp Continental C912F four-cylinder engine. It is of mixed construction with a fabric-covered welded steel-tube fuselage. The wings are built with two wooden spars, aluminum ribs, and fabric covering. The Tri-Traveller was widely used by flying schools as a trainer.

CHANCE-VOUGHT F4U "CORSAIR" 1941–57

STANDARD DATA: Seats 1. Gross wt. 12,309. Empty wt. 8,694. Engine 2,250-hp Pratt & Whitney. PERFORMANCE: Top mph 425. Cruise mph 350. Stall mph 80. Initial climb rate 3,120. Range 1,560. Ceiling 44,100.

The prototype XF4U4 was delivered to the Navy in 1940, and after extensive testing the Corsair entered quantity production in the fall of 1941. The Corsair was the first United States fighter to exceed 400 mph, and the airplane achieved an outstanding record as a carrier fighter during World War II and as a ground attack weapon in Korea. During the record period of production that extended from 1941 to 1957, over 12,000 of the type were built, several of which are currently active in civilian hands.

CONSOLIDATED VULTEE (CONVAIR) L-13 1945

STANDARD DATA: (L-13) Seats 3. Gross wt. 2,900. Empty wt. 2,070. Fuel capacity 60–112. Engine 245-hp Franklin. PERFORMANCE: Top mph 115. Cruise mph 92. Stall mph 43. Initial climb rate 1,050. Ceiling 15,000. Range 368–750. Takeoff distance (50') 561. Landing distance (50') 483.
STANDARD DATA: (Centaur) Seats 6. Gross wt. 3,550. Empty wt. 2,300. Engine 300-hp Lycoming. PERFORMANCE: Top mph 121. Cruise mph 100. Stall mph 46. Initial climb rate 750. Ceiling 13,100. Range 850. Takeoff distance (50') 725. Landing distance (50') 700.

First built in 1945, the L-13 was intended to meet military requirements for a general-purpose liaison, observation, photographic, and ambulance aircraft. By 1947, 300 aircraft were delivered; twenty-eight were adapted for Arctic use on wheels, skis, or floats. Standard seating was for one pilot, an observer, and a third member aft. As an ambulance airplane, the L-13 carried a pilot, medical attendant, and two casualty stretchers. Power was supplied by a 245-hp Franklin flat six-cylinder engine. The aircraft payload was 833 pounds. As is often the case with military observation/liaison, several companies have produced civilian versions. Most conversions are fitted with 300-hp Lycoming radial engines, such as the Centaur 101 (originally the Longren Centaur). This model can seat up to six persons and has double loading doors in the starboard side. The Caribbean Traders Husky Mk II is similarly powered but makes use of an extended vertical stabilizer and can accommodate up to eight persons. Another firm, L-13 Inc., built a 300-hp version that could carry up to one ton of cargo in addition to the pilot. Its structure is reinforced, but otherwise it is similar to the Centaur 101 and the Husky.

CONSOLIDATED VULTEE BT-13 "VALIANT" 1941–45

STANDARD DATA: Seats 2. Gross wt. 4,360. Empty wt. 3,345. Fuel capacity 120. Engine 450-hp Pratt & Whitney.

PERFORMANCE: Top mph 166. Cruise mph 140. Stall mph 75. Initial climb rate 1,562. Range 516. Ceiling 16,500.

Almost 10,000 BT-13 basic trainers were manufactured for the Army Air Corps before and during World War II, but relatively few remain active. Designed by the Vultee Aircraft Division of the Aviation Manufacturing Corp., the airplane soon took the parent name of Convair as the former company merged with the Consolidated Aircraft Corp. to become Consolidated Vultee Aircraft Corp. (Convair). The airplane was officially named the Valiant, universally dubbed the "Vibrator," but fly it did, behind a 450-hp Pratt & Whitney Wasp Junior nine-cylinder engine or a Wright Whirlwind of the same power. Similar in many respects to the much more prevalent T-6, except for fixed landing gear and generally lower performance, the BT-13 was used by the Air Corps as a "halfway house" on the training road between biplane and civilian light-plane training and the advanced instruction given in the AT-6. Those who enjoy restoring older aircraft can have a field day with the Valiant, several hundred of which exist in out-of-license condition and needing major repair. Plenty of airframes exist for parts sources, and the Wasp that powered most Valiants is one of the best engines ever built; parts and service are available almost anywhere in the free world. The Valiant is relatively easy to fly but weighs almost as much as the Cessna 310 or Beech Baron when everything is full, so it can't be treated like an Aircoupe.

CULVER DART
MODEL G
1938–41, 1946

STANDARD DATA: Seats 2. Gross wt. 1,550. Empty wt. 910. Engine 90-hp Lambert. **PERFORMANCE:** Top mph 132. Cruise mph 112. Initial climb rate 850. Range 580. Ceiling 14,800.

The Dart Model G two-seat light cabin monoplane, designed by Al Mooney, was originally produced as the Lambert

Monosport by Lambert Aircraft Corp., which later became the Monocoupe Corp. Designs and rights were later acquired by the Dart Manufacturing Corp. and then ultimately held by Culver Aircraft. Production of the Model G began in 1938s. A 90-hp Lambert five-cylinder radial air-cooled engine provided the power. Variations of the Dart were designated by engine type and an alpha code after the G prefix. For example, the Dart GK was powered by a 90-hp Ken Royce five-cylinder radial, and the Dart GW was equipped with a 90-hp Warner Scarab Junior radial swinging a Hamilton Standard aluminum prop. The Model GC was subsequently produced with a 100-hp Continental. All Dart Model Gs were of mixed construction with welded steel-tube fuselages and wooden wings. Seating was for two in side-by-side fashion with dual controls. In all, 51 Darts were manufactured and of the 21 left in existence, approximately one dozen Model Gs are still active.

CULVER CADET
1939–41

STANDARD DATA: Seats 2. Gross wt. 1,305. Empty wt. 730. Fuel capacity 20. Engine 80-hp Franklin or 75-hp Continental. **PERFORMANCE:** (LFA) Top mph 140. Cruise mph 120. Stall mph 45. Initial climb rate 800. Range 600. Ceiling 17,500.

The Culver Aircraft Co. was formed to take over Dart Manufacturing Corporation's production of the Dart Model G in 1939. A new aircraft, similar to the Dart in appearance, but smaller, was designed and soon became known as the Cadet. The aircraft was modified and in 1940 became the Model LCA. Production of the wooden aircraft lasted until the next year when the Culver company closed its civilian works to concentrate on military contracts. The LCA was powered by a 75-hp Continental engine, while a similar version, the LFA, was powered by an 80-hp Franklin four-cylinder engine. Approximately 50 Cadets are currently active and not infrequently found on the used-plane market.

CULVER NR-D

STANDARD DATA: Seats 1. Gross wt. 1,830. Engine 150-hp Franklin. **PERFORMANCE:** Top mph 175. Cruise mph 160. Initial climb rate 800. Range 512.

The Culver NR-D was initially a radio-controlled target airplane intended to simulate enemy attacks. Its design was derived from that of the Culver Cadet. A unique feature in comparison to other target planes was that it was built with a single-seat cockpit and could be flown manually. When the surplus planes became available to private owners, the cockpit made the conversion to conventional private use very easy. The radio-controlled equipment was removed, and the interiors were refinished. There are currently a dozen NR-Ds registered in this country out of the 750 or so examples produced for the Air Force and Navy.

CULVER MODEL V
1946–62

STANDARD DATA: Seats 2. Gross wt. 1,600. Empty wt. 1,030. Fuel capacity 32. Engine 90-hp Continental. **PERFORMANCE:** Top mph 135. Cruise mph 130. Stall mph 55. Initial climb rate 750. Range 700. Ceiling 13,100. Takeoff run 800. Takeoff distance (50') 1,600.

The Model V was introduced in 1946 by the Culver Aircraft Corp., but few were produced before the company went bankrupt in the same year. In those years, power was supplied by an 85-hp Continental engine. In 1956, Superior Aircraft Co. was founded to acquire Culver Aircraft and reinstate production of the Model V under the name Superior Satellite. The Satellite used a 90-hp Continental engine, but otherwise retained the same basic structure as the Model V. The fuselage and wings were constructed from resin-bonded spruce and plywood. Nearly 30 Satellites and Model Vs are still active in the United States.

CURTISS JN-4D
"JENNY"
1914

STANDARD DATA: Seats 2. Gross wt. 2,130. Empty wt. 1,580. Engine 90-hp Curtiss OX-5. **PERFORMANCE:** Top mph 75. Cruise mph 65. Stall mph 35. Initial climb rate 250.

The Curtiss Jenny was America's first mass-produced commercially viable airplane. Designed in 1914 to lower the accident record being rolled up by the U.S. Army in earlier pusher airplanes, the Jenny went on to become the standard U.S. military trainer throughout World War I and for five years thereafter. Nearly 7,000 were built, and surplus Jennies began showing up in civilian hands by 1919. For around $6,000 you could buy a crated Jenny, put it together, and start your own barnstorming business. Many took up the challenge with varying degrees of success. The fatal flaw of the Jenny (aside from a vicious stall-spin characteristic) was the powerplant. Literally dozens of things could (and did) go wrong with the OX-5, and an engine failure every 10 hours was not uncommon. By the close of the 1920s, wrecks, and rot had begun to take a toll on the original 7,000. Less than a dozen Jennies remain today.

CURTISS-WRIGHT C1
"ROBIN"
1928–30

STANDARD DATA: Seats 3. Gross wt. 2,620. Empty wt. 1,710. Fuel capacity 35. Engine 90-hp Curtiss OX-5 or 225-hp Continental W-670K. **PERFORMANCE:** (90 hp). Top mph 100. Cruise mph 84. Initial climb rate 400. Range 800. Ceiling 10,200. **PERFORMANCE (225 hp):** Top mph 126. Cruise mph 104. Initial climb rate 800. Range 410. Ceiling 14,250.

The design and production of the first Curtiss Robin three-seat monoplanes was begun by the Curtiss Aeroplane and Motor Co. in Garden City, New York. It was soon decided that producing a commercial machine in a factory primarily equipped for military aircraft was impractical; thus, the Curtiss-Robertson Airplane Manufacturing Corp. was formed in 1928 to take over production of the Curtiss Robin C-1. The first Robin's modest price was primarily due to its use of cheap, surplus 90-hp OX-5 engines. Sales were excellent, and the type became the first cabin three-seater to be mass-produced. During the plane's production life, several variations were produced with different engines, but today about half of the Robins still in service are powered by 225-hp Continentals. As the supply of the OX-5 engines diminished, the Robin was introduced with the new Curtiss Challenger 165-hp engine. This combination proved to be the most popular of the last several Robin models, and over 750 were sold. In the last year of production, a four-place variant of the type was introduced as the Robin 4C-1A but failed to achieve much of a following; only 25 of this type were produced.

CURTISS-WRIGHT P-40 "HAWK"
1938–44

STANDARD DATA: Seats 1. Gross wt. 6,789. Empty wt. 5,381. Engine 1,200-hp Allison liquid-cooled V-12. **PERFORMANCE:** Top mph 365. Cruise mph 315. Landing mph 72.5. Range 945. Ceiling 35,000.

The P-40 Warhawk saw wider service than any other fighter during World War II. It was present on every front throughout the world from 1939 to 1945, and it flew under the colors of 28 allied nations. The Warhawk was the only Army Air Corps fighter in service during the first month of the war, and it (along with the British Spitfire and the Grumman Wildcat) bore the bulk of the responsibility for meeting the enemies' attack until late in 1942. The Warhawk fought in Africa, England, Australia, China, and Russia. A total of 13,783 P-40s were produced during the war. Power was supplied by a single 1,200-hp Allison 12-cylinder liquid-cooled engine.

DAVIS D1-W
1930

STANDARD DATA: Seats 2. Gross wt. 1,460. Empty wt. 925. Engine 125-hp Warner Scarab. **PERFORMANCE:** Top mph 142. Cruise mph 122. Initial climb rate 1,360. Ceiling 14,800.

Davis Aircraft Corp. produced three models of the D4 series two-seat light monoplanes in the early 1930s. Neither of

the first two models, the D-1-85 with an 85-hp Le Blond engine or the D-1-K with a 100-hp Kinner engine, can be found active today. The third model, the D1-W was equipped with a 125-hp Warner Scarab seven-cylinder radial air-cooled engine. Very few D-1-W models can be found still active. Easily identified by the large "Parasol" type wing and what looks like an over-sized engine for its small, open-cockpit fuselage, the D-1-W features complete dual controls for its tandem seats. The aircraft has a steel-tube fuselage covered with fabric and a two-spar wing.

DE HAVILLAND DH-4
1917–24

STANDARD DATA: Seats 2. Gross wt. 3,740. Empty wt. 2,440. Engine 420-hp Liberty. **PERFORMANCE:** Top mph 124. Cruise mph 115. Stall mph 55. Initial climb rate 1,000. Range 350.

The DH-4 was the first combat plane to go into production in the United States. Over 3,400 of the type were built before production ceased at the war's end in 1918. Armed with two Vickers guns on the cowl, two Lewis guns at the rear cockpit and 220 pounds of bombs in the wing racks, it became the first and only American-built plane to fly over enemy territory in World War I. After the Armistice, variations of the DH-4 remained with the military services as observation or transport planes until 1932. During the 1920s, DH-4s also achieved prominence as airmail carriers piloted by such luminaries as Charles Lindbergh. Generally, the type was very serviceable with tremendous load-carrying capability and good reliability; however, its early versions quickly achieved the inglorious title of "Flaming Coffins" because the fuel tanks had a habit of exploding. Though the problem was satisfactorily resolved after the first year of production, the title stuck. Scant few exist today.

DE HAVILLAND DH-60 "GIPSYMOTH"
1925–32

STANDARD DATA: Seats 2. Gross wt. 1,750. Empty wt. 920. Engine 120-hp de Havilland Gipsy II. **PERFORMANCE:** Top mph 107. Cruise mph 85. Initial climb rate 720. Range 320. Ceiling 18,000.

The de Havilland Moth series of two-seat light biplanes began with the flight of the DH-60 in 1925. The original Moths had a wooden fuselage structure and were powered by engines ranging from the 60-hp A.D.C. Cirrus I to the 105-hp Cirrus

Hermes. As production of the early models tapered off, the improved DH-60 GM Gipsy Moth was introduced in 1928. The Gipsy featured a welded steel-tube fuselage, folding wings, and engine options up to 120-hp. About 1,700 DH-60s were built in England during the seven years of production, with an additional 150 built by Moth Aircraft Co. of Lowell, Massachusetts. Less than a dozen are reported active in the United States.

DE HAVILLAND DH-82 "TIGER MOTH"
1931–45

STANDARD DATA: Seats 2. Gross wt. 1,825. Empty wt. 1,115. Engine 130-hp Gipsy Major I. **PERFORMANCE:** Top mph 109. Cruise mph 90. Stall mph 43. Initial climb rate 673. Range 300. Ceiling 13,600.

The Tiger Moth was the final refinement of the two-place Moth series. Distinguished in part from its predecessors by its swept-back folding wings and more powerful Gipsy Major engine, the Tiger Moth first flew in October 1931, and more than 1,000 had been delivered by the outbreak of World War II. During the war, the British government adopted the biplane as a primary trainer for military flying schools throughout the Commonwealth. Between 1939 and 1945, de Havilland built 4,005 Tiger Moths in the United Kingdom and a further 1,747 in Canada. After the plane was declared surplus in 1947, it became perhaps the most widely operated biplane in Canada and Europe. Several examples have recently been imported into the United States and are finding great favor for their aerobatic capability and antiquated appearance.

DE HAVILLAND CANADA DHC-1 "CHIPMUNK"
1946–53

STANDARD DATA: Seats 2. Gross wt. 1,930. Empty wt. 1,158. Fuel capacity 30. Engine 145-hp D.H. Gipsy Major.

PERFORMANCE: Top mph 139. Cruise mph 124. Stall mph 50. Initial climb rate 900. Range 485. Ceiling 17,200. Takeoff distance (50') 870. Landing distance (50') 930.

The Chipmunk was designed by the Canadian de Havilland company for use as a primary trainer in both Canada and the United Kingdom. Slightly over 200 machines were produced in Canada, but over 1,000 were manufactured in Britain. A further 60 Chipmunks were produced in the late 1950s under license in Portugal. Few of these airplanes have made their way into the United States, but of those that have, most have been extensively modified for aerobatic and airshow work. Seating is tandem fashion under a sliding bubble canopy. A 145-hp Gipsy Major four-cylinder engine turns either a fixed-pitch wood propeller or a metal Fairey-Reed airscrew. The fuselage and wings are of all-metal construction, but the ailerons, elevators, and rudder are fabric covered.

DE HAVILLAND CANADA DHC-2 "BEAVER"
1948–69

STANDARD DATA: (Mk I) Seats 7. Gross wt. 5,100. Empty wt. 3,000. Fuel capacity 95–138. Engine 450-hp Pratt & Whitney. **PERFORMANCE:** Top mph 140. Cruise mph 135. Stall mph 60. Initial climb rate 1,020. Range 778. Ceiling 18,000. Takeoff distance (50') 1,015. Landing distance (50') 1,000.
STANDARD DATA: (Mk III) Seats 7–9. Gross wt. 5,370. Empty wt. 2,760. Fuel capacity 191. Engine 578-eshp Pratt & Whitney turboprop. **PERFORMANCE:** Top mph 170. Cruise mph 157. Stall mph 60. Initial climb rate 1,185. Range 677. Ceiling 20,500. Takeoff distance (50') 920. Landing distance (50') 870.

The Beaver first entered production in March 1948 and was the first in a family of STOL utility aircraft designed primarily for use in the Canadian bush. Since that time it has found great favor in a variety of civilian and military roles throughout the world. Beavers have had an excellent reputation of performing under the most difficult conditions, especially in Northern Canada, Alaska, Korea, and Vietnam and are noted for their ruggedness and short-field capability. The Mark I Beaver was the first in the series and was powered by a 450-hp nine-cylinder radial. The Mark III, which first became available in 1964, was designated the TurboBeaver. Accommodations were altered to seat up to nine passengers, and a 578-eshp (estimated shaft horsepower) turboprop with increased fuel capacity was installed. The starboard seat in the pilot's compartment is removable, and the cabin floor is stressed to handle freight. The Beaver's controls feature dual rudder pedals and a Y-type control column with a throw-over wheel.

DE HAVILLAND CANADA DHC-3 "OTTER"
1952–67

STANDARD DATA: Seats 9–10. Gross wt. 8,000. Empty wt. 4,431. Fuel capacity 214. Engine 600-hp Pratt & Whitney. **PERFORMANCE:** Top mph 160. Cruise mph 132. Stall mph 58. Initial climb rate 850. Range 875. Ceiling 18,800. Takeoff distance (50') 1,155. Landing distance (50') 880.

The Otter began production in 1951 as a larger complement to the Beaver. Like the Beaver, it has found favor with military as well as civilian operators who demand a great deal from their airplanes. By early 1966, a total of 460 Otters had been produced, many of which went to the U.S. Army under the U-1B designation. The R.C.A.F. uses Otters in Arctic search and rescue missions, paratroop drops, and aerial photographic duties. The United States has employed them in a wide range of areas from the Antarctic to Vietnam.

DIAMONA AIRCRAFT DA-20 "KATANA"
1994–95

STANDARD DATA: Seats 2. Gross wt. 1,610. Empty wt. 1,090. Fuel capacity 20.9. Engine 80-hp liquid-cooled Rotax 912.A3. **PERFORMANCE:** Top mph 155. Cruise mph 147. Initial climb rate 780. Ceiling 16,500. Range 490. Takeoff distance (50') 720. Landing distance (50') 800.

Originally introduced to the United States as the Diamona DV-20, the Katana is an all-composite, two-place, side-by-side training aircraft that was designed and produced in Europe by HOAC of Austria. HOAC has been a leading producer of sailplanes and motorgliders in Europe and has produced the Katana for a number of years abroad. Recognizing

that general aviation production in the United States was all but dead, HOAC opened a production facility in Ontario, Canada, with hopes of supplying North America with a much needed training aircraft. The Katana has enjoyed surprising acceptance in the United States and Canada as a well-crafted high-performance trainer.

The Katana was subsequently awarded Type 23 certification as a full production aircraft by the FAA and began to appear at flight schools around the country. Because of its lightweight composite construction, the Katana makes full use of minimum horsepower to give surprising performance and economy. Stressed to +4.4 and –2.2 Gs, the Katana is approved for limited aerobatics, which adds to the fun quotient. The Katana's motorglider heritage is evident with a wingspan of over 36 feet, which makes for a very stable training platform.

DOUGLAS "DAUNTLESS"
1941–44

STANDARD DATA: Seats 2. Gross wt. 10,500. Empty wt. 6,450. Engine 1,200-hp Wright Cyclone. **PERFORMANCE:** Top mph 255. Cruise mph 185. Stall mph 78. Initial climb rate 1,428. Ceiling 25,200. Range 773.

The Dauntless was produced in land-based and shipboard attack bomber variations. The two scout and dive bomber aircraft differed from each other only in minor items of equipment and in the elimination of carrier arrester gear on the land-based versions. The A-24 was built for the U.S. Army Air Force from 1941–43, and 863 were delivered for service. The Dauntless was powered by a 1,200-hp Wright Cyclone nine-cylinder radial engine and could achieve a top speed of 255 mph at 14,000 feet. Seating was in tandem fashion, and the rear cockpit was fitted with two machine guns on flexible mounts. Other armament included two fixed .50-caliber guns mounted in the fuselage, which were synchronized to fire through the propeller. A swinging bomb cradle for one bomb in the 500–1,000-pound class was carried underneath the fuselage, while other bomb racks were attached under the wing roots. Hydraulically operated dive brakes above and below the trailing edges of the outer wings and the center section of the fuselage set it apart as a dive bomber. By 1944, 5,936 Dauntlesses had been built and put into service. It was replaced by other advanced aircraft in the middle 1940s, but many stayed active.

DRIGGS DART I, II

STANDARD DATA: Seats 2. Gross wt. 820. Empty wt. 450. Engine 35-hp Anzani. **PERFORMANCE:** Top mph 85. Cruise mph 80. Landing mph 30. Initial climb rate 550. Range 250. Ceiling (absolute) 18,000.

The Driggs Dart was a light two-seat biplane first built in 1928. Original power was supplied by a French-built Anzani three-cylinder radial engine fed by a main fuel tank in the fuselage just behind the engine. Its tandem cockpits were fitted with dual controls, and its airfoils were of unequal span. The Driggs Aircraft Corp. was founded in Lansing, Michigan, by Ivan Driggs who had been previously associated with the Dayton-Wright Co. and the Johnson Airplane and AA Supply Co. In addition to the Dart, Driggs also built a lightplane designated the Skylark, which was fitted with a 60-hp Rover four-cylinder in-line inverted powerplant and could achieve a top speed of 110 mph.

EMIGH "TROJAN"
1948–51

STANDARD DATA: Seats 2. Gross wt. 1,450. Engine 90-hp Continental. **PERFORMANCE:** Top mph 130. Cruise mph 115. Landing mph 48. Range 550. Ceiling 13,000.

The Emigh Trojan was built in small numbers between 1948 and 1950 by the Emigh Aircraft Corp. and later the Emigh Trojan Aircraft Co. Its unique feature is the simplified construction methods used in its assembly. The metal fuselage of the Trojan is made up of two identical halves that are joined along their horizontal centerline. Its wingtips, tail surfaces, and ailerons are all interchangeable. This side-by-side two-seat cabin airplane can still be seen at airports around the country. Over 30 examples are listed in the United States civil aircraft register.

ERCOUPE, AIRCOUPE
1937–67

STANDARD DATA: (Aircoupe) Seats 2. Gross wt. 1,450. Empty wt. 930. Fuel capacity 25. Engine 90-hp Continental. **PERFORMANCE:** Top mph 129. Cruise mph 114. Stall mph 48. Initial climb rate 640. Range 615. Ceiling 17,300. Takeoff run 540. Landing roll 350.
STANDARD DATA: (Ercoupe) Seats 2. Gross wt. 1,400. Empty wt. 838. Fuel capacity 25. Engine 85-hp Continental. **PERFORMANCE:** Top mph 125. Cruise mph 110. Stall mph 47. Initial climb rate 560. Ceiling 11,000. Range 430.
STANDARD DATA: (Mooney Cadet) Seats 2. Gross wt. 1,450. Empty wt. 950. Fuel capacity 24. Engine 90-hp Continental. **PERFORMANCE:** Top mph 118. Cruise mph 110. Stall mph 46. Initial climb rate 835. Ceiling 12,500. Range 480. Takeoff distance (50') 953. Landing distance (50') 1,016.

In the late 1930s, the Ercoupe was designed as a stall-proof, spinproof airplane that had no rudder pedals. An interconnection between the ailerons and limited-travel rudders made flying the Ercoupe as easy as steering a car. Prevention of stalls was accomplished by blocking elevator travel before stall angle was achieved. Dubbed the model 415, the low-wing two-seater was produced from 1937 until World War II. None of the twin-tailed models were built during the war, but production resumed in 1945 with models 41 SE, F, and G appearing between 1947 and 1949. Finally, in 1951, production ceased, but in 1955, Fornaire Aircraft resurrected the Ercoupe calling it the F-1 Aircoupe. Air Products took over production between 1960 and 1962, and then it passed to Alon Aircraft in 1964.

Alon called its airplane—still virtually unchanged from the original Ercoupe—the Aircoupe A-2. The Alon version did, however, have rudder pedals and a modified landing gear, which on some models is a backward-bending spring-steel gear leg rather than an oleo strut. The Alon A-2 also featured a blown sliding-bubble canopy instead of the lift-up type fitted on earlier models. Alon Aircoupes had extremely attractive upholstery, and all flight gauges were shock-mounted on a floating subpanel in front of the pilot. Dual toe brakes were standard, operated by a bar running across and above the rudder pedals.

Alon was not the end of the Ercoupe history. Mooney Aircraft purchased the Aircoupe rights in 1968, changed the double tail to a single tail and sold the airplane with the name of Mooney Cadet. The A-2 Cadet and M10 Cadet were produced until 1970 when Mooney sold out to Aerostar.

FAIRCHILD 71 MONOPLANE
1928

STANDARD DATA: Seats 6. Gross wt. 5,500. Empty wt. 3,135. Fuel capacity 160. Engine 410-hp Pratt & Whitney Wasp radial. **PERFORMANCE:** Top mph 138. Cruise mph 102. Landing mph 55. Initial climb rate 900. Range 850. Ceiling 17,000.

The Fairchild 71 was designed as an improved version of the popular FC-2W2 and was first introduced in 1928. In the following year, Fairchild Aviation Limited began building this six-passenger lightweight commercial airplane in Canada and designated it the Model 71C and 71CM. The Model 71CM differed from the 71C by its metal fuselage skin rather than the standard fabric covering. All Fairchild 71s are of mixed construction with wooden wings and steel-tube fuselage structures. The enclosed cabin houses six passengers and a pilot. The pilot is in a single seat at the front of a cabin that narrows considerably at the nose. Several Model 72s are registered in the United States.

FAIRCHILD F-45
1936

STANDARD DATA: Seats 5. Gross wt. 4,000. Empty wt. 2,474. Fuel capacity 90. Engine 370-hp Wright Whirlwind. **PERFORMANCE:** Top mph 170. Cruise mph 164. Stall mph 49. Initial climb rate 1,140. Range 840. Ceiling 19,000.

First introduced in 1936, the F-45 was a five-seat cabin monoplane intended as a high-performance personal transport aircraft. Primarily used as an executive aircraft, it was built with a mixed construction that made use of a fabric-covered steel-tube fuselage and a wooden outer wing section. While the prototype was powered by a 220-hp Jacobs radial engine, subsequent production models received the 370-hp Wright Whirlwind seven-cylinder radial engine. Many reengined versions are still in active service powered by 450-hp Pratt & Whitney Wasp Juniors and 475-hp Wright Whirlwinds. Original Model 45s were capable of cruising at 164 mph at 75 percent power and 8,000 feet. Accommodations provided for two at the controls and three on a cross-seat in the back of the cab. A door on each side of the cabin made for easy entry.

FAIRCHILD PT-19/-23/-26
1939-45

STANDARD DATA: (PT-26) Seats 2. Gross wt. 2,741. Empty wt. 2,022. Fuel capacity 45. Engine 200-hp Ranger. **PERFORMANCE:** Top mph 126. Cruise mph 114. Stall mph 53. Initial climb rate 675. Range 450. Ceiling 17,300.

The Fairchild PT-19 was designed as a tandem two-seat primary trainer for use in the United States and Canada. Full-

scale production began early in 1940, and by the end of the war 5,401 PT-19s had been built in Canada, the United States, and Brazil. PT-19s were operated by Civilian Pilot Training schools throughout the war in conjunction with the Army Air Force, the principal user. In Canada, the aircraft was known as the Cornell. The PT-19 was powered by a 175-hp six-cylinder in-line inverted Ranger engine and could cruise at 113 mph for about 430 miles. Two other versions of the basic airframe also were produced. These were the PT-26, which featured an enclosed cockpit and a 200-hp Ranger engine, and the PT-23, which resembled the original PT-19 but utilized a 220-hp Continental radial engine. A few civilian models of the Cornell were also produced and were known as M-62s. Around 120 of the Fairchild aircraft are flying today, and many of these have been extensively rebuilt because the wooden center section of the fuselage has a propensity to rot.

FAIRCHILD F-22
1931-36

STANDARD DATA: Seats 2. Gross wt. 1,750. Empty wt. 1,102. Engine 145-hp Warner Scarab. **PERFORMANCE:** Top mph 133. Cruise mph 115. Initial climb rate 900. Ceiling 20,000. Range 350 mph.

The Kreider-Reisner Division of Fairchild produced this tandem two-seat parasol monoplane in 1931. It has the distinction of being one of the first successful light monoplanes that was built in quantity. During the five years that it was produced, a variety of engines were used. One of the most common powerplants was the 145-hp Warner Scarab seven-cylinder radial air-cooled engine; other engines included the 125-hp Warner Scarab, the 95-hp A.C.E. Cirrus, and the 90-hp Wright Gipsy.

FAIRCHILD F-24
1939-46

STANDARD DATA: Seats 4. Gross wt. 2,882. Empty wt. 1,813. Fuel capacity 60. Engine 200-hp Ranger. **PERFORMANCE:** Top mph 124. Cruise mph 112. Landing mph 57. Range 465. Ceiling 12,700.

Fairchild's 24R four-seat cabin monoplane first appeared in 1939 and was produced for the civilian aircraft market until the United States entered World War II. In 1942, production of the F-24R was shifted to a military version, which was designated UC-61K. The F-24R is equipped with a 175-hp Ranger six-cylinder, air-cooled engine that delivers a near 120-mph cruise speed for more than 600 miles. Other versions of the F-24 were powered by 145- or 165-hp Warner Super Scarab radials, 200-hp inline Ranger, and 450-hp Pratt & Whitney Wasp Junior.

A close look at the landing gear assembly reveals Fairchild's wide stance. Turns while taxiing are accomplished through the use of a steerable tailwheel, a point which challenges some of the F-24's pilots because of the rearward location of the center of gravity. Construction of the F-24 is a steel-tube fuselage, heavily faired to shape with formers and spruce longerons. Wings are wooden with fabric covering.

FAIRCHILD HILLER TURBO-PORTER (PILATUS PORTER)
1960–80

STANDARD DATA: (PC-6/B2) Seats 10. Gross wt. 4,850. Empty wt. 2,601. Fuel capacity 170. Engine 550-shp Pratt & Whitney turboprop. **PERFORMANCE:** Top mph 174. Cruise mph 161. Stall mph 52. Initial climb rate 1,580. Range 634. Ceiling 30,025. Takeoff distance (50') 620. Landing distance (50') 560.
STANDARD DATA: (PC-6/C) Seats 10. Gross wt. 4,850. Empty wt. 2,612. Fuel capacity 170–270. Engine 575-shp AiResearch turboprop. **PERFORMANCE:** Top mph 174. Cruise mph 164. Stall mph 52. Initial climb rate 1,607. Ceiling 27,875. Range 683–1,044. Takeoff distance (50') 600. Landing distance (50').

Fairchild Hiller produced the first series of Pilatus Turbo-Porters under license from the Pilatus Flugzeugwerke AG of Switzerland. This single-engine utility STOL aircraft was originally called the Heli-Porter and was powered by a 575-shp Pratt & Whitney. Other models produced by both the Fairchild Hiller and Pilatus companies include the PC-6/B1 Turbo-Porter and the PC-6/C Turbo-Porter. The PC-6/B1 utilizes a 550-shp Pratt & Whitney. The PC-6/1C is the later version of the first Heli-Porters and is now powered by a 575-shp AiResearch turboprop engine. The Turbo-Porter's STOL characteristics enable it to operate from small airfields.

Its easily removable seats allow it to be rapidly changed from a passenger carrier to a cargo carrier. Other jobs performed by the Pilatus are ambulance duties, aerial photogra-

phy, supply dropping, parachute training, and agricultural dusting. Current models of the Turbo-Porter have forward-opening doors on both sides of the cockpit, a large sliding door on the starboard side of the fuselage, and a double door on the portside. Currently, Fairchild continues to produce the Porter utility aircraft for agencies of the United States government. This version is powered by a Pratt & Whitney turboprop flat-rated at 550-shp with 680-shp available for takeoff. Also under production is the Peacemaker, housing a 650-shp Garrett turboprop and used primarily for counter-insurgency operations. Fairchild Hiller discontinued building and marketing the Turbo-Porter in the United States; however, the airplane continues to be produced by its parent company in Switzerland.

FLEET MODEL 1 and 2
1929–41

STANDARD DATA: Seats 2. Gross wt. 1,530. Empty wt. 976. Fuel capacity 24. Engine 110-hp Warner Scarab seven-cylinder radial. **PERFORMANCE:** Top mph 111. Cruise mph 90. Stall mph 46. Initial climb rate 930. Range 350. Ceiling 16,000.

The Fleet Aircraft Division of the Consolidated Aircraft Corp. was formed in Buffalo, New York, in 1929 specifically to undertake production of the Fleet Trainer. Prior to 1932, the Fleet 1 (110-hp Warner), the Fleet 2 (100-hp Kinner), and the Fleet 7 (125-hp Kinner) outsold any other make in their class and also proved to be popular overseas, particularly in China and Latin America. In all, about 600 Fleets were produced in the United States before production was terminated in 1935.

In the late 1930s, Fleet Aircraft of Canada acquired the manufacturing rights to the design and began producing an improved version of the Fleet 1 under the designation Fleet 16B Finch II. These models were equipped with 125-hp Kinners, and over 600 were delivered to the R.C.A.F. as basic trainers during the early part of the war. Most of these Canadian models are equipped with a sliding canopy to replace the open cockpit of the earlier models. Perhaps 30 Fleets exist today in the United States, with a few more active in Canada and other countries.

FLEET 80 "CANUCK"
1945–47

STANDARD DATA: Seats 2. Gross wt. 1,480. Empty wt. 858. Engine 85-hp Continental. **PERFORMANCE:** Top mph 111. Cruise mph 100. Range 400. Ceiling 12,000.

A favorite with Canadian pilots, this lightweight side-by-side two-seater can be fitted with wheels, floats, or skis. The

FLEET 80 "CANUCK"

sturdy all-metal frame, covered with fabric, is powered by a Continental four-cylinder 85- or 90-hp engine. A total of 210 Canucks were built in two years by Fleet Manufacturing, Ltd. in Fort Erie, Ontario, and of those a healthy percentage are still in flying condition. Most of the Fleet 80s flying today have been modified with improved heaters and cowling systems, updated Ceconite covering, and additional gyros and radios. Designed especially for Canadian flying conditions, the Canuck is still traded fairly regularly in Canada, and many a Canadian pilot has received primary pilot training in this Fleet airplane.

FLEETWINGS "SEA BIRD"

STANDARD DATA: Seats 4. Gross wt. 3,750. Empty wt. 2,450. Fuel capacity 70. Engine 285-hp Jacobs. **PERFORMANCE:** Top mph 150. Cruise mph 135. Initial climb rate 900. Range 540. Ceiling 14,500. Takeoff run 29 secs.

The "Sea Bird" amphibian was the first stainless-steel airplane to receive approved certification in the United States. In 1929, Fleetwings, Inc. began design and research work in stainless-steel construction. In 1934, the firm acquired Keystone Aircraft Corp. and built all-stainless-steel wings for the U.S. Army's Douglas "Dolphin." The "Sea Bird" is powered by a single 285-hp seven-cylinder radial engine in a nacelle mounted above the fuselage on steel-tube struts. A hatch on the port side provides entrance to both the forward stowage area and the cabin, where seating is for four in two pairs. The landing lights, water rudder, tailwheel, and main gear are all retractable. Of the six Sea Birds built, two are known to exist and one is currently active.

FOKKER D VII
1917–29

STANDARD DATA: Seats 1. Gross wt. 1,984. Engine 185-hp BMW or 160-hp Mercedes. **PERFORMANCE:** Top mph 117. Cruise mph 100. Stall mph 45. Range 150. Ceiling 19,680.

Only a few of the original single-seat German World War I fighters exist today. The Fokker D VII was chosen by the chief of the German air service, General Von Hoeppel, as the plane that could outmaneuver the Spad and the Sopwith in aerial combat. Fokker delivered the first D VII to the Von Richthofen unit within two months after the original order of 400 had been placed. Although the famous Von Richthofen chose to stick with the Fokker Triplane, eventually he was shot down while flying a D VII. The D VII ultimately became the favorite of many a German pilot.

Fitted with twin Spandau guns, the thick-winged fighter could almost hang by its prop at 45 degrees yet maintain excellent controllability. Its fuselage was made of welded and braced steel tube in box girder structure and covered with metal panels forward and a fabric-ply combination in the rear. The wooden cantilevered wings required no external wire bracing, and struts really weren't needed but were added to give the pilots some moral support. Both the 160-hp Mercedes D III and the BMW III 185-hp engines were six-cylinder in-line water cooled.

Perhaps the easiest to fly of all the World War I fighters, the Fokker D VII could execute rapid, smooth turns and was quite sensitive on the elevators. After the war, Fokker continued to build the D VII, selling the coveted plane to Holland, Belgium, Poland, Sweden, Italy, and Spain. The United States received 142 D VIIs that served with the military until the mid-1920s when a lack of spare parts forced their grounding.

FUNK MODEL B
1939

STANDARD DATA: Seats 2. Gross wt. 1,350. Empty wt. 890. Fuel capacity 20. Engine 75-hp Lycoming or 85-hp Continental. **PERFORMANCE:** (85-hp). Top mph 115. Cruise mph 100. Stall mph 37. Initial climb rate 800. Range 350. Ceiling 15,000. Takeoff run 348.

Originally produced by Akron Aircraft Co., the Model B was kept in production by the Funk Aircraft Co. after the latter company replaced Akron in 1941. The two-seat cabin monoplane, first made in 1939, had been equipped with a 65-hp Funk four-cylinder engine but in 1941 featured a 75-hp Lycoming engine and the designation 75L. After World War II, production continued on the Model B, this time with a Continental 85-hp engine and called the B-85C. The Model B has fabric-covered wooden wings and a steel-tube fuselage, also covered with fabric. Many present-day Funk owners have replaced the original fabric with strong Ceconite fabric and added other features such as hydraulic brakes and wheel pants. Over 100 Model Bs are active today and are fairly easily found for sale.

GREAT LAKES SPORT TRAINER
1929–32/1974–78/1980–94

STANDARD DATA: (1932) Seats 2. Gross wt. 1,580. Empty wt. 910. Engine 90-hp Cirrus. PERFORMANCE: Top mph 116. Cruise mph 100. Stall mph 40. Initial climb rate 1035. Range 400. Ceiling 21,000.

STANDARD DATA: Seats 2. Gross wt. 1,800. Empty wt. 1,230. Fuel capacity 26. Engine 180-hp Lycoming. PERFORMANCE: Top mph 132. Cruise mph 118. Stall mph 54. Initial climb rate 1,150. Ceiling 17,000. Range 300. Takeoff distance (50') 825. Landing distance (50') 825.

The original Great Lakes Model 2T-1 Sport Trainer was built by the Great Lakes Aircraft Corp. in Cleveland, Ohio, in 1929. Between 1929 and 1932, the company built more than 200 of them, and they quickly became a great favorite of aerobatic pilots. The designer, Charles W. Meyers, raced a customized Great Lakes with considerable success during the early 1930s, and the legendary Tex Rankin flew one in airshows throughout the country before World War II, setting records for both inside and outside loops. After the war, enthusiasm for the airplane continued and many airframes were converted to accept larger engines, particularly Warner radials. During the past several years, factory blueprints of the design have been available to homebuilders from the resurrected Great Lakes Aircraft Co., also of Cleveland, and several are under construction utilizing various modern engines.

In 1972, the design rights were sold to the Great Lakes

Aircraft Co. of Wichita, Kansas, and Enid, Oklahoma. In 1973, the Model 2T-1A-1 was certified with a 140-hp Lycoming, and the Model 2T-1A-2 (with a 180-hp Lycoming) was produced for the first time in 1974. In 1980, after more than 50 years, the legendary Great Lakes biplane found a new home in Eastman, Georgia. R. Dean Franklin, a Great Lakes pilot, set up a modern production facility after acquiring production rights, type certificates, and other assets of the Great Lakes Aircraft Co. The Great Lakes is the oldest certificated airplane still in production, and its manufacture closely follows the basic specifications of the original design.

GRUMMAN J2F "DUCK"
1933–45

STANDARD DATA: Seats 2. Gross wt. 7,290. Empty wt. 5,445. Fuel capacity 150. Engine 1,050-hp Wright Cyclone nine-cylinder radial. PERFORMANCE: Top mph 190. Cruise mph 106. Initial climb 1,330. Range 850. Ceiling 21,000.

Production of this general utility amphibian began in 1933 when the first prototype flew, and production continued until 1945. In all, nine series of the Duck were built. The J2F-6 was by far the most common. It featured aerodynamic improvements over the previous models, including a long-cord engine cowling. Only two Ducks are known to be active, though several more are registered. The amphibian was originally used for photography, target-towing, scouting, and rescue work. Although the Duck is normally flown as a two-seater in tandem fashion, a folding floor in the rear cockpit gives access to a lower compartment for use in rescue work and the like; the lower compartment could house either two extra crew members or a stretcher. Some models of the Duck were powered by the 725-hp Wright Cyclone engine.

GRUMMAN F4F "WILDCAT"
1941–45

STANDARD DATA: Seats 1. Gross wt. 5,876. Empty wt. 4,425. Fuel capacity 160. Engine 1,000-hp Wright Cyclone or 1,050-hp Pratt & Whitney Twin wasp. PERFORMANCE: (Wright Cyclone) Top mph 325. Cruise mph 285. Landing mph 66. Initial climb rate 3,300. Range 1,150. Ceiling 28,000.

Designed in 1937 by Robert L. Hall, designer of the famous Gee Bee racers of the early 1930s, the Wildcat first entered production in 1941. By 1942, Wildcats equipped all carrier fighter squadrons and remained our sole carrier fighter

GRUMMAN F4F " WILDCAT"

in action until mid-1943. Of all the U.S. wartime fighters, Wildcats were the slowest, even among the carrier-based varieties, yet they compensated for this defect in part by their good rate of climb and maneuverability. Though inferior to the Mitsubishi Zero in performance, Wildcats managed to score many crucial victories over the Japanese in the Pacific. This was due to good armament, firepower, and outstanding piloting techniques. At first, Wildcats were powered by 1,000-hp Wright Cyclones and 900-hp Twin Wasps. Those craft were designated F4F-4 and F4F-3 respectively. Later, the FM-2 Wildcat standardized the use of the 1,350-hp Cyclone engine. It was the last version to be built.

GRUMMAN F6F "HELLCAT"
1942–45

STANDARD DATA: Seats 1. Gross wt. 12,500. Empty wt. 9,153. Engine 2,000-hp Pratt & Whitney. **PERFORMANCE:** Top mph 400. Initial climb rate 3,000. Range 1,800. Ceiling 37,800.

The Hellcat single-seat shipboard fighter is easily recognizable by its landing gear that retracts into the center section as opposed to the Wildcat with gear that retracts into the fuselage just forward of the wings. It also differs from the later Bearcats in that it lacks the Bearcat's 360-degree vision canopy. The prototype of the Hellcat first flew in 1942. The shipboard fighter saw its first action in an attack on Marcus Island in 1943. Later Hellcats differ from their predecessors by having a redesigned engine cowling, improved windshield and tail surfaces, additional armor, and a waxed glossy skin. Bulletproof fuel tanks were housed in the wings, and an auxiliary drop tank could be added. Armament included six .50-caliber machine guns in the wings.

GRUMMAN F8F "BEARCAT"
1944–49

STANDARD DATA: Seats 1. Gross wt. 9,300. Empty wt. 7,070. Fuel capacity 185, two drop tanks 150 gals. each. Engine 2,100-hp Pratt & Whitney 18-cylinder radial. **PERFORMANCE:** Top mph 425. Cruise mph (economy) 163. Initial climb rate 5,700. Range 1,105. Ceiling 42,300.

The Grumman F8F Bearcat was originally designed as a replacement for the Hellcat, and it was hoped that the Bearcat would have better maneuverability and be able to operate from the smallest Navy carriers. The Bearcat was small, limited in weight and armed with four .50-caliber guns and external fittings for two 1,000-pound bombs, drop tanks, or four rockets. It was powered by a 2,100-hp Pratt & Whitney 18-cylinder radial engine, which accounts for an exceptional climb rate. Contracts for 2,023 Bearcats were approved in October 1944, and deliveries started in February 1945. The end of the war reduced the contract for the F8F-1D, and a total of 1,263 were produced. Surplus Bearcats designated F8F-1D and fitted with a modified fuel system were used in the Indochina war by the French Armee de l'Air. A number of Bearcats were later transferred to the Vietnam Air Force. The Bearcat was the last of Grumman's piston-engine carrier fighters.

GRUMMAN AMERICAN TRAINER
1967–79

STANDARD DATA: (Trainer) Seats 2. Gross wt. 1,560. Empty wt. 975. Fuel capacity 24. Engine 108-hp Lycoming. **PERFORMANCE:** Top mph 138. Cruise mph 124. Stall mph 60. Initial climb rate 705. Range 435. Ceiling 12,750. Takeoff distance (50') 1,590. Landing distance (50') 1,100.
STANDARD DATA: (Yankee) Seats 2. Gross wt. 1,500. Empty wt. 963. Fuel capacity 24. Engine 108-hp Lycoming. **PERFORMANCE:** Top mph 144. Cruise mph 134. Stall mph 66. Initial climb rate 710. Ceiling 11,000. Range 515. Takeoff distance (50') 1,615. Landing distance (50') 1,245.

The American AA-1 Yankee and its improved version, the AA-1A Trainer, started out as the James Bede-designed BD-1. After acquiring the design from Bede in 1964, American Aviation did some extensive redesign work and put the two-place Yankee into production in 1967. Conceived as a low-cost sport or utility aircraft, the Yankee incorporated several new construction techniques, including the use of aluminum honeycomb panels as the primary structural members and metal-to-metal bonding instead of rivets or bolts. The wing spar is a heavy aluminum tube that also houses the fuel supply. The wing ribs are bonded to the spar. Large bonded-on skin panels virtually eliminate all seams, and there are no protruding rivet heads to create drag.

The AA-1A Trainer was introduced in 1971 and soon replaced the Yankee. It incorporated a modified wing with improved low-speed characteristics, some changes in optional equipment, and a propeller with improved cruising performance. Grumman American Aircraft Corp. ultimately took over the production of the Trainer and added more versions based on the basic airframe design.

GRUMMAN AMERICAN TR-2
1971–79

STANDARD DATA: Seats 2. Gross wt. 1,560. Empty wt. 1,039. Fuel capacity 24. Engine 108-hp Lycoming. **PERFORMANCE:** Top mph 144. Cruise mph 133. Stall mph 60. Initial climb rate 660. Range 463. Ceiling 11,550. Takeoff distance (50') 1,590. Landing distance (50') 1,100.

Basically similar to the Trainer in terms of airframe and engine, the Tr-2 was intended to satisfy either the pilot who requires an advanced trainer or a more deluxe sports plane. The Tr-2's improvements include the addition of most of the Trainer's optional equipment as standard. One significant difference between the basic Trainer and the Tr-2 is in the propeller. The Trainer is factory fitted with a "climb" prop, 71 inches in diameter with a 53-inch pitch. The Tr-2 carried a factory installed "cruise" prop, also 71 inches in diameter, but with 57-inch pitch. This cruise propeller accounts for the in-

crease in top and cruise speed plus about 30 additional miles in total range; however, the Tr-2 suffers in the climb department with a 660-fpm capability compared to the Trainer's 705-fpm climb speed. Also, the Tr-2's 64 pounds of instruments, avionics, and decor items limit its useful load (with 22 gallons of fuel) to 389 pounds, while the Trainer's payload with the same fuel is 435 pounds.

GULFSTREAM AMERICAN "CHEETAH"
1972–79

STANDARD DATA: (Cheetah) Seats 4. Gross wt. 2,200. Empty wt. 1,362. Fuel capacity 38–52. Engine 150-hp Lycoming. **PERFORMANCE:** Top mph 157. Cruise mph 147. Stall mph 60. Initial climb rate 660. Range 589–830. Ceiling 12,650. Takeoff distance (50') 1,600. Landing distance (50') 1,100.
STANDARD DATA: (Traveler) Seats 4. Gross wt. 2,200. Empty wt. 1,180. Fuel capacity 37. Engine 150-hp Lycoming. **PERFORMANCE:** Top mph 150. Cruise mph 140. Stall mph 61. Initial climb rate 660. Ceiling 12,650. Range 627. Takeoff distance (50') 1,420. Landing distance (50') 1,052.

The AA-5 Traveler is essentially an enlarged version of the AA-1A Trainer. Given an increased wingspan and 32 more horsepower on an extended fuselage, the Traveler is a full four-place airplane. Production first began in late 1971 and was facilitated by the fact that the Trainer and the Traveler share nearly two thirds of their parts in common. Introduced by Grumman American, the Cheetah includes as standard equipment that which is usually optional on the Trainer. Also added were: electric flaps, increased tailplane dimensions, a baggage allowance of 120 pounds, and optional fuel capacity of 52 gallons (as opposed to the standard 38-gallon tankage).

At 75 percent power at 8,500 feet, the Cheetah will true 147 mph. Drop down to a more normal 6,500 feet and a more economical 65-percent power setting, and it will pull a true of 133 mph. Clean surfaces and clean design are behind the Cheetah's super speed figures. A rugged, chemical, metal-to-metal bonding process is used in place of rivets. It was a fairly new manufacturing process that other manufacturers were beginning to use on their expensive twins. Grumman American redesigned the old AA-5 Traveler's engine cowling for reduced drag, streamlined the main gear fairings and eliminated the ventral fin, all of which were speed-helping changes. Other improvements over the old AA-5 were engine cooling baffles, a long-range fuel tank option, a better exhaust system, a redesigned nose strut, and a 30-percent larger tail surface. The larger tail surface allowed the aft center-of-gravity loading to be extended and markedly improved control response. The Cheetah was finally manufactured by Gulfstream American Corp.

GULFSTREAM AMERICAN "TIGER" 1974–79

STANDARD DATA: Seats 4. Gross wt. 2,400. Empty wt. 1,400. Fuel capacity 52. Engine 180-hp Lycoming. **PERFORMANCE:** Top mph 170. Cruise mph 160. Stall mph 61. Initial climb rate 850. Range 752. Ceiling 13,800. Takeoff distance (50') 1,550. Landing distance (50') 1,120.

For the most part, the Tiger is a new-engine version of the four-seat Traveler. Its cruise speed, rate of climb, and 110-pound useful load put it in the class of many higher priced aircraft, including some light retractables. The Tiger features fold-down rear seats for increased baggage space and a redesigned engine cowl for easier removal. Still in use are the honeycomb box section and the extruded tubular alloy spar in the wing, the virtually rivetless resin-bonded skin, and castering nosewheel to facilitate steering in tight places. Airflow has been smoothed by adding new wheel fairings and a recontoured spinner cowl area. Though the year 1979 saw the company name change from Grumman American to Gulfstream American, there were no significant changes in the Tiger itself. Production was halted during 1980.

GULFSTREAM AMERICAN "SUPER AG-CAT" 1957–81

STANDARD DATA: Seats 1. Gross wt. 4,500. Empty wt. 2,690. Fuel capacity 80. Engine 450-hp Pratt & Whitney radial. **PERFORMANCE:** Top mph 147. Cruise mph 90. Stall mph 67. Initial climb rate 1,800. Range 400. Ceiling 14,000. Takeoff distance (50') 1,360. Landing distance (50') 750.

The Grumman Super AG-Cat is a beefed-up version of the regular G-164 AG-Cat built under contract by Schweizer Aircraft in Elmira, New York. The specialized agricultural sprayer flew for the first time in 1957, with first deliveries in 1959. Designed with a maximum-lift wing using minimum wingspan, the powerful biplane can make a continuous 1.5G turn at dusting speed even at gross weight. The wings are constructed of Duralumin with fabric covering, and the fuselage is made with steel tube covered with Duralumin sheet metal. The upper and lower wings of the biplane are interchangeable. An enclosed cockpit canopy is optional; otherwise, the single-seat cockpit is open and a reinforced fairing aft of the cockpit provides "turnover" protection. The Super AG-Cat will carry up to 2,000 pounds or 247 gallons of agricultural chemicals in a fiberglass hopper. Power was originally supplied by a 220-hp Continental. Until 1969 the 220-hp Continental, 300- or 275-hp Jacobs, or 450-hp Pratt & Whitney were used. Since 1969, engine options have been limited to the 600 or 450-hp Pratt & Whitneys.

HARLOW PJC-2 1938–41

STANDARD DATA: Seats 4. Gross wt. 2,600. Empty wt. 1,700. Engine 145-hp Warner Super-Scarab seven-cylinder radial. **PERFORMANCE:** Top mph 150. Cruise mph 135. Landing mph 53. Initial climb rate 660. Range 500. Ceiling 15,500.

The Harlow Engineering Corp. of Alhambra, California, began production of the Harlow PJC-2 in 1938. In the following year, the company changed its name to the Harlow Aircraft Co. The Model PJC-2 was a four-seat cabin-monoplane of all-metal construction and was fitted with retractable landing gear. The Harlow was under development for three years and submitted to over a year of flight testing before it was placed on the market. Production was continued in small numbers until 1941. In that same year, a two-seat training version was produced under the designation of PC-5A. It differed mainly by having a narrower fuselage and a 165-hp Warner Super-Scarab engine. PC-5A production lasted until 1942.

HAWKER "HURRICANE" 1937–44

STANDARD DATA: (Hurricane II) Seats 1. Gross wt. 7,014. Empty wt. 5,454. Engine 1,185-bhp Rolls-Royce Merlin XX. **PERFORMANCE:** Top mph 320. Initial climb rate 2,950. Ceiling 33,000.

During the Battle of Britain, Hurricanes accounted for more victories over Luftwaffe aircraft than any other fighter—1,500 in all. The first Hurricane flew in October 1937. Designated the Hurricane I, it was outfitted with a Rolls-Royce Merlin II or III engine, fabric-covered wings, and a wooden prop. It lacked armor and self-sealing fuel tanks. Hurricanes saw action throughout the war from the skies over Great Britain to Norway, Italy, North Africa, and Burma. They carried out missions as fighters, fighter-bombers, tank-busters, catapult fighters, and carrier fighters. The first Hurricane II went into production in 1940 and was powered by a Merlin XX V-12-cylinder liquid-cooled engine. Improvements included wing alterations for increased armament, redesigned engine mount, strengthened fuselage, and tanks protected with self-sealing rubber. In all, over 15,000 Hurricanes were built by the time production ceased in 1944.

HAWKER "SEA FURY"
1944–53

STANDARD DATA: Seats 1. Gross wt. 12,350. Empty wt. 9,240. Fuel capacity 240. Engine 2,560-hp Bristol Centaurus 18-cylinder radial. **PERFORMANCE:** Top mph 450. Cruise mph (30,000 ft.) 415. Initial climb rate 4,320. Range 1,630. Takeoff run 960.

The Hawker Sea Fury was the last piston-engine fighter to serve the Royal Navy. It was designed in 1942, primarily as a lighter version of the Tempest although it didn't enter production in time to see action in World War II. Sea Fury airplanes were used in Korea where they often had to engage Soviet-built Mig-15 jet fighters and succeeded in scoring a few victories against their faster opponents. A total of 860 Sea Fury airplanes were built, including a number of tandem two-seat trainers. This type exists in very small numbers in the United States where modified versions have scored notable wins on the air-racing circuit.

HELIO COURIER H-295/395/391
1955–78

STANDARD DATA: (H-295) Seats 4–6. Gross wt. 3,400. Empty wt. 2,080. Fuel capacity 120. Engine 295-hp Lycoming. **PERFORMANCE:** Top mph 167. Cruise mph 165. Stall mph 30. Initial climb rate 1,150. Range 660. Ceiling 20,500. Takeoff distance (50') 610. Landing distance (50') 520.
STANDARD DATA: (H-250) Seats 6. Gross wt. 3,400.

Empty wt. 1,890. Fuel capacity 120–270. Engine 250-hp Lycoming. **PERFORMANCE:** Top mph 160. Cruise mph 152. Stall mph 31. Initial climb rate 830. Ceiling 15,200. Range 644–1,288. Takeoff distance (50') 750. Landing distance (50') 520.

The Helio Courier, which has the ability to take off and land at 30 mph on unimproved landing strips less than 500 feet long, has established itself firmly in the general aviation market. A certificated STOL (**S**hort **T**ake **O**ff and **L**and) aircraft, the Courier series displays an aptitude for safe, almost stall-proof, slow-speed flight, as well as the range and cruising speed of comparable conventional aircraft. Leading-edge wing slats automatically extend or retract in response to changes in air pressure to prevent stalls or spins. Aileron-linked airflow interceptors provide excellent lateral control while large slotted flaps on the trailing edge, working in conjunction with the slats on the leading edge, double the lift of the wing.

Also, its full cantilever construction eliminates the wasteful drag created by strut braces. With an all-moving stabilator for pitch control and a tall, swept fin, and rudder for its direction control, the two Courier models possess maximum stability during slow flight. The original Courier prototype was a converted Piper Vagabond; from this was created the H-391, which was powered by a 260-hp Lycoming and offered seating for four to five. The H-395 followed in 1959 with its 295-hp engine and five seats. The H-295 first appeared in 1965 and featured increased seating and the same 295-hp engine. Its counterpart was the H-250 powered by the 250-hp Lycoming.

The two current commercial versions of the Helio are the Super Courier H-295 with nonretractable conventional landing gear and the Tri-gear 54-Courier HT-295 with nonretractable tricycle gear. Three models are flown, by the U.S. Air Force: the U-10A with a fuel capacity of 60 gallons; the U-lOB, a long-range version with tankage for 120 gallons; and the U-1OD, an improved long-range version with a fuel capacity of 120 gallons and a gross weight boosted to 3,600 pounds.

HELIO H-550A "STALLION"
1966–76

STANDARD DATA: Seats 8–10. Gross wt. 5,100. Empty wt. 2,860. Fuel capacity 120. Engine 680-ehp United Aircraft of Canada turboprop. **PERFORMANCE:** Top mph 216. Cruise mph 206. Minimum mph 42. Initial climb rate 2,200. Range 445. Ceiling 25,000. Takeoff distance (50') 660. Landing distance (50') 750.

The Stallion is specifically designed for operation from unprepared fields and is equipped with a full complement of STOL devices. Design of the Stallion began in 1963, and the first models were produced in 1966. The Helio Aircraft Corp.

HELIO H-550A "STALLION"

was founded in 1948, and its first prototype was a converted Piper Vagabond. Then Helio became a part of the General Aircraft Corp. and produced the Super Courier and the Stallion. Both aircraft are similar in construction. The Stallion is powered by a single 680-ehp turboprop engine driving a three-blade reversible-pitch prop and fed by wing tanks with a capacity of 120 gallons.

Its all-metal cantilevered wings are equipped with high-lift slotted all-metal flaps, fabric-covered balanced ailerons, and full-span automatic leading-edge slats. The tail unit features a one-piece horizontal surface with combined trim and antibalance tab. The cabin is protected by a crash-resistant tubular frame. The Stallion's accommodations provide for a pilot and copilot up front with either eight passengers on bench seats or six passengers seated individually. Access is made through a door on the port side near the pilot, an optional starboard door, and a double cargo door on the port side. The double door is in two sections—the forward half hinges and the rear half slides. The rear half can be opened during flight for cargo drops or parachutists.

HOWARD DGA-15P
1939–42

STANDARD DATA: Seats 5. Gross wt. 4,350. Empty wt. 2,700. Fuel capacity 150. Engine 450-hp Pratt & Whitney Wasp Junior 9-cylinder radial. **PERFORMANCE:** Top mph 201. Cruise mph 191. Landing mph 61. Range 1,263. Ceiling 21,500.

First produced by the Howard Aircraft Corp. in 1939, the DGA-15 was modeled after the Bendix Trophy winner DGA-6 "Mr. Mulligan" of 1934–35. It was a progressive development of the DGA-8 and the DGA-9. Four variations of the DGA-15 were the DGA-15P with a 450-hp Wasp Junior, the DGA-15W with a 350-hp Wright engine, the DGA-15J with a 350-hp Jacobs engine, and finally the GH-1 produced for the U.S. Navy as a four-seat personnel transport. Approximately 70 DGA-15s are active today, and at least one will show up at any respectable fly-in.

INTERSTATE S1B
"CADET"
1940/1969–80

STANDARD DATA: (102 hp). Seats 2. Gross wt. 1,650. Empty wt. 1,103. Fuel capacity 15. Engine 102-hp Franklin. **PERFORMANCE:** Top mph 114. Cruise mph 105. Stall mph 38. Initial climb rate 900. Range 540. Ceiling 16,500. **STANDARD DATA:** (150 hp). Gross wt. 1,900. Empty wt. 1,100. Fuel capacity 40. Engine 150-hp Lycoming. **PERFORMANCE:** Top mph 115. Cruise mph 110. Stall mph 39. Range 650. Initial climb rate 1,000. Takeoff run 350.

In 1940, the Interstate Aircraft & Engineering Corp. began production of the Interstate Cadet. The S1B was a member of a family of taildraggers, such as the Piper Cub, Taylorcraft, Luscombe, and Aeronca Champ that served many a weekend pilot with fun-filled hours during the late 1930s and early 1940s. The original Cadet was produced in a number of versions using engines from 65 hp to 102 hp. Most popular was the S5B using a 102-hp four-cylinder Franklin. The tandem two-seater was modified for the military at the beginning of the war and called the L-6 liaison plane. This version was equipped with a glazed canopy that extended well aft toward the tail.

In 1969, production of the Interstate Cadet was resurrected by Bill and Jan Diehl, owners of Arctic Aircraft Co. in Anchorage, Alaska. The one family operation has modified the Cadet to become a lightweight bush plane. Installation of a 150-hp Lycoming engine has markedly increased performance and useful load. Large, high flotation tires permit safe landings on beaches or riverbeds. Construction is of chromoly tubing covered with Dacron. All control cables, brake cables, fuel lines, and the like are completely exposed. The revived Cadet, now dubbed the S2B2, has been certificated for aerobatics, and even snap maneuvers are approved.

JOHNSON
"ROCKET 185"/
"TEXAS BULLET"
1946–51

STANDARD DATA: Seats 4. Gross wt. 2,250. Empty wt. 1,550. Fuel capacity 55. Engine 185-hp Lycoming/185-hp Continental. **PERFORMANCE:** Top mph 207. Cruise mph 185. Stall mph 50. Initial climb rate 900. Ceiling 24,500. Takeoff run 600. Landing roll 400.

This high-performance, three-seat, cabin monoplane was first built in 1946 by Johnson Aircraft, Inc. and was ultimately manufactured in small numbers. The quick and light aircraft was built of all-metal construction with a fabric-covered fuselage. Two persons are seated side-by-side with full dual controls while the third is seated centrally just behind the

JOHNSON "ROCKET"

JOHNSON "TEXAS BULLET"

front seats. In 1950, Aircraft Manufacturing Co. acquired the rights to produce a refined four-seat version of the Rocket, which it called the Texas Bullet.

The original Rocket was powered by a 185-hp four-cylinder Lycoming engine; the Texas Bullet changed over to a Continental of the same rating. Also, the fabric covering of the Rocket was traded for an all-metal, flush-riveted skin, and a redesigned tail was added. The Bullet sported a top speed of 210 mph, a cruise speed of 183 mph, and a climb rate of 900 fpm. Overall, the new refinements added only 100 pounds to the empty weight, and 50 pounds were added to the fully loaded weight. Exhaust gasses from the engine of the Rocket and Bullet were led into a unique "jet assist" cylinder below the fuselage. It was claimed that the device converted engine exhaust into useful thrust at speeds faster than 40 mph. Also, both aircraft made use of a Hartzell hydro-selective two-blade variable-pitch propeller.

KINNER "SPORTSTER"
1932

STANDARD DATA: Seats 2. Gross wt. 1,875. Empty wt. 1,218. Engine 100-hp Kinner. **PERFORMANCE:** Top mph 104. Cruise mph 90. Initial climb rate 800. Ceiling 14,000. Range 340.

Kinner Airplane and Motor Corp. is better-known for radial engines used in many World War II primary trainers, including the Meyers OTW and the Ryan PT-22, but Kinner also introduced an airplane of its own design in 1932. As might be expected, the side-by-side two-seat Sportster series of low-

wing taildraggers was powered by 100-hp Kinner five-cylinder radial engines. Some of the Sportsters that are still active have opted for the 125-hp Kinner. The aircraft employed a mixed construction with the conventional fabric-covered wooden wings and fabric-covered steel-tube fuselage combination. Another version, named the Playboy, was a cabin model powered by a 160-hp Kinner. It featured wire-braced rather than strut-braced wings; otherwise, construction was essentially the same.

LAKE "BUCCANEER"/ "RENEGADE"
1957–94

STANDARD DATA: (Buccaneer) Seats 3–4. Gross wt. 2,690. Empty wt. 1,555. Fuel capacity 54. Engine 200-hp Lycoming. **PERFORMANCE:** Top mph 154. Cruise 150. Stall mph 45. Initial climb rate 1,200. Range 825. Ceiling 14,700. Takeoff run (water) 1,100. Takeoff run (land) 600. Landing run (water) 600. Landing roll (land) 475.
STANDARD DATA: (LA-4) Seats 4. Gross wt. 2,400. Empty wt. 1,600. Fuel capacity 40. Engine 180-hp Lycoming. **PERFORMANCE:** Top mph 135. Cruise mph 131. Stall mph 51. Initial climb rate 800. Ceiling 14,000. Range 627. Takeoff run (land) 650. Takeoff run (water) 1,125. Landing roll (land) 475. Landing run (water) 600.

LAKE "BUCCANEER"

LAKE "RENEGADE"

The Lake Amphibian is the only plane of its type currently manufactured in the United States. It is a development of a plane formerly known as the Skimmer, which was built by Colonial Aircraft Corp. Various versions of the Skimmer were produced in the 1950s in limited quantities. In 1959, the name of the plane was changed to the Lake, and improvements were introduced. From 1958 to 1970, the standard engine was a 180-hp Lycoming, and the airplane was designated the LA-4 Amphibian. In 1970, Lake removed the retractable gear from some LAAs and offered them as seaplanes with detachable beaching gear.

Also in 1970, Lake fitted a 200-hp fuel-injected Lycoming engine to the LA-4 and renamed it the Buccaneer. Performance increased substantially, as did the price tab. Lake has since discontinued the LA-4 and the Seaplane and is concentrating on production of the Buccaneer and the Renegade. Standard fuel tanks in the Lake were 40 gallons until someone decided that the pontoons could also be used as fuel tanks. The new auxiliary tanks took 7½ gallons on each side, and the total capacity increased to 55 gallons. The extra 20 hp in the 200-hp Buccaneer has increased cruising speed by 12 mph and top speed by 14 mph. Allowable gross weight also increased an additional 200 pounds.

LINCOLN-PAGE
1928

STANDARD DATA: Seats 3. Gross wt. 2,500. Empty wt. 1,380. Fuel capacity 67. Engine 150-hp water-cooled Hispano Suiza 8-cylinder. **PERFORMANCE:** Top mph 127. Cruise mph 111. Landing mph 38. Initial climb rate 1,000. Ceiling 18,400.

The Lincoln-Page LP-3 was the principal product of the Lincoln Aircraft Co. located in Lincoln, Nebraska. Its president, Victor H. Roos, later named the company when Lincoln and American Eagle merged. The LP-3 was a three-seat open-cockpit biplane in the same class as the Lairds, Swallows, and Eaglerocks. It was powered by any of three different engines: the 150-hp Hispano Suiza eight-cylinder water-cooled engine, the 150-hp Axelson seven-cylinder radial air-cooled engine, or the 90-hp Curtiss OX-5 engine. Its tandem cockpits sat two occupants in the front and one in the rear. The Lincoln-Page featured mixed construction with wooden wings and a steel-tube fuselage. Kin to the LP-3 was the Trainer, a two-seat training biplane. It housed the OX-5 powerplant and could attain a top speed of 105 mph.

LOCKHEED "VEGA"
1927–33

STANDARD DATA: Seats 5–7. Gross wt. 4,750. Empty wt. 2,725. Engine 450-hp Pratt & Whitney Wasp SC-1. **PERFORMANCE:** Top mph 195. Cruise mph 170. Stall mph 59. Initial climb rate 1,250. Range 550. Ceiling 55,000.

During the late 1920s and early 1930s, the Vega was the favorite of many of the world's most renowned aviators. Such greats as Roscoe Turner, Wiley Post, and Charles Lindbergh used the Vega and its variations to break all existing records for speed, altitude, distance, and endurance. Post, flying his beloved "Winnie Mae," climbed to the astonishing altitude of 55,000 feet in 1935. He pioneered the pressure suit to make the record-setting flight. Meanwhile, Lindbergh and his wife Anne were busy flying a Sirus, which is a sistership to the Vega, setting distance records that would stand for 30 years. Turner and his faithful lion cub flew a Vega to new transcontinental victories in the United States. Several offshoot versions of the Vega were also named for stars such as Orion and Sirus. The Vega was the first airplane to be produced by the Lockheed Aircraft Co. and stands in front of a long line of great Lockheed airplanes to follow. Lockheed first produced the high-wing cabin monoplane in 1927 and by the time production ceased in 1933 a total of 131 had been made. Only a few of the great record-makers are still active today.

LUSCOMBE "PHANTOM"
1934–37

STANDARD DATA: Seats 2. Gross wt. 1,725. Empty wt. 960. Fuel capacity 30. Engine 145-hp Warner "Super-Scarab" seven-cylinder radial engine. **PERFORMANCE:** Top mph 132. Cruise mph 120. Stall mph 40. Initial climb rate 850. Ceiling 15,000. Range 600.

The Phantom was a side-by-side, two-seat cabin monoplane that first appeared as a product of the newly formed Luscombe Airplane Corp. Its president was Donald A. Luscombe, formerly president and chief engineer of the Monocoupe Corp., which pioneered the development of die-cut metal construction. This method helped to make production with interchangeable parts possible. The Phantom is of all-metal construction and was an advanced airplane for its time, making use of a stressed-skin Duralumin fuselage. Its production was also unusual in that Luscombe subcontracted all components from specialist manufacturers; only assembly and finish work were performed by the parent company. Power was supplied by a single 145-hp Warner "Super-Scarab" seven-cylinder radial engine, and dual controls were standard.

LUSCOMBE 8A-8F
"SILVAIRE"
1937–60

STANDARD DATA: (8F) Seats 2. Gross wt. 1,400. Empty wt. 870. Fuel capacity 25. Engine 90-hp Continental. **PER-**

FORMANCE: Top mph 128. Cruise mph 120. Stall mph 40. Initial climb rate 900. Range 500. Ceiling 17,000. Takeoff run 550. Landing roll 450.

STANDARD DATA: (8-A) Seats 2. Gross wt. 1,200. Empty wt. 650. Fuel capacity 14. Engine 65-hp Lycoming. **PERFORMANCE:** Top mph 110. Cruise mph 104. Stall mph 37. Initial climb rate 900. Ceiling 15,000. Range 350. Takeoff distance (50') 1,950. Landing distance (50') 1,540.

Luscombe's Model 8 Silvaire first appeared in 1937, and the first 50-hp production models were on the market in 1938. In March 1939, the 8A, with a 65-hp Lycoming, and the 8B, with a 65-hp Continental engine, were introduced. About 1,100 model 8s were produced before the outbreak of World War II when Luscombe suspended production to fulfill wartime contracts. Production was resumed after the war with all-metal versions of the Silvaire, the 8E and 8F. Side-by-side two-seaters, the postwar models used a Continental 90-hp engine and were claimed to be aerobatic. Over 6,000 postwar Silvaires were built, and more than 2,000 are currently rated airworthy. Luscombe was acquired by Temco Aircraft Corp. in 1948, but only some 50 Silvaires were manufactured before the line was suspended for a second time due to military commitments. The final models of the 8F were produced by Silvaire Aircraft Co. between 1946 and 1960 when their production was discontinued permanently.

LUSCOMBE 11-A "SEDAN"
1948–50

STANDARD DATA: Seats 4. Gross wt. 2,280. Empty wt. 1,280. Fuel capacity 42. Engine 165-hp Continental. **PERFORMANCE:** Top mph 145. Cruise mph 130. Landing mph 58. Initial climb rate 900. Range 500. Ceiling 17,000. Takeoff run 800. Landing roll 500.

In 1948, the four-place, 165-hp Luscombe Silvaire 11-A Sedan was introduced and then discontinued the following

year. The 11-A was essentially a four-seat redevelopment of Luscombe's Model 8 with a deeper fuselage. Constructed of all-metal, the Sedan can be used to carry cargo. The rear seats are removable, and tiedown straps are provided to hold a maximum 600 pounds of cargo in place. The Sedan was manufactured in only limited numbers both under Luscombe and Temco Aircraft Corp., the company that purchased Luscombe in 1948.

MAULE M-4/M-5
1962–85

STANDARD DATA: (M-4 Jetasen) Seats 4. Gross wt. 2,100. Empty wt. 1,100. Fuel capacity 42. Engine 145-hp Continental. **PERFORMANCE:** Top mph 157. Cruise mph Stall mph 40. Initial climb rate 700. Ceiling 12,000. Range 750. Takeoff distance 585. Landing distance (50') 600.

STANDARD DATA: (M-4 Rocket) Seats 4. Gross wt. 2,100. Empty wt. 1,190. Fuel capacity 42. Engine 210-hp Continental. **PERFORMANCE:** Top mph 170. Cruise mph 165. Stall mph 40. Initial climb rate 1,250. Range 680. Ceiling 18,000. Takeoff distance (50') 585. Landing distance (50') 600.

STANDARD DATA: (M-5-210C) Seats 4. Gross wt. 2,300. Empty wt. 1,350. Fuel capacity 42. Engine 210-hp Continental. **PERFORMANCE:** Top mph 158. Cruise mph Stall mph 56. Initial climb rate 1,250. Ceiling 18,000. Range 600. Takeoff distance (50') 600. Landing distance (50') 600.

STANDARD DATA: (M-5-235C) Seat 4. Gross wt. 2,300. Empty wt. 1,400. Fuel capacity 42. Engine 235-hp Lycoming. **PERFORMANCE:** Top mph 172. Cruise mph 160. Stall mph 56. Initial climb rate 1,350. Range 550. Ceiling 20,000. Takeoff distance (50') 600. Landing distance (50') 600.

The Maule offers performance and economy for its power and size. Praised by bush pilots in Canada and Alaska, it is one of the few airplanes that combines true STOL characteristics with low cost and high-speed economical cruise. The welded steel-tube fuselage is covered with fiberglass, and the short-span wing is all metal with a thick, high-lift airfoil. The airplane accomplishes its short-field performance with two-position flaps of an unusually high-lift capability and without the elaborate spoilers, slots, and other items normally associated with STOL design. The Maule was produced in five versions: Jetasen, Astro-Rocket, Rocket, Strata-Rocket and Lunar-Rocket.

The original M-4 was powered by a 145-hp Continental engine and was produced until 1966 when it became the Jetasen. During the previous year, the Rocket entered production with a 210-hp Continental powerplant and a constant-speed propeller. The Astro-Rocket was a deluxe version of the Jet-asen, housing a 180-hp Franklin. In 1967, the Strata-Rocket was introduced into the line. Basically similar to the Rocket, it was powered by a 220-hp Franklin. All aircraft mentioned thus far shared the same M-4 designation.

The first M-5 Lunar-Rockets were delivered in 1974 as M-5-210Cs with 210-hp Continental engines. As expected, the M-5-220C houses a 220-hp Franklin. These models differ from the earlier M-4s by having four cabin doors for hauling cargo as the "C" in the model number implies; otherwise, the M-5 has a 30-percent increase in flap area and enlarged tail surfaces to enhance its short-field performance. The 220-hp version was discontinued when the Franklin engine was no longer available, and the M-5-235C was added to the line in 1976 employing a 235-hp Lycoming.

MESSERSCHMITT BF-108 "TAIFUN"
1934–44

STANDARD DATA: Seats 3. Gross wt. 3,087. Empty wt. 1,887. Engine 240-hp Argus. **PERFORMANCE:** (240 hp) Top mph 189. Cruise mph 161. Initial climb rate 1,030. Range 620. Ceiling 20,340.

The BF-108 Taifun (Typhoon) is a three-seat cabin monoplane built by the Bayerische Flugzeugwerke. The design by Prof. Willy Messerschmitt in 1933 was the forerunner of the famous BF-109 Messerschmitt fighter that ruled Axis skies during World War II. A few of the all-metal Taifuns were owned by wealthy Europeans before the war, but most of the 885 airplanes built entered service in Luftwaffe training schools. They were also extensively used for liaison and communication missions. After the war, France continued production of the BF-108 (by then Me 108 and Me 208), using the designation of Nord 1000 for the Me 108 and Nord 1100 for the Me 208. Both were fitted with 220-hp Renault engines, and the Me 208 featured a tricycle landing gear.

MESSERSCHMITT BF-109
1935–44

STANDARD DATA: Seats 1. Gross wt. 6,090. Empty wt. 4,180. Fuel capacity 106. Engine 1,200-hp Mercedes-Benz inverted 12-cylinder. **PERFORMANCE:** Top mph 390. Cruise mph 310. Initial climb rate 3,320. Range 440. Ceiling 37,000.

The Messerschmitt 109 was Germany's primary front-line fighter throughout World War II. Designed between 1933 and 1935, the first production models began reaching Luftwaffe units in mid-1937. By the outbreak of the war, there were only 235 in service, but within a short time production

was drastically accelerated. By the war's end, around 35,000 of the type had been manufactured, making it the most numerous fighter of the conflict.

Performance and maneuverability were outstanding and proved generally superior against all types of opposing fighters in the European Theater, with the probable exception of the Spitfire. Some later models, particularly the 109G, suffered performance problems due to design changes, and in the later stages of the war, Allied fighters succeeded in effectively dealing with the type. After the war, Czechs undertook production of the design, and 109s served in the Czechoslovakian Air Force until 1952. The Israel Defense Force also made good use of the Czech-made 109s during the late 1940s. Few of the original 35,000 survive today, and anyone showing up at a fly-in these days in a Messerschmitt can count on gathering a crowd.

MESSERSCHMITT 209 "MONSUN"
1970–80

STANDARD DATA: Seats 2. Gross wt. 1,807. Empty wt. 1,067. Fuel capacity 37. Engine 150-hp to 160-hp Lycoming. **PERFORMANCE:** (160 hp). Top mph 170. Cruise mph 158. Stall mph 62. Initial climb rate 1,180. Range 745. Ceiling 18,100. Takeoff run 590. Landing roll 655.

The 209 Monsun is built by the largest aerospace company in Germany, the Messerschmitt Bolkow-Blohm Gmbh. The Messerschmitt part of the name comes from the company that produced the famous ME-109 during World War II. MBB's light two-seater called the Monsun (Monsoon) is produced in three versions: the BO209-150 with a 150-hp Lycoming engine, the BO209-160 with a 160-hp fuel-injected Lycoming, and the BO209S, which is the trainer model with a nonretractable nosewheel and the choice of a 125-hp Lycoming or a 130-hp Rolls-Royce/Continental engine.

Flown for the first time in 1969 and produced in 1970, the low-wing Monsun features tricycle gear with retractable nose gear as an option. The main gear is nonretractable. Wings on the 150 and 160 models can be unbolted and folded back along the fuselage for ease in storage or for towing the airplane behind a car. The control lines to the ailerons and flaps automatically dismount and reconnect when the wings are folded and unfolded. With a large clear bubble canopy, the visibility in the 209 is excellent. Construction is all metal except for a fiberglass cowling.

MEYERS OTW
1939–44

STANDARD DATA: Seats 2. Gross wt. 1,910. Empty wt. 1,340. Fuel capacity 26. Engine 160-hp Kinner five-cylinder radial. **PERFORMANCE:** Top mph 120. Cruise mph 105. Landing mph 40. Initial climb rate 1,200. Range 400. Ceiling 17,500.

This popular two-seat biplane was introduced in 1939 as a primary trainer. The first model was the OTW-125, powered by a 125-hp Warner Scarab engine and constructed with a metal fuselage and wooden wings. A year later, Meyers installed a 145-hp Scarab and gave the tandem-seat airplane the OTW-145 designation. The OTW-160 soon followed and featured a 160-hp Kinner. In 1943, the entire production of the Meyers plant in Tecumseh, Michigan, was concentrated on the Model OTW-160, and the total output was delivered to schools operating under C.A.A. War Training Service. All three models of the OTW can still be found flying in the United States and Canada.

MITSUBISHI NAVY "ZERO"
1942

STANDARD DATA: Seats 1. Gross wt. 5,140. Engine 1,100-hp Nakajima Sakae 21 14-cylinder radial. **PERFORMANCE:** (Zeke) Top mph 325. Cruise mph 265. Range 590. Ceiling 36,000.

The Mitsubishi Navy ZERO was a single-seat fighter powered by a 1,100-hp Nakajima powerplant of 14-cylinders

in two rows. It had three unprotected fuel tanks, one in the fuselage and one in each wing. The pilot's cockpit was located over the center section of the wing and was under a raised transparent canopy with no armor protection. The ZERO fighter was produced in two versions, the Mk. I, code-named "Zeke," and the Mk. II, code-named "Hamp." The only difference was that the Mk. II had a redesigned wing with smaller span and blunt wingtips. Both fighters' armament consisted of two 20mm cannon in the leading edge of the wings, outboard of the prop disc, and two 7.7mm machine guns mounted in the top cowling, firing through the airscrew. One 500-pound bomb could be carried in place of a fuel drop tank.

MONOCOUPE 90A
1930–42/1947–50

STANDARD DATA: Seats 2. Gross wt. 1,610. Empty wt. 1,000. Fuel capacity 14. Engine 115-hp Lycoming. **PERFORMANCE:** Top mph 156. Cruise mph 135. Stall mph 40. Initial climb rate 1,100. Range 600.

Introduced by the Monocoupe Corporation in 1930, the Model 90A two-seat cabin monoplane was progressively improved until production was suspended in 1942. These early Monocoupes were powered by various engines, including the 90-hp Lambert, the 90-hp Franklin, and the Warner 125-hp Scarab or 145-hp Super Scarab. The main tanks were mounted in the wing roots, providing gravity feed to the engine. Seating was for two in side-by-side fashion with access by means of doors on either side. The fuselage was of welded steel-tube construction, while the wings were of wood. All surfaces, save the aluminum leading wing edges, were fabric covered. After a five year lapse in production, the Monocoupe was again built utilizing the same basic airframe but changing to either the 125- or 115-hp Lycoming horizontally opposed air-cooled engine.

MOONEY M-18 "MITE"
1947–54

STANDARD DATA: Seats 1. Gross wt. 780. Empty wt. 520. Fuel capacity 14. Engine 65-hp Continental. **PERFORMANCE:** Top mph 138. Cruise mph 125. Stall mph 43. Initial climb rate 1,090. Range 440. Ceiling 19,400. Takeoff distance (50') 525. Landing distance (50') 860.

The Mooney Mite, first flown in 1947, was constructed by Mooney Aircraft, a company formed by two former executives of the defunct Culver Aircraft Corp. This single-seat monoplane was originally powered by a converted 25-hp Crosley automobile engine. With this engine, the Mite had a top speed of over 100 mph, a cruising speed of 85 mph, and a climb rate of 400 fpm. To improve the aircraft's takeoff and

MOONEY M-18 "MITE"

initial rate of climb performance, the company installed 55- and 65-hp Lycoming engines and designated it the M-18L. The final engine was the 65-hp Continental in the M-18C.

The Mite included "safe-trim," a trim-control system that consisted of a gear linking the tail trim with the wingflaps. It automatically established proper settings for takeoff climb, approach, and landing. The little personal plane was constructed with a single spruce-and-plywood D-spar wing structure with fabric covering aft of the spar. It had a metal-covered steel-tube fuselage forward and a wooden structure aft.

MOONEY MARK 20 SERIES "201/231"/ "RANGER"/ "CHAPARRAL" 1954–95

STANDARD DATA: (Ranger) Seats 4. Gross wt. 2,575. Empty wt. 1,525. Fuel capacity 52. Engine 180-hp Lycoming. **PERFORMANCE:** Top mph 169. Cruise mph 165. Stall mph 57. Initial climb rate 800. Ceiling 16,500. Range 1,047. Takeoff distance (50') 1,395. Landing distance (50') 1,550.
STANDARD DATA: (201) Seats 4. Gross wt. 2,740. Empty wt. 1,640. Fuel capacity 64. Engine 200-hp Lycoming. **PERFORMANCE:** Top mph 201. Cruise mph 195. Stall mph 61. Initial climb rate 1,030. Ceiling 18,800. Range 1,295. Takeoff distance 870. Landing roll 770.
STANDARD DATA: (231) Seats 4. Gross wt. 2,900. Empty wt. 1,800. Fuel capacity 75.6. Engine 210-hp turbocharged Continental. **PERFORMANCE:** Top mph 231. Cruise mph 210. Stall mph 66. Initial climb rate 1,080. Ceiling 24,000. Range 1,258. Takeoff distance (50') 2,060. Landing distance (50') 2,280.
STANDARD DATA: (Chaparral) Seats 4. Gross wt. 2,575. Empty wt. 1,600. Fuel capacity 52. Engine 200-hp Lycoming. **PERFORMANCE:** Top mph 195. Cruise mph 182. Stall mph 57. Initial climb rate 1,400. Ceiling 18,800. Range 1,015. Takeoff distance (50') 1,010. Landing distance (50') 1,360.

MOONEY "CHAPARRAL"

MOONEY "201"

MOONEY "231"

MOONEY "252 TSE"

The Mooney lineage is hard to trace. It helps to remember that the Mooney Mark 20, Mark 21, and Ranger are essentially the same aircraft. In 1955, Mooney introduced the Mark 20 as a low-wing aircraft with retractable landing gear. This early version was powered by a 150-hp Lycoming. Its wings were constructed of wood and fabric, while its tail unit was a plywood structure with steel-tube framed control surfaces. The Mark 20A entered production in 1958 offering a 180-hp Lycoming engine as an option. These two aircraft continued in production until 1960, when the Mark 20 was discontinued, and 1961, when the Mark 20A was replaced by the Mark 21.

The Mark 21 was the first Mooney to feature all-metal construction but was otherwise the same airplane. In 1963, the Master was offered as a nonretractable version of the Mark 21, and in 1964, the Super 21 entered production with its fuel-injected 200-hp Lycoming. The Ranger replaced the Mark 21 and Master in 1967. It differed from earlier models by the addition of a one-piece windshield and the elimination of the dorsal fin. That same year the Statesman was added to the line with its longer fuselage and extra passenger windows; the Executive 21 was also introduced, utilizing the Statesman's fuselage with a 200-hp fuel-injected engine.

In November 1969, the Mooney Aircraft Corp. was purchased by Butler Aviation International, and the name of the company was changed to Aerostar Mooney. The Ranger (M20C) and Executive (M20F) were continued under the same names, and the Super 21 was reinstated as the Chaparral.

Production of all aircraft ceased in 1972, soon after the purchase, but in 1974, Republic Steel assumed control, and production was put into motion under the name of Mooney Aircraft once again. The most recent versions are the Model 201, 231, 252, 301, and the Ovation.

In order to achieve more speed from the basic airframe, it was put through an extensive aerodynamic clean-up program. The previously uncovered gear wells were fitted with complete doors. A McCauley paddle-blade prop yielded increased efficiency at the blade extremities. A super-slick engine cowling shape provided minimum drag at cruise, while new cowl flaps were reworked to open wide during climb to keep down engine temperatures. The windshield was streamlined. The use of flush riveting was expanded to the leading 60 percent of the wing chord, and fiberglass fairings were used on all hinges.

The addition of turbocharging might seem a rather meager justification for calling an airplane "new," but in the case of the Mooney 231, turbocharging was a big deal. When the 201 was first introduced in 1976, there was little question that a turbo version would follow. Like Rajay's Piper Lance system, the Mooney installation is a sea-level unit designed to deliver 30 inches of manifold pressure right up to the critical altitude. Maximum operation altitude for the 231 has been established at 23,000 feet. It flies at approximately 207 mph at 75 percent power. Of special note is the fact that 1980 was the first year Mooney surpassed Piper Arrow in sales since the single-engine retractable-gear Piper took the number one sales position away from Mooney.

For 1981, the Model 201 featured sculptured wingtips with integral navigation and strobe lights. First introduced on the 231, the new tips reduce parasite drag and help provide better roll response. They're made of tough and resilient fiberglass. Improvement to range and payload for the Turbo 231 results from redesign of the fuel tanks. Eight gallons of unusable fuel have been reduced to three gallons; this and other changes result in a 35-pound increase in payload. Total usable fuel is up from 72 to 75.6 gallons.

MOONEY M-20R "OVATION" 1994

STANDARD DATA: Seats 4. Gross wt. 3,368. Empty wt. 2,200. Fuel capacity 95. Engine 280-hp Continental IO-550G. **PERFORMANCE:** Top mph 227. Cruise mph 220. Initial climb rate 1,000. Ceiling 21,000. Range 900. Takeoff distance (50') 1,700. Landing distance (50') 1,600.

The latest in the ever-increasing model line at Mooney Aircraft is the Ovation. The Ovation is the fastest nonturbo Mooney, but its performance figures are well into the range of a turbocharged aircraft. Disregarding altitude limitations, if you need to get there fast and you don't want to go on oxygen, then this ship is just the ticket. Because of the width of the IO-550G, the cabin at the firewall has been widened about two inches to accommodate a smooth cowling-to-fuselage transition thus eliminating the "heavily-cheeked" look of the TLS.

MOONEY M20J "MSE" 1990-95

STANDARD DATA: Seats 4. Gross wt. 2,900. Empty wt. 1,726. Fuel capacity 65. Engine 200-hp Lycoming IO-360-A3B6D. **PERFORMANCE:** Top mph 197. Cruise mph 191. Initial climb rate 780. Ceiling 18,600. Range 925. Takeoff distance (50') 2,400. Landing distance (50') 2,200.

Mooney has been well known for building fast and efficient airplanes. The MSE (Mooney Special Edition) is certainly no exception; in fact, it is the most efficient four-place normally aspirated single in general aviation. The MSE can realize 18 nm to the gallon at max cruise and well over 20 mpg at more conservative settings. The rest of the aircraft is typical Mooney, and it can effectively carry 596 pounds in the cabin with the tanks topped. This roughly translates to three 170-pounders with 86 pounds of stuff or two average couples and toothbrushes, still not too bad in the world of four-place retractables.

MOONEY MARK 22 "MUSTANG" 1967-69

STANDARD DATA: Seats 5. Gross wt. 3,680. Empty wt. 2,440. Fuel capacity 52. Engine 310-hp fuel-injected Lycoming. **PERFORMANCE:** Top mph 256. Cruise mph 230. Stall mph 67. Initial climb rate 1,125. Range 1,493. Ceiling 24,000. Takeoff distance (50') 1,870. Landing distance (50') 1,520.

The Mooney Mark 22 was the most radical in its class in that it offered the only pressurized cabin in a commercial single-engine plane. The Mustang was first introduced in 1967 and was dropped when Butler Aviation took over the Mooney line. The engine is a 310-hp Lycoming that is turbocharged for high-altitude operation and adequate power. The Mustang has flight characteristics similar to other Mooneys; however, special pilot training is required to assure proper management of the cabin pressurization system. Mooney had engineered all the necessary safety features into the cabin and door, which had to provide a good seal against the loss of air. Because the Mark 22 can be operated so easily and so high, it offers very fast airspeeds at very reduced fuel consumption.

MOONEY M20M "TLS" 1989-95

STANDARD DATA: Seats 4. Gross wt. 3,368. Empty wt. 2,268. Fuel capacity 89. Engine 270-hp Lycoming TIO-540 AF1A. **PERFORMANCE:** Top mph 253. Cruise mph 223. Initial climb rate 1,350. Ceiling 5,000. Range 1,015. Takeoff distance (50') 1,700. Landing distance (50') 1,600.

When first introduced to the Mooney line, the TLS was touted as being the highest, farthest, fastest, and most luxurious production Mooney of all time. Mooney has been well-known for producing compact four-place speed-demon aircraft that squeeze every ounce of speed from their available horsepower. The TLS has lived up to all of Mooney's claims. The fuselage length has been lengthened by 18 inches to give greater leg accommodation for rear passengers. A 350-hp Lycoming was derated 270 hp, and it provides effortless 223-knot high-speed high-altitude cruising that in turn makes trips of more than 1,000 miles a reality.

NAKAJIMA NAVY 97 "KATE" 1942

STANDARD DATA: Seats 2–3. Engine 700-hp Nakajima Hikari nine-cylinder radial. **PERFORMANCE:** Top mph 225. Cruise mph 205. Range 600.

The Nakajima Navy 97 was a single-engine torpedo bomber and was code-named "Kate." Housing a 700-hp nine-cylinder air-cooled radial engine, the Model 97 is easily identified by its continuous canopy under which two to three crewmen were seated. This torpedo plane also featured cantilevered wings with taper on both the leading and trailing edges and dihedral on the outer sections only. Its flaps were exceptionally short. The main landing gear were inward-retractable, and the tail wheel was nonretractable. Armament consisted of two 7.7mm machine guns mounted in the cowling and one or two movable machine guns of the same caliber in the rear cockpit. An 18-inch torpedo or bombs up to 1,100 lbs. could be carried under the fuselage.

NAKAJIMA "OSCAR"

STANDARD DATA: Seats 1. Gross wt. 5,500. Empty wt. 1,150-hp Nakajima Type 2. **PERFORMANCE:** Top mph 333. Cruise mph 265. Range 1,000.

The Japanese Army designation for this single-seat fighter was Type 1 fighter, Model 2; the popular name was "Haya-busa" meaning peregrine falcon, and the Americans call it "Oscar." Its wings taper in chord and thickness, and the landing gear retracted inward into recesses in the underside of the wings. The powerplant was one 1,150-hp Nakajima Type 2 14-cylinder twin-row radial engine. It was fitted with a two-

speed supercharger and turned a three-blade constant-speed propeller. The fuel tanks were in the wings, protected by self-sealing rubber. Standard armament was two 12.7mm machine guns in the fuselage that were synchronized to fire through the prop. The pilot sat under a sliding "bubble" canopy and was protected by armor to the rear.

NAVAL AIRCRAFT FACTORY N3N-3 1940–52

STANDARD DATA: Seats 2. Gross wt. 2,780. Empty wt. 2,050. Engine 235-hp Wright Whirlwind. **PERFORMANCE:** Top mph 118. Cruise mph 98. Initial climb rate 800. Range 470. Ceiling 13,700.

In 1935, the Naval Aircraft Factory in Philadelphia began design of the N3N primary trainer. The government-owned company finally began production in April 1940 and produced a total of 816 two-seaters before production ceased in 1942. The tandem biplane, nicknamed the "Yellow Peril," was built both as a landplane and floatplane; many of the latter were used at Annapolis until retired in 1959. The original Yellow Peril was powered by a 235-hp seven-cylinder Wright Whirlwind radial engine although many of the trainers that found themselves in civilian hands were fitted with other engines such as the 459-hp Pratt & Whitney Wasp Junior, the 600-hp Wasp, or smaller Continental engines of 220 to 250 hp. Almost 150 N3N biplanes are active today, many of them serving faithfully as agricultural aircraft.

NAVION "RANGEMASTER" 1961–78

STANDARD DATA: (285 hp) Seats 5. Gross wt. 3,315. Empty wt. 1,950. Fuel capacity 108. Engine 285-hp Continental. **PERFORMANCE:** Top mph 197. Cruise mph 191. Stall mph 59. Initial climb rate 1,375. Range 1,800. Ceiling 21,500. Takeoff distance (50') 920. Landing distance (50') 980.

The Rangemaster is a refinement of the earlier North American/Ryan Navion design. It is quite a different airplane despite the fact that it retains the original Navion wing, undercarriage, and fuselage. In the early 1960s, the production of Navions was taken over by the Navion Aircraft Corp., which was made up of members of the American Navion Society. The first Rangemaster took to the air in 1960, and production began in 1961. The first model was designated the Rangemaster G and retained the 260-hp Continental. The Rangemaster G-1 followed in 1962 with redesigned smaller tail surfaces. Rangemasters get their name from the excellent range provided by the extra fuel that can be carried in the two centerline fuel tanks mounted on the tip of each wing. These 34-gallon tip tanks are in addition to the main 40-gallon tank. In 1966, the Rangemaster H was unveiled with its 285-hp powerplant. It quickly became known for its speed, short-field performance, and of course its exceptional range.

NEW STANDARD D-25
1929

STANDARD DATA: Seats 5. Gross wt. 3,400. Empty wt. 2,010. Fuel capacity 62. Engine 200-hp Wright Whirlwind. **PERFORMANCE:** Top mph 105. Cruise mph 85. Stall mph 40. Initial climb rate 800. Ceiling 17,800.

The D-25 was a further development of the Gates-Day GD-24. This five-seat general-purpose commercial biplane accommodated four persons in side-by-side pairs in the forward of two tandem cockpits; the pilot sat in the aft cockpit. Power was supplied by a 200-hp Wright Whirlwind J-5 radial fed by a 62-gallon fuel tank. In 1929, a fleet of D-27 Mail Planes was delivered to Clifford Ball who operated the Cleveland-Pittsburgh-Washington mail route. Another version was the D-26, in which two of the front four seats were removed.

The D-27 Mail Plane differed by having all four seats removed and the forward cockpit covered over. The D-28 was a twin-float seaplane. Most of the D-25s that have survived have been put into service as agricultural aircraft with the dust hopper or spray tank replacing the forward cockpit. The fuselage was built from Duralumin angles and channels riveted or bolted together. The wings were made from basswood and plywood and covered with fabric.

NOORDUYN "NORSEMAN" (C.C.F.)
1935–59

STANDARD DATA: Seats 6–8. Gross wt. 7,540. Empty wt. 4,700. Fuel capacity 120. Engines 550-hp Pratt & Whitney Wasp. **PERFORMANCE:** Top mph 155. Cruise mph 141. Stall mph 68. Initial climb rate 714. Range 464. Ceiling 17,000.

The Norseman was designed by Robert B.C. Noorduyn in 1934 and entered production in Montreal, Canada, in 1935. Designed primarily for use in the Canadian bush as a lightweight freighter and transport, the Norseman IV with the Pratt & Whitney Wasp engine was used during World War II by both the R.C.A.F. and the U.S. Air Corps as a utility transport and navigational trainer. Altogether 759 aircraft were supplied to the Air Corps under the UC-64 designation. After the war, the Canadian Car and Foundry Co. acquired the assets of the Noorduyn Co. and continued production of an improved Norseman until 1959. Many have remained active in Canada as bush planes, and several are equipped with floats.

NORTH AMERICAN AT-6 "TEXAN"
1941–54

STANDARD DATA: Seats 2. Gross wt. 5,300. Empty wt. 4,158. Fuel capacity 111. Engine 550-hp Pratt & Whitney Wasp. **PERFORMANCE:** Top mph 205. Cruise mph 170. Landing mph 67. Initial climb rate 1,600. Range 750. Ceiling 21,500.

This is one of the most popular and widely used of military surplus aircraft in general aviation. It was manufactured in greater quantities than any other basic training plane. One of the great virtues of the AT-6 is the fact that it is an all-metal plane, which eliminates any concern over deterioration. The AT-6 is not difficult to fly and generally is the first step in ratings for any pilot who wishes to move up to faster surplus military aircraft. It is known under a variety of names and designations, including Texan, Harvard, AT-6, and SNJ-4. More than 10,000 were built by the United States and allied countries during the span of its lifetime. AT-6 was the army designation, and SNJ-4 was the navy designation. The name Harvard applied to those built by the Noorduyn factory in Canada; the Harvard differed only in its lack of armament equipment. The AT-6 was later modernized and used in Korea as a spotter plane. It had slightly more power and better visibility from both seats.

NORTH AMERICAN T-28 "TROJAN"
1950–58

STANDARD DATA: Seats 2. Gross wt. 6,759. Empty wt. 5,111. Fuel capacity 125. Engine 800-hp Wright radial. **PERFORMANCE:** Top mph 288. Cruise mph 190. Stall mph 72. Initial climb rate 2,570. Range 1,008. Ceiling 29,800. Takeoff distance (50') 1,308.

The North American T-28 was the first U.S. military trainer to be outfitted with tricycle landing gear. It was designed for the U.S. Air Force as a replacement for the AT-6 as an advanced trainer. Production began in 1950 and was discontinued eight years later. Several different versions of the T-28 exist. Some of the original T-28s were built for the air force, while others were constructed for the navy. A number of them were subsequently supplied to foreign countries. Finally, the latest version with a 1,425-hp engine was constructed for counterinsurgency warfare in the early 1960s. Another version produced during the same period was powered by a 2,450-shp Lycoming turboprop engine to increase the aircraft's maximum speed to 360 mph and gross weight to 15,530. The T-28 is considered to be easy to fly so long as the engine is operating at full power. When power is reduced, the rate of descent is spectacular.

NORTH AMERICAN P-51 "MUSTANG"
1943–46

STANDARD DATA: (P-51D) Seats 1–2. Gross wt. 11,600. Empty wt. 7,125. Fuel capacity 269–489. Engine 1,720-hp Rolls-Royce/Packard Merlin. **PERFORMANCE:** Top mph 437. Cruise mph 362. Initial climb rate 3,475. Range 2,300. Ceiling 41,900.

Many experts agree that the North American P-51 Mustang is the world's finest fighter plane in its class. Most air races around closed circuits include a large percentage of Mustangs. Quite a few P-51s have been converted to seat two persons. Although the Mustang went out of production in 1946, it still functions as a first-line fighter plane for many of

the small countries of the world. By civilian aircraft standards, the Mustang is a difficult plane to fly; it is considered especially tricky on takeoffs when the engine torque requires expert pilot handling. Designed originally for the V-12 Allison engine, the P-51's high-altitude and power performance did not live up to expectations. So, the 1,450-hp Packard Merlin became the standard powerplant.

There are several models of the Mustang, but the F-51 D was the first version to feature the trimmed-down rear fuselage and bubble canopy. Earlier Mustangs looked similar to the Spitfire. Today many Mustangs have been modified to handle engines with an output of over 2,000 hp. An interesting mutation of the P-51 was the F-82 "Twin Mustang." Essentially, it was two Mustang fuselages joined by a constant-chord center section and a rectangular tailplane. It was used as a two-seat long-range escort fighter and had a maximum speed of over 475 mph.

NORTHWEST "RANGER"
1961–72

STANDARD DATA: Seats 6–8. Gross wt. 4,700. Empty wt. 2,848. Fuel capacity 91. Engine 520-hp Lycoming. **PERFORMANCE:** Top mph 170. Cruise mph 166. Stall mph 62. Initial climb rate 1,475. Range 530. Ceiling 20,000. Takeoff distance (50') 915. Landing distance (50') 920.

Originally designed by Lockheed Aircraft as the Model 60 light utility transport, the eight-seat Ranger was also manufactured under license by Aeronautica Macchi of Italy with the name "Conestoga." In 1968, marketing and production rights were acquired by Northwest Industries, Ltd. of Edmonton, Alberta. The versatile high-wing airplane was certified as either a land plane with tricycle or conventional gear, or a floatplane on Edo floats, or a ski plane on Fluidyne wheel skis. The original model was powered by a large 400-hp eight-cylinder fuel-injected Lycoming and had a maximum speed of 156 mph. Without the drag brought about by floats, the Ranger can climb at 1,080 fpm at sea level. Entrance to the large cabin is through a giant passenger/cargo door or through the pilot's door beside the left front seat. In 1970, the Ranger received a 520-hp Lycoming engine to increase its climb rate and cruise speed when used with floats.

PASPED "SKYLARK"
1936

STANDARD DATA: Seats 2. Gross wt. 1,885. Empty wt. 1,288. Engine 125-hp Warner Scarab. **PERFORMANCE:** Top mph 139. Cruise mph 125. Stall mph 35. Initial climb rate 850. Ceiling 16,000. Range 650.

In 1936, the Pasped Aircraft Co. of Glendale, California, introduced a two-seat side-by-side cabin monoplane called the Skylark. Its engine was a 125-hp Warner Scarab radial engine housed in a low-drag cowling. The fuselage was a rectangular steel-tube welded structure covered with Duralumin metal panels forward and fabric aft. The wings were wire-braced from above, had plywood leading edges, and were covered with both fabric and Duralumin (the latter only at the center section). The single surviving example still flying is fitted with a 175-hp Warner Super Scarab.

PIPER J-3 "CUB"
1938–47

STANDARD DATA: Seats 2. Gross wt. 1,200. Empty wt. 680. Fuel capacity 9. Engine 40-hp to 65-hp Continental. **PERFORMANCE:** (65 hp). Top mph 87. Cruise mph 75. Stall mph 38. Initial climb rate 450. Range 206. Ceiling 11,500. Takeoff run 700. Landing roll 800.

The Piper J-3, developed in 1937, made the name "Cub" a household word. It became one of the most popular of the inexpensive "flivver" aircraft that were intended to bring amateur flying within the reach of the average man. The J-3 was a classic learn-to-fly plane that was originally derived from the similar J-2 Cub of 1936 vintage. The 40-hp J-3 first appeared

in 1938, and more than 5,500 of these tandem two-seat fabric-covered flying machines were built before production was temporarily suspended in 1942. The J-3s were back in production again in 1945 powered by a 65-hp Continental. In 1947, several revisions changed the nomenclature to PA-11 Cub Special. Although parts for the old J-3s are becoming harder to obtain, many of these aircraft are changing hands every year. It is one of the lowest priced used airplanes on the market, but is rapidly gaining appeal as a near-classic.

PIPER J-4 "CUB COUPE"
1939–42

STANDARD DATA: Seats 2. Gross wt. 1,400. Empty wt. 865. Fuel capacity 16. Engine 75-hp Continental. **PERFORMANCE:** Top mph 100. Cruise mph 96. Landing mph 40. Initial climb rate 450. Range 455. Ceiling 12,000.

The J-4 Coupe was the first Piper monoplane to have side-by-side seating. First flown in 1938 and produced from 1939 to 1942, the light high-wing monoplane with enclosed cabin was often used in flight training schools and in the Civilian War Training Program. Very similar in structure to the J-3 Cub, the J-4 was powered by a 75-hp four-cylinder Continental engine. Cub Coupe features included hydraulic brakes, a more complete instrument panel, and navigation lights. Fuel capacity and overall size of the J-4 was also increased over its predecessor, the J-3. Construction was welded steel-tube fuselage, and wings are made from spruce spars and aluminum alloy. Almost 200 Coupes are still active.

PIPER PA-15 "VAGABOND"/ PA-16 "CLIPPER"/ PA-17 "PACER"
1948–49

STANDARD DATA: (PA-15) Seats 2. Gross wt. 1,100. Empty wt. 620. Fuel capacity 36. Engine 65-hp Continental. **PERFORMANCE:** Top mph 100. Cruise mph 90. Stall mph 45. Initial climb rate 510. Range 250. Ceiling 10,000. Takeoff run 900. Landing roll 300.
STANDARD DATA: (PA-16) Seats 4. Gross wt. 1,500. Empty wt. 800. Fuel capacity 36. Engine 115-hp Lycoming. **PERFORMANCE:** Top mph 125. Cruise mph 112. Stall mph 50. Initial climb rate 600. Range 480. Ceiling 11,000. Takeoff run 720. Landing roll 600.
STANDARD DATA: (PA-17) Top mph 100. Cruise mph 90. Stall mph 45. Initial climb rate 530. Ceiling 10,500. Range 250. Takeoff run 800. Landing roll 300.

The PA-15 entered production in 1948 and was one of the first to appear after Piper had temporarily suspended its activi-

PIPER PA-16 " CLIPPER"

ties. Originally powered by a 65-hp Lycoming engine, the PA-15 Vagabond was a side-by-side two-seater and a forerunner of a new series that would come to include the Clipper, Pacer, and ultimately the Tri-Pacer. The PA-17, introduced in 1949, was primarily intended to serve as a trainer and with a 65-hp Continental installed. The PA-15 and PA-17 were not built in large quantities, perhaps due to the four-seat PA-16 Clipper, which was also produced in 1949. The PA-16 housed a 115-hp Lycoming engine and subsequently evolved into the PA-20 Pacer.

PIPER J-5 "CUB CRUISER"/PA-12 "SUPER CRUISER" 1946-48

STANDARD DATA: (Super Cruiser) Seats 3. Gross wt. 1,390. Empty wt. 490. Fuel capacity 30. Engine 108-hp Lycoming. **PERFORMANCE:** Top mph 115. Cruise mph 105. Stall mph 49. Initial climb rate 600. Range 600. Ceiling 12,600. Takeoff distance (50') 720. Landing distance (50') 470. **STANDARD DATA:** (J-5) Seats 3. Gross wt. 1,450. Empty wt. 830. Fuel capacity 25. Engine 75-hp Continental. **PERFORMANCE:** Top mph 100. Cruise mph 85. Landing mph 39. Initial climb rate 450. Range 450. Ceiling 10,000.

The Piper J-5 Cruiser, one of the many J-3 derivatives, entered production in 1946. It differed from the earlier Cub by having increased seating with a single forward seat and a side-by-side seat aft. Also featured was increased engine size from the J-3's 65-hp engine to either a 75-hp or 100-hp Lycoming engine. The PA-11 was similar to the J-5 but was powered by a 90-hp engine. The PA-12 Super Cruiser was powered by a 108-hp Lycoming four-cylinder engine and was also designed to carry three persons. A later version of the Cruiser line was

the PA-14 Family Cruiser, which was designed to carry four persons and sported flaps on its wings. The PA-12 Super Cruiser, typical of the J-3 Cub derivatives, is still extremely common throughout the United States.

PIPER PA-18 "SUPER CUB" 1949-94

STANDARD DATA: Seats 3. Gross wt. 1,750. Empty wt. 930. Fuel capacity 36. Engine 150-hp Lycoming. **PERFORMANCE:** Top mph 130. Cruise mph 115. Stall mph 43. Initial climb rate 960. Range 460. Ceiling 19,000. Takeoff distance (50') 500. Landing distance (50') 725.
STANDARD DATA: Seats 2. Gross wt. 1,500. Empty wt. 800. Fuel capacity 18. Engine 90-hp Continental. **PERFORMANCE:** Top mph 112. Cruise mph 100. Stall mph 42. Initial climb rate 710. Ceiling 15,750. Range 360. Takeoff distance (50') 750. Landing distance (50') 800.

Piper's PA-18 Super Cub first appeared in 1949 as a replacement for the J-3 and PA-11 series. It follows the same basic design as the older Cubs while offering a more powerful engine. Between 1949 and 1955, the power was gradually increased through several different engines from 90 hp to 150 hp. Some of the earlier models of the Super Cub (PA-18A) had dusting and spraying equipment installed and were used as agricultural aircraft. Other versions, designated L-18 and L-21, were designed for the military as liaison aircraft and have been used as observation planes in Southeast Asia. Along with the increase in engine power, the fuel capacity was quadrupled over that of its predecessor, extending the maximum range to more than 400 miles.

Although its top speed leaves something to be desired, the design of this airplane meets the purpose for which it was intended. After 45 years of production, Piper decided to leave the Super Cub well enough alone. Piper sells every one that it makes, particularly in South America, Asia, and Africa—anywhere a pilot needs to lift off from an unimproved airstrip in 500 feet carrying 820 pounds of people, fuel, and baggage. The PA-18 has earned the distinction of being the longest production run of any single model airplane in the history of aviation. As of 1980, over 30,000 had been built.

PIPER PA-20 "PACER" 1950-54

STANDARD DATA: Seats 4. Gross wt. 1,950. Empty wt. 1,010. Fuel capacity 36. Engine 135-hp Lycoming. **PERFORMANCE:** Top mph 139. Cruise mph 125. Stall mph 48. Initial climb rate 620. Range 580. Ceiling 15,000. Takeoff distance (50') 1,600. Landing distance (50') 1,280.

The PA-20 Pacer was first introduced in 1949 as the PA-16 Clipper, a development of the PA-15 Vagabond. The "Clipper" name lasted only a year because Pan Am owned rights to that trademark. As the first four-seater to be built on the "short" Piper wing, the PA-16 featured a 115-hp Lycoming engine. In 1950, the PA-20 Pacer appeared with a larger tail, larger fuel tanks, wheel controls (versus a stick), and balanced elevators. The PA-20 was then produced in several versions, each featuring slight differences in engine size. Between 1950 and 1951, it was built with either the 115-hp or 125-hp Lycoming engine. From 1952 until production ceased in 1954, the 125-hp and 135-hp Lycoming powerplants were used.

PIPER PA-22 "TRI-PACER" 1951–60

STANDARD DATA: Seats 4. Gross wt. 2,000. Empty wt. 1,104. Fuel capacity 36. Engine 150-hp Lycoming. **PERFORMANCE:** Top mph 140. Cruise mph 130. Stall mph 49. Initial climb rate 800. Range 536. Ceiling 16,000. Takeoff distance (50') 600. Landing distance (50') 1,280.
STANDARD DATA: Seats 4. Gross wt. 1,950. Empty wt. 1,040. Fuel capacity 36. Engine 135-hp Lycoming. **PERFORMANCE:** Top mph 137. Cruise mph 132. Stall mph 48. Initial climb rate 620. Ceiling 15,000. Range 580. Takeoff distance (50') 1,600. Landing distance (50') 1,280.
STANDARD DATA: Seats 4. Gross wt. 2,000. Empty wt. 1,110. Fuel capacity 36. Engine 160-hp Lycoming. **PERFORMANCE:** Top mph 141. Cruise mph 134. Stall mph 48. Initial climb rate 800. Ceiling 16,500. Range 536. Takeoff distance (50') 1,480. Landing distance (50') 1,280.

Piper's Tri-Pacer came to life in 1951 as a redesigned PA-20 Pacer. The conventional-gear Pacer had a tendency to swerve when landing in a crosswind, so Piper Aircraft went to the drawing boards and came up with a tricycle landing gear version. Originally equipped with a 125-hp engine, the power was increased on subsequent models approximately every two years: 135 hp, 150 hp, and 160 hp. When the 160-hp version was introduced in 1958, the 150-hp model also remained in production. To distinguish the two models, the 150-hp version was called the "Caribbean" during 1959 and 1960. The four-seater (really a three-placer) proved very popular with pilots during the 1950s and is continuing to serve faithfully today.

Of fabric-covered tubular construction, the Tri-Pacer was never known for outstanding speed, but it does perform surprisingly well against newer aircraft in its class. In comparison with Piper's 180 and Cessna's 172, the Tri-Pacer takes off in less distance, climbs faster, carries almost as much weight, and cruises a little faster than the 172. In spite of its stubby appearance, there are many pilots/owners who speak fondly of these sturdy little birds. Besides, they weren't designed to win any beauty contests; they were designed to carry four people through the sky from point A to point B, and they do just that very well.

PIPER PA-22-108 "COLT" 1961–63

STANDARD DATA: Seats 2. Gross wt. 1,650. Empty wt. 940. Fuel capacity 36. Engine 108-hp Lycoming. **PERFORMANCE:** Top mph 120. Cruise mph 108. Stall mph 54. Initial climb rate 610. Range 648. Ceiling 12,000. Takeoff distance (50') 1,570. Landing distance (50') 1,250.

The Piper Colt, introduced in 1961, is primarily intended for use by clubs and flying schools. It is identical in many ways to the Tri-Pacer and employs the same undercarriage, engine mounts, seats, windshield, door, tail surfaces, struts, and instrument panel. This two-seater aircraft is powered by a 108-hp Lycoming four-cylinder engine. The Colt features an all-metal airframe with fabric covering and was available in many Custom and Super Custom versions. Over 2,000 Piper Colts were built during the two years of production, and many of those are still very active.

PIPER "TOMAHAWK" 1978–82

STANDARD DATA: Seats 2. Gross wt. 1,670. Empty wt. 1,064. Fuel capacity 32. Engine 112-hp Lycoming. **PERFOR-**

MANCE: Top mph 130. Cruise mph 125. Stall mph 53. Initial climb rate 718. Ceiling 12,000. Range 502. Takeoff distance (50') 1,460. Landing distance (50') 1,374.

The sleek all-metal Tomahawk was the first trainer to meet all FAA requirements of FAR 23-Amendment 16. It combines a number of innovative design elements, including a jet-age T-tail that positions the fixed horizontal stabilizer and interchangeable elevators in air undisturbed by propeller slipstream. The T-tail facilitates quieter, smoother, and more stable flight with minimal pitch change at any speed. As an end plate for the vertical fin, the "T" also provides more positive rudder control. The "T" permits precise spin training, and the positive response gives the student excellent conditions for practicing stalls.

The Tomahawk's modern low-wing design is an adaptation of NASA's Whitcomb airfoil and provides optimum in-flight visibility, ground handling, safety, and landing ease. The design consists of a constant thickness and a rectangular planform with a high aspect ratio chosen for its low drag that permits excellent speed and high lift. The Tomahawk also features a bubble canopy and a door both sides of the cabin. For cost- and time-efficient maintenance, the Tomahawk's engine is accessible through a wide double opening cowling, and if necessary, the engine can be removed without detaching the propeller. The most significant refinement for the Tomahawk in 1980 was the reduction in the forces necessary to extend the flaps, carried out with the intention of reducing the student pilot's workload. In keeping with the T-tail design, there is no pitch-up tendency with flap extension.

PIPER "CHEROKEE"/ "CRUISER"/"WARRIOR" 1964–92

STANDARD DATA: (Warrior) Seats 2. Gross wt. 2,325. Empty wt. 1,342. Fuel capacity 50. Engine 160-hp Lycoming. **PERFORMANCE:** Top mph 146. Cruise mph 141. Stall mph 58. Initial climb rate 710. Ceiling 13,000. Range 730. Takeoff distance (50') 1,490. Landing distance (50') 1,115.
STANDARD DATA: (140) Seats 2. Gross wt. 1,950. Empty wt. 1,180. Fuel capacity 36–50. Engine 140-hp Lycoming. **PERFORMANCE:** Top mph 144. Cruise mph 134. Stall mph 52. Initial climb rate 820. Ceiling 15,000. Range 560–780. Takeoff distance (50') 1,700. Landing distance (50') 1,080.
STANDARD DATA: (160) Seats 4. Gross wt. 2,200. Empty wt. 1,215. Fuel capacity 36–50. Engine 160-hp Lycoming. **PERFORMANCE:** Top mph 146. Cruise mph 137. Stall mph 55. Initial climb rate 730. Ceiling 15,800. Range 545–735. Takeoff distance (50') 1,660. Landing distance (50') 1,090.

The Cherokee 140 was introduced in 1964 to meet the demand for an efficient low-wing trainer. Initially powered by a 140-hp Lycoming engine, the smallest Cherokee graduated to 150 hp in 1966, and an optional two-passenger rear seat was also made available. Licensed in the utility category, Piper's learn-to-fly airplane is also approved for aerobatic maneuvers such as lazy eights, chandelles, steep turns, and spins when operating below 1,950 pounds gross weight. When trimmed properly, the Cherokee is a very stable airplane and can be flown with aileron control alone.

The plane was sold in three versions: the Cherokee 140D, the Custom Cherokee 140D, and the Executive Cherokee 140D. The versions differed in the amount of optional equipment added. The 1973 models of the 140 were called the Cruiser and the Flite Liner, the latter being the trainer version. In 1975, the names were again changed. The Cruiser became the trainer version and the Warrior is the spacious sportster. The Warrior differs from the trainer by having a longer range, higher gross weight, longer wingspan, and more room. Because the same engine is used, the Warrior's performance suffers a little by comparison.

Mechanically, the Cruiser has changed little from 1976; however, 1977 refinements include new easy-to-close doors, a one-piece stabilator, and a sophisticated power console with a T-shaped throttle. In 1978, the Warrior flew almost seven mph faster as a result of overall drag reductions, a refined powerplant, and new high-performance speed fairings for the gear. An additional benefit is an increase in range by five percent.

By 1979, the Cruiser was discontinued as Piper's trainer airplane, replaced by the T-tail Tomahawk. Virtually unchanged, the Warrior continued as the airplane with the greatest useful load and lowest base price in its class. The Warrior boasts 983 pounds of useful load. As for fuel economy, the Warrior's 160-hp Lycoming sips only 6.6 gph at 55 percent power. When set up for best economy at 75 percent power, the four-seater can cover 679 miles with a 45-minute reserve.

PIPER PA 28-161 "WARRIOR II" 1978–95

STANDARD DATA: Seats 4. Gross wt. 2,440. Empty wt. 1,348. Fuel capacity 50. Engine 160-hp Lycoming O-320-D3G. **PERFORMANCE:** Top mph 146. Cruise mph 140. Initial climb rate 644. Ceiling 11,000. Range 640. Takeoff distance (50') 1,650. Landing distance (50') 1,160.

Through the early 1990s, Piper Aircraft stove off a Chapter 11 bankruptcy and managed to reorganize to keep production up and running. By 1995, the Warrior II and a stripped down trainer version, the Cadet, were being sold. The

Cadet is essentially the same aircraft minus the creature comforts and two seats. With a standard useful load of 1,099 pounds, the Warrior II continues to be a rugged sportplane capable of carrying four 180-pound adults and 80 pounds of baggage. As a trainer, the Cadet sold for around $100,000 in early 1995, and well-appointed versions of the Warrior II started at around $130,000.

PIPER CHEROKEE 180 "ARCHER"
1963–92

STANDARD DATA: Seats 4. Gross wt. 2,550. Empty wt. 1,414. Fuel capacity 50. Engine 180-hp Lycoming. **PERFORMANCE:** Top mph 153. Cruise mph 147. Stall mph 61. Initial climb rate 740. Range 774. Ceiling 13,650. Takeoff distance (50') 1,625. Landing distance (50') 1,550.

The 180-hp Cherokee 180 was unveiled in 1963, one year before the Cherokee 140 made its debut. It uses the same basic Cherokee airframe and wing that serves the entire series from the 140-hp two-seat trainer to the 300-hp fuel-injected Cherokee Six. The Model 180 utilizes a slightly longer wing, a wider horizontal stabilator, and a more spacious cabin. In recent models, handling and stability improved, while the heavy airliner feel changed to a light control response. The first year in which the Cherokee 180 received a name was 1973, it was dubbed the Challenger. The following year it was renamed Archer, and in 1976 it became Archer II. The 1976 Archer can carry up to 1,160 pounds of people, luggage, and fuel.

Also, late model Archers utilize an advanced semitapered wing. This wing deserves much of the credit for the 180's payload and speed. Like all Cherokee models, the Archer features a glare-reducing panel and a T-shaped throttle on a compact power console. In 1978, the Archer's speed was increased by almost seven mph and its range was improved by almost five percent as a result of overall drag reductions, a refined powerplant, and new high-performance speed fairings for the landing gear. With 1,136 pounds of useful load, a 6.3

gph fuel consumption rate at 55 percent power, four seats, and 26 cu. ft. for baggage, the Archer is an efficient hauler.

PIPER CHEROKEE "ARROW"/ "TURBO ARROW"/"ARROW II"
1967–90

STANDARD DATA: (Arrow) Seats 4. Gross wt. 2,750. Empty wt. 1,593. Fuel capacity 77. Engine 200-hp Lycoming. **PERFORMANCE:** Top mph 175. Cruise mph 165. Stall mph 63. Initial climb rate 831. Ceiling 17,000. Range 932. Takeoff distance (50') 1,600. Landing distance (50') 1,525.
STANDARD DATA: (Turbo Arrow) Seats 4. Gross wt. 2,900. Empty wt. 1,638. Fuel capacity 77. Engine 200-hp turbocharged Continental. **PERFORMANCE:** Top mph 205. Cruise mph 198. Stall mph 66. Initial climb rate 940. Ceiling 20,000. Range 897. Takeoff distance (50') 1,620. Landing distance (50') 1,555.

PIPER "ARROW IV"

PIPER TURBO ARROW

Piper's Cherokee Arrow takes the thinking out of flying a retractable. When the Arrow first appeared in 1967, it included a sensing device on the exterior of the fuselage that measured airspeed, and when the speed reached a predetermined minimum level, the landing gear on the Arrow automatically extended. The great benefit in this, of course, is that it reduced situations in which pilots forgot to lower the gear, thereby preventing many wheel-up landings. The Arrow also has a control quadrant in much the same style as that used in multiengine aircraft.

First introduced with a 180-hp Lycoming, Piper offered a 200-hp Arrow in the latter half of 1969. Both the 180-hp and 200-hp Arrows were sold through 1971, but in 1972 an all-new Arrow II was announced in Lock Haven. The Arrow II had a number of refinements over the former Arrows. The fuselage was stretched for more passenger leg room, a bigger stabilator was added for stability and better control, a modified upswept rudder was added, and the wing span was increased by two feet to increase gross weight, takeoff run, and rate of climb. Wider cabin windows, a wider cabin door, and a new paint job improved the exterior cosmetics of the Arrow II.

The Arrow IV and Turbo Arrow IV for 1979 received the T-tail pioneered by several other models in 1978. The long-popular, high-performance Arrow benefited with advanced handling characteristics and reduced cabin noise. Placement of the horizontal stabilator up out of the prop wash and wing airflow made the improvements possible. The Arrow continued to feature the long-span, semitapered wing introduced in 1977 when the Arrow became the Arrow III. And for an even quieter and smoother flight, the Turbo Arrow IV offers an optional three-blade propeller. A built-in oxygen system on the Turbo Arrow is similar to that introduced during 1980 on the Turbo Seminole. The oxygen system consists of a rear-mounted bottle with easy-to-reach overhead outlets, night-lighted pressure gauge, masks, and control-wheel microphone button.

PIPER CHEROKEE 235 "DAKOTA/PATHFINDER" 1964–95

STANDARD DATA: (Dakota) Seats 4. Gross wt. 3,000. Empty wt. 1,633. Fuel capacity 77. Engine 235-hp Lycoming. **PERFORMANCE:** Top mph 170. Cruise mph 166. Stall mph 64. Initial climb rate 965. Ceiling 17,900. Range 800. Takeoff distance (50') 1,300. Landing distance (50') 1,740.
STANDARD DATA: (Pathfinder) Seats 4. Gross wt. 3,000. Empty wt. 1,565. Fuel capacity 84. Engine 235-hp Lycoming. **PERFORMANCE:** Top mph 161. Cruise mph 153. Stall mph 65. Initial climb rate 800. Range 915. Ceiling 13,550. Takeoff distance (50') 1,410. Landing distance (50') 1,740.

This middle-of-the-line Cherokee (formerly the Charger) is powered by a 235-hp engine and ranks between the Archer and the bigger Cherokee Six. Piper apparently planned the entire Cherokee series so that even a student could work his or her way up the line progressively to constant-speed-prop retractables with a minimum of transitioning difficulty. The 235 is of fixed-gear variety, but a constant-speed prop is offered as one of the many factory options.

The main difference between the Pathfinder and the other Cherokees is its powerful 540 cu. in. Lycoming beneath the fiberglass cowl. It is a true four-place airplane in every sense of the word and excels in the fixed-gear category with a capability of carrying a useful load that is greater than its empty weight. The 235 Pathfinder can take off with four adults, 200 pounds of baggage, 84 gallons of fuel, and still be under the approved gross weight limitations. Couple this with its range of just under 1,110 miles at 55 percent power, and it can readily be seen why the 235 Pathfinder outranks many other aircraft in the same class.

In 1979, Dakota became the name of Piper's 235-hp four-seater. Along with its new name, the Dakota came outfitted with the same semitapered wings that had graced earlier model Arrow IIIs, Warrior Is, and Archer IIs. The Dakota boasts more useful load and range plus a shorter takeoff distance and faster cruise than any plane in its class. Further aerodynamic streamlining is also accomplished with the introduction of the same speed fairings used on several other single-engine models. The Dakota's cowl design includes a streamlined close-fitting cowl and oversized spinner to better cut through the air.

PIPER CHEROKEE SIX 260/300 1965–79

STANDARD DATA: (260) Seats 6–7. Gross wt. 3,400. Empty wt. 1,779. Fuel capacity 84. Engine 260-hp Lycoming. **PERFORMANCE:** Top mph 170. Cruise mph 158. Stall mph 63. Initial climb rate 775. Ceiling 12,800. Range 828. Takeoff distance (50') 1,800. Landing distance (50') 1,000.
STANDARD DATA: (300) Seats 6–7. Gross wt. 3,400. Empty wt. 1,846. Fuel capacity 84. Engine 300-hp Lycoming. **PERFORMANCE:** Top mph 180. Cruise mph 170. Stall mph 63. Initial climb rate 1,050. Ceiling 16,250. Range 840. Takeoff distance (50') 1,350. Landing distance (50') 1,000.
STANDARD DATA: (300) (1979) Seats 6–7. Gross wt. 3,400. Empty wt. 1,837. Fuel capacity 98. Engine 300-hp Lycoming. **PERFORMANCE:** Top mph 179. Cruise mph 175. Stall mph 63. Initial climb rate 1,050. Ceiling 17,100. Range 856. Takeoff distance (50') 1,350. Landing distance (50') 1,000.

The big Six is a prodigious people packer. Resembling a stretched version of the basic Cherokee airframe, it provides slight twin performance with single-engine economy. The Six was introduced in 1965 with a 260-hp engine, which some pilots seem to feel was not quite enough power. So the people at Piper decided to offer the option of the 300-hp powerplant up front in 1970. Basically a six-seater, the largest of the Cherokees is easily converted to handle a large amount of cargo loaded through its spacious rear double doors; thus, it performs as a double-duty passenger utility airplane. Besides the standard six-seat arrangement with center aisle, there is a seventh-seat option.

In 1978, increased speeds of seven mph made the Cherokee Sixes the fastest planes in their class. A five-percent increase in range is also a product of overall drag reductions, a refined powerplant, and new Piper-engineered speed fairings. In 1979, the single-engine workhorse was fitted with a 98-gallon capacity fuel tank and structurally integrated fuel system popularized by the Lance. The new fuel system increased the Six's range by over 100 miles at many power settings. At 65 percent best power, the Six's range is 923 miles.

PIPER "LANCE"/ "TURBO LANCE" 1977–84

STANDARD DATA: (Lance) Seats 6–7. Gross wt. 3,600. Empty wt. 2,011. Fuel capacity 98. Engine 300-hp Lycoming. **PERFORMANCE:** Top mph 190. Cruise mph 181. Stall mph 80. Initial climb rate 1,000. Ceiling 14,600. Range 994. Takeoff distance (50') 1,690. Landing distance (50') 1,710.
STANDARD DATA: (Turbo Lance) Seats 6–7. Gross wt. 3,600. Empty wt. 2,071. Fuel capacity 98. Engine 300-hp turbocharged Lycoming. **PERFORMANCE:** Top mph 222. Cruise mph 201. Stall mph 80. Initial climb rate 1,000. Ceiling 20,000. Range 937. Takeoff distance (50') 1,660. Landing distance (50') 1,710.

Piper's Lance is essentially a Cherokee Six with retractable landing gear. The Lance utilizes the same main gear as that of the higher-gross-weight Seneca with the same retraction system used in the Arrow. The Lance's 1,690-pound useful load is a healthy allowance for passengers, fuel, and luggage. As with the Cherokee Six 300, the dependable 300-hp engine is fuel injected. Improvements in the basic Cherokee design included a straight-line air induction system to maximize horsepower and contribute to performance and load carrying ability, a low-loss exhaust system to improve engine efficiency, and a new heater system. The Lance's distinction is that it is the first airplane to make the step from fixed-gear super-hauler to high-performance retractable.

Because the Six's strongest selling point was useful load, Piper had to look for ways to improve the Lance's carrying ability in order to make room for the added weight of the new gear without sacrificing payload. Piper did this by refining the intake and exhaust systems to achieve more horsepower from the venerable Lycoming engine. With added effective power and the increased aerodynamic efficiency of retractable gear, it was possible to up the gross from 3,400 to 3,600; thus, the Lance still retains a 114-pound useful-load advantage over the Six, even with its retractable gear.

Lance changes in 1978 included the addition of a turbocharged version as well as the use of a T-tail on both models. The Turbo Lance, with its turbocharged 300-hp Lycoming cruises at 201 mph at 16,000 feet. Maximum continuous power is provided to 15,000 feet. The T-tail design reduces noise and vibration levels, increases stability by diminishing longitudinal trim changes as power and flap settings are changed, and increases the center-of-gravity envelope.

PIPER "COMANCHE" 1958–72

STANDARD DATA: (260) Seats 4–6. Gross wt. 3,100. Empty wt. 1,728. Fuel capacity 90. Engine 260-hp Lycoming. **PERFORMANCE:** Top mph 195. Cruise mph 185. Stall mph 61. Initial climb rate 1,370. Range 1,190. Ceiling 20,000. Takeoff distance (50') 1,040. Landing distance (50') 1,015.
STANDARD DATA: (250) Seats 4. Gross wt. 2,900. Empty wt. 1,690. Fuel capacity 60. Engine 250-hp Lycoming. **PERFORMANCE:** Top mph 190. Cruise mph 180. Stall mph 61. Initial climb rate 1,350. Ceiling 19,800. Range 748. Takeoff distance (50') 1,650. Landing distance (50') 1,015.
STANDARD DATA: (400) Seats 4. Gross wt. 3,600. Empty wt. 2,110. Fuel capacity 130. Engine 400-hp Lycoming. **PERFORMANCE:** Top mph 233. Cruise mph 202. Stall mph 68. Initial climb rate 1,600. Range 1,540. Ceiling 19,500. Takeoff distance (50') 1,500. Landing distance (50') 1,820.
STANDARD DATA: (180) Seats 4. Gross wt. 2,550. Empty wt. 1,475. Fuel capacity 60. Engine 180-hp Lycoming. **PERFORMANCE:** Top mph 167. Cruise mph 150. Stall mph 61. Initial climb rate 910. Ceiling 18,500. Range 705. Takeoff distance (50') 2,240. Landing distance (50') 1,015.

The Comanche was once the top of Piper's single-engine lineup. It was introduced in 1958 as the PA-24 with a 250-hp Lycoming powerplant. A 180-hp version was also offered as an option. The Comanche continued to be produced in these two models until 1964 when a third Comanche option was introduced as the Comanche 400 powered by a 400-hp eight-cylinder engine, it was claimed to be the world's fastest single, piston-engine airplane of the day. The airframe was basically the same except for structural allowances for catering to its higher gross weight and increased airspeed. Its larger tail unit had horizontal surfaces similar to those used on the Aztec. By 1966, the single-engine Comanche line was limited to the Model 260 version only; the 180 was discontinued in 1964, the 250 was replaced by the 260 in 1965, and the 400 was discontinued in 1966. Also in 1966, the seating was increased by adding an optional third row of seats, and the gross takeoff weight was boosted from 2,900 pounds to 3,100 pounds.

PIPER "PAWNEE"/ "BRAVE" 1959–81

STANDARD DATA: (Brave restricted category) Seats 1. Gross wt. 4,400. Empty wt. 2,225. Fuel capacity 89. Engine

300-hp Continental. **PERFORMANCE:** Top mph 125. Cruise mph 106. Stall mph 67. Initial climb rate 355. Range 515. Take-off distance (50') 2,600. Landing distance (50') 1,470.
STANDARD DATA: (Pawnee D with duster) Seats 1. Gross wt. 2,900. Empty wt. 1,479. Fuel capacity 38. Engine 235-hp Lycoming. **PERFORMANCE:** Top mph 110. Cruise mph 100. Stall mph 46. Initial climb rate 500. Range 255. Takeoff distance (50') 1,470. Landing roll 850.

Piper's version of an agricultural duster-sprayer is the PA-25 Pawnee. First produced in August 1959, the single-seat chemical applicator was designed especially to give maximum pilot safety. The pilot sits high, gaining good visibility both forward and rearward. Safety exits are installed on both sides of the specially strengthened enclosed cockpit, and a steel-tube "turnover" structure is built in. A wire cutter is mounted on the center of the windshield, and there is a cable from the top of the cockpit to the top of the rudder to deflect wires or cables. Inside the cockpit, a rounded sheet-metal cushion above the instrument panel protects the pilot's head in case of a crash. The Pawnee is built with rectangular-section welded steel tube with fabric covering and Duraclad plastic finish. The chemical hopper in the Pawnee D carries 150 gallons or 1,200 pounds of chemicals, and the power to deliver it comes from either a 235- or 260-hp Lycoming. In 1975, the Pawnee Brave entered the lineup with its 285-hp Continental, a hopper with a capacity of 1,900 pounds or 225 gallons, and a larger sprayer.

PIPER "SARATOGA"/ "TURBO"/"SP"/ "TURBO SP" 1980–84

STANDARD DATA: (SP) Seats 6. Gross wt. 3,600. Empty wt. 1,986. Fuel capacity 107. Engine 300-hp Lycoming. **PERFORMANCE:** Top mph 189. Cruise mph 183. Stall mph 66. Initial climb rate 1,010. Ceiling 16,700. Range 995. Takeoff distance (50') 1,759 (two-blade), 1,573 (three-blade). Landing distance (50') 1,612.
STANDARD DATA: (Turbo SP) Seats 6. Gross wt. 3,600. Empty wt. 2,073. Fuel capacity 107. Engine 300-hp turbocharged Lycoming. **PERFORMANCE:** Top mph 224 (three-blade), 220 (two-blade). Cruise mph 204. Stall mph 64. Initial climb rate 1,120. Ceiling 20,000. Range 971. Takeoff

distance (50') 1,590 (two-blade), 1,420 (three-blade). Landing distance (50') 1,640.
STANDARD DATA: (Saratoga) Seats 6. Gross wt. 3,600. Empty wt. 1,920. Fuel capacity 107. Engine 300-hp Lycoming. **PERFORMANCE:** Top mph 176. Cruise mph 173. Stall mph 66. Initial climb rate 990. Ceiling 15,900. Range 972. Takeoff distance (50') 1,740. Landing distance (50') 1,700.
STANDARD DATA: (Turbo) Seats 6. Gross wt. 3,600. Empty wt. 2,000. Fuel capacity 107. Engine 300-hp turbocharged Lycoming. **PERFORMANCE:** Top mph 209 (three-blade), 205 (two-blade). Cruise mph 190. Stall mph 66. Initial climb rate 1,075. Ceiling 20,000. Range 1,001. Takeoff distance (50') 1,590 (two-blade), 1,420 (three-blade). Landing distance (50') 1,700.

PIPER "SARATOGA"

PIPER "TURBO SARATOGA"

PIPER "SARATOGA SP"

PIPER "TURBO SARATOGA SP"

In order to organize and improve its "workhorse" lineup, Piper introduced the Saratoga models in 1980 to replace the Cherokee Six and Lance models. The Saratoga brand actually applies to four separate airplanes. Beginning with the junior model in the brood, we have the basic Saratoga, a six-place fixed-gear 300-hp version. Next is the Saratoga SP, which is everything the basic Saratoga is except that the feet tuck away in flight. For the rare-air set, there is the turbocharged version of the stiff-legged model, designated the Turbo Saratoga. With retractable gear, the high-sky version becomes the Saratoga SP. Possibly the most significant aerodynamic change is the move from the stubby airfoil of the Cherokee line to a state-of-the-art semitapered wing that is gracefully slender and powerfully long.

After all the hoopla that surrounded the introduction of the T-tail on the Lance, returning to the full-span stabilator was a move for which a variety of reasons were offered. According to Piper, the new wing is so aerodynamically efficient and docile that it simply doesn't need the T-tail to help, and since the T-tail is inherently more expensive to produce, there was no need to keep it. An optional three-blade propeller for all models reduces cabin noise, delivers peak performance on takeoff and climbout, and offers better clearance when taxiing. Double rear doors make loading easy and helps owners take advantage of the Saratoga's substantial cargo capacity.

While the designation SP basically means retractable gear, it literally translates to "Special Performance." The aerodynamic profile is exceptionally clean by combining tuckaway gear with semitapered wings, which cut parasite drag to a minimum, and flush riveting on the leading edge. The Turbo SP is approved for flight into known-icing conditions with the optional deice package, and both SP models can be equipped with RCA Weather Scout I radar. The latest model Saratogas have been equipped with Dyna-Cushion engine mounts. With the addition of the new mounts, the Saratoga provides a remarkably quiet and comfortable environment, closer to that usually associated with large multiengine aircraft.

PORTERFIELD 65 "COLLEGIATE"/ 90 "FLYABOUT"
1935–39

STANDARD DATA: (65) Seats 2. Gross wt. 1,200. Empty wt. 700. Fuel capacity 13. Engine 65-hp Continental. PERFORMANCE: Top mph 108. Cruise mph 103. Landing mph 40. Initial climb rate 900. Range 325. Ceiling 16,000.
STANDARD DATA: (90) Seats 2. Gross wt. 1,326. Empty wt. 823. Fuel capacity 18. Engine 90-hp Warner Scarab Junior. PERFORMANCE: (90) Seats 2. Gross wt. 1,326. Stall mph 40. Initial climb rate 1,050. Ceiling 20,000. Range 336.

The Porterfield Aircraft Corp. was founded in 1934 by E.E. Porterfield, once president of the American Eagle Aircraft Corp. In the following year, it began producing the Porterfield two-seat monoplane. Designations included the 35-70 (70-hp Le Blond), 35-90 (90-hp Warner Scarab Junior), 35-65 (65-hp engine), and 35-75 (75-hp engine). The company introduced the CP-series in 1939, which included the CP-50, CP-55, CP-65, FP-65, and LP-65. The initials refer to the type of engine—Continental, Franklin or Lycoming—and the numbers refer to the horsepower. The Collegiate CP-65 was the most popular of the series. A substantial number of these two-seat training planes are still in flyable condition.

PORTERFIELD 65 "COLLEGIATE"

PORTERFIELD 90 "FLYABOUT"

PORTERFIELD MODEL 35-70/35-90
1935

STANDARD DATA: Seats 2. Gross wt. 1,326. Empty wt. 823. Fuel capacity 18. Engine 90-hp Warner Scarab Junior. PERFORMANCE: Top mph 135. Cruise mph 120. Stall mph 40. Initial climb rate 1,050. Ceiling 20,000. Range 336.

Both Porterfield models entered production in 1935 and were powered by either the 70-hp LeBlond five-cylinder or the 90-hp Warner Scarab Junior five-cylinder radial engines; thus, the numerical designations 35-70 and 35-90 apply. The Porterfield Aircraft Corp. of Kansas City, Missouri, had been founded one year, and the development work was done by E.E. Porterfield, who was formerly president of the American Eagle Aircraft Corp. Other versions of the first Porterfields were built with 50-, 65-, and 75-hp Continental or Lycoming engines. The enclosed cabin for two persons had dual controls, but they were quickly removable from either seat. Wing construction was two spruce spars, spruce and plywood ribs, and fabric covering. The fuselage was a fabric-covered steel-tube structure.

PZL-104 WILGA "THRUSH"
1964–80

STANDARD DATA: Seats 4. Gross wt. 2,755. Empty wt. 1,624. Fuel capacity 51. Engine 230-hp Continental. PERFORMANCE: Top mph 127. Cruise mph 93. Stall mph 40. Initial climb rate 865. Range 390. Ceiling 12,075. Takeoff distance (50') 625. Landing distance (50') 780.

The PZL-104 Wilga (Wilga translates to Thrush) is built in Warsaw, Poland, by WSK-Okecie. (The WSK stands for a company name that no Westerner would even attempt to pronounce.) The first PZL-104 Wilga-1 flew in 1962 and was immediately followed by the Wilga-2 and Wilga-3 as design modifications were made. The Wilga 32 and 35 were further improvements to incorporate a redesigned landing gear, a more comfortable cabin, and a fiberglass-laminated tailwheel leg. The Wilga 32 is fitted with a six-cylinder 230-hp Continental engine, and the Wilga 35 has a 260-hp Ivchenko nine-cylinder radial engine. Various models were sold for various purposes, such as glider towing (32A), passengers (32P), or ambulance use (32S). The Polish taildragger features a cantilevered high wing without the need for wing struts. Construction is all metal with a beaded metal skin.

REARWIN 8135 "CLOUDSTER" 1940

STANDARD DATA: Seats 2 or 3. Gross wt. 1,800. Empty wt. 1,100. Fuel capacity 34. Engine 120-hp Ken Royce seven-cylinder radial. **PERFORMANCE:** Top mph 135. Cruise mph 120. Landing mph 48. Initial climb rate 910. Range 609. Ceiling 16,300.

The Cloudster was preceded by the 8090 and 8125 versions with two seats each. The 8090 and 8125 were powered by 90-hp and 120-hp Ken Royce engines respectively. The three-seat Cloudster 8135 was introduced in 1940 and was powered by the same 120-hp engine as the 8125. The two planes were produced side-by-side to provide buyers with a two or three-seat option. Another model of the Cloudster was the 8135T. This two-seat tandem trainer was specially designed for instrument training in cooperation with Pan American Airways. It had two separate compartments, one behind the other, each with its own door, flying controls, and instruments. Included was a set of blind-flying instruments such as the Sperry directional gyro, artificial horizon, and a Lear radio transmitter and receiver.

REARWIN 7000 "SPORTSTER" 1935–42

STANDARD DATA: Seats 2. Gross wt. 1,460. Empty wt. 861. Fuel capacity 24. Engine 70-hp Ken Royce five-cylinder radial. **PERFORMANCE:** Top mph 115. Cruise mph 103. Landing mph 38. Initial climb rate 670. Range 500. Ceiling 15,000.

The first Rearwin 7000 Sportsters appeared in 1935 and were powered by 70-hp LeBlond radials. The Model 8500 Sportster with an 85-hp LeBlond was also introduced in 1935. The Model 9000 version of the Sportster was powered by ei-

ther a 90-hp Warner, Ken Royce, or LeBlond, which increased the top speed of the aircraft to 123 mph. The tandem two-seat cabin monoplane was produced for five years. During this time, Rearwin Airplanes, Inc. was taken over by the Rearwin Airplanes partnership of R.A. Rearwin, Royce S. Rearwin, and Kenneth R. Rearwin. They bought all the assets of the LeBlond Aircraft Corp. in 1937 and began producing their own engines that carried their name, Ken Royce. From then on all Rearwin Sportsters were provided with Ken Royce engines. The Rearwin company was bought in 1942 and the name changed to the Commonwealth Aircraft Inc.

REARWIN 185 "SKYRANGER" 1940–47

STANDARD DATA: Seats 2. Gross wt. 1,450. Empty wt. 910. Fuel capacity 48. Engine 80-hp Continental. **PERFORMANCE:** Top mph 114. Cruise mph 103. Stall mph 40. Initial climb rate 650. Range 500. Ceiling 14,000.

Rearwin Aircraft and Engines introduced the Skyranger in 1940 as a side-by-side two-seat cabin monoplane. This aircraft was first produced in four versions: the 175 with a 75-hp Continental, the 180 with an 80-hp Continental, the 180F with a 80-hp Franklin, and the 190F powered by a 90-hp Franklin engine. After World War II, the aircraft was reintroduced as the Skyranger 185 by Commonwealth Aircraft, a company created from Rearwin in 1941. Its production was terminated in 1947. The Skyranger 185 differs from its predecessors in only one respect, an 85-hp Continental engine.

REPUBLIC "SEABEE" 1944–47

STANDARD DATA: Seats 4. Gross wt. 2,600. Empty wt. 1,775. Engine 215-hp Franklin. **PERFORMANCE:** Top mph 120. Cruise mph 103. Landing mph 53. Initial climb rate 700. Range 560. Ceiling 12,000.

About 200 Seabees are currently flying in the United States, with approximately 130 others active in other countries. First made in 1944 and placed into full-scale quantity production in 1946, a total of 1,060 aircraft were produced before Republic Aviation abandoned civilian aircraft production in 1947. The relatively low-cost amphibian is still a favorite among sea-rated pilots, and current used prices reflect its popularity. Design of the four-seat flying boat is unique. The RC-3 Seabee's single six-cylinder engine is mounted behind and on top of the cabin so that the pusher propeller spins about halfway back the length of the fuselage. The original Seabee prototype used a 175-hp Franklin engine and first flew in 1944. Numerous changes in design and components reduced empty weight and production costs before the final RC-3 model was approved.

REPUBLIC P-47 "THUNDERBOLT" 1942–45

STANDARD DATA: Seats 1. Gross wt. 12,500. Empty wt. 9,900. Fuel capacity 270–370. Engine 2,300-hp Pratt & Whitney Double Wasp. **PERFORMANCE:** Top mph 440. Cruise mph 350. Landing mph 100. Initial climb rate 2,500. Range 650. Ceiling 40,000.

The Thunderbolt had a reputation as the toughest, heaviest single-engine fighter used in World War II. It could take punishment like no other and packed a battery of eight .50-caliber machine guns along with a greater load of armament than any other fighter in its day. In the air, the P-47 had an outstanding record. For every one shot down, it destroyed five enemy aircraft. Because its size and rugged construction allowed it to survive heavy battle damage, all leading Thunderbolt aces survived the war. The product of several years of development, the P-47 first flew in May 1941 and entered production the following year. It was initially employed chiefly for long-range fighter sweeps and escort duty, but later models also saw action as fighter bombers. More P-47s were produced than any other Army Air Force fighter, with the final total numbering 15,600.

ROCKWELL COMMANDER 112/112TC/114 1973–94

STANDARD DATA: (112) Seats 4. Gross wt. 2,800. Empty wt. 1,173. Fuel capacity 48–68. Engine 200-hp Lycoming. **PERFORMANCE:** Top mph 173. Cruise mph 163. Stall mph 62. Initial climb rate 1,020. Range 592–880. Ceiling 13,900. Takeoff distance (50') 1,585. Landing distance (50') 1,310. **STANDARD DATA:** (112TC) Seats 4. Gross wt. 2,950. Empty wt. 1,834. Fuel capacity 48–68. Engine 210-hp turbocharged Lycoming. **PERFORMANCE:** Top mph 195. Cruise mph 181. Stall mph 58. Initial climb rate 1,023. Range 510–823. Ceiling 20,000. Takeoff distance (50') 1,780. Landing distance (50') 1,221. **STANDARD DATA:** (114) Seats 4. Gross wt. 3,140. Empty wt. 1,790. Fuel capacity 48–68. Engine 260-hp Lycoming. **PERFORMANCE:** Top mph 191. Cruise mph 185. Stall mph 63. Initial climb rate 1,160. Range 720. Ceiling 17,000. Takeoff distance (50') 1,650. Landing distance (50') 1,318. **STANDARD DATA:** (Alpine) Seats 4. Gross wt. 2,950. Empty wt. 2,035. Fuel capacity 48–68. Engine 210-hp turbocharged Lycoming. **PERFORMANCE:** Top mph 197. Cruise mph 188. Stall mph 62. Initial climb rate 914. Ceiling 20,000. Range 529–764. Takeoff distance (50') 1,750. Landing distance (50') 1,275. **STANDARD DATA:** (Gran Turismo) Seats 4. Gross wt. 3,272. Empty wt. 2,070. Fuel capacity 68. Engine 260-hp Lycoming. **PERFORMANCE:** Top mph 191. Cruise mph 181. Stall mph 62. Initial climb rate 1,030. Ceiling 16,500. Range 722. Takeoff distance (50') 2,150. Landing distance (50') 1,200.

ROCKWELL COMMANDER 112

ROCKWELL COMMANDER

ROCKWELL " GRAN TURISMO" COMMANDER

The first deliveries of the Model 112 began in the summer of 1972 under the name of Aero Commander. A product of extensive consumer research, it was a four-seat, retractable-gear aircraft, originally powered by a 180-hp Lycoming engine. A fixed-gear version of this low-priced Aero Commander was called the Model 111, but its production life span was short. The Model 112 features the most spacious cabin of any four-seat, single-engine production aircraft, and for convenience it has a passenger access door on each side. Many new construction procedures were developed to facilitate assembly and reduce drag while retaining the plane's structural integrity.

The new manufacturing process included the use of large single assemblies rather than small pieces riveted together. The reduced number of rivets together with beaded skins improved airflow over the 112's surfaces. Subsequent additions to the line include the 112TC and the 114. The TC designation of the former means turbocharged, and the added boost helps the 112TC climb to 10,000 feet in 10 minutes. Even at 14,000 feet, the airplane can continue to climb at a rate of 900 fpm. The Model 114 utilizes a 260-hp normally-aspirated engine to provide a useful load with enough allowance for four persons, full fuel, a full radio package, and 100 pounds of baggage.

One change in the single-engine lineup was an emphasis on reduced drag by the elimination of certain scoops and the addition of several fairings. The result is a slight increase in speed for the 114, 112TC, and the 112B. The 112B also received new disc brakes and larger wheels. Both the 112 models were increased by over 100 pounds.

The 200-hp Rockwell 112 was dropped from the lineup of single-engine aircraft in 1979, and the names of the 112TC and the 114 were changed to the Alpine Commander and Gran Turismo Commander, respectively. These aircraft display slightly differing specification and performance figures, as reflected in the introductory summaries. The Gran Turismo is a three-blade 260-hp model, and the Alpine is a 210-hp turbocharged wide-body Commander. They were offered fully IFR-equipped by Rockwell with King avionics and a Century III autopilot. The McCauley three-blade prop improves sound and vibration levels.

Rockwell discontinued production of the single-engine line by 1980. In 1988, the rights for the Commander 112/114 were bought by a new company called Commander Aircraft, which allowed that company to maintain the existing fleet. Certification for a newly redesigned 114B was granted in 1991 and full production began once more with the 1992 model year. The aircraft proved reasonably successful even during the unfavorable economic climate of the 1990s.

ROCKWELL COMMANDER "THRUSH" 1965–80

STANDARD DATA: (600) Seats 1. Gross wt. 6,000. Empty wt. 3,700. Fuel capacity 100. Engine 600-hp Pratt & Whitney. **PERFORMANCE:** Top mph 140. Cruise mph 124. Stall mph 55. Initial climb rate 900. Range 402. Ceiling 15,000. Takeoff run 775. Landing roll 500.
STANDARD DATA: (800) Seats 1. Gross wt. 6,000. Empty wt. 4,100. Fuel capacity 100. Engine 800-hp Pratt & Whitney. **PERFORMANCE:** Top mph 155. Cruise mph 137. Stall mph 57. Initial climb rate 1,600. Range 330. Ceiling 25,000. Takeoff run 600. Landing roll 500.

Aero Commander's entries into the agricultural aircraft market were in three basic sizes. The Sparrow was the smallest of the lot with a payload of 1,400 pounds and utilizing a 235-hp engine. The Quail was an intermediate model using the same airframe as the Sparrow but with engine power increased to 290 hp. The Thrush Commander was not only the largest of the Aero Commander line but also was the largest specially designed agricultural craft in production in the United States. With 600 hp, this impressive aircraft can carry a payload up to 3,280 pounds and fuel capacity double that of any other ag plane. With that big Pratt & Whitney pulling it along through the air, it can probably use all the fuel it can get.

The Thrush 800 utilizes an impressive 800-hp Pratt & Whitney radial engine. It has a useful load of 1,900 pounds and a hopper capacity of 400 gallons. Marsh Aviation Co. builds a modification of the Thrush, called the S2R-T Turbo Thrush, in which turbine power replaces piston power. For standard use, the AiResearch turboprop is derated to 600-shp; however, maximum 778-shp output is available for emergencies. One advantage other than additional power is that normal automotive diesel fuel can be used if jet fuel is not at hand. Top speed is increased to 205 mph, and climb rate is boosted to 3,000 fpm.

RYAN SC/SCW 1937–41

STANDARD DATA: Seats 3. Gross wt. 2,150. Empty wt. 1,350. Engine 145-hp Warner Super Scarab radial or 150-hp Supercharged Menasco. **PERFORMANCE:** Top mph 152. Cruise mph 140. Stall mph 45. Initial climb rate 900. Ceiling 19,400. Range 520.

The Ryan Aeronautical Co. was the successor to the old Ryan Company that produced Charles Lindbergh's *Spirit of St. Louis*. The original company, known as Ryan Airlines, began operations in 1922, and rapid expansion took place after their transatlantic success; however, the Depression took its toll, and in 1931 T. Claude Ryan reentered the industry by forming the Ryan Aeronautical Co. Production of the SC all-metal three-seat cabin monoplane began in 1938. The aircraft was either fitted with the 145-hp Warner Super Scarab seven-cylinder radial or the 150-hp Menasco supercharged in-line engine. The wings were detachable, supported by an all-metal structure and covered by stressed Alclad metal. Accommodations were for three under a sliding canopy: two up front and one in the rear.

RYAN STM-2
1934–42

STANDARD DATA: Seats 2. Gross wt. 1,600. Empty wt. 1,027. Fuel capacity 24. Engine 125-hp Menasco C-4. **PERFORMANCE:** Top mph 150. Cruise mph 127. Stall mph 42. Initial climb rate 1,200. Range 350. Ceiling 17,500.

The Ryan Aeronautical Co. was a successor to the Ryan Co. that produced the aeroplane Charles Lindbergh used to cross the Atlantic. The company benefited from the airplane boom that followed but succumbed to the Depression in 1931. In 1934, the company was revived and began building the ST two-seat monoplane series. There were three models: the ST with a 95-hp Menasco, the STA with a 125-hp Menasco, and the STA Special with a 150-hp Menasco. For military purposes, the STM-1 was built with the 150-hp engine and sold to many Latin American countries. It was followed by the STM-2, which embodied several modifications specified by the U.S. Army Air Corps and was designated the PT-20. Numerous aircraft of this type are still active.

RYAN PT-22
1939–42

STANDARD DATA: Seats 2. Gross wt. 1,860. Empty wt. 1,313. Fuel capacity 24. Engine 160-hp Kinner. **PERFOR-**

MANCE: Top mph 131. Cruise mph 123. Landing mph 54. Initial climb rate 1,000. Range 352. Ceiling 15,500.

The Ryan PT-22 is another surplus military trainer of the World War II era that is still reasonably available on the used market. It is quite easy to operate and maintain. The fuselage is metal, but the wings are covered with fabric. The earliest versions had a Menasco engine, but the PT-22 trainers available in the largest numbers are powered by a Kinner radial engine. Beginning in 1941, the first model was the PT-21 powered by a 132-hp Kinner five-cylinder radial. The later version with a 160-hp engine was designated as the PT-22. Although the performance and range characteristics of these planes are too limited to make them practical, they are still popular with weekend pilots. The 160-hp Kinner engine is also a five-cylinder type, and the supply of surplus parts for it and the earlier versions are still ample.

RYAN "NAVION"
1946–51

STANDARD DATA: (205 hp) Seats 4. Gross wt. 2,750. Empty wt. 1,782. Fuel capacity 40. Engine 205-hp Continental. **PERFORMANCE:** Top mph 163. Cruise mph 155. Stall mph 75. Initial climb rate 1,110. Range 500. Ceiling 15,600. Takeoff distance (50') 1,100. Landing distance (50') 1,110.
STANDARD DATA: (Super Navion) Seats 4. Gross wt. 2,850. Empty wt. 1,930. Fuel capacity 40–60. Engine 260-hp Lycoming. **PERFORMANCE:** Top mph 174. Cruise mph 170. Stall mph 55. Initial climb rate 1,250. Ceiling 18,000. Range 415–640. Takeoff run 399. Landing run 468.

The Navion has been built at intervals by several companies. It began in 1946 as an original design by the North American Aviation Co. It is believed that many of the features were borrowed from North American's highly successful fighter plane, the P-51 Mustang. North American was involved in the production for a relatively short time, and manufacture was transferred to the Ryan Co. The Navion of this era was powered by a 185-hp Continental. The engine was later boosted to 205 hp in the Navion A and 260 hp in the Navion B. North American and Ryan turned out over 1,000 Navions each from 1946 to 1951. Further development of the Navion design was carried out by the Navion Aircraft Co. established in 1961. Over 1,200 Ryan Navions are still active.

SHINN 2150-A
1959–62

STANDARD DATA: Seats 2. Gross wt. 1,817. Empty wt. 1,125. Fuel capacity 35. Engine 150-hp Lycoming. **PERFORMANCE:** Top mph 148. Cruise mph 135. Stall mph 52. Initial climb rate 1,450. Range 525. Ceiling 22,000. Takeoff distance (50') 440. Landing distance (50') 450.

Originally designed and built by W.J. Morrisey of Morrisey Aviation, Inc. the Model 2150 was built and sold by Shinn Engineering in Santa Ana, California, after the latter company purchased manufacturing and sales rights from Morrisey in 1960. Morrisey's original prototypes were known as the Model 2000, using a 95-hp Continental engine or a 108-hp Lycoming engine. When Shinn began production of the tandem two-seater in May 1961, the airplane became known as the Shinn 2150-A. Shinn included a number of refinements over the Morrisey, yet production of the tricycle-gear airplane stopped in 1962. The aircraft is now produced in kit form through Morrisey aviation in Arizona.

SIAI-MARCHETTI
PN 333 "RIVIERA"
1962–66

STANDARD DATA: Seats 4. Gross wt. 3,270. Empty wt. 2,300. Fuel capacity 37–64. Engine 250-hp Continental. **PERFORMANCE:** Top mph 177. Cruise mph 164. Stall mph 68. Initial climb rate 1,220. Range 560. Ceiling 18,500. Ground takeoff run (50') 1,400. Water takeoff run 1,565. Ground landing distance (50') 1,100. Water landing distance 625.

Originally developed by the Nardi Company, the Riviera amphibian first flew in December 1952. Siai-Marchetti purchased manufacturing rights from Nardi and placed the four-seater into production in 1960. A New Jersey firm handled all

United States sales, and the Rivieras were assembled by Southwest Airmotive. The four-seater is powered by a 250-hp six-cylinder Continental engine mounted on top of the fuselage behind the cabin in a pusher-prop arrangement. For water use, the landing gear folds up into the fuselage behind the cabin, and the small nose gear is hidden behind nose gear doors. Forward visibility through a large bubblenose windshield is excellent. Production of the Riviera ended in early 1966 after 30 airplanes had been built.

SIAI-MARCHETTI
S.205 (WACO 5.220)/S.208
1966–81

STANDARD DATA: (S.205-20/R) Seats 4. Gross wt. 2,755. Empty wt. 1,630. Fuel capacity 56. Engine 200-hp Lycoming. **PERFORMANCE:** Top mph 174. Cruise mph 159. Stall mph 52. Initial climb rate 865. Range 940. Ceiling 17,650. Takeoff distance (50') 1,340. Landing distance (50') 1,540.
STANDARD DATA: (S.202-22/R) Seats 4. Gross wt. 2,755. Empty wt. 1,653. Fuel capacity 56. Engine 220-hp Franklin. **PERFORMANCE:** Top mph 183. Cruise mph 175. Stall mph 52. Initial climb rate 1,160. Range 823. Ceiling 20,330. Takeoff distance (50') 1,240. Landing distance (50') 1,540.
STANDARD DATA: (S.208) Seats 4. Gross wt. 3,306. Empty wt. 1,785. Fuel capacity 117. Engine 260-hp Lycoming. **PERFORMANCE:** Top mph 199. Cruise mph 187. Stall mph 58. Range 1,250. Ceiling 17,725. Takeoff distance (50') 1,640. Landing distance (50') 1,310.

The Siai-Marchetti S.205 was built in several versions, all differing in engine size and gear type. For this reason, the airplane's uses can range from the most economical touring craft to a high-performance executive craft. It is designed to house engines varying in size from 180 to 300 hp. All Siai-Marchetti aircraft make use of honeycomb panels to give the airframe an exceptionally rigid structure. The first examples were completed in 1965, and were all powered by 180-hp Lycoming engines.

Later models included the S.205-10/F, S.205-1 8/R, S.205-20/F, S.205-20/R, S.205-22/R, and S.202-22/M. The numbers following the dash refer to the engine size (10 = 100 hp, 18 = 180 hp, etc.) and the letter refers to retractable, fixed, or military. The Model S.202-22/R was powered by a Franklin engine and utilized retractable gear; it was also assembled in the United States by Allied Aero Industries as the Waco Vela S.220. All the variations went out of production in 1972 except the 20/F and 20/R. The S.208 entered production in 1968 and shared nearly 60 percent of the S.206's structural components. It is powered by a 260-hp Lycoming and features retractable landing gear.

SIAI-MARCHETTI SF.260
1967–81

STANDARD DATA: Seats 3. Gross wt. 2,430. Empty wt. 1,543. Fuel capacity 63. Engine 260-hp Lycoming. **PERFORMANCE:** Top mph 235. Cruise mph 214. Stall mph 65. Initial climb rate 1,770. Range 1,275. Ceiling 21,370. Takeoff distance (50') 1,390. Landing distance (50') 1,610.

The Siai-Marchetti SF.260 looks very much like the Procaer Picchio except for its wingtip fuel tanks and rearward one-piece sliding canopy. The prototype of the aircraft was built by Aviamilano and flew for the first time in 1964. It was powered by a 250-hp Lycoming engine. Production of the airplane was subsequently taken over by the Siai-Marchetti Co. and the SF.250 was upgraded to a 260-hp Lycoming, thus the designation SF.260. The cabin has accommodations for three occupants, one in the rear seat and two in the front seats. Two small children can be carried in the back seat as long as their combined weight does not exceed 250 pounds. Construction of the Siai-Marchetti is all metal with four fuel tanks (two in the wings and two tip tanks). Its landing gear is a retractable tricycle type. The SF.260 holds two FAI speed records in the C-I-b class and are listed under the aircraft's United States designation: Waco Meteor.

SOCATA "RALLYE"/ WACO "MINERVA"
1966–81

STANDARD DATA: (150) Seats 4. Gross wt. 1,920. Empty wt. 1,170. Fuel capacity 47. Engine 150-hp Lycoming. **PERFORMANCE:** Top mph 134. Cruise mph 124. Stall mph 52. Initial climb rate 870. Ceiling 13,000. Range 622. Takeoff run 420. Landing roll 390.
STANDARD DATA: (180) Seats 4. Gross wt. 2,315. Empty wt. 1,260. Fuel capacity 60. Engine 180-hp Lycoming. **PERFORMANCE:** Top mph 150. Cruise mph 140. Stall mph 57. Initial climb rate 760. Ceiling 11,800. Range 805. Takeoff run 445. Landing roll 425.
STANDARD DATA: (235) Seats 4. Gross wt. 2,640. Empty wt. 1,525. Fuel capacity 71. Engine 230-hp Lycoming. **PERFORMANCE:** Top mph 171. Cruise mph 152. Stall mph 58. Initial climb rate 980. Ceiling 14,800. Range 810. Takeoff run 490. Landing roll 425.

SOCATA (Societe de Construction d'Avions de Tourisme et d'Affaires), a subsidiary of Aerospatiale, had reintroduced its Rallye line of airplanes to the American market. In 1963, development of the Rallye series was taken over by S.E.E.M.S. (Societe d'Exploitation des Establissements Morane-Saulnier). This company was soon taken over by G.E.M.S. (Gerance des Establissements Morane-Saulnier),

which was controlled by Sud-Aviation, and Sud-Aviation ultimately became Aerospatiale and formed the SOCATA subsidiary to produce the Rallye. Then in the late 1960s and early 1970s, the Waco Aircraft Co., a subsidiary of Allied Aero Industries, produced and marketed the Rallye Commodore (220-hp Franklin) in the United States as the Waco Minerva. After 1971, Waco discontinued its involvement.

The entire Rallye line consists of 12 models:

- 100S (Sport) has a 100-hp Rolls-Royce Continental, two seats, and is cleared for spins.
- 100T (Tourisme) has the same Rolls-Royce engine and three to four seats.
- 100ST can be operated as a two-seater cleared for spins or a four-seater not cleared for spins.
- 150CT has a 150-hp Lycoming and improved design.
- 150T is similar to the 100T except for its 150-hp Lycoming.
- 150ST is a high-performance version for flying clubs.
- 180CT has a 180-hp Lycoming and constant-speed prop.
- 180T is specialized for towing.
- 235CT has seating for four and a 235-hp Lycoming.
- 235CA is an agricultural version.
- 235C is a taildragger.
- 235G is a military variant.

Only the 150ST, 18OCT, and 235CT were marketed in the United States.

All Rallyes have full STOL capabilities as a result of full-span automatic antistall leading-edge slats plus slotted Fowler flaps and generously sized control surfaces. The 150 is one of the few trainers with seats for four, and all Rallyes feature sliding canopies for easy entrance. Both the 180 and 235 have larger airframes, a strengthened structure, wheel fairings, more prop clearance, larger rudder and ailerons, modified cockpit canopy, and larger baggage compartment.

SOPWITH "CAMEL"
1917–19

STANDARD DATA: Seats 1. Gross wt. 1,453. Empty wt. 929. Fuel capacity 31.5. Engine 130-hp Clerget, 110-hp Le Rhone Rotary, 150-hp Dentley, 100-hp Monosoupape. **PERFORMANCE:** (130 hp). Top mph 113. Initial climb rate 1,080. Range 300. Ceiling 19,000.

The Sopwith Camel holds the unique distinction of having achieved the highest number of aerial victories in World War I. This is especially amazing because the Camel entered combat during the latter part of 1917 when the war was just about over. During those final months, the Sopwith shot down 1,294 enemy fighters, bombers, and Zeppelins. The Camel received its nickname because the receivers of the two Vickers machine guns

SOPWITH "CAMEL"

were covered by two humplike projections. It was the most highly maneuverable fighter of the war but quite tricky to master. The short and compact airframe coupled to the large torque-producing rotary engine made right-hand turns occur incredibly fast.

SPAD 5 XIII

STANDARD DATA: Seats 1. Gross wt. 1,862. Engine 220-hp Hispano 8B. **PERFORMANCE:** Top mph 139. Initial climb rate 1,500. Range 185. Ceiling 21,800.

This famous World War I French fighter was designed and built by the Societes des Productions Armand Deperdussin and thus received the abbreviated nickname SPAD. The model S13 became available to French, British, American, and Italian squadrons in May 1917. It had considerable power and range for its time and carried two 7.65mm Vickers machine guns. The SPAD achieved numerous victories in the competent hands of such Allied aces as Eddie Rickenbacker, Guynemer, Rene Fonck, and Frank Luke. The total production of the SPAD XIII reached 8,440 before armistice.

SPARTAN C.3
1928

STANDARD DATA: Seats 3. Gross wt. 2,150. Empty wt. 1,310. Engine 120-hp Walter. **PERFORMANCE:** Top mph 105. Cruise mph 92. Landing mph 45. Initial climb rate 500.

The Spartan C-3 was one of the three-seat open-cockpit biplanes that were highly popular in the Midwest during the late 1920s. The tandem cockpits had accommodations for one pilot

in the rear and two side-by-side passengers sitting in the front. The powerplant was a Walter nine-cylinder radial. The Spartan's wings were of equal-span design and utilized hollow box spars with spruce flanges and two-ply diagonal mahogany-planked sides. The main fuel tanks were housed in the top wings. The suspension was cushioned by a rubber shock-absorber cord. A later refinement of the C-3 called for either the 150-hp Wright Whirlwind J-6 or the 170-hp Curtiss Challenger. Improvements included increased cockpit protection, zippered inspection openings in the tail, the lower wings faired into the fuselage, a booster magneto, and a Hamilton Standard metal airscrew. The Challenger engine boosted the Spartan's maximum speed to 115 mph and climb rate to 900 fpm.

SPARTAN 7-W "EXECUTIVE"
1936–40

STANDARD DATA: Seats 5. Gross wt. 4,400. Empty wt. 2,987. Engine 450-hp Pratt & Whitney Wasp Junior. **PERFORMANCE:** Top mph 212. Cruise mph 200. Landing mph 65. Initial climb rate 1,430. Range 900. Ceiling 24,000.

This speedy low-wing cabin airplane received its performance from 450 hp supplied by a Pratt & Whitney nine-cylinder Wasp Junior radial engine. The Spartan 7-W Executive was produced during 1937 to 1940, and an attempted revival, called the Model 13 Executive, appeared in 1946. Only the prototype of the fixed-gear Model 12 flew; no production was ever undertaken. The Executive had a retractable conventional gear, a thick wing, and a relatively small tail for the amount of power it carried up front. Several Executives served during World War II using the "UC-71" designation.

SPORTAVIA AVION-PLANEUR RF4D
1966–80

STANDARD DATA: Seats 1. Gross wt. 804. Empty wt. 584. Fuel capacity 10. Engine 40-hp Volkswagen. **PERFORMANCE:** Top mph 122. Cruise mph 112. Stall mph 46. Initial climb rate 690. Range 422. Ceiling 19,700. Takeoff run 427. Landing roll 328.

Although the Sportavia RF4D had been around since 1966, it wasn't too widely known until May 1969 when Mira Slovak flew one across the Atlantic to win the 1,000£ prize offered by the *London Evening News* for the best performance by a light aircraft under 5,000 pounds in the Daily Mail Air Race. Using a converted engine, the RF4D was preceded by models RF-01, RF-2, and RF-3 during the years 1960 through 1966. The all-wood single-seater is rated fully aerobatically and combines the characteristics of a sailplane and a small powered sportplane. A single main landing wheel retracts forward manually into a fiberglass cowling. The small tailwheel is steerable, and there is a manually operated brake on the main wheel.

STINSON (VULTEE) V-74/L-1 "VIGILANT"
1940

STANDARD DATA: (L-1) Seats 2. Gross wt. 3,332. Empty wt. 2,593. Fuel capacity 48. Engine 285-hp Lycoming radial. **PERFORMANCE:** Top mph 122. Cruise mph 110. Initial climb rate 1,160. Range 280. Ceiling 12,800.

The Stinson Vigilant is a two-seat liaison/observation plane powered by a Lycoming nine-cylinder radial engine rated at 285 hp. Its two occupants sit in tandem fashion surrounded by window side panels that slope outward to facilitate downward vision. The domed roof is made from transparent plastic material. In 1940, the Army Air Corps ordered better than 140 V-74s and gave them the designation of L-1. These were followed by a larger order of L-1As with their longer fuselage and increased gross weight. Other versions of the Vigilant were used as ambulances, glider pickup trainers, and

floatplanes. Very few of these high-wing monoplanes are still active.

STINSON 76/L-5 "SENTINEL"
1941–44

STANDARD DATA: Seats 2. Gross wt. 2,158. Empty wt. 1,472. Fuel capacity 36. Engine 190-hp Lycoming. **PERFORMANCE:** Top mph 130. Cruise mph 112. Initial climb rate 975. Ceiling 15,800. Range 275. Maximum range 420.

The V-76 Sentinel two-seat liaison and observation airplane was developed from the Model 105 Voyager in 1941 by the Stinson Division of Consolidated Vultee. The first deliveries to the U.S. Army were made in 1942. Deliveries of the initial version, the L-5, totalled 1,731, and subsequent orders brought the total production to 3,283. In 1943, changes in the electrical system resulted in the designation L-5A. The L-5B version was an ambulance modification with the addition of a special downfolding door aft of and adjoining the standard backseat door. When both rear doors were opened, a single stretcher could be loaded. Other versions included the L-5C with a reconnaissance camera, the L-5F with drooping ailerons, and the L-5G with a 190-hp Lycoming. Fuel was carried in two tanks, one in each wing. The spruce wing spars and ribs were fabric covered. The same materials were used for the tail. The fuselage was fabric-covered steel tube.

STINSON "RELIANT"
1934–42

STANDARD DATA: (SR.10) Seats 5. Gross wt. 4,000. Empty wt. 2,810. Engine 290-hp Lycoming. **PERFORMANCE:** Top mph 141. Cruise mph 130. Initial climb rate 850. Ceiling 14,000.

The first model of the Reliant was the SR with a wingspan of 36 feet 3 inches; 88 were built. The Reliant underwent various minor changes that resulted in the SR-1 through SRA. The SR-S, still a four-seater, was introduced in 1934 with a 41-foot wingspan, and 145 subsequently were built. The SR-6 was next, and 50 ships were built. All these early Reliants had evolved from the Stinson S.M. series and had straight wings.

The first taper-wing (gull-wing) Reliant was the SR-7, which had a span of 41 feet. This characteristic wing also gave the Reliant the nickname of Stinson "Gullwing." The SR-8 was the first to feature five seats. The SR-9 was produced in 1937 making use of the same 285-hp Lycoming nine-cylinder radial engine as the SR-8, as well as a 450-hp Pratt & Whitney or a 350-hp Wright Whirlwind. The SR-10, introduced in 1938, was fitted with the same three engines. Vultee Aircraft bought the Stinson Aircraft Co. in 1940, and the Reliant became the V-77, and about 500 were completed.

STINSON 10A "VOYAGER" 1940–41

STANDARD DATA: Seats 3. Gross wt. 1,625. Empty wt. 948. Fuel capacity 20. Engine 90-hp Franklin. **PERFORMANCE:** Top mph 115. Cruise mph 109. Initial climb rate 600. Range 380. Ceiling 13,000.

The 10 Voyager was the improved successor to the 105 Voyager. Introduced in 1940, the new airplane differed only by its increased cabin width and other minor structural changes. Several versions of the Model 10 were built during its short life span. The 10 housed an 80-hp Continental, the 10A used the 90-hp Franklin, and the 10B was powered by the 75-hp Lycoming. Wing construction consisted of spruce spars and aluminum ribs covered with fabric. The fuselage was built from a welded steel-tube frame covered with fabric. The enclosed cabin had seating for three, two side-by-side and one behind on the port side. Two doors provided access on either side of the plane. Though production of this light private plane ceased in 1941, it remained in wide use in the Civilian Pilot Training Program. The Voyager also formed the basis for the L-Sentinel liaison/observation plane.

STINSON 108 "VOYAGER" 1946–50

STANDARD DATA: Seats 4. Gross wt. 2,400. Empty wt. 1,300. Fuel capacity 50. Engine 150-hp to 165-hp Franklin. **PERFORMANCE:** Top mph 143. Cruise mph 121. Stall mph 65. Range 510. Initial climb rate 850. Takeoff run 1,400. Landing roll 1,500. Ceiling 16,500.

After the war, production of civil aircraft resumed, and the 108 Voyager appeared in 1946. It was an improved four-seat version of the prewar Model 10 and was powered by a 150-hp Franklin engine. Subsequently, a 165-hp powerplant was used. The final version of the Voyager was produced in late 1948; the Model 108-3 with the larger fuel tank and in-creased vertical tail are symbolic of the Stinson line. Piper Aircraft acquired the tooling and manufacturing rights in December 1948, and a few additional Voyagers were built before production was discontinued in 1950. Piper also produced the Stinson Station Wagon that was a light freighter version of the Voyager. By removing the two rear seats, space was made available for up to 640 pounds of cargo. The Station Wagon had a slightly lighter empty weight.

SUPERMARINE "SPITFIRE" 1945

STANDARD DATA: (Spitfire I) Seats 1. Gross wt. 5,332. Fuel capacity 102. Engine Rolls-Royce Merlin III. **PERFORMANCE:** Top mph 367. Initial climb rate 3,000. Range 500. Ceiling 40,000.

Six years of war proved the basic Spitfire design to be highly successful. In actuality, the first Spitfire was a low-winger outfitted with a 600-hp Goshawk engine and fixed landing gear. The name was later transferred to the more familiar aircraft that was the product of high-speed design features borrowed from three successive Schneider Cup Trophy Contest winners that set three world speed records. Powered by one of the earliest Merlin engines turning a fixed-pitch prop, the prototype classed itself as the fastest military plane of its day.

The Spitfire I saw the early Merlin replaced by a Merlin III and the two-blade wooden prop exchanged for a three-blade controllable-pitch metal prop. Subsequent Spitfires housed Merlin XII, 32, 45, 46, 47, 61-66, 70, 71, 77, Griffon III, IV, and 65 engines. Standard wings were elliptical in design; however, some were fitted with shorter square-tipped or pointed wings. Some later versions were equipped with a bubble-type rearview canopy.

TAYLORCRAFT
1939–58

STANDARD DATA: (Model 19) Seats 2. Gross wt. 1,500. Empty wt. 860. Fuel capacity 18. Engine 85-hp Continental. **PERFORMANCE:** Top mph 120. Cruise mph 110. Stall mph 38. Initial climb rate 700. Range 300. Ceiling 17,000.
STANDARD DATA: (Ranch Wagon) Seats 2. Gross wt. 1,150. Empty wt. 670. Fuel capacity 12. Engine 65-hp Lycoming. **PERFORMANCE:** Top mph 105. Cruise mph 95. Stall mph 35. Initial climb rate 450. Ceiling 17,000. Range 250.
STANDARD DATA: (Model 15) Seats 4. Gross wt. 2,200. Empty wt. 1,275. Fuel capacity 42. Engine 145-hp Continental. **PERFORMANCE:** Top mph 132. Cruise mph 120. Stall mph 136. Initial climb rate 700. Ceiling 16,000. Range 500. Takeoff run 500.

C.G. Taylor, who designed and developed what is now known as the Piper Cub, later formed another company and produced a second outstanding aircraft in the Taylorcraft series. All "T-Crafts" had welded steel-tube fuselages and wooden-spar wings. Most had fabric covering, but a few four-place Ranch Wagons (Model 20) were built with molded fiberglass wings and fuselage coverings. Power started with a Continental engine of 40-hp and in ensuing years Lycoming, Franklin, and Continental engines of 50, 65, and 85 hp were used in the two-seater models (Models A, B, and D).

The four-seat Tourist Model 15 (1950) had a 145-hp Continental, and the Ranch Wagon (1955) had a 225-hp Continental. Taylorcrafts were built in considerable numbers during World War II as military spotter aircraft, and most of T-Crafts seen flying today are ex-GI planes. These featured 65 hp, cruised at just over 90 mph, and were labeled 0-57. After the war, Taylorcraft slicked up the design, added an 85-hp Continental, and produced the Model 19 Sportsman version, which was good for a 110-mph cruise. A development of this model has been put back into production by Taylorcraft Aviation Corp. of Alliance, Ohio.

TEMCO/GLOBE "SWIFT"
1945–51

STANDARD DATA: Seats 2. Gross wt. 1,710. Empty wt. 1,139. Fuel capacity 26. Engine 125-hp Continental. **PERFORMANCE:** Top mph 150. Cruise mph 140. Stall mph 50. Initial climb rate 1,000. Range 420. Ceiling 16,000. Takeoff run 684. Landing roll 381.

In 1947, the Texas Engineering and Manufacturing Co. bought all tooling, patents, and manufacturing rights for the two-seat all-metal Globe Swift from the Globe Aircraft Corp.

Before Globe had gone bankrupt, Temco had been building Swifts under a subcontract. After Globe collapsed, Temco continued to produce the Swift under its own name. Taking to the air for the first time in 1945, the Swift was originally powered by an 85-hp Continental. The later model Swift produced by Temco utilized a 125-hp Continental engine and was built from 1947 to 1951, when production ceased. Despite the fact that the Swift hasn't been built since that time, there are still upwards of 600 aircraft active in this country.

TEMCO "BUCKEROO"
1949

STANDARD DATA: (TE-18) Seats 2. Gross wt. 1,975. Empty wt. 1,350. Fuel capacity 32. Engine 165-hp Franklin. **PERFORMANCE:** Top mph 156. Cruise mph 145. Initial climb rate 1,000. Ceiling 17,000. Takeoff distance (50') 875. Landing distance (50') 740.

The Temco Buckeroo was built in two versions, the Model TE-1A using a 145-hp Continental and the TE-1B with a 165-hp Franklin. The Model TE-lA Buckeroo tandem two-seat basic trainer was introduced in 1949. It was a tandem-seat version of the Swift and made use of about 80 percent of the Swift's tooling. The Buckeroo was developed to meet the need for an airplane with a low initial cost and economical operation while maintaining the high-performance characteristics required of a military trainer. In 1951, after the Swift was discontinued to concentrate on emergency defense orders, Buckeroo production continued as the Model TE-1B. Under the Air Force designation YT-35, this primary trainer also proved itself to be an adequate ground-support aircraft. Few Buckeroos remain active today.

ARCTIC "TERN"

STANDARD DATA: Seats 2. Gross wt. 1,900. Empty wt. 1,073. Fuel capacity 40. Engine 160-hp Lycoming. **PERFORMANCE:** Top mph 117. Cruise mph 112. Stall mph 34. Initial climb rate 1,275. Ceiling 21,000. Range 650. Takeoff (50') 500. Landing (50') 350.

The old tandem Interstate trainer was reborn when the Arctic Aircraft Co. decided to develop the Tern bush plane. The Interstate's rugged design and construction make it ideal for operating in remote areas on unimproved fields, sandbars,

ARCTIC "TERN"

and beaches. Manufactured in Alaska, there are several features that bring the old trainer up to date. The Tern features a high gross weight (1,900 pounds under State of Alaska commercial requirements) and large balanced control surfaces. Its NACA 23012 airfoil design affords a wide center of gravity range with the famous floating characteristic of the Taylorcraft. A semi-Fowler slotted flap gives the pilot complete control and allows the slowest flight and slowest stall speed available in the light-plane field. The Tern is also designed for the mechanic because all components are readily accessible for inspection and maintenance. It can be easily fitted with floats, skis, or high-flotation tires to meet the bush pilot's choice of terrain.

TRAVEL AIR 6000
1928

STANDARD DATA: Seats 6. Gross wt. 3,725. Empty wt. 2,350. Engine 220-hp Wright Whirlwind. **PERFORMANCE:** Top mph 126. Cruise mph 108. Landing mph 53. Initial climb rate 750. Range 678. Ceiling 15,000.

Travel Air Manufacturing Co., of which Walter H. Beech was an officer, introduced the Travel Air 6000 in 1928. It was a six-seat commercial-cabin monoplane and a more recent development of the Travel Air 5000. The airplane housed either a 220-hp Wright Whirlwind, a 300-hp Whirlwind, or a 410-hp Pratt & Whitney. The 220-hp Whirlwind was the original powerplant. When Travel Air merged with the Curtiss-Robertson Division of Curtiss-Wright, the aircraft's designation was changed to Travel Air Model 6. Construction was mixed: fabric-covered wooden wings and a welded steel-tube fuselage covered by fabric. The wings utilized box spars with spruce flanges, plywood sides, and built-up Warren-truss-type ribs.

TRIDENT 320
"TRIGULL"
1977–79

STANDARD DATA: Seats 4. Gross wt. 3,800. Empty wt. 2,500. Fuel capacity 100. Engine 285-hp Continental Tiara.

PERFORMANCE: Top mph 165. Cruise mph 154. Stall mph 56. Initial climb rate 1,030. Ceiling 16,000+. Range 795. Takeoff run (land) 520. Takeoff run (water) 790. Landing roll (land) 570. Landing (water) 490.

A product of Trident Aircraft Ltd., Vancouver, British Columbia, the Trigull 320 has been in the research, testing, and construction stage since 1971. The Trigull has been considered Canada's answer to the old Republic RC-3 SeaBee, the Lake Buccaneer, the Italian Riviera, and other amphibians that have been developed over the years. It is a pusher, which has many advantages over a tractor. The rearward location of the propeller and engine offers a more practical location of the center of gravity. Unique features include retractable wing floats that serve double duty as wing-lifting areas, a nosewheel that can act as a bumper, drooping ailerons with flap extension, Continental's tried and proven Tiara engine, retracting water rudder, and ample cabin and baggage space. The Trident's 285-hp powerplant turns a constant-speed reversible-pitch propeller and can produce up to 320 hp for five minutes. Seating is for a pilot and up to five passengers. Entrance is through three doors: one on each side of the cabin and one bow door.

VARGA KACHINA

STANDARD DATA: Gross wt. 1,817. Empty wt. 1,125. Fuel capacity 35. Wingspan 30'. Length 21'2". Engine 150-hp Lycoming. **PERFORMANCE:** Top mph 148. Cruise mph 130. Stall mph 52. Climb rate 1,450. Ceiling 22,000. Takeoff distance (50') 440. Landing distance (50') 450. Range 525.

Veteran Douglas test pilot William Morrisey guessed that the thousands of returning World War II pilots would be eager to climb into a tandem sport plane that had all the charisma of a military trainer. After battling the FAA's red tape for some years, Morrisey sold out to Clifford Shinn, who built some 35 planes before quitting. The tandem two-seater was renamed Kachina and marketed by George Varga. The fuselage is built of chrome moly tubing with removable metal side and bottom panels for quick inspection. The left side of the greenhouse canopy swings open for entrance to the cockpit. The Kachina's big appeal is not only reasonable cost but sheer fun of flying.

WACO OPEN COCKPIT BIPLANES
1931–42

STANDARD DATA: (UPF) Seats 2. Gross wt. 2,650. Empty wt. 1,870. Fuel capacity 50. Engine 220-hp Continental. **PERFORMANCE:** Top mph 138. Cruise mph 123. Climb to 9,000 in 15 minutes. Ceiling 15,800.

WACO 1BA

WACO UPF-7

Waco open-cockpit biplanes were first produced in 1923. The most popular and common survivor is the UPF-7 (PT-14) because it was produced in the largest numbers as a primary trainer from 1937 to 1942. The Waco F series was the replacement for the older 1928 O series and was put into production in 1930. The F series airplanes represent the majority of Wacos still seen flying. The first to be assembled were the INF and the KNF, which housed 125-hp and 100-hp Kinners respectively. In subsequent years, numerous models were added, each differing for the most part by the powerplant: in 1931, the PCF (170-hp Jacobs) and QCF (165-hp Continental); in 1932, the PBF (170-hp Jacobs) and UBF (210-hp Jacobs); in 1934, the UMF (210-hp Continental) and YMF (225-hp Jacobs); and in 1935, the CPF (250-hp Wright) and YPF (225-hp Jacobs).

An explanation is necessary for an understanding of the Waco designation pattern. In the case of the UPF-7, the U stands for the 220-hp Continental engine, the P stands for the Waco wing that was used, the F indicates the model with twin open cockpits and seating for three, and the 7 means it is the

seventh in the series of this basic type. After 1930, the third letter designations indicating year of introduction and style were as follows: F, 1930 with seating for three in two open cockpits; G, 1930 single-seat; C, 1931 standard cabin model until 1935 when it became the custom model (20 mph faster); M, 1931 mail plane version; A, 1932 single open cockpit with side-by-side seats; D, 1934 military export open or closed tandem cockpits; C-2, 1935 Standard model; S, 1935 Standard cabin model with four seats; F, 1939 cabin model with five seats; and N, 1939 tricycle version of the C.

The first letter engine designations are as follows: A, 330-hp Jacobs; B, 165-hp Wright; C, 250-hp Wright; D, 285-hp Wright; F, 350-hp Wright; H, 300-hp Lycoming; I, 125-hp Kinner; J, 365-hp Wright; K, 100-hp Kinner; M, 125-hp Menasco; O, 210-hp Kinner; P, 170-hp Jacobs; Q, 165-hp Continental; R, 110–125-hp Warner Scarab; S, 420-450-hp Pratt & Whitney Wasp Junior; U, 220-hp Continental; V, 240-hp Continental; W, 450-hp Wright; Y, 225-hp Jacobs; and Z, 285-hp Jacobs.

Waco construction generally consisted of a wooden wing structure with metal leading edge covered in fabric and a steel-tube fuselage also covered with fabric.

WACO CABIN BIPLANES
1935–45

STANDARD DATA: (E) Seats 4. Gross wt. 4,200. Empty wt. 2,563. Fuel capacity 125. Engine 300-hp Jacobs radial. **PERFORMANCE:** Top mph 185. Cruise mph 177. Initial climb rate 1,170. Range 600. Ceiling 18,000.
STANDARD DATA: (S series) Seats 5. Gross wt. 3,250. Empty wt. 1,945. Fuel capacity 70. Engine 225-hp Jacobs. **PERFORMANCE:** Top mph 144. Cruise mph 135. Initial climb rate 750. Ceiling 12,500.

The heart of the Waco cabin biplane family is the C series. It was first introduced in 1935 and remained in production until 1939. The first models received the designation of PDC and employed a Jacobs radial rated at 170 hp. The subsequent model that was produced in the greatest numbers during 1931 was the QDC, which was powered by a 165-hp Continental. Other engines used were the 165-hp Wright, 210-hp Kinner, and 210-hp Continental. The design of the C series continued unchanged until 1935 when its constant-cord wing design was swapped for an elliptical design. After that, the various models were powered by the 320-hp Wright Whirlwind and the 330-hp and 285-hp Jacobs.

The N series appeared in 1937 and was essentially the same as the C series with the exception of tricycle landing gear. The F series was intended to replace the C series by virtue of its design refinements. The most noticeable of these changes was the elimination of the slanting wing struts and the use of wires instead. The S series was put into production in 1935 when the C series changed to the elliptical wing design. The S series was initiated to take the place of the old C series and retained the use of a constant-chord wing structure.

WREN 460
1963–75

STANDARD DATA: Seats 4. Gross wt. 2,800. Empty wt. 1,690. Fuel capacity 65. Engine 230-hp Continental. **PERFORMANCE:** Top mph 160. Cruise mph 151. Stall mph 31. Initial climb rate 1,080. Range 1,150. Ceiling 19,200. Takeoff run 270. Landing roll 250.

Until the first part of 1972, the Wren Aircraft Corp. in Fort Worth, Texas, manufactured a STOL light aircraft using a new Cessna 182 airframe. With a design developed by James Robertson, the Wren 460 uses four Wren devices to provide the 182 with slow-flight and STOL capability. The four devices are (1) full-span double-slotted flaps to increase lift coefficient, (2) an increased wing section nose radius to postpone wing stall to 20 degrees angle of attack, (3) two small horizontal control surfaces—known as the Robertson ultralow-speed nose control system—mounted on both sides of the cowling immediately behind the propeller to use the propeller slipstream in slow flight pitch control, and (4) five feathering drag plates—known as "Wren's teeth"—added to each upper wing surface to overcome adverse aileron yaw and decrease lift and increase drag on the low wing during a turn.

An optional Hartzell/Wren Beta reversible-pitch propeller gives the 460 the ability to clear a 500-foot obstacle yet still come to a full stop in 1,000 feet. The added lift devices permit amazing slow-flight capability. In fact, the Wren is more maneuverable at slow speeds than at faster cruising speeds. With 20 degrees of flaps and an airspeed of 70 mph, the engine is at 21 percent power, thus allowing an endurance of over 15 hours.

ZLIN Z 526 L
1966–77

STANDARD DATA: (526 L) Seats 2. Gross wt. 2,150. Empty wt. 1,521. Fuel capacity 24. Engine 200-hp Lycoming. **PERFORMANCE:** Top mph 158. Cruise mph 140. Stall mph 56. Initial climb rate 1,378. Range 310. Ceiling 22,300. Takeoff distance (50') 1,050. Landing distance (50') 1,345.

The Zlin's impressive record in aerobatic competition includes awards for first place in the World Aerobatic Championships of 1960, '62, '64, and '68, plus the Lockheed Trophy in Britain in 1957, '58, '61, '63, '64, and '65. Production of the Czechoslovakian training and aerobatic planes started in 1947 and includes the 726, 126, 226, 326 and 526. The Z 526 L is for all practical purposes a development of the Zlin Z 526 F Trener, the major difference between them being the 526 L's use of a 200-hp Lycoming in place of the usual 180-hp Avia M 137 engine. Both aircraft were designed to perform duties as ab initio or advanced trainers, aerobatic trainers, competition planes, and glider towplanes. The pilot and passenger are seated in tandem fashion under a continuous sliding canopy. The main landing gear retract backward into the wings, and the tires protrude slightly to reduce damage in the event of a wheels-up landing.

Section 2

Multiengine aircraft

As aircraft design evolved, the search for more power and greater performance led to multiengine airframe formats. Rapidly progressing aircraft technology walked hand-in-hand with lightweight engine technology making possible aircraft that were increasingly fast and more powerful. The technological frontier was new ways to utilize the airplane, which could be used for carrying people and for hauling cargo great distances. Then the goal became more people, more cargo, and greater distances. And of course the airplane could be used as an instrument of war and carry large quantities of bombs to faraway lands. In many designer's minds, multiple engines were the answer to safety concerns, their reasoning being that if one engine quit there would be another or more to keep the aircraft airborne. This was a good selling point in theory but, as it proved in most cases, results were more along the line of an extended glide to a safer emergency landing site.

Multiengine safety has remained a major focal point for manufacturers worldwide, and the theory has been proven. The multiengine aircraft has become the international workhorse and have proven its worth above and beyond what was once envisioned. In the pages before you, we illustrate the multiengine aircraft and their specific roles that have made their existence a worthy addition to the development of international aviation.

AERO COMMANDER
L 3805
1948

STANDARD DATA: Seats 6–7. Gross wt. 4,600. Empty wt. 2,800. Fuel capacity 100. Engines two 190-hp Lycomings. **PERFORMANCE:** Top mph 181. Cruise mph 165. Stall mph 57. Initial climb rate 1,450. Ceiling 24,400. Range 850. Takeoff run 780. Landing roll 849.

The Aero Design and Engineering Corp., the predecessor of the Aero Commander Company, was formed in 1944, and its president was Theodore (Ted) R. Smith, more recently of Aerostar fame. The company's first production model was the Aero Commander 3805, which first flew on April 23, 1948. In all, three prototypes of the six-seat light transport were built. The cabin accommodated six persons seated in side-by-side pairs with the full-width rear seat possibly being used for a seventh person. The wings were of all-metal construction with built-up spars and hydraulic flaps. The fuselage was also of all-metal construction. This first of a highly successful family of high-wing twins could cruise at 165 mph at 75 percent power at sea level. Its service ceiling was 24,400 feet, and its single-engine ceiling was 8,700 feet. Subsequently, the L 3805 underwent considerable design changes before going into production as the Aero Commander 520.

AERO COMMANDER
520
1951–54

STANDARD DATA: Seats 6–7. Gross wt. 5,400. Empty wt. 3,800. Fuel capacity 150. Engines two 260-hp Lycomings. **PERFORMANCE:** Top mph 211. Cruise mph 196. Stall mph 57. Initial climb rate 1,800. Ceiling 24,400. Range 850. Takeoff distance (50') 950.

By 1951, Ted Smith was general manager of the Aero Commander company and the Model 520 had entered into production. Its twin 260-hp Lycomings turning Hartzell two-blade props enabled the Commander to cruise at 196 mph at 10,000 feet and 60 percent power. Like its predecessor, it

seated six to seven people, but the rear seat was optional. The landing gear was a retractable tricycle type, and fuel was carried in baglike wing cells. The company adopted a policy of assigning numbers to their aircraft that corresponded to the total horsepower of the model, and in 1952, the first Model 520 was delivered. By the time production subsided in 1954 and the Model 560 came into being, approximately 150 examples of the 520 were built.

AERO COMMANDER
560
1954–65

STANDARD DATA: Seats 5–7. Gross wt. 7,000. Empty wt. 4,690. Fuel capacity 223. Engines two 350-hp Lycomings. **PERFORMANCE:** Top mph 288. Cruise mph 230. Stall mph 73. Initial climb rate 1,587. Range 1,705. Ceiling 21,900. Takeoff distance (50') 1,350. Landing distance (50') 1,375.
STANDARD DATA: Seats 5–7. Gross wt. 6,500. Empty wt. 4,300. Fuel capacity 223. Engines two 295-hp Lycomings. **PERFORMANCE:** Top mph 222. Cruise mph 210. Initial climb rate 1,450. Stall mph 66. Ceiling 22,500. Range 1,625. Takeoff distance (50') 1,452. Landing distance (50') 1,625.

The Aero Commander 560 had a production run of 11 years, starting in 1954. It replaced the Model 520 in the Aero Commander line. For the first three years, it used the 44½-foot wing, but, in 1957, acquired the 49½-foot wing now common to all the light Commander twins. The 560 featured a new tail unit with swept surfaces, more power, a greater all-up weight, and higher performance. Engine power was rated at 270 hp in 1954, increased to 295 hp in 1956, and boosted again in 1961 to 350 hp. It was the highest performance twin ever made in this Commander class. Top speed reached 248 mph, which is over 30 mph more than the Shrike Commander. Standard seating provided for five persons with optional seating for seven. Later, the 560F was available in an eight-seat high-density arrangement. The standard fuel tanks had a capacity of 223 gallons, but optional long-range tanks with a capacity of 285 gallons could be installed.

AERO COMMANDER
680/"COURSER"
1955–69

STANDARD DATA: Seats 5–11. Gross wt. 8,500. Empty wt. 5,600. Fuel capacity 223. Engines two 380-hp Lycomings. **PERFORMANCE:** Top mph 265. Cruise mph 240. Stall mph 82. Initial climb rate 1,285. Range 1,495. Ceiling 28,500. Takeoff distance (50') 1,560. Landing distance (50') 1,450.
STANDARD DATA: Seats 5–11. Gross wt. 7,000. Empty wt. 4,330. Fuel capacity 233. Engines two 340-hp Lycomings.

PERFORMANCE: Top mph 260. Cruise mph 230. Stall mph 71. Initial climb rate 1,600. Ceiling 24,200. Range 1,480. Takeoff distance (50') 1,575. Landing distance (50') 1,630.

The Aero Commander 680 and Grand Commander are two of the larger versions of the basic Aero Commander design that appeared in profusion during the nearly two decades of type production. These particular models are king-sized with greater gross weight and more seating capacity. There is also a pressurized version. The basic characteristics, allowing for differences due to larger dimensions, are essentially similar to the more familiar, but smaller, Commander twins. Ease of handling in the air, exceptional short-field ability for the bulk and performance, and good economy at fast cruising speeds are notable, plus even greater pilot and passenger comfort. All Commander twins came off the same production line in Oklahoma.

The engines on the Commander 680 have always been supercharged, and the very earliest versions have some reputation for engine malfunctions if not operated with care. From 1955 to 1960, the Super and 680E were powered by 340-hp Lycomings. The 380-hp engines were first used in 1960, and the designation was changed to 680F or 680FL Grand Commander. In 1962, pressurization became available as an option. Another major option became available in 1967, a choice of turboprop power in place of the conventional reciprocating engines. Finally, in 1968, the 680 designation was dropped and the name changed to Courser for the last two years of production, 1968–69.

AEROSPACE LINES "GUPPY" 1962–75

STANDARD DATA: (201) Gross wt. 170,000. Empty wt. 100,000. Fuel capacity 7,582. Engines four 4,912-eshp Allison turboprops. **PERFORMANCE:** Top mph 288. Cruise mph 253. Stall mph 117. Initial climb rate 1,500. Range 505. Ceiling 25,000. Takeoff distance (50') 8,500. Landing distance (50') 6,750.

Aerospace Lines of Santa Barbara, California, builds some funky-looking airplanes for very special purposes. Originally designed to carry large booster stages or other partially assembled rockets for United States space programs, the Guppy is now used to haul portions of wide-bodied jets in production. The Guppy is unique in design, looking like it could hardly even lift off the ground much less reach a cruising speed of 280 mph. But the shape of the huge fuselage itself acts as a lifting device, thus overcoming the great structural drag. The Guppy-101 model splits in the center (swing-nose) to allow loading of its valuable cargo. Other Guppy models, including the Pregnant Guppy and Mini Guppy, have a removable tail section to allow straight-in loading. All Guppy models use the Boeing 377 Stratocruiser fuselage.

AMERICAN JET INDUSTRIES "HUSTLER" 400/500 1978–81

STANDARD DATA: (500) Seats 7–9. Gross wt. 9,500. Empty wt. 4,681. Fuel capacity 500. Engines one 850-shp Pratt & Whitney Aircraft of Canada turboprop and one 2,200-lb s.t. Pratt & Whitney Aircraft of Canada turbofan. **PERFORMANCE:** Maximum cruise mph 460. Economy cruise mph 403. Stall mph 88. Initial climb rate 4,950. Ceiling (forward engine only) 25,000. Ceiling (both engines) 40,000. Range (both engines) 1,290. Range (forward engine only after reaching cruising altitude) 2,875. Takeoff distance (50') 1,500. Landing distance (50') 1,500.
STANDARD DATA: (400) Seats 7. Gross wt. 6,000. Empty wt. 3,500. Fuel capacity 290. Engines one 850-shp Pratt & Whitney Aircraft of Canada turboprop and one 640-lb s.t. Teledyne turbojet. **PERFORMANCE:** Maximum cruise mph 400. Economy cruise mph 292. Stall mph 68. Initial climb rate 3,500. Ceiling (forward engine only) 35,000. Range 2,400. Takeoff distance (50') 900. Landing distance (50') 1,000.

The prototype of the Hustler 400 first flew in 1978. Its unique powerplant setup allows the cruising economy of a single-engine turboprop with the safety of a twin and the landing/takeoff performance of a STOL airplane. Up front is a turboprop rated at 850-shp turning a four-blade constant-speed reversible prop. Aft is a standby power source in the form of a 640-pound s.t. turbojet intended to enhance safety by enabling the Hustler to maintain 170 mph at an altitude of 15,000 feet with the nose propeller feathered. Also, on takeoff, the aft jet is activated automatically by a torque-sensing device on the turboprop. In situations where a short-field forewarns of the need for extra boost, the aft jet can be left at idle.

The cabin is pressurized to permit operation at altitudes up to 35,000 feet. STOL operation is made possible by a supercritical wing with full-span Fowler trailing edge flaps and spoilers in place of ailerons for lateral control. For the Model 500, the fuselage was extended to make room for a larger, 2,200-pound s.t. turbofan engine, and wingtip tanks were added to augment the standard fuel supply. Also, ailerons were added, thereby requiring that the full-span flaps be trimmed. The larger aft turbofan makes it possible for the Model 500 to be certified as a twin-engine airplane.

ANTONOV AN-22 "ANTHEUS"
1967–81

STANDARD DATA: Seats 29. Gross wt. 551,160. Empty wt. 251,325. Fuel capacity 14,500. Engines four 15,000-shp Kuznetzov turboprops. **PERFORMANCE:** Top mph 460. Range 6,800. Takeoff run 4,260. Landing roll 2,620.

Designed by Oleg Antonov, the AN-22 was first introduced to the western world at the Paris Salon Air Show in June 1965. The long-range passenger/cargo transport went into production in 1967, and Soviet plans were to sell the huge airplane to other countries. Such was not to be the case, or else no other countries were interested in the twin-tailed airliner. Aeroflot, Russia's state airline, remains the only airline using the Antheus. The AN-22 is powered by four 15,000-shaft-horsepower engines, each driving a pair of four-blade contrarotating propellers. A cabin for 28 or 29 passengers is located aft of the flight deck and separated from the main cargo cabin by a bulkhead. A 727-passenger two-deck version of the Antheus was studied in 1966, but no further development occurred. The Soviet Air Force is using most of the AN-22s produced mainly as cargo or missile carriers. Aeroflot uses the large transport in underdeveloped areas of Siberia.

BAUMANN "BRIGADIER"
1947

STANDARD DATA: Seats 5. Gross wt. 3,500. Empty wt. 2,200. Fuel capacity 76. Engines two 145-hp Continentals. **PERFORMANCE:** Top mph 175. Cruise mph 155. Stall mph 55. Initial climb rate 1,250. Ceiling 18,000. Range 750.

From outside appearances, the Brigadier looks like an early Aero Commander with pusher engines. Baumann Aircraft Company was formed by J.B. Baumann in 1945, and its first product was the 250. This soon evolved into the B-290. Like the Aero Commander Company, the Baumann Company derived its numerical designations from the total horsepower of the aircraft; thus, the B-250 was powered by twin 125-hp Continentals and the B-290 was propelled by twin 145-hp Continentals. In both cases, the engines were installed in a pusher configuration. Construction was all-metal, and the landing gear were retractable tricycle type. The prototype of the five-seat B-250 was ultimately sold to Piper Aircraft for use as a test vehicle.

BEAGLE B.206 "BASSET"
1964–70

STANDARD DATA: Seats 5–8. Gross wt. 7,125. Empty wt. 4,380. Fuel capacity 234. Engines two 340-hp Rolls-Royce/Continentals. **PERFORMANCE:** Top mph 258. Cruise mph 220. Stall mph 80. Initial climb rate 1,590. Range 1,600. Ceiling 27,100. Takeoff distance (50') 2,390. Landing distance (50') 2,485.

The Beagle B.206 was built in several versions, of which the most prominent are the Series I, Series II, and Basset C.C.1, the latter being the military version. The Series II differs from the Series I in that it is powered by twin 340-hp engines instead of the smaller 310-hp engines used in Series I. This Beagle is basically a light twin-engine transport with accommodations for five to eight persons. The first prototype flew in 1961. The first flight of the Series II was in June 1965. The most current version of the Series II has an extended cabin with an additional rear window and a large passenger or cargo door on the port side. The Beagle B.218 closely resembles the B.206 but is considerably smaller in overall size. Accommodations provide for four (seated in pairs), and power is supplied by two 145-hp Rolls Royce/Continentals. Plastics are used extensively in the airframe where stress is not a problem.

BEECH "BARON"
1961–95

STANDARD DATA: (B55) Seats 6. Gross wt. 5,100. Empty wt. 3,256. Fuel capacity 100–136. Engines two 260-hp Continentals. **PERFORMANCE:** Top mph 231. Cruise mph 216. Stall mph 84. Initial climb rate 1,693. Ceiling 19,300. Range 918. Takeoff distance (50') 2,154. Landing distance (50') 2,148.

STANDARD DATA: (E55) Seats 4–6. Gross wt. 5,300. Empty wt. 3,236. Fuel capacity 100–136. Engines two 260-hp Continentals. **PERFORMANCE:** Top mph 239. Cruise mph 230. Stall mph 84. Initial climb rate 1,682. Ceiling 19,100. Range 1,074. Takeoff distance (50') 2,050. Landing distance (50') 2,202.

STANDARD DATA: (56TC) Seats 4–6. Gross wt. 5,990. Empty wt. 3,700. Fuel capacity 142–204. Engines two 380-hp turbocharged Lycomings. **PERFORMANCE:** Top mph 290. Cruise mph 284. Stall mph 84. Initial climb rate 2,020. Ceiling 32,200. Range 1,070. Takeoff distance (50') 1,420. Landing distance (50') 2,080.

STANDARD DATA: (58) Seats 4–6. Gross wt. 5,400. Empty wt. 3,361. Fuel capacity 136–194. Engines two 285-hp Continentals. **PERFORMANCE:** Top mph 239. Cruise mph 230. Stall mph 85. Initial climb rate 1,660. Ceiling 18,600. Range 1,275. Takeoff distance (50') 2,101. Landing distance (50') 2,498.

STANDARD DATA: (58P) Seats 4–6. Gross wt. 6,100. Empty wt. 4,018. Fuel capacity 160–190. Engines two 325-hp turbocharged Continentals. **PERFORMANCE:** Top mph 300. Cruise mph 277. Stall mph 90. Initial climb rate 1,475. Ceiling 25,000+. Range 1,160. Takeoff distance (50') 2,643. Landing distance (50') 2,427.

STANDARD DATA: (58TC) Seats 4–6. Gross wt. 6,200. Empty wt. 3,793. Fuel capacity 160–190. Engines two 325-hp turbocharged Continentals. **PERFORMANCE:** Top mph 300. Cruise mph 277. Stall mph 90. Initial climb rate 1,475. Ceiling 25,000+. Range 1,160. Takeoff distance (50') 2,643. Landing distance (50') 2,427.

BEECH "BARON" B55

BEECH "BARON" 58

The Beech Baron is a beautiful-to-fly airplane, outstanding even among other "royalty" in the Beechcraft line. The first Barons appeared in 1961 with 260-hp Continentals and a list price of only $58,000. The original 55 Baron became the A55 model and is still in production with the same engines as the B55. In 1966, the C55 was introduced with the 285-hp power-plants,

and in the following year, the turbocharged 56TC entered production with its formidable 380-hp Lycomings. The C55 became the D55 and finally the E55, Beechcraft's high-performance, high-payload Baron. The Baron 58 became a part of the lineup in 1970, replacing the 56TC, and used the 285-hp Continental engine. In addition to these popular twins, Beechcraft has added two new versions, the 58P for over-the-weather pressurized comfort and the Baron 58TC for high-altitude performance. Both these additions use the same 310-hp turbocharged Continental engines, enabling them to have a service ceiling of 25,000 feet and above. All Baron 58s have accommodations for four to six passengers with optional club seating where the rear two pairs face other. An increase in structural capacity allows the 58TC to carry 350 pounds more than the Baron 58.

In 1977, a new three-blade propeller was standard on the 58P. Two inches shorter, it improved maximum speed and increased the climb rate by more than 100 fpm. That year, club seating in all models, simplified fuel management, and increased optional fuel capacities were added. More than 4,700 Barons have been delivered. Optional equipment on the 58E55 and B55 are heavy-duty brakes that offer up to 50 percent greater stopping power.

In 1979, the pressurized Baron's performance was enhanced by an increase in horsepower from 310 to 325 with the Continental TSIO-520WB six-cylinder engines. Providing a higher degree of performance, the turbocharged, fuel-injected engine is exclusively a Beech powerplant shared only by the 58TC. With the additional horsepower, the Baron 58P has a top speed approaching 300 mph. Maximum cruise speed for the 58TC was increased to 277 mph. Pressurization differential in the 58P was increased from 3.7 psi to 3.9 psi, providing a sea-level cabin up to 8,350 feet. At 25,000 feet, the Baron's service ceiling, the cabin is a comfortable 11,900 feet. The latest improvements to the Baron line include 50-amp alternators as standard equipment, with 60-amp and 100-amp alternators for those aircraft fitted with abundant options. Redesigned sidewall panels and a one-piece headliner provide more headroom and elbowroom while reducing cabin noise levels.

BEECH 76 "DUCHESS" 1978–82

STANDARD DATA: Seats 4. Gross wt. 3,900. Empty wt. 2,460. Fuel capacity 100. Engine two 180-hp Lycomings. **PERFORMANCE:** Top mph 197. Cruise mph 191. Stall mph 69. Initial climb rate 1,248. Ceiling 19,650. Range 717. Takeoff distance (50') 2,119. Landing distance (50') 1,881.

This low-priced twin is fitted with two 180-hp Lycoming engines and is designed to carry four people with 180 pounds of luggage and optional equipment at 185 mph for more than 800 miles. The twin includes doors on both sides of the cabin. Optional avionics are similar to those on the Beechcraft Sierra. The Model 76 makes use of honeycomb-bonded wings for a smoother airfoil design with less drag and a lower manufacturing cost. Unlike other Beech twins, it was marketed through the Aero Centers because its economical and easy-to fly operation made it ideal for multiengine training, charter, and personal transportation.

Outstanding design characteristics of the Duchess include an aerodynamically advantageous T-tail, which places the horizontal surfaces above the propeller slipstream for better stability and handling, and opposite-rotating propellers to eliminate the "critical engine" aspect of multiengine flying. In 1980, a 28-volt electrical system was added to provide increased cranking power in cold weather, more power for avionics, and improved parts commonality with other Beech products. The most recent improvements to the Duchess included a "Throttle Q Switch" that prevents the landing-gear warning horn from sounding when the throttle is retarded if the airspeed is kept above 99 knots; this allowed the pilot to reduce power during descent without having to listen to the gear horn. Also, RCA Weather Scout II radar was available as an option.

BEECH "TRAVEL AIR"
1958–68

STANDARD DATA: (E95) Seats 4–5. Gross wt. 4,200. Empty wt. 2,650. Fuel capacity 112. Engines two 160-hp Lycomings. **PERFORMANCE:** Top mph 240. Cruise mph 200. Stall mph 75. Initial climb rate 1,250. Range 1,035. Ceiling 18,100. Take-off distance (50') 1,280. Landing distance (50') 1,590.

The Beechcraft Travel Air was the lowest priced light twin in the post-World War II lineup from the Wichita airframe maker. When the Model 95 Travel Air was in its prototype stage in 1956, it was known as the Badger. It entered production in 1958 with a factory list price of $49,500. In the 10 following years, the Travel Air was subject to a few major changes. Engine power output remained at 180 hp on all models, with carburetors being replaced by fuel injectors in 1964. In that same year, the cabin was stretched an additional 20 inches. The factory list price rose in 1968 to $153,500 including avionics. For this kind of money, the Travel Air, on a competitive basis, was an excellent value. In all these years and changes, the basic performance figures of the Travel Air differed only slightly. Top speed varied only by a mile per hour

or so, cruise rose from 195 to 200, and range and altitude held constant. A limitation of the Travel Air to some pilots was the low single-engine ceiling of 4,400 feet. Obviously in some sections of the United States, mostly in the West, this would be inadequate for terrain clearance.

BEECH "TWIN BONANZA"
1950–63

STANDARD DATA: (150) Seats 6–7. Gross wt. 7,300. Empty wt. 4,460. Fuel capacity 230. Engines two 340-hp Lycomings. **PERFORMANCE:** Top mph 235. Cruise mph 223. Stall mph 82. Initial climb rate 1,270. Range 1,650. Ceiling 29,150. Take-off distance (50') 1,450. Landing distance (50') 1,840.
STANDARD DATA: (D50A–E) Seats 6. Gross wt. 6,300. Empty wt. 3,981. Fuel capacity 180. Engines two 295-hp Lycomings. **PERFORMANCE:** Top mph 214. Cruise mph 203. Stall mph 71. Initial climb rate 1,450. Ceiling 20,000. Range 1,650. Takeoff distance (50') 1,260. Landing distance (50') 1,452.
STANDARD DATA: (C50) Seats 4–6. Gross wt. 5,500. Empty wt. 3,800. Fuel capacity 33. Engines two 275-hp Lycomings. **PERFORMANCE:** Top mph 205. Cruise mph 182. Stall mph 64. Initial climb rate 1,450. Ceiling 20,000. Range 920. Takeoff distance (50') 1,350. Landing distance (50') 1,210.

Not until late 1958 when the Queen Air flew did Beech introduce an airplane heavier than the Twin Bonanza, which began its life in 1949. It was the first postwar light twin to reach quantity production in the United States, and late models grossed 7,300 pounds. Built with 260-, 275-, 295-, and 340-hp Lycoming engines, the Twin Bonanza design has proved highly versatile. Beech produced the military U8 Seminole, the civil Queen Air and early King Airs from the Twin Bonanza wing. Swearingen marketed a conversion of the basic Twin Bonanza as the Caliber. The design started life as a six-seater, and a seventh seat was added on the model in 1960. There is so much room inside that numerous luxury executive interiors have been custom-installed. The aircraft has also been successful as an ambulance plane with room for a stretcher and medical attendants, in addition to the crew.

The weight it can haul seems limited only by power and federal regulation; the 65-90 King Air, with the same basic wings, grosses more than a ton heavier than the Twin Bonanza. The airplane did not have particularly sparkling climb performance on the smaller engines, and single-engine ceiling also was poor, but more power cures these faults and makes a used Twin Bonanza highly competitive in performance against later, smaller, and more expensive twins. With a useful load of up to

1,840 pounds and two separate baggage compartments, there's plenty of room for your personal gear.

BEECH "DUKE"
1968–82

STANDARD DATA: (B60) Seats 4–6. Gross wt. 6,775. Empty wt. 4,423. Fuel capacity 142–232. Engines two 300-hp turbocharged Lycomings. **PERFORMANCE:** Top mph 283. Cruise mph 275. Stall mph 84. Initial climb rate 1,601. Ceiling 30,000. Range 1,203. Takeoff distance (50') 2,626. Landing distance (50') 3,065.

If you need to operate at altitudes above 31,000 feet or travel 286 mph at 23,000 feet, the fully pressurized Beech Duke will meet your needs. You can have seating for four to six, and on some versions the center row of seats faces aft. Custom interiors might include a toilet, refreshment bar, and writing desk. Powered by turbocharged 300-hp Lycomings, the Duke uses turbo bleed air to obtain 4.6 psi cabin pressure, which will maintain a 10,000-foot cabin altitude all the way to 24,800 feet. Either engine can do the job alone if needed. Two separate baggage compartments in the nose and aft fuselage handle 500 and 315 pounds of luggage, respectively. The spacious Duke cabin provides a center aisle separating the seats, and dividers are between the flight deck and passenger cabin.

Pilots will like the Duke's single-engine ceiling of 15,700 feet at gross. This airplane has so much power (the loading is only 8.5 pounds/hp) that it can cruise for 1,021 miles at 210 mph on a mere 45 percent of its rated output. Improvements in 1976 were a 20-percent increase in range and new landing lights on the retractable gear. As an option, the pressurized twin can hold up to 232 gallons of usable fuel by adding wet wingtips; this boosts the fuel load by 90 gallons over the 142-gallon standard fuel load. The previous option allowed a maximum of 202. In 1977, the Duke advertised a higher cruise speed, improved exterior lighting, and a standard Collins avionics package. In 1980, a Hoskins fuel-flow system indicated flow in gallons and pounds per hour, plus fuel remaining. Timing modes calculated flying time remaining and elapsed time since engine start. In 1981, the air-conditioning system was refined to provide for greater cooling capacity.

BEECH "QUEEN AIR"
1960–81

STANDARD DATA: (B80) Seats 6–11. Gross wt. 8,800. Empty wt. 5,312. Fuel capacity 214–264. Engines two 380-hp supercharged Lycomings. **PERFORMANCE:** Top mph 247. Cruise mph 225. Stall mph 81. Initial climb rate 1,275. Ceiling 26,800. Range 1,102. Takeoff distance (50') 2,556. Landing distance (50') 2,572.

STANDARD DATA: (70) Seats 7–11. Gross wt. 8,200. Empty wt. 4,995. Fuel capacity 214. Engines two 340-hp Lycomings. **PERFORMANCE:** Top mph 240. Cruise mph 209. Stall mph 79. Initial climb rate 1,375. Ceiling 26,800. Range 1,295. Takeoff distance (50') 1,675. Landing distance (50') 2,017.

STANDARD DATA: (65) Seats 6–7. Gross wt. 7,700. Empty wt. 4,640. Fuel capacity 230. Engines two 340-hp Lycomings. **PERFORMANCE:** Top mph 240. Cruise mph 209. Stall mph 80. Initial climb rate 1,300. Ceiling 27,000. Range 1,205. Takeoff distance (50') 1,700. Landing distance (50') 1,980.

The Beech Queen Airs come in a dizzying variety of models: 65, 80, and 88. The Model 65 is the original and least expensive version. It dates from 1960 when it emerged as a six- to nine-place light twin powered by 340 hp and offering good comfort and performance. Two years later, a 380-hp option was available and designated as the Model 80. The Model 88 is a pressurized version of the Model 80. The single-engine service ceiling of the Queen Air 65 is a truly remarkable 15,500 feet. Also notable are the relatively short takeoff and landing distances over 50-foot obstacles. Air-conditioning is optional equipment.

At only 45 percent power, a Model 65 will cruise at 171 for 1,660 miles at 10,000 feet using only 23 gph of fuel. This includes warmup, taxi, takeoff and climb, plus a reserve of 45 minutes. In 1971, the Excalibur Aviation Company and Swearingen Aircraft acquired the rights to build and market a modified version of the Queen Air. Called the Queenair 800, it employs two 400-hp Lycoming eight-cylinder engines with modified low-drag engine nacelles and three-blade Hartzell propellers. Deliveries of Queen Airs became limited to overseas markets, and sales in the United States were essentially discontinued.

BEECH MODEL 18
1937–69

STANDARD DATA: (D18S) Seats 5–7. Gross wt. 8,750. Empty wt. 5,770. Fuel capacity 206–286. Engines two 450-hp Pratt & Whitney Wasp Juniors. **PERFORMANCE:** Top mph 230. Cruise mph 211. Stall mph 77. Initial climb rate 1,190. Range 985. Ceiling 20,500. Takeoff distance (50') 1,760. Landing distance (50') 1,460.

The Model 18 was introduced before World War II and was subject to so many modifications, both civilian and military, that its variety is almost infinite. Some later Model 18s were optionally equipped with tricycle gear, turbines, new nose sections, and the like to such a degree that they are identified under other names. Few aircraft, however, can boast of such dependability and comfort. Some pilots find the tailwheel version tricky, but there are still executives of major companies who have a choice of more modern aircraft and still prefer the Model 18. Beech thought several times it could quietly discontinue the Model 18, but demand warranted keeping it available. Finally, in 1969, the last 10 planes were sold to the Japanese, ending a 32-year production cycle. Military versions of the Model 18 were designated C-45 and were primarily used as utility transports.

BEECH H18 "SUPER-LINER" 1964–69

STANDARD DATA: Seats 9–10. Gross wt. 9,900. Empty wt. 5,845. Fuel capacity 198–318. Engines two 450-hp Pratt & Whitneys. **PERFORMANCE:** Top mph 256. Cruise mph 220. Stall mph 87. Initial climb rate 1,400. Range 1,530. Ceiling 21,400. Takeoff distance (50') 2,072. Landing distance (50') 1,850.

The H18 Super-Liner is an advanced version of the Beechcraft Model 18 series. It has more engineering improvements than any previous model, including electric cowl flaps, a redesigned exhaust system, lightweight props, and automatic oil coolers. In 1963, factory-installed tricycle landing gear became optional equipment. Both the tricycle gear and the pointed nose are borrowed from the Volpar-modified version of the Beech 18. Other options included fuel injection, air-conditioning, an autopilot, and weather radar. Several companies produced variations of the Model 18. Pacific Airmotive Corp. built the Tradewind, a remanufactured D-18 offering tricycle gear, new windscreen, increased fuel capacity, and other updated equipment. Volpar Inc. originally marketed tricycle landing gear kits and later introduced kits for installing 705-eshp AiResearch turbine engines. Volpar also produced a stretched version called the Turboliner with accommodations for 15 passengers. The Dumod Corp. also built a 15-seat version with

larger windows and glass-fiber control surfaces. Another reengined Model 18 is the Hamilton Westwind III powered by 579-shp United Aircraft of Canada turboprops.

BEECH 99 "AIRLINER" 1968–95

STANDARD DATA: (B99) Seats 15–17. Gross wt. 10,955. Empty wt. 5,777. Fuel capacity 368. Engines two 688-shp Pratt & Whitney reverse-flow free-spool turbines. **PERFORMANCE:** Cruise mph 285. Stall mph 87. Initial climb rate 2,090. Ceiling 26,313. Range 1,035. Takeoff distance (50') 2,480. Landing distance (50') 1,810.
STANDARD DATA: (99) Seats 15–17. Gross wt. 10,400. Empty wt 5,675. Fuel capacity 374. Engines two 550-shp Pratt & Whitney turboprops. **PERFORMANCE:** Cruise mph 250. Stall mph 75. Initial climb rate 1,910. Ceiling 25,000, Range 960. Takeoff distance (50') 3,200. Landing distance (50') 2,470.

The Beechcraft 99 Airliner was the first turbine-powered retractable-landing-gear aircraft to meet FAA approval for commuter air carrier service. First delivered in 1968, the Model 99 was powered by twin 550-shp Pratt & Whitney turboprops driving reversible propellers. The Beechcraft 99 cruises at more than 250 mph and pulls a gross load of 10,200 pounds or more. Introduced in 1969, the 99A Airliner housed 680-shp Pratt & Whitney free-shaft turbines flat rated at 550-shp. Except for the engines, the 99A is identical to the original 99. The 99B, announced in 1972, featured engineering improvements for increased reliability, maintainability, and passenger comfort. The ship has an air-conditioning unit as an option with its high-pressure continuous-flow oxygen system. Also, an optional cargo door and a cargo pod—the pod is installed beneath the fuselage—increase its cargo capability. Seating can be varied to suit specific needs. Production ceased in 1978, but renewed interest in turboprop aircraft and the subsequent rapid growth in the commuter airline field caused Beech to reinstate production of the 99 Airliner.

BEECH "KING AIR" 1965–95

STANDARD DATA: (B90) Seats 6–10. Gross wt. 9,650. Empty wt. 5,685. Fuel capacity 384. Engines two 500-shp Pratt & Whitney turboprops. **PERFORMANCE:** Cruise mph 260. Stall mph 87. Initial climb rate 1,900. Ceiling 27,000. Range 1,480. Takeoff distance (50') 1,420. Landing distance (50') 2,300.
STANDARD DATA: (C90) Seats 6–10. Gross wt. 9,650. Empty wt. 5,765. Fuel capacity 384. Engines two 550-shp

Pratt & Whitney reverse-flow, free turbines. **PERFORMANCE:** Cruise mph 256. Stall mph 87. Initial climb rate 1,955. Ceiling 28,100. Range 1,384. Takeoff distance (50') 2,261. Landing distance (50') 1,672.

STANDARD DATA: (E90) Seats 6–10. Gross wt. 10,100. Empty wt. 6,052. Fuel capacity 474. Engines two 550-shp Pratt & Whitney reverse-flow free turbines. **PERFORMANCE:** Cruise mph 287. Stall mph 89. Initial climb rate 1,870. Ceiling 27,620. Range 1,507. Takeoff distance (50') 2,024. Landing distance (50') 2,110.

STANDARD DATA: (F90) Seats 7–10. Gross wt. 10,950. Empty wt. 6,549. Fuel capacity 470. Engines two 750-shp Pratt & Whitney PT6A-135 jetprops. **PERFORMANCE:** Cruise mph 307. Stall mph 89. Initial climb rate 2,380. Ceiling 29,802. Range 1,657. Takeoff distance (50') 2,856. Landing distance (50') 2,275.

STANDARD DATA: (A100) Seats 8–15. Gross wt. 11,500. Empty wt. 6,797. Fuel capacity 470. Engines two 680-shp Pratt & Whitney reverse-flow free turbines. **PERFORMANCE:** Cruise mph 285. Stall mph 86. Initial climb rate 1,963. Ceiling 24,850. Range 1,481. Takeoff distance (50') 2,681. Landing distance (50') 2,109.

STANDARD DATA: (B100) Seats 8–15. Gross wt. 11,800. Empty wt. 7,088. Fuel capacity 470. Engines two 715-shp AiResearch fixed-shaft turbines. **PERFORMANCE:** Cruise mph 305. Stall mph 96. Initial climb rate 2,139. Ceiling 28,138. Range 1,455. Takeoff distance (50') 2,694. Landing distance (50') 2,679.

STANDARD DATA: (A200) Seats 6–13. Gross wt. 12,500. Empty wt. 7,437. Fuel capacity 544. Engines two 850-shp Pratt & Whitney reverse-flow free turbines. **PERFORMANCE:** Top mph 333. Cruise mph 328. Stall mph 86. Initial climb rate 2,450. Ceiling 33,880+. Range 2,185. Takeoff distance (50') 2,579. Landing distance (50') 2,074.

BEECH "KING AIR" C90

BEECH "KING AIR" E90

BEECH "KING AIR" F90

BEECH "KING AIR" B100

One out of every four turbine-powered aircraft—turboprop and pure jet—in business and executive use in the United States is a King Air. Many are in commercial airline, government, or military use in the United States and internationally. This impressive record is a tribute to the outstanding qualities of the King Air. A full range of optional avionics includes autopilot and complete Category II landing system capability. The 90, A90, and B90 are all powered by 500 shp. In 1970, the B90 was fitted with a 550-shp Pratt & Whitney, which was subsequently used on the C90. The 100 series was introduced in 1969, and the E90 became part of the lineup in 1972. Both employed the same 680-shp Pratt & Whitney turboprops. All have full-feathering reversible propellers. The pressurized three-compartment interior can be maintained at sea-level atmosphere pressure to flight levels as high as 10,500 feet.

The C90 is one of the industry's lowest priced turboprops, and the E90 is virtually a more powerful version of the C90. The higher-capacity versions are the A100 (discontinued) and B100, with the latter being the first King Air to be outfitted with Garrett turboprops. Power-to-weight ratio in the B100 permits essentially instantaneous acceleration from flight idle to full power. The T-tail Super King Air, with its two 850-shp Pratt & Whitney engines, can be operated from smaller airports; taking off and landing over a 50-foot obstacle can be accomplished in 2,579 and 2,845 feet respectively, without prop reversing upon landing.

The King Air F90 is a fuel-efficient version, thanks in part to the Pratt & Whitney engines with improved turbine blades that extract more power from the engine. At 300 mph true air speed, it burns less than 70 gallons per hour. Slower-turning props also reduce interior noise levels. The F90 was the first King Air in the 90 series to make use of the T-tail that has long graced the Super King Air. The dual-wheel gear are fitted with brake deice systems. The pressurization differential of 5.0 pounds/sq. in. provides a sea-level cabin at 11,000 feet. The Super King Air Model 200C has large cargo doors for specialized missions, and the Model 200T was modified for missions such as special maritime patrol, thunderstorm research, photography, and the like. As the world's most popular turboprop, it retains 93.6 percent of its original purchase price after three years of ownership.

BEECHCRAFT "SUPER KING AIR 300/350"

STANDARD DATA: Seats 8–12. Gross wt. 14,100. Empty wt. 8,490. Fuel capacity 539. Engines two 1,050-shp Pratt & Whitney PT6A-60A reverse-flow free turbines. **PERFORMANCE:** Top mph 365. Cruise mph 354. Initial climb rate 2,844. Ceiling 33,000+. Range 2,255. Takeoff distance (50') 1,992. Landing distance (50') 2,907.

BEECH "SUPER KING AIR"

BEECH "SUPER KING AIR 350"

Beechcraft's top-of-the-line answers to the business propjet market are the Super King Air 300 and the Super King Air 350. With executive seating for 8–12 in many specified and custom arrangements, the Super 300/350 can accommodate most business travel applications. Standard Collins avionics packages could be considered on the deluxe side for heavy IFR flight with dual communication and navigation units, autopilot, ADF, DME, all-weather radar, inverters, and transponders. The Super 300's cabin is pressurized at a 6.5 differential, which maintains an 8,500-foot cabin at 30,000 feet.

BEECHCRAFT "STARSHIP" 1989–94

STANDARD DATA: Seats 8–10. Gross wt. 14,610. Empty wt. 10,085. Fuel capacity 534. Engine two 1,200-shp Pratt & Whit-

ney PT6A-67A free turbines. **PERFORMANCE:** Top mph 385. Cruise mph 377. Initial climb rate 2,969. Ceiling 34,800. Range 1,633. Takeoff distance (50') 4,093. Landing distance (50') 2,630.

The Beech Starship is perhaps the most technologically advanced aircraft to ever hit the business aviation scene. Its twin-turbine pusher and canard-wing configuration is a direct development from the innovative efforts of design pioneer Burt Rutan. Rutan is famous for his unconventional proof-of-concept aircraft that have become some of the most popular kitbuilt and plans-built airplanes to grace homebuilt aviation. Starship is built entirely of composites such as carbon-graphite, Kevlar, and E-glass, which make for an exceptionally strong and light aircraft that is not subject to the same inherent long-term weaknesses found in aluminum airframes. The structure will not fatigue, crack, rot, and is impervious to attack by most chemical substances. The composite makeup of the airframe does not transmit noise or vibration from its twin 1,200-shp Pratt & Whitney engines, thus keeping interior cabin sound levels extremely low. Because of its canard configuration, the design is virtually impossible to stall, and the stock aircraft was equipped with an impressive avionics suite. Starship was definitely a ground-breaking step into the future of business-aviation transportation; unfortunately production ceased approximately 10 years after its introduction.

BOEING B-17 "FLYING FORTRESS" 1935–45

STANDARD DATA: Seats 5. Gross wt. 49,650. Empty wt. 30,620. Fuel capacity 1,700. Engines four 1,200-hp Wright Cyclone radials. **PERFORMANCE:** Top mph 323. Cruise mph 250. Climb to 25,000 ft. in 41 min. Range 3,400. Ceiling 37,000.

The tremendously tough B-17 flew the 8th Air Force's first combat mission out of England in August, 1942. The British were skeptical about daylight bombing, but the American strategy was made possible by the ruggedness built into high-flying bombers like the B-17 and by the deadly accuracy of the Norden bombsight. Used as the spearhead of the U.S. Army Air Force's attacks in Europe, the aircraft also saw combat duty in all theaters of war. Three days after Pearl Harbor, the Japanese convoys en route to Luzon in the Philippines were met by Flying Fortresses. Designed by Boeing in 1934, the four-engine bomber made its first flight in July 1935. The first model to see action was the B-17C, powered by Wright Cyclone nine-cylinder radial engines. Several versions of the basic B-17 were produced throughout the war, differing in armament, performance, and gross weight. A total of 12,731 Flying Fortresses were built between 1935 and 1945.

BOEING A-314 "CLIPPER" 1938

STANDARD DATA: Seats 74. Gross wt. 84,000. Empty wt. 48,400. Fuel capacity 5,408. Engines four 1,600-hp Wright Cyclone radials. **PERFORMANCE:** Top mph 210. Cruise mph 188. Range 4,900.

Boeing flying boats, known as "California Clippers," operated over the South Pacific Ocean routes for Pan American Airlines. One such "California Clipper" flew from Los Angeles Harbor to Auckland, New Zealand, an 8,000-mile, 50-hour route with night layovers at Honolulu, Canton Island, and Noumea, New Caledonia. On two decks, an upper or control deck and a passenger deck, there were accommodations for a crew of 11 and 68 passengers or 36 sleeping passengers. The passenger deck was divided into nine sections, including a lounge, six separate passenger compartments, a specially furnished deluxe compartment, a galley, and restrooms. The flying boat was propelled by four 1,600-hp Wright Cyclone twin-row 14-cylinder radial engines turning full-feathering constant-speed airscrews. The fuel tanks were housed in the wings and hydrostabilizers. In 1938, they were the largest airplanes built in the United States. They were tested to a maximum loaded weight of 82,500 pounds, the greatest weight ever carried aloft by any of the world's heavier-than-air craft to that date, with the exception of the German Dornier DO-X and the Russian Maxim-Gorky.

CAMAIR "TWIN NAVION" 1953–61

STANDARD DATA: Seats 4. Gross wt. 4,500. Empty wt. 3,000. Fuel capacity 188–200. Engines two 300-hp fuel-injected Continentals. **PERFORMANCE:** Top mph 215. Cruise mph

200. Stall mph 60. Initial climb rate 2,000. Ceiling 22,000. Range 900. Takeoff run 400. Landing roll 600.

The Camair flew for the first time in 1953 and was designed to meet the requirements of the Cameron Iron Works. The company was so pleased with the results of the prototype (powered by two 225-hp Continentals) that it decided to produce similar conversions of the Navion single-engine airplane on a commercial basis. The designation Camair 480 indicates the combined power of the twin 240-hp Continental powerplants used in the production model. Starting with a North American/Ryan Navion, structural modifications were carried out to allow for the increased horsepower and weight of the two engines, while aerodynamic, comfort, and styling refinements were added. Building of new aircraft has been suspended; however, the Camair Aircraft Corp. continues to supply spare parts to Twin Navion owners. In all, four models were built: the Model A prototype with two 225-hp Continentals, the Model B with twin 240-hp Continentals, the Model C with twin 260-hp Continentals, and the Model D with two 300-hp Continentals.

CASA "COMMUTER"

STANDARD DATA: Seats 26. Gross wt. 16,091. Empty wt. 9,072. Fuel capacity 555. Engines two 908-shp Garrett-AiResearch turboprops. **PERFORMANCE:** Top mph 242. Initial climb rate 1,730. Ceiling 28,000. Range 1,070. Takeoff distance (50') 1,588. Landing distance (50') 1,700.

The CASA Commuter is a product of Construcciones Aeronauticas, S.A. of Spain. It has been in service with several European and African airlines as well as the Spanish Air Force and is used by certain commuter airlines in the United States. The airplane's high-lift wing and 908-shp Garrett-AiResearch TPE331 turboprop engines allow it to operate from unimproved 2,000-foot strips, yet the airplane can carry up to 28 passengers and a crew of two on stage lengths of 320 nm and cruise at 210 knots. Alternatively, the utilitarian CASA 200 may be converted to an all-cargo configuration that provides room for a small car plus other freight. The generous cabin dimensions allow a comfortable seating arrangement for passengers, and its height permits full stand-up headroom. The high wing design provides ample viewing for all 28 passengers. Simplicity is the basic design philosophy of the CASA airframe, with conventional skin-stringer-frame construction. Though such an airframe lacks bonding and special processes, safety and simplicity are still maximized.

CENTURY "JETSTREAM III" 1966–81

STANDARD DATA: (Jetstream) Seats 4–18. Gross wt. 12,500. Empty wt. 8,450. Fuel capacity 456. Engines two 850-eshp Turbomeca Astazou turboprops. PERFORMANCE: Top mph 345. Cruise mph 306. Stall mph 84. Initial climb rate 2,100. Ceiling 30,000. Range 1,900. Takeoff distance (50') 2,490. Landing distance (50') 2,300.

STANDARD DATA: (Jetstream III) Seats 4–18. Gross wt. 12,500. Empty wt. 8,200. Fuel capacity 426. Engines two 902-eshp Garrett AiResearch turboprops. PERFORMANCE: Cruise mph 300+. Range 1,920. Takeoff distance (50') 2,500. Landing distance (50') 1,000.

The Jetstream was originally built by Handley Page in Great Britain. Work began in 1966 and 165 aircraft had been built by 1967. Powered by twin 850-eshp Turbomeca Astazou turboprops in Europe or 895-eshp Garrett AiResearch turboprops in the United States, the Jetstream had accommodations for a crew of two plus flight attendant and 4–18 passengers. With a diameter of 6 feet, a length of 24 feet, and 613 cu. ft. of usable cabin space, the Jetstream has the largest interior in its class. There is stand-up headroom, ample walk-around space, and 14 windows. The most recent version of the Jetstream was marketed by Century Aircraft Corp. of Amarillo, Texas, and was designated the Jetstream III. Powered by Garrett AiResearch turboprop engines delivering 904-eshp each, the Jetstream III is air-conditioned and pressurized at 6.5 psi. The conversion to Garrett engines allows the jet to squeeze 1,920 miles out of a 426-gallon fuel capacity. The engine conversions were performed by Volpar, Inc. in Van Nuys, California.

CESSNA T-50 "BOBCAT" 1939–44

STANDARD DATA: Seats 4–6. Gross wt. 5,700. Empty wt. 4,050. Fuel capacity 120–160. Engines two 245-hp Jacobs radi-

als. PERFORMANCE: Top mph 179. Cruise mph 165. Landing mph 65. Initial climb rate 1,525. Range 750. Ceiling 15,000.

World War II is responsible for most of the Bobcats still flying. It is unlikely that the more than 5,000 of these five-passenger twins would have been built without a military requirement for twin-engine trainers. Several hundred remain on the United States civil register. Originally built with 245-hp Jacobs radial engines, some Bobcats later got 295-hp Lycomings, and others have since been reengined with 300-hp Jacobs powerplants. With the addition of an exit-hatch window to meet safety requirements, some also have been converted to six-seaters, though normal seating is two pilots and three passengers on a single bench-type rear seat. The Bobcat is of fabric-covered steel-tube construction, the fuselage being faired with spruce stringers that gave way to the ship's nickname, "the Bamboo Bomber." The wing also is fabric-covered over heavy wooden spars. The landing gear retracts upward into the nacelles and remains partly exposed so that belly landings can be made with little or no damage if the flaps are up. An unusual feature of the Jacobs engine is that it operates on only one magneto, plus battery ignition. It is started on the battery, then switched to the mag. Both engines turn generators, and they run smoothly on ignition if a mag fails. Bobcats have a large rudder, but the vertical stabilizer is small and minimum single-engine control speed is 90 mph. At 10,000 feet, full throttle gives 20" of manifold pressure, and 1,900 RPM on the Hamilton Standard constant-speed props will yield 143 mph indicated.

CESSNA 303 "CRUSADER" 1982–84

STANDARD DATA: Seats 6. Gross wt. n/a. Empty wt. n/a. Fuel Capacity n/a. Engines Two 250-hp turbocharged Continentals. PERFORMANCE: Top mph 247. Cruise mph 207. Stall mph n/a. Initial climb rate 1,400. Ceiling 25,000. Range n/a. Takeoff distance (50') 1,993. Landing distance (50') n/a.

Not since the 240-hp 310 was discontinued in 1958 has Cessna produced a conventionally configured twin as lightweight as the Crusader, which is powered by two 250-hp turbocharged Continentals. Set alongside the likes of Piper's Apache and Twin Comanche or the Seneca and Seminole, the Beech Duchess, and the (Grumman American) Gulfstream Cougar, the Crusader would appear to have an abundance of horsepower. But for Cessna, a total of 500 hp for an airplane with wing-mounted powerplants and seating for six is light! Outstanding features of the Crusader include a new airfoil, a wide-oval fuselage with comfortable seating, and counterrotating propellers. Performance figures for the Crusader post a 247-mph maximum speed at 20,000 feet and a maximum cruise of more than 207 mph at 10,000 feet. Maximum certified altitude is 25,000 feet, and the single-engine service ceiling is more than 13,000 feet. At sea level, a 1,400 fpm rate of climb can be achieved, and takeoff over a 50-foot obstacle can be accomplished in under 2,000 feet.

CESSNA 310
1954–81

STANDARD DATA: (310R) Seats 4–6. Gross wt. 5,500. Empty wt. 3,358. Fuel capacity 102–207. Engines two 285-hp fuel-injected Continentals. **PERFORMANCE:** Top mph 238. Cruise mph 224. Stall mph 81. Initial climb rate 1,662. Ceiling 19,750. Range 568–1,303. Takeoff distance (50') 1,700. Landing distance (50') 1,790.
STANDARD DATA: (T310R) Seats 4–6. Gross wt. 5,500. Empty wt. 3,467. Fuel capacity 102–207. Engines two 285-hp turbocharged Continentals. **PERFORMANCE:** Top mph 273. Cruise mph 231. Stall mph 81. Initial climb rate 1,700. Ceiling 27,400. Range 568–1,322. Takeoff distance (50') 1,662. Landing distance (50') 1,790.
STANDARD DATA: (310) Seats 5. Gross wt. 4,700. Empty wt. 2,695. Fuel capacity 102. Engines two 240-hp Continentals. **PERFORMANCE:** Top mph 232. Cruise mph 213. Stall mph 102. Initial climb rate 1,660. Ceiling 20,500. Range 800. Takeoff distance (50') 1,405. Landing distance (50') 1,720.
STANDARD DATA: (310/260-hp) Seats 4–6. Gross wt. 5,200. Empty wt. 3,110. Fuel capacity 184. Engines two 260-hp fuel-injected Continentals. **PERFORMANCE:** Top mph 237. Cruise mph 222. Stall mph 72. Initial climb rate 1,495. Range 1,082. Ceiling 19,500. Takeoff distance (50') 1,795. Landing distance (50') 1,697.

There probably isn't a pilot who at one time or another hasn't burned with the desire to have a Cessna 310. Over the years it has been refined and acquired even more rakish lines. Models prior to 1960 have the square dorsal fin, the swept style having been introduced in 1960. Horsepower rating is 240 for each engine through 1958. In 1959, fuel-injected Continental engines rated at 260 hp were installed. From 1954 through 1957, the 310 had no alphabet designation. Starting in 1958 and continuing through 1971, each annual model was identified, beginning with the 310-B; however, there is no 310-E or 310-M in volume production due to engineering changes. The alphabet designation was dropped in 1972.

Two major changes in the 1956 model year were an increase in the number of windows and an improved Continental engine that was available. Earlier versions of the 310 are a little more difficult to pilot due to imbalance caused by fuel distribution. Since this has been revised, its maneuvering characteristics have improved. The 310 also yields more hard landings per pilot than other twins because flying speed is lost more quickly on flareout. The latest versions were available with turbocharged engines of the exhaust-driven type. The newer models featured a larger windshield and a new back window giving more cabin light and better passenger/pilot visibility. The nose of the most recent 310s has been extended 32 inches to add room for up to 350 pounds of avionics and/or cargo. Optionally available fuel tank capacity is up to 207 gallons and 285-hp injected powerplants provide a total of 50 horses more than before.

For 1977, the 310 was equipped with several new refinements, including improved cabin ventilation, a redesigned escape hatch, increased capacity of the circuit breaker panel by 30 percent, and simplified maintenance with a one-piece autopilot assembly. The wing locker fuel tanks now have tear-resistant bladders and a new metal containment canister. Newer model 310s benefited from a one-year warranty on the airframe, the avionics, and the engine. Also, new threadless blade propellers were standard; each is six pounds lighter than the previous prop, for a total of 12 pounds per aircraft.

CESSNA 320
"SKYKNIGHT"
1962–68

STANDARD DATA: (320F) Seats 4–6. Gross wt. 5,300. Empty wt. 3,273. Fuel capacity 102–184. Engines two 285-hp turbo-supercharged Continentals. **PERFORMANCE:** Top mph 275. Cruise mph 256. Stall mph 78. Initial climb rate 1,924. Range 845. Ceiling 29,000. Takeoff distance (50') 1,190. Landing distance (50') 1,513.
STANDARD DATA: (320A–C) Seats 5. Gross wt. 4,990. Empty wt. 3,190. Fuel capacity 102–133. Engines two 260-hp Continentals. **PERFORMANCE:** Top mph 265. Cruise mph 245. Stall mph 77. Initial climb rate 1,850. Ceiling 27,200. Range 855–1,430. Takeoff distance (50') 1,470. Landing distance (50') 1,770.

The Cessna Skyknight, which has the numerical designation of 320, was an attempt by Cessna to establish a heavier version of the 310 design. The original Skyknight was developed from the 310 with supercharged engines giving increased performance. In 1963, the canted wingtip tanks were added. Horsepower was boosted in 1966 from 260 to 285. The more recent models also had extended engine nacelles to increase baggage capacity, a stretched cabin with greater glass area, and other refinements. Despite all these extras, the Skyknight actually has a gross weight of only 100 pounds greater than that of the comparable Cessna 310 and an empty weight differential of only 100 pounds more. Further, the fuel consumption at economical throttle settings was not substantially different. Yet the Skyknight offered a cruise speed almost 17 percent greater due to its ability to operate efficiently at higher altitudes. Starting in 1963, its second model year, the Skyknight also carried alphabetic designations, beginning as the 320-A and continuing without interruption through the 320-F in 1968.

CESSNA 335
1980

STANDARD DATA: Seats 6. Gross wt. 5,990. Empty wt. 3,749. Fuel capacity 102–207. Engines two 330-hp fuel-injected Continentals. **PERFORMANCE:** Top mph 265. Cruise mph 247. Stall mph 82. Initial climb rate 1,400. Ceiling 26,800. Range 429–1,168. Takeoff distance (50') 2,365. Landing distance (50') 1,850.

While the Cessna 310 celebrated its Silver Anniversary and the 1,000th Model 340 rolled off the assembly line, the Model 335 was introduced to challenge its two stalwart brothers on home turf. Billed as the lowest-priced cabin-class business twin, it offered six-place seating and a service ceiling of 26,800 feet to put it above weather situations. The Model 335 was powered by two 300-hp Teledyne Continental fuel-injected TSIO-520EB engines. Its cruise speed is judged to be 224 mph at 74 percent power and 10,000 feet. Maximum fuel range proves to be 1,372 miles at 194 mph and 20,000 feet. The 335 over powers the 310 by 30-hp and lags behind the 340 by 20-hp total. The 335 was expected to replace the 310's, Barons and Aztecs in the field, and possibly do the same for the 340 in years to come. Unexpectedly, its production was short-lived when it evidently didn't offer the flying/buying public what it wanted.

CESSNA 337
"SKYMASTER"/
"PRESSURIZED SKYMASTER"
1964–80

STANDARD DATA: (337) Seats 4–6. Gross wt. 4,630. Empty wt. 2,790. Fuel capacity 90–150. Engines two 210-hp fuel-injected Continentals. **PERFORMANCE:** Top mph 206. Cruise mph 194. Stall mph 70. Initial climb rate 1,100. Range 1,139. Takeoff distance (50') 1,675. Landing distance (50') 1,650. **STANDARD DATA:** (Pressurized) Seats 5. Gross wt. 4,700. Empty wt. 3,061. Fuel capacity 150. Engines two 225-hp turbocharged Continentals. **PERFORMANCE:** Top mph 250.

Cruise mph 236. Stall mph 71. Initial climb rate 1,250. Range 1,133. Ceiling 30,300. Takeoff distance (50') 1,500. Landing distance (50') 1,675. **STANDARD DATA:** (T337) Seats 4–6. Gross wt. 4,500. Empty wt. 2,795. Fuel capacity 131. Engines two 210-hp turbocharged Continentals. **PERFORMANCE:** Top mph 231. Cruise mph 224. Stall mph 68. Initial climb rate 1,155. Ceiling 30,100. Range 1,200. Takeoff distance (50') 1,595. Landing distance (50') 1,520.

CESSNA "SKYMASTER"

CESSNA "PRESSURIZED SKYMASTER"

You know this machine by the thrumming "electric mixer" sound as it speeds overhead. The Cessna Skymaster 337 is the unique tandem twin, with one engine in the nose as a puller and the second at the rear of the cabin as a pusher. Dual rudders extend to the rear on booms, which also support the horizontal elevators. The engine arrangement gives it especially easy-to-fly characteristics for a light twin, particularly in regard to engine-out operation. Pilots have no control problems when flying on one engine. For this reason, the FAA issues a special center-thrust rating for those without a multiengine rating who then qualify for this type. The original Skymaster was designated 336 and was fitted with fixed gear. Retractable gear was introduced in 1965, and the model number changed to 337. The following year turbocharging was added as an option, and pressurization became available in 1973. Both the standard and turbocharged Skymaster utilize the 210-hp engine; only the Pressurized Skymaster makes use of the 225-hp turbocharged Continental.

For both 1975 and 1976, Skymasters offer improved range plus the addition of two new specially-equipped IFR models, the Skymaster II and Pressurized Skymaster II. The "II" versions incorporated as standard equipment an extensive package of avionics and accessories usually ordered by owners. In 1976, flap extension speeds were reduced, and aerodynamics and soundproofing improved.

The 1977 Skymaster was the first general aviation aircraft with a nose-mounted engine to be radar-equipped. The Skymasters are fitted with a Bendix weather radar mounted in a fiberglass pod that is attached to the front and rear spars below the right wing. The pod is located just outboard of the wing strut and in no way alters flight characteristics. This unit means additional safety and utility for the business or pleasure pilot. In addition, front engine propeller blades have an improved airfoil that significantly improves single-engine performance. In 1980, United States production of the Skymaster line was discontinued to make room for the 303 Crusader. Production of the Skymaster was limited to facilities in Reims, France.

CESSNA 340
1972–84

STANDARD DATA: Seats 6. Gross wt. 5,990. Empty wt. 3,921. Fuel capacity 102–207. Engines two 310-hp turbocharged Continentals. **PERFORMANCE:** Top mph 281. Cruise mph 231. Stall mph 82. Initial climb rate 1,650. Ceiling 29,800. Range 506–1,325. Takeoff distance (50') 2,175. Landing distance (50') 1,850.

The Cessna 340 is a pressurized six-place twin featuring center-aisle seating, an air-stair door, and top cruise performance. Developed from the 310, it utilizes a similar landing gear and tail unit. Its wings are borrowed from the Model 414. Until 1976, power for the 340 was generally quoted as 285 hp. It used the same turbocharged engines as the T310. But power in subsequent models is rated at 310 hp during takeoff for the 285-hp engine. Propellers with a shorter diameter were added for 1976 to reduce tip speeds, thereby lowering sound levels. In addition, a propeller synchrophaser maintains phase of the blades engine-to-engine by controlling prop RPM.

With a fuselage five feet longer than the 310, the 340's big selling point is a spacious interior with pressurization. It was the first light twin to offer pressurization, and it was Cessna's hope that the 340 would make this option accessible to light-twin owners. Allowable baggage in the airplane is 930 pounds with storage bins located in the nose, behind the seats, and in nacelle lockers. Since 1975, the Model 340 II and 340 III were added to the line with their packages of special avionics and instruments. For 1981, a McCauley threadless-blade propeller had become standard, resulting in a 12-pound weight saving per airplane.

CESSNA 401/402
1966–85

STANDARD DATA: (402 C Businessliner) Seats 6–10. Gross wt. 6,885. Empty wt. 4,069. Fuel capacity 213. Engines two 325-hp turbocharged Continentals. **PERFORMANCE:** Top mph 266. Cruise mph 224. Stall mph 78. Initial climb rate 1,450. Ceiling 26,900. Range 461–1,101. Takeoff distance (50') 2,195. Landing distance (50') 2,485.
STANDARD DATA: (401) Seats 6–8. Gross wt. 6,300. Empty wt. 3,904. Fuel capacity 102–207. Engines two 300-hp

turbocharged Continentals. **PERFORMANCE:** Top mph 263. Cruise mph 221. Stall mph 79. Initial climb rate 1,610. Ceiling 26,180. Range 489–1,242. Takeoff distance (50') 2,220. Landing distance (50') 1,765.

Derived from the Model 411, the Cessna 401 and 402 are essentially the same aircraft put to two different uses. The 401, introduced in 1966 and discontinued in 1972, was basically designed as a medium to light executive transport. The 402, introduced in conjunction with the 401 and in production until 1985, was intended for the third-level airline market and featured a cabin that was easily converted from cargo/utility to passenger seating. Both aircraft were aimed at owners/pilots who want to move up from the light twins to a somewhat heavier model. The 401/402 has excellent single-engine performance, yet can operate as a marginal small commercial feeder-type airliner. All versions are powered by twin 300-hp turbo-supercharged Continental engines, the smallest of all the 411 derivatives, turning three-blade constant-speed full-feathering propellers.

The 402 was available in two versions: the Utililiner and the Businessliner. The former features a 10-place high-density seating arrangement for commuter operations. These seats can be easily removed for conversion to an all-cargo configuration. The Businessliner has six- to eight-place executive seating in a variety of arrangements. On late models, the cruise RPM of the turbo system powerplants was lowered to 75 percent power, which results in quieter operation. A propeller synchrophaser maintains propeller synchronization and controls blade phase angles engine-to-engine to reduce cabin sound level and vibrations.

The 402C, introduced in 1979, has an increased useful load of 349 pounds and two more passengers with added performance due to an engine upgrade to a 325-hp turbocharged Continental. The airplane accomplishes its increased payload feat by a lengthened bonded wet wing, rivet elimination, drag minimization, increased aspect ratio, and elimination of tip tanks. Its wing also enables fuel capacity to be increased to 213 gallons. The more powerful engine substantially increases single-engine rate of climb from 225 to 301 fpm. Maximum cruise was upped by two mph at 10,000 feet. Also, the engines were moved outboard more than five inches for greater propeller-to-fuselage clearance, resulting in a quieter cabin. The 402C has borrowed its landing gear from the Chancellor, giving it a faster retraction time and simplified rigging. Time between overhauls is extended to 1,600 hours. Also, McCauley threadless-blade propellers result in a 12-pound weight savings and require no special tools for installation.

CESSNA 411/414 CHANCELLOR 1965–85

STANDARD DATA: (Chancellor) Seats 8. Gross wt. 6,750. Gross wt. 6,750. Empty wt. 4,357. Fuel capacity 213. Engines two 310-hp turbocharged Continentals. **PERFORMANCE:** Top mph 275. Cruise mph 258. Stall mph 83. Initial climb rate 1,580. Ceiling 31,350. Range 600–1,507. Takeoff distance (50') 2,595. Landing distance (50') 2,393.
STANDARD DATA: (411) Seats 6–8. Gross wt. 6,500. Empty wt. 3,865. Fuel capacity 202. Engines two 340-hp turbocharged Continentals. **PERFORMANCE:** Top mph 268. Cruise mph 223. Stall mph 82. Initial climb rate 1,900. Ceiling 26,000. Range 1,284. Takeoff distance (50') 2,010. Landing distance (50') 1,815.

The Cessna 411, first delivered in 1965, was one of Wichita's first ventures into the "airliner" market. The cabin is separated from the passenger compartment by a divider. Seating is spacious and available in a variety of arrangements. Built-in airlinelike stairs are in the door. Power was provided by twin 340-hp Continental engines, supercharged with AiResearch exhaust-driven compressors and turning full-feathering constant-speed propellers. The 411A, produced from 1967–68, featured a redesigned nose and more baggage space. The model 414, a 411 derivative introduced in 1970, utilized the 421's fuselage and tail unit with the 401's wings.

The six- to seven-seat pressurized light transport is a step up for owners of the pressurized 340 and is fitted with the same 310-hp turbocharged engines. For 1976 the airplane was equipped with a propeller synchrophaser to control propeller RPM and phase relationship of the blades, engine-to-engine. Baggage capacity of the 414 is 930 pounds, and cabin seating is available with an array of executive options.

The Chancellor replaced the former 414 in 1978 and offered a new level of payload performance, range, and fuel efficiency. The maximum takeoff weight went up to 400 pounds to yield a higher useful load. The airplane's bonded wet wing is 4½ feet longer than previous models and lifts an airframe which is 2 feet 8 inches longer from nose to tail. In addition, the Chancellor's wet wing has an increased fuel capacity of 106 gallons of usable fuel. A cabin differential of 5.0 psi allows a 10,000 foot cabin at 26,500 feet. Propeller-to-fuselage clearance is more than 31 inches for a very quiet cabin.

The twin turbocharged 310-hp engines provide sea-level power to 20,000 feet, while the twin-engine rate of climb is 1,580 fpm, and the single-engine rate is 290 fpm. The Chancellor utilizes the hydraulic components of the Golden Eagle gear and features a five-second retraction time. For 1981, Chancel-

lor refinements included a heated fuel manifold, frost panes for cockpit side windows, and threadless-blade propellers.

CESSNA 421 "GOLDEN EAGLE" 1967–85

STANDARD DATA: Seats 6–8. Gross wt. 7,450. Empty wt. 4,640. Fuel capacity 213–270. Engines two 375-hp turbocharged Continentals. **PERFORMANCE:** Top mph 297. Cruise mph 277. Stall mph 85. Initial climb rate 1,940. Range 1,099–1,377. Ceiling 30,200. Takeoff distance (50') 2,323. Landing distance (50') 2,293.

The Cessna 421 evolved from the Cessna 411 design and represents the firm's effort to produce a pressurized light twin at a reasonable price. The pressurization system employed on the Cessna 421 is a standard type that operates off the engine turbochargers; it is not otherwise linked, either mechanically or hydraulically, to the Continental 375-hp powerplants. This system maintains sea-level pressure inside the cabin up to 9,000 feet. The 421B Golden Eagle, first produced in 1970, featured an increase in overall length, principally due to an enlarged nose section to make room for more baggage and avionics. The wingspan was increased to maintain takeoff and cruise performance.

The 421B Executive Commuter made use of easy-to-remove seats to provide alternative cargo/passenger capability; however, maximum fuel capacity was reduced to 225 gallons. For 1976, a wet-wing design increased standard fuel capacity on the 421C and saved some 30 pounds to be added to useful load. A new turbocharger increased critical altitude by 2,000 feet. Wide-blade propellers reduced noise levels. An extended vertical fin and rudder improved directional control. The Golden Eagle distinguished itself by successfully competing with turboprops by providing superior speed, useful load, and cabin size.

Its fuel efficiency is unmatched at low and high altitudes. With six people on board, it typically cruises at 275 mph over a distance of 1,118 miles at 25,000 feet. A new landing gear in 1980 gave the Golden Eagle a higher stance, a more level ground attitude, and softer touchdowns. An optional direct-current electric windshield was certified for service throughout the entire deice envelope. Improvements for 1981 were a refined fuel injection system, a heated fuel manifold, and frost panes for crew windows. The new injection system makes use of an engine-driven fuel pump that maintains pressure with a regulator referenced to the engine turbocharging system. A priming system independent of the fuel injection system enhances engine starting during temperature extremes.

CESSNA "TITAN"
1977–81

STANDARD DATA: Seats 6–10. Gross wt. 8,400. Empty wt. 4,861. Fuel capacity 348. Engines two 375-hp turbocharged Continentals. **PERFORMANCE:** Top mph 267. Cruise mph 251. Stall mph 81. Initial climb rate 1,575. Ceiling 26,000. Range 739–1,755. Takeoff distance (50') 2,367. Landing distance (50') 2,130.

All-new planes added to the Cessna twin-engine lineup for 1977 were the Titan Ambassador, Titan Courier, and Freighter. All were designed to carry big loads with exceptional fuel efficiency. Courier versions provide high-density seating that can be removed to allow room for cargo. Operators can choose the combination of seats and cargo space that suits their missions. The Ambassador executive versions of the Titan have luxurious interiors with room to work en route. The cabin volume of the Titan is 316 cu.ft., and its length is nearly 19 feet with 14 feet behind the crew.

Optional double doors allow for the loading of "D" size shipping containers and other oversized bundles. With a useful load of more than 3,500 pounds, the Ambassador can carry combinations of people (10 maximum), cargo, and fuel up to 2,040 pounds. A bonded wet wing holds 340 gallons of usable fuel. At 10,000 feet, 65 percent power, and peak exhaust gas temperature, the Titan Courier can carry up to 2,500 pounds of cargo 802 miles at 207 mph. With 2,000 pounds of passengers and baggage it will travel 1,308 miles at 208 mph. An optional propeller synchrophaser in recent models incorporates identical governors to eliminate the slaved combination used on previous systems. One significant change for 1981 was an extension of TBO time to 1,600 hours. The extension applied to engines on newer Titans and also to those previously manufactured.

CESSNA 441 "CONQUEST"
1978–86

STANDARD DATA: Seats 11. Gross wt. 9,850. Empty wt. 5,687. Fuel capacity 481. Engines two flat-rated 635-shp Garrett AiResearch turboprops. **PERFORMANCE:** Top mph 339. Cruise mph 337. Stall mph 86. Initial climb rate 2,435. Ceiling 35,000+. Range 1,380–2,524. Takeoff distance (50') 2,465. Landing distance (50') 1,875.

Cessna entered the propjet market in 1977 with deliveries of the Conquest. Since the first flight of the Conquest in August 1975, it underwent a series of design improvements, including an increase in wing aspect ratio and improved engine performance. The Conquest is positioned at the top end of the turboprop market in performance; however, its modest price, low fuel consumption, and low operating costs make it

CESSNA "CONQUEST"

CESSNA "CARAVAN II"

competitive across the entire market of full-sized executive aircraft. The higher aspect-ratio wing also has greater fuel capacity. Usable fuel volume was boosted to a total 475 usable.

Its Garrett AiResearch powerplants are each flat-rated at 625-shp and yield a single-engine service ceiling of 21,380 feet and a single-engine climb rate of 715 fpm. Cruising at 33,000 feet with six people and baggage on board, the Conquest has a range of 2,237 miles plus reserves at an average speed of 312 mph.

Modification of the Conquest tail assemblies was necessary to comply with an airworthiness directive issued by the FAA in 1979. The company decided to provide all Conquest owners with a redesigned horizontal tail assembly and update all Conquests in the field to 1980 configuration. Conquest's certified altitude was raised in 1981 to 35,000 feet from the previous 33,000-foot limit. This became effective with serial number 173. At the higher certified maximum altitude, cruise fuel flows are decreased and range is extended.

CESSNA CORSAIR
1980–86

STANDARD DATA: Seats 6–8. Gross wt. 8,200. Empty wt. 4,846. Fuel capacity 367. Engines two 450-shp Pratt & Whitney turbines. **PERFORMANCE:** Top mph 304. Initial climb rate 1,888. Ceiling 34,000. Range 1,621.

Cessna's second entry into the propjet market came in 1980 with the introduction of the Corsair. Its seating for up to eight and 8,200-pound maximum takeoff weight made it the lightest propjet on the market. Powered by two Pratt & Whitney PT6A-112 turbine engines flat-rated at 450 shp, the Corsair has a maximum cruise speed of 304 mph at 18,700 feet and can climb directly from sea level to 26,000 feet in less than 20 minutes. Service ceiling is rated at 34,000 feet. Its usable fuel supply of 367 gallons and useful load of 3,429 pounds allows the Corsair to carry eight adults plus baggage for 898 miles. With passengers and crew trimmed to four, the range is extended to 1,622 miles.

The Corsair's pressurized cabin makes high altitude travel quiet and comfortable. Cabin pressure differential is 5.0 psi, providing a 10,000-foot cabin at 26,500 feet or an 11,900-foot cabin at 30,000 feet. Slow-turning propellers along with propeller tip placement two feet from the fuselage combine to reduce cabin noise. The Corsair's trailing-link main landing gear allows wheels to pivot vertically and longitudinally for soft landings. Wide-chord three-blade propellers are reversible to aid short-field landings and extend brake life. The props are equipped with deice protection, a synchronizer to minimize noise, and automatic feather to match blade angle to engine power.

CONSOLIDATED VULTEE PBY-5A CATALINA
1943–45

STANDARD DATA: Gross wt. 34,000. Empty wt. 17,564. Fuel capacity 1,750. Engines two 1,200-hp Pratt & Whitneys. **PERFORMANCE:** Top mph 196. Cruise mph 125. Stall mph 76. Initial climb rate 1,111. Range 2,520. Ceiling 15,800.

The more familiar PBY-5A is simply the amphibian version of the PBY-5 flying boat. The original flying boat went into service in the U.S. Navy in 1939 and was soon adopted by the RAF, which in turn dubbed it the "Catalina." This name was later recognized by the U.S. Navy in 1941. In addition to the aircraft's primary role as a patrol bomber, the Catalina has been used as a torpedo carrier, night bomber, antisubmarine weapon, long-range reconnaissance plane, and air/sea rescue plane. Catalinas also have exceptional load carrying ability with a cargo capacity of 15,000 pounds. Due to their versatility, PBYs have been widely used commercially and militarily throughout the world.

CHAMPION LANCER
1963–65

STANDARD DATA: Seats 2. Gross wt. 2,450. Empty wt. 1,790. Fuel capacity 60. Engines two 100-hp Continentals. **PERFORMANCE:** Top mph 130. Cruise mph 120. Stall mph 62. Initial climb rate 642. Range 510. Ceiling 12,900. Takeoff run 500.

The Champion Lancer was (during its production run) the least expensive twin produced in this country. Champion's aim was to offer a twin with design simplicity, easy maintenance, and low operational costs. The Lancer was also designed to handle unimproved landing strips. It flew for the first time in 1961, but production didn't start until 1963. Several revisions were made in the interim including the relocation of the engine nacelles to a position above the wing. Construction of the Lancer was all-metal with a fiberglass covering. Thirty-six Lancers rolled off the production line in the first year.

CONVAIR 240/340/440
1947–58

STANDARD DATA: (240) Seats 44. Gross wt. 41,790. Empty wt. 27,682. Fuel capacity 1,550. Engines two 2,100-hp Pratt & Whitney Twin-row Wasps. **PERFORMANCE:** Top mph 347. Cruise mph 291. Landing mph 88. Initial climb rate 1,520. Ceiling 30,000. Range 1,800. Takeoff distance (50') 2,760. Landing distance (50') 3,970.
STANDARD DATA: (340) Seats 44. Gross wt. 47,000. Empty wt. 29,486. Fuel capacity 1,750. Engines two 2,400 Pratt & Whitneys. **PERFORMANCE:** Cruise mph 284. Range 2,015. Takeoff run 4,675. Landing roll 4,500.
STANDARD DATA: (440) Seats 44–52. Gross wt. 49,100. Empty wt. 31,305. Fuel capacity 1,730. Engines two 2,400 Pratt & Whitneys. **PERFORMANCE:** Top mph 309. Cruise mph 289. Stall mph 85. Initial climb rate 1,192. Range 1,040. Ceiling 25,500. Takeoff run 4,930. Landing roll 3,980.

CONVAIR CV-240

CONVAIR 540

CONVAIR 580

Flown for the first time on March 16, 1947, the CV-240 was Convair's first postwar commercial transport. Three basic versions were produced in subsequent years, each differing in the location and type of passenger and loading facilities with the addition of minor refinements. The aircraft was originally designed to carry 44 passengers plus crew. It employed two Pratt & Whitney 18-cylinder radial engines rated at 1,900 hp in low blower, 1,700 hp in high blower, and 2,100 hp available at takeoff with water injection. The CV-240 with an increased wingspan and longer fuselage for a larger payload became the Convair-Liner 340, flown for the first time in 1951.

The CV-440 Metropolitan was merely a refinement of the CV-340 featuring modifications to increase speed, reduce the noise level in the cabin, and provide for up to 52 passengers. It was also available with twin Pratt & Whitneys that produced 2,500 hp at takeoff. The CV-580 was a conversion of the piston-engine CV-340 or CV-440 powered by Allison 501-D13 turboprops rated at 3,750 shp each. The conversion was developed by the Pacific Airmotive Corp. and received certification in 1960. Normal cruising speed was 348 mph, maximum range was 1,620 miles, and gross weight was increased to 53,200 pounds.

CURTISS-WRIGHT C46 "COMMANDO"
1940

STANDARD DATA: Seats 40. Gross wt. 45,000. Empty wt. 29,483. Fuel capacity 1,400–2,200. Engines two 2,000-hp Pratt & Whitney Twin Wasps. PERFORMANCE: Top mph 265. Cruise mph 227. Landing mph 71. Climb to 10,000 13.5 minutes. Range 2,994. Ceiling 24,500.

The first Curtiss-Wright C-46 production models were delivered in 1941 to help fulfill the needs of the Air Transport Commands during World War II. In its military transport configuration, it can carry 16,000 pounds of cargo or 50 fully equipped troops. The civilian version contains 36 passenger seats. Nearly 400 commercial models remain in service in North and South America. A total of 3,180 "Commandos" were produced during World War II, and a large number of

these serve in Chinese, Japanese, Korean, and South American Air Forces. In appearance, the C-46 is very similar to the Douglas DC-3, but the Curtiss's greater wing area, larger fuselage, and 1,600 extra horsepower made the C-46 a much more versatile workhorse.

DE HAVILLAND CANADA DHC-7 (DASH 7)

STANDARD DATA: Seats 52. Gross wt. 43,500. Empty wt. 25,800. Fuel capacity 1,480. Engines four 1,120-shp Pratt & Whitney Aircraft of Canada turboprops. PERFORMANCE: Top mph 271. Cruise mph 265. Initial climb rate 1,270. Ceiling 23,600. Takeoff run 5,700. Landing roll 3,040. Range 810–1,300.

Design of the Dash 7 STOL airliner began in 1972 in response to a market survey of short-haul transport requirements. The first production example took to the air in 1977, and certification followed within that same year. Each of the four turboprop engines (two on each wing) drives a Hamilton constant-speed full-feathering reversible-pitch four-blade propeller made from fiberglass. The props are slow-turning to reduce noise levels, so that the landing approach noise level on a three-degree glideslope is 92.4 EPNdB. Maximum seating is for 50 passengers divided on either side of a center aisle, a flightcrew of two, and two cabin attendants. Up to five standard pallets can be carried by the Dash 7 in an all-cargo configuration.

DE HAVILLAND "DRAGON"/"RAPIDE"
1934–45

STANDARD DATA: Gross wt. 5,550. Empty wt. 3,230. Fuel capacity 76. Engines two 200-hp D.H. Gipsy-Sixes. PERFORMANCE: Top mph 157. Cruise mph 132. Initial climb rate 867. Range 556. Ceiling 16,700. Takeoff run 870. Landing roll 510.

The Dragon/Rapide was a twin-engine passenger or freight carrier designed by de Havilland Aircraft Company and flown for the first time in 1934. Production continued until 1945, and 737 of the airplanes were built including the D.H. 89A that was adopted by the R.A.F. and named the "Dominie." It was the radio training and communications version; 475 of these were built. It accommodated a pilot, who sat far up in the nose of the plane, and seats and freight space as desired. The main cabin was entered by a large door on the port side. Construction consisted of a boxlike structured fuselage with plywood paneling on the inside and fabric covering on the outside. Wings had wooden spars and fabric covering. Dragons and Rapides still in service have usually changed to the Gipsy Queen 2 engines.

DE HAVILLAND DHC-6 "TWIN OTTER"
1965–94

STANDARD DATA: Seats 11–22. Gross wt. 12,500. Empty wt. 7,320. Fuel capacity 382. Engines two 652-shp Pratt & Whitney Aircraft of Canada turboprops. **PERFORMANCE:** Top mph 210. Stall mph 67. Initial climb rate 1,600. Range 794. Ceiling 26,700. Takeoff distance (50') 1,200. Landing distance (50') 1,050.

This popular STOL transport is used by a number of feeder airlines around the world. Its short- and soft-field capability gives the versatile Twin Otter room to spare on even the shortest of underdeveloped strips. Produced in Canada, the DHC6 300 series is powered by two Pratt & Whitney/United Aircraft of Canada turboprops, each capable of 652 shp. The 300S model features several improvements: high-capacity brakes, an antiskid system, wing spoilers, refined electrical and hydraulic systems, propeller automatic feather, and improved fire protection. Earlier models, the series 100 and 200, were fitted with 570-shp engines. Access to the two-man cockpit is through a carlike door on each side or through the cabin. The standard "Commuter" version will accommodate 20 passengers, but optional arrangements are available.

DORNIER DO 28 D-1 "SKYSERVANT"
1967–81

STANDARD DATA: Seats 12–13. Gross wt. 8,470. Empty wt. 5,066. Fuel capacity 236. Engines two 380-hp Lycomings.

PERFORMANCE: Top mph 202. Cruise mph 170. Stall mph 65. Initial climb rate 1,180. Range 1,255. Ceiling 25,200. Takeoff distance (50') 1,020. Landing distance (50') 1,000.

Professor Claude Dornier started his first aircraft company in 1922 as the successor to the "Do" division of the Zeppelin Werke, GmbH. When the manufacture of aircraft became forbidden in Germany after World War II, Dornier continued his design work in Spain. There he developed the Do 25, a general-purpose airplane that later evolved into the Do 27. The Do 28, a twin-engine version of the Do 27, was produced until 1971. The light utility transport Do 28 Skyservant was built starting in 1971. The Skyservant was a completely new design, retaining only the basic configuration of the earlier aircraft and featuring STOL capabilities. The high-wing airplane is adaptable to a variety of uses including ambulance and military surveys. For photographic missions, the Skyservant can be equipped with a darkroom and camera doors in the under fuselage. The Skyservant's twin Lycomings and landing gear are mounted on stub wings that protrude from the lower fuselage directly underneath the main wings.

DOUGLAS B-26 INVADER
1942

STANDARD DATA: Seats 3. Gross wt. 37,000. Empty wt. 22,370. Engines two 2,000-hp Pratt & Whitney 18-cylinder radials. **PERFORMANCE:** Top mph 345. Cruise mph 284. Initial climb rate 1,250. Range 1,400. Ceiling 22,100.

The B-26 Invader was originally built in three different prototypes, one as a light bombardment and attack airplane, one as a modification for use as a night fighter, and one attack bomber with a large-caliber mounted cannon. The prototype of the basic bomber and attack plane was flown for the first time in 1942. In testing, it actually carried nearly twice the bomb load required by the original specifications submitted by the military. In addition, it exceeded every performance guarantee and was 700 pounds under its designed empty weight. The Invader went into action with the Ninth Air Force in the European Theater in 1944.

Its armament included six fixed .50-caliber machine

guns in the nose, eight paired .50-caliber guns under the wings, and two two-gun electrically-operated turrets. One turret was above and one turret was below the fuselage; both turrets were remotely controlled from a gun-sighting position behind the wings. The upper gun turret could be locked in the forward position and fired by the pilot. The Invader also had internal bomb bays, external bomb racks, and self-sealing fuel tanks.

DOUGLAS DC-3
1936–46

STANDARD DATA: Seats 28–30. Gross wt. 25,200. Empty wt. 16,865. Fuel capacity 411. Engines two 1,200-hp Pratt & Whitney Twin-Wasps. **PERFORMANCE:** Top mph 230. Cruise mph 207. Stall mph 67. Initial climb rate 1,130. Range 2,125. Ceiling 23,200.

The DC-2 was developed from the DC-1. The DC-2 first flew in 1934, and production continued until 1936 when it was replaced by the DC-3. The DC-2 was powered by two Wright engines rated at 710 hp each. It was later modified by the U.S. Air Force under the designation C-39. The C-39 was essentially the DC-2 with DC-3 wing and tail assemblies and two 975-hp Wright engines. Construction was all-metal with a semimonocoque fuselage. The DC-3 replaced the DC-2 in 1935 and was ultimately built in larger numbers than any other transport either before or after. It provided for 21 passengers or an optional 28 to 30 and was powered by 1,000- or 1,100-hp Wright Cyclones or 1,200-hp Pratt & Whitney radials. The DC-3, currently the most widely used of the early Douglas transports, is a postwar conversion of the World War II military C-47.

DOUGLAS DC-4/C-54
1939

STANDARD DATA: Seats 42. Gross wt. 65,000. Empty wt. 35,000, Fuel capacity 2,100. Engines four 1,000-hp Pratt & Whitney Twin-Wasps. **PERFORMANCE:** Top mph 285. Cruise mph 222. Stall mph 80. Initial climb rate 1,200. Range 3,500. Ceiling 25,000.

The DC-4 design was the product of a group effort involving the technical departments of five of the largest airline companies in the United States in 1939. Its service tests were carried out under the supervision of United Airlines. The first model had seating for more than 50 passengers and was powered by Pratt & Whitney Twin-Wasp engines. Unfortunately, it was sold to Japan where it was involved in a crash. Its extensive service testing resulted in a somewhat

smaller design with seating for approximately 40 passengers. This version was placed in production in 1940. At the outbreak of World War II, the military ordered large-scale production of the DC-4 and gave it the designation of C-54. The military version was powered by 1,350-hp Twin-Wasps and was outfitted to carry troops, trucks, and other heavy equipment. The C-54 was also provided with its own facilities for field loading.

DOUGLAS DC-6/DC-7
1947–58

STANDARD DATA: (DC-6) Seats 64–92. Gross wt. 106,000. Empty wt. 49,767. Fuel capacity 3,992–5,512. Engines four 2,500-hp Pratt & Whitney Double Wasps. **PERFORMANCE:** Top mph 360. Cruise mph 307. Landing mph 93. Initial climb rate 1,120. Range 3,860. Takeoff distance (50') 4,500. Landing distance (50') 3,010.

STANDARD DATA: (DC-7) Seats 62–99. Gross wt. 143,000. Empty wt. 72,763. Fuel capacity 7,824. Engines four 3,400-hp Wright Turbo Compound radials. **PERFORMANCE:** Top mph 406. Cruise mph 346. Stall mph 97. Climb rate (20,000 ft.) 240. Range 4,635. Ceiling 21,700. Takeoff distance (50') 6,360. Landing distance (50') 5,100.

The Douglas DC-6 is essentially a stretched, more powerful, and pressurized version of the DC-4 with three-blade props. The DC-7 is merely a stretched DC-6 with four-blade props and retaining all aerodynamic and structural features. The only difference between the DC-6 and the DC-4 in exterior appearance is that the DC-6 is extended an additional seven feet and the windows are square instead of the earlier porthole style. This new version also provides for up to 62 passengers, 20 more than the DC-4. The DC-7 was increased 3 feet 4 inches longer than the DC-6. It provided for the accommodation of 69 first-class passengers or 95 coach passengers. The DC-7's engines further increased its gross weight. The DC-7B, a later version, was basically an intercontinental aircraft.

EMBRAER "BANDEIRANTE"
1972–86

STANDARD DATA: Seats 21. Gross wt. 12,500. Empty wt. 7,857. Fuel capacity 440. Engines two 750-shp Pratt & Whitney turboprops. **PERFORMANCE:** Top mph 286. Cruise mph 259. Stall mph 82. Initial climb rate 1,788. Ceiling 24,100. Range 1,180. Takeoff distance (50') 2,215. Landing distance (50') 2,790.

The Bandeirante from Brazil is a commuter airliner powered by two Pratt & Whitney PT6A-34 free-turbine turboprop engines flat-rated at 750 shp maximum continuous power at 2,200 propeller RPM. The propellers are three-blade Hartzells with automatic synchronization and full beta-control reversing. Standard seating is for 18 passengers with maximum provisions for 21. There is a crew/passenger door at the front and passenger/baggage door at the rear, both on the port side. The first prototype flew in 1968, with the first production model flying in 1972. By the beginning of 1979, 219 Bandeirantes of various models had been sold to some 40 operators around the world. The Bandeirante is available in more than 14 versions, differing in their equipment for specialized missions.

EVANGEL 4500 STOL
1969–76

STANDARD DATA: Seats 9. Gross wt. 5,500. Empty wt. 3,530. Fuel capacity 111. Engines two 300-hp Lycomings. **PERFORMANCE:** Top mph 230. Cruise 182. Stall mph 67. Initial climb rate 1,500. Range 637. Ceiling 21,030. Takeoff distance (50') 1,125. Landing distance (50') 1,140.

Few light twins can carry a full-sized refrigerator, two full 55-gallon drums, five adults, and a goat, and still fly in and out of 1,000-foot jungle strips. The Evangel 4500 STOL does it with ease. It derives its power from two direct-drive fuel-injected Lycoming engines rated at 300 hp each. Only rectangular sections are used for construction of the main fuselage; therefore, optimum utilization of space can be made. The Evangel's cargo doors, one on each side, are the full height of the fuselage side and twice as wide (compared to height). The main landing gear retracts rearward into the wings just below the engine nacelles, but the tires are allowed to protrude in order to provide some protection for wheels-up landings. A turbocharged version, the 4500-300-II, entered production in 1974 to increase the maximum takeoff weight to 5,700 pounds.

FAIRCHILD HILLER
FH-227 (FOKKER)
1958–94

STANDARD DATA: (FH-227) Seats 44–52. Gross wt. 43,500. Empty wt. 22,923. Fuel capacity 1,364. Engines two 2,300-eshp Rolls-Royce Dart turboprops. **PERFORMANCE:** Top 294. Cruise 270. Stall mph 87. Initial climb rate 1,560. Range 1,655. Ceiling 28,000. Takeoff run 3,950. Landing roll 4,100.

STANDARD DATA: (F27 Mk 600) Seats 44 plus crew. Gross wt. 45,000. Empty wt. 22,786. Fuel capacity 1,357–2,463. Engines two 2,140-shp Rolls-Royce Dart turboprops. **PERFORMANCE:** Cruise mph 298. Initial climb rate 1,480. Ceiling 29,500. Takeoff distance 2,310. Landing distance 3,290.

The original Fokker F-27 Friendship was built in Holland. Fairchild has built the F-27 under license from Fokker since 1958, and both companies continue to build the short-to-medium-range airliner on special order. The first F-27 models had a maximum gross weight of 40,500 pounds and seated 44 passengers. Power was supplied by twin 1,720-eshp Dart turboprops. When Fairchild merged with Hiller Aircraft, the designation of the airplane was changed to FH-227 and the fuselage was stretched by six feet, giving increased cabin space for passengers and freight. The stretched airliner will accommodate up to 52 passengers. In 1960, power was increased to 2,105 eshp. The stretched version was fitted with 2,250-eshp engines, and ultimately the FH-227 received a redesigned windshield, stronger landing gear, strengthened rear fuselage, heavier wing skin, propellers of increased diameter, and a more powerful 2,300-eshp Dart turboprop. Fairchild discontinued building the FH-227 under license from Fokker in 1975; however, the Fokker-VFW F27 Friendship continues to be built in the Netherlands. There are 13 versions of the F27.

FORD TRI-MOTOR
1926

STANDARD DATA: Seats 15. Gross wt. 13,250. Empty wt. 7,800. Engines three 425-hp Pratt & Whitneys. **PERFORMANCE:** Top mph 140. Cruise mph 115. Landing mph 60. Range 500. Ceiling 20,000.

The "Tin Goose" is perhaps the most important aircraft in United States airline history. The original Stout Metal Airplane Company was purchased in 1925 by Henry Ford. The new division of the Ford Motor Company produced three versions of the Tri-Motor monoplane. The 4-AT-E was fitted with three 300-hp Whirlwinds. The 6AT utilized the same engines

FORD TRI-MOTOR

but had a larger wing area and accommodations for 13 instead of 11 passengers. The 5-AT-B was outfitted with the same wings and number of seats but differed by having the more powerful 425-hp Pratt & Whitney "Wasp" engines. The Tri-Motor's fuselage was constructed from a series of transverse duralumin bulkheads covered with corrugated metal skin. One engine was mounted in the nose, while the other two were suspended underneath the wings.

GAF NOMAD

STANDARD DATA: (N22B) Seats 13. Gross wt. 8,500. Empty wt. 4,613. Fuel capacity 269–363. Engines two 420-shp Allison turboprops. **PERFORMANCE:** Cruise mph 193. Stall mph 75. Initial climb rate 1,460. Ceiling 21,000. Range 840. Takeoff (50') 1,180. Landing (50') 1,110. Takeoff run (STOL) 600. Landing run (STOL) 250.
STANDARD DATA: (N24A) Seats 17. Gross wt. 9,400. Empty wt. 5,241. Fuel capacity 269–363. Engines two 420-shp Allison turboprops. **PERFORMANCE:** Cruise mph 193. Stall mph 75. Initial climb rate 1,280. Ceiling 20,000. Range 840. Takeoff (50') 1,710. Landing (50') 1,380.

The Nomad is designed and built by the Government Aircraft Factories in Australia in two models. These are the short-takeoff-and-landing (STOL) Nomad N22B and the Nomad N24A commuter aircraft. Variations on the basic aircraft include the Mission Master, the Search Master for maritime surveillance work, and a photographic and mapping model. The aircraft have been proved successful in many countries, often flying over rugged terrain in climates ranging from tropical to subarctic. The N22B, capable of carrying up to 12 passengers, can take off in only 800 feet. The STOL capability of this aircraft, originally developed for Australian military use, has made it ideal for operations in rugged areas such as the highlands of

Papua, New Guinea. The larger N24A is a later development of the basic aircraft capable of carrying more passengers and cargo. The Nomad is characterized by simplicity of construction and systems, which contribute to its economy of operation. Its two Allison 250-B17C turboprops are rated at 420 shp, producing more than two horsepower per pound of engine weight. The B17C offers an improved single-engine high-altitude performance capability and a more rugged gearbox.

GRUMMAN GOOSE/WIDGEON 1937–46

STANDARD DATA: (Goose) Seats 4–6. Gross wt. 8,000. Empty wt. 5,425. Fuel capacity 220. Engines two 400-hp Pratt & Whitney Wasp Juniors. **PERFORMANCE:** Top mph 201. Cruise mph 191. Initial climb rate 1,100. Range 640. Ceiling 21,000.
STANDARD DATA: (Widgeon) Seats 4–5. Gross wt. 4,525. Empty wt. 3,240. Fuel capacity 108. Engines two 200-hp Rangers. **PERFORMANCE:** Top mph 153. Cruise mph 138. Initial climb rate 700. Range 920. Ceiling 14,600.

Seaplanes take a ferocious pounding, and it is a tribute to the way Grumman builds airplanes that these two continue to serve so well. More than 300 of the G-21A Goose series with 450-hp Pratt & Whitney engines were built just before and during World War II, of which about 80 remain active in the United States and Canada. Production of the smaller Widgeon, with 200-hp Ranger inline engines, totaled more than 200, with a further 40 license-built in France and later resold to the United States.

The Goose has proved a popular "back country" airplane in Canada, where remote lakes and waterways serve as landing sites. A number had executive interiors installed by United States corporations whose vice presidents liked to fish in the northern woods. The Widgeon originally seated four, but the G-44A was built with five seats, and some have been converted to seat six with the middle row of seats facing aft and their backs against the wheelwells. The McKinnon Turbo Goose is a modified version of the Goose featuring twin 680-shp Pratt & Whitney powerplants, increased fuel capacity, retractable wing floats, plus other improvements. McKinnon also produces a "Super Widgeon" powered by 270-hp Lycomings.

GRUMMAN "GULFSTREAM I" 1959–68

STANDARD DATA: Seats 10–24. Gross wt. 35,100. Empty wt. 21,900. Fuel capacity 1,550. Engines two 2,210-eshp Rolls-

Royce Darts. **PERFORMANCE:** Top mph 348. Cruise mph 288. Initial climb rate 1,900. Approach speed 128. Range 2,540. Ceiling 33,600. Takeoff run 2,550. Landing roll 1,525.

The Gulfstream I is a business transport designed to carry a crew of two with 10 to 14 passengers. Power is provided by twin Rolls-Royce Dart turboprop engines turning four-blade Rotol constant-speed propellers. The Gulfstream I first flew in 1958 and was the first United States twin-engine business aircraft to be certificated to cruise at 30,000 feet. A later version received certification as a 24-passenger variation for feeder-line use. Two Gulfstream offspring were enlisted for military use: the VC-4A was a U.S. Coast Guard transport and the TC-4C was an "avionics classroom" for the U.S. Navy.

GULFSTREAM "COUGAR" 1978–79

STANDARD DATA: Seats 4. Gross wt. 3,800. Empty wt. 2,588. Fuel capacity 80–118. Engines two 160-hp Lycomings. **PERFORMANCE:** Top mph 193. Cruise mph 184. Stall mph 72. Initial climb rate 1,160. Ceiling 17,400. Range 609–966. Takeoff distance (50') 1,850. Landing distance (50') 1,330.

Several twins were called "light" in 1977, but only two were genuinely entitled to the term: the centerline-thrust Cessna Skymaster and the Piper Seneca. Grumman American (now Gulfstream American) entered this uncrowded field late in January 1977 with its Cougar. Competition had grown considerably by 1979. Gulfstream's fuel-stingy four-place retractable is powered by a pair of 160-hp Lycoming engines, long favored by pilots for their 2,000-hour recommended overhaul period. A single-engine minimum control speed that is slower than its stall speed at maximum gross weight with flaps extended puts the Cougar amongst the safest multiengine airplanes.

Fully fueled and cruising at optimum altitude (8,500 feet) on 75 percent power, the Cougar can cover 970 miles while retaining a 45-minute reserve. The maximum-range power setting (45 percent power) yields 1,350 miles. Seating is for four, but the Cougar's cabin is easily large enough to accommodate six. Like single-engine models in the Gulfstream line, the light twin makes use of the same space-age metal-to-metal bonding construction techniques throughout. It also incorporates such sophisticated materials as a high-strength honeycomb "aluminum sandwich" slab that is extensively used in many high-performance military jets.

HAWKER SIDDELEY "DOVE" 1945

STANDARD DATA: Seats 117. Gross wt. 13,500. Empty wt. 6,325. Engines two 400-hp Bristol Siddeley Gipsy Queens. **PERFORMANCE:** Top mph 230. Cruise mph 187. Stall mph 74. Initial climb rate 1,135. Range 880. Ceiling 21,700.

Originally manufactured by the de Havilland Aircraft Company, the Dove took to the air for the first time in 1945. Since that time it has been made available in numerous variations, and its production was ultimately taken over by Hawker Siddely. The light transport is powered by two six-cylinder air-cooled Gipsy Queen engines, each putting out 400 hp. The first Doves housed 340-hp Gipsy Queens that were later replaced by 380-hp models. Doves in the United States were marketed as the Custom 800 executive carriers and were equipped with all the usual appointments.

The R.A.F. and Royal Navy versions were called the "Devon" and "Sea Devon," respectively. The Dove utilizes a unique cockpit/canopy design in order to provide extra headroom and increase visibility for the pilots. For a time, Riley Turbostream Corp. of Waco, Texas, built a remanufactured Dove called the Turbo Exec 400 powered by twin turbocharged fuel-injected engines. Another version of the Dove was produced by Texas Airplane Manufacturing Co. that employed 705-eshp turboprops and a stretched fuselage.

HAWKER SIDDELEY "HERON"

STANDARD DATA: Seats 14–17. Gross wt. 13,500. Empty wt. 8,484. Fuel capacity 494. Engines four 250-hp Bristol Siddeley Gipsy Queens. **PERFORMANCE:** Top mph 190. Cruise mph 183. Stall mph 75. Initial climb rate 1,075. Range 1,550. Takeoff distance (50') 2,424. Landing distance (50') 2,065.

The Heron is basically an enlarged version of the Dove. The original Heron Series I had fixed tricycle landing gear, but that plane was soon replaced by the Series II, which was equipped with retractable gear. The Heron is equipped to seat 14 passengers in single seats on each side of the central aisle. Two alternative arrangements allow for either 17 passengers with no toilet facilities or luxurious executive appointments for six to eight. Four 250-hp Gipsy Queen six-cylinder inline direct-drive unsupercharged engines are fitted with bracket-type constant-speed two-blade airscrews. The Riley TurboSkyliner was one modification of the Heron; four 290-hp Lycoming engines with turbochargers were used in place of the originals.

LOCKHEED P-38
"LIGHTNING"
1939–45

STANDARD DATA: Seat 1. Gross wt. 21,600. Empty wt. 12,780. Engines two 1,425-hp Allisons. **PERFORMANCE:** Top mph 414. Cruise mph 285. Range 460. Ceiling 35,000.

The P-38 Lightning was the first completely military aircraft built by the Lockheed Aircraft Corp. It was produced in no less than 12 versions differing from each other by engine size, use, and armament. The most numerous model was the P-38L powered by the same 1,425-hp engine as the P-38H, but with improved performance ratings. When needed, the engine could produce a "war emergency" 1,600 hp. A bulletproof window was installed, the radiators in the twin tail-booms were increased in capacity, and fuel tanks were placed in the leading-wing edges. The Lightning's armament included one 20mm cannon and four .50-caliber machine guns in the nose along with racks to carry up to 1,600 pounds of bombs.

The P-38 was used as a single-seat fighter, a light bomber, a rocket carrier, and a photographic/reconnaissance plane. It utilized a unique fuel system with separate fuel tanks for each

engine. Each tank was divided into three cells, all self-sealing. Two main tanks were in the center fuselage and one tank was in each leading wing edge. The entire system was interconnected so that fuel from any tank, except the outer wing tanks, could be routed to either engine.

LOCKHEED MODEL 10
"ELECTRA"/MODEL 18
"LODESTAR"

STANDARD DATA: Seats 8–14. Gross wt. 24,000. Empty wt. (avg.) 15,000. Power two 1,200-hp Wright Whirlwind or 2,000-hp Pratt & Whitney Wasp engines. **PERFORMANCE:** Top mph 321. Cruise mph 280. Initial climb rate 1,494. Range 2,800. Ceiling 22,950.

In the 1930s and 1940s, Lockheed built a series of twins that still remain active in the general aviation fleet. Approximately 20 Model 10 Electras and 30 small Model 12s remain registered in the United States, but several hundred of the big Model 18 Lodestars remain, many of which have been extensively modernized. Both of the smaller ships used Wasp Juniors; late models standardizing on the 450-hp version. The Electra carried 10 passengers, and the Model 12 carried six passengers, the latter being considerably faster with a 225-mph top speed and 202-mph cruise. The Lodestar and its derivatives were highly successful commercial carriers and served as the basis of the Hudson series of World War II lightweight bombers and the Model 37 Ventura patrol bombers. More than 100 converted Venturas also appear on the U.S. civil register. The Lodestar used 1,200-hp Pratt & Whitney Double Wasps.

LOCKHEED MODEL 12
"ELECTRA JR."
1936

STANDARD DATA: Seats 8. Gross wt. 8,650. Empty wt. 6,090. Fuel capacity 200. Engines two 420-hp Wright Whirlwinds. **PERFORMANCE:** Top mph 217. Cruise mph 220. Stall mph 65. Initial climb rate 1,460. Ceiling 21,300. Range 784.

Housing a crew of two and six passengers, the Model 12 was designed as a lighter, smaller version of the Model 10 Electra. It was first introduced in 1936 with a choice of two powerplants: twin 400-hp Wasp Juniors or twin 420-hp Wright Whirlwinds. The largest engine installed in later years was the 450-hp Pratt & Whitney Wasp Junior; this version of the lightweight Lockheed survives in the greatest numbers. In 1936, the Model 12 had the distinction of being the fastest airplane in its class (commercial twin) produced in the United States. The Model 212-A was a military version fitted with a dorsal gun turret and supplied to several foreign countries, including the Netherlands East Indies.

LOCKHEED "CONSTELLATION" 1943–58

STANDARD DATA: Seats 94. Gross wt. 133,000. Empty wt. 73,016. Fuel capacity 6,550. Engines four 3,250-hp Wright Turbo Compound radials. **PERFORMANCE:** Top mph 352. Cruise mph 331. Stall mph 99. Initial climb rate 1,140. Range 4,820. Ceiling 23,000. Takeoff distance (50') 4,600. Landing distance (50') 3,550.

The Lockheed Constellation L.749 variation was a long-range version of the earlier L.049. The earliest Constellation was initially flown in January 1943. Designed for commercial transport, the first Constellations were produced for the U.S. Air Force as C-29s. The first Constellation placed in airline service was the L.749 series. This aircraft differed from earlier versions in its increased fuel capacity and takeoff weight. The L.749 provided for 44 to 64 passengers and was powered by four 2,500-hp Wright Cyclone 18-cylinder air-cooled engines.

A stretched version of the L.749, the L.1049 Super Constellation, was introduced in 1950. Gross weight was increased substantially when the fuselage was expanded by 18.4 feet and 3,250-hp Wright engines were fitted. The stretched "Connie" held up to 91 passengers; with tip tanks, range was increased to 5,840 miles. The L.1049C model had structural modifications to allow a gross weight of 150,000 pounds, provided that more powerful engines were available. Lockheed built 286 Super "Connies," then followed with production of the L.1619 Starliner, the ultimate in Constellation design. With a range of 7,200 miles, the Starliner became popular on long international routes for TWA and Air France. Only 43 Starliner Constellations were built, and most of those were short lived, bowing out gracefully for the introduction of the jet age. Few Constellations of any of the models remain active today, most having been robbed of engines and left to rot away. One air-

plane has been the focus of a restoration group seeking to preserve a flying example.

LOCKHEED L.188 "ELECTRA" 1958–63

STANDARD DATA: Seats 74–98. Gross wt. 116,000. Empty wt. 57,300. Fuel capacity 5,520. Engines four 3,750-eshp Allison turboprops. **PERFORMANCE:** Top mph 448. Cruise mph 405. Stall mph 107. Initial climb rate 1,970. Range 2,770. Ceiling 28,400. Takeoff run 4,720. Landing roll 4,300.

Electras were produced in two versions, the L.188 and the L.188C. The L.188C was fitted with new tanks for increased fuel capacity and longer range. Initially developed according to specifications ordered by American Airlines to meet its need for a medium-range airliner, the Electra first took to the air in 1957. Most were equipped to carry about 74 passengers, but 98 could be packed in if necessary. Several crashes occurred in 1959 that caused Lockheed Corp. to make a few improvements including a stronger wing structure and engine nacelles plus thicker wing skins. The Electra is still used by many airlines around the world on their shorter routes.

MARTIN M-130, 156 1936

STANDARD DATA: (M-156) Seats 46. Gross wt. 63,000. Empty wt. 30,414. Engines four 1,000-hp Wright Cyclones. **PERFORMANCE:** Top mph 190. Cruise mph 156. Takeoff mph 70. Range 2,410. Ceiling 15,500.

The first aircraft to span the Pacific Ocean in scheduled commercial operations was the Martin 130 flying boat. It became famous in 1936 as the "China Clipper" when it was used to open Trans-Pacific service by Pan American World Airways. The giant Martin Clipper carried 10 passengers on overseas flights with a range of 3,200 miles. On shorter routes, its capacity was 48 passengers. The M-130 had a cruising speed of 163 mph, weighed 53,000 pounds when fully loaded, and a wingspan of 130 feet. The Model 156, a later development, was built for Pan American Airways. Lateral buoyancy was provided by seawings rather than conventional sponsons or outboard floats. Interior furnishings provided for either a maximum of 46 passengers or a more luxurious arrangement allowing for night sleeping for a reduced number of passengers. Four 1,000-hp nine-cylinder radial engines were mounted in nacelles on the leading edge of the center section.

MARTIN 202
1946–50

STANDARD DATA: Seats 40. Gross wt. 39,900. Empty wt. 26,930. Engines two 2,100-hp Pratt & Whitney. **PERFORMANCE:** Top mph 311. Cruise mph 286. Stall mph 76. Initial climb rate 2,200. Range 635. Ceiling 33,000. Takeoff distance (50') 1,565. Landing distance (50') 1,720.

The prototype of the Martin 22 flew in 1946. Power was provided by twin Pratt & Whitney 18-cylinder air-cooled radial engines capable of developing a normal output of 1,800 hp, 2,100 hp for takeoff or 2,400 hp with water injection. The engines turned Hamilton Standard three-blade reversible-pitch airscrews. The "Two-O-Two" was the first twin-engine airliner of postwar design to receive certification for airline use. Accommodations provided for a crew of three or four plus 36 to 40 passengers. Another version of the 202 was outfitted with larger fuel tanks to increase its range to 2,365. The subsequent 4-0-4 was introduced in 1950 with a fuselage 39 inches longer, slightly more powerful engines, and pressurization.

MITSUBISHI MU-2
1967–85

STANDARD DATA: (MU-2L) Seats 6–14. Gross wt. 11,575. Empty wt. 6,975. Fuel capacity 366. Engines two 715-shp AiResearch turboprops. **PERFORMANCE:** Cruise mph 340. Stall mph 115. Initial climb rate 2,630. Ceiling 29,600. Range 1,450. Takeoff distance (50') 2,170. Landing distance (50') 1,880.
STANDARD DATA: (MU-2M) Seats 7–11. Gross wt. 10,470. Empty wt. 6,090. Fuel capacity 366. Engines two 724-shp AiResearch turboprops. **PERFORMANCE:** Cruise mph 365. Stall mph 112. Initial climb rate 2,840. Ceiling 32,200. Range 1,680. Takeoff distance (50') 1,800. Landing distance (50') 1,600.
STANDARD DATA: (Solitaire) Seats 8–9. Gross wt. 10,470. Empty wt. 7,010. Fuel capacity 403. Engines two 727-eshp AiResearch turboprops. **PERFORMANCE:** Top mph 370. Cruise mph 360. Stall mph 84. Initial climb rate 2,350. Ceiling 33,500. Range 1,840. Takeoff distance (50') 1,800. Landing distance (50') 1,950.
STANDARD DATA: (Marquise) Seats 9–11. Gross wt. 11,575. Empty wt. 7,650. Fuel capacity 403. Engines two 778-eshp AiResearch turboprops. **PERFORMANCE:** Top mph

355. Cruise mph 340. Stall mph 87. Initial climb rate 2,200. Ceiling 29,750. Range 1,600. Takeoff distance (50') 2,170. Landing distance (50') 2,200.

MITSUBISHI "SOLITAIRE"

MITSUBISHI "MARQUISE"

The Mitsubishi MU-2 is a high-performance turboprop with an extraordinary top speed of 370 mph. It can cruise at an exceptional 360 mph. Much of this outstanding performance apparently is the result of rather compact overall dimensions for a turboprop twin. Before the earlier versions of the MU-2 had established a substantial penetration of the United States market, certain features of the aircraft were modified to make it more suitable and competitive. The Japanese manufacturer, Mitsubishi, made highly successful aircraft of its own design and of the designs of United States plane makers. The MU-2 is unusual in that it is one of the few high-wing turboprops.

Models B and D were powered by 605-eshp and seated 7–9 passengers. The Model F represented a boost in power to 705-eshp, and the Model G featured increased seating capacity for up to 11 people. In 1972, Models J and K were added to the line, both utilizing 724-eshp turboprops and offering seating arrangements that corresponded to Models F and G, respectively. The MU-2L is powered by 776-shp Garrett AiResearch turboprops and carries nine passengers. Its counterpart, the MU-2M, is a continuation of the Model K. The MU-2L and MU-2M were discontinued in 1976 and replaced by the MU-2N and MU-2P, which evolved into the Solitaire (standard fuselage) and Marquise (stretched fuselage), respectively.

The Solitaire is powered by two turboprops producing 727 eshp at maximum continuous power or 689 eshp at recommended cruise power of 96 percent RPM. Each engine turns a Hartzell 98-inch four-blade prop and provides a 475-fpm single-engine rate of climb when loaded to full gross. With a cabin pressurization differential of 6.0 psi, a sea-level cabin can be maintained up to 14,000. The Marquise, which is 6 feet 2 inches longer, is powered by two turboprops, each producing 778 eshp for takeoff or maximum continuous operation and 738 eshp at recommended cruise power. Single-engine rate-of-climb is 410 fpm at full gross, and cabin pressurization differential is the same as the Solitaire.

NORTH AMERICAN B-25 "MITCHELL"
1942

STANDARD DATA: Crew 6. Gross wt. 33,500. Empty wt. 21,100. Engines two 1,708-hp Wright Cyclones. **PERFORMANCE:** Top mph 303. Cruise mph 230. Landing mph 95. Initial climb rate 1,110. Range 1,350. Ceiling 24,200.

The prototype of the B-25 was flown for the first time in 1940. It and the first few B-25s off the production line had wings with a constant dihedral from the fuselage to the tips. Only after the 10th one were the wings redesigned with the characteristic gull configuration. Its armament included four .30-caliber machine guns, one in the nose and three amidships, and a single .50-caliber gun in the tail. The usual bomb load was 2,000 pounds with a maximum overload of 3,600 pounds. Several models of the B-25 were produced in subsequent years. The B-25A was fitted with self-sealing fuel tanks and armor for the pilot. The B replaced the midship and tailguns with electrically operated turrets. Each turret had two .50-caliber machine guns. The lower turret was remote-controlled.

The C and D were provided with automatic flight control equipment. The E and F were fitted with experimental deicing equipment. The G was the first model to carry a 70mm cannon. The H increased its armament to four .50-caliber guns in an armored nose and two pairs of .50-caliber guns on each side of the fuselage. The B-25J was produced in the largest numbers. It was the precision bomber version of the H; the crew increased to six to include a bombardier.

PILATUS BRITTEN-NORMAN
1967-86

STANDARD DATA: (Islander) Seats 10. Gross wt. 6,600. Empty wt. 3,738. Fuel capacity 137–196. Engines two 300-hp Lycomings. **PERFORMANCE:** Top mph 180. Cruise mph 164. Stall mph 49. Initial climb rate 1,130. Range 900. Ceiling 18,000. Takeoff distance (50') 1,100. Landing distance (50') 1,170.
STANDARD DATA: (Trislander) Seats 18. Gross wt. 10,000. Empty wt. 5,843. Fuel capacity 197. Engines three 260-hp Lycomings. **PERFORMANCE:** Top mph 180. Cruise mph 166. Initial climb rate 980. Ceiling 13,150. Takeoff distance (50') 1,950. Landing distance (50') 1,445.

The Britten-Norman Islander is a popular, fixed-gear twin for commuter/feeder work. With accommodations for up to nine passengers plus a pilot, the Islander can also be operated as a freighter carrying more than a ton of cargo. The high-wing twin has three forward opening doors, two on the port side and one on the starboard. Passenger baggage is stored in a large 30-

cu.-ft. bin behind the cabin with an access door on the port side. Delivery of the Islander began in August 1967, but the great number of orders from over 50 countries forced Britten-Norman to subcontract manufacture of a number of the miniairliners to the British Hovercraft Corporation. Others were produced in Romania by IRMA. Buyers were able to choose Lycoming engines: 260 or 300 hp. A Rajay turbocharging unit increased the Islander's twin-engine ceiling to 26,000.

A choice of wings was offered, so the plane could be fitted with the standard 49-foot-span wings or extended 53-foot wings, using raked tips and auxiliary fuel tanks. In 1970, Britten-Norman introduced an enlarged version of the twin-engine Islander with a third engine mounted high on the tail in a tractor position. The three engines were 260-hp O-540-E4C flat-sixes turning Hartzell two-blade constant-speed fully feathering propellers. Three versions of the Trislander are the BN-2A Mk 111-2 (a standard version with extended nose baggage compartment), the BN-2A Mk 111-3 (with an automatic feathering system for the props), and the BN-2A Mk 111-4 (with a rocket engine for additional thrust if an engine fails on takeoff). In 1978, Pilatus Aircraft Ltd. of Switzerland acquired all the assets of Britten-Norman Ltd., including the facilities on the Isle of Wright. Final takeoff took place in 1979.

PIPER "APACHE"
1954-66

STANDARD DATA: (160 hp). Seats 4–5. Gross wt. 3,800. Empty wt. 2,280. Fuel capacity 72–108. Engines two 160-hp Lycomings. **PERFORMANCE:** Top mph 183. Cruise mph 173. Stall mph 61. Initial climb rate 1,260. Range 1,260. Ceiling 17,000. Takeoff run 1,190. Landing roll 750.
STANDARD DATA: (235 hp). Seats 4–5. Gross wt. 4,000. Empty wt. 2,735. Fuel capacity 144. Engines 235-hp Lycomings. **PERFORMANCE:** Top mph 202. Cruise mph 191. Stall mph 62. Initial climb rate 1,450. Range 980. Ceiling 17,200. Takeoff run 830. Landing roll 880.

The Piper Apache is generally credited as being the first successful light twin. While Apaches are no longer in production, they were made in such great numbers that the supply is plentiful, and they should be plentiful for many years to come.

It all began in 1952 with the introduction of the Twin-Stinson, the first Piper of Stinson lineage to be produced since the Piper/Stinson Flying Station Wagon. It was powered by twin 125-hp Lycoming engines. The following year Piper introduced the PA-23 Apache, a vast improvement on the Twin-Stinson concept.

The Apache featured a conventional single rudder tail unit rather than the Twin-Stinson's twin-tail configuration, and power was boosted with the use of 150-hp Lycomings. The new Piper also utilized all-metal construction and retractable landing gear. In 1958, 160-hp engines were added, and in 1963, the 235-hp Lycoming became the standard powerplant to meet requirements for better single-engine performance. This later model was the first to sport swept tail surfaces and was quite similar to the Aztec of the same vintage, except for the Apache's smaller engines and shorter nose. The Apache became the "basic bread-and-butter" light twin for trainer use; quite a few have been modified with higher performance engines or other improvements. Not only are Apaches inexpensive to purchase, but operating costs are low.

PIPER PA-30/39 "TWIN COMANCHE" 1963–72

STANDARD DATA: Seats 4. Gross wt. 3,725. Empty wt. 2,210. Fuel capacity 30. Engines two 160-hp Lycomings. **PERFORMANCE:** Top mph 205. Cruise mph 194. Stall mph 69. Initial climb rate 1,460. Range 948. Ceiling 18,600. Takeoff run 950. Landing roll 700.

The Twin Comanche was a derivative of the single-engine Comanche and was introduced in 1963 as a replacement for the Apache H. Little was done to the original Comanche fuselage when it was adapted for use in the Twin Comanche in order to simplify tooling and assembly operations. The PA-30 was offered in four models: Standard, Custom, Sportsman, and Turbo. The latter differed in engine power, and the rest contained different interior appointments, electronics, and instrumentation. Piper announced the end of PA-30 production in 1970 and introduced a new PA-39 line. The new Twin Comanche was fitted with counterrotating props to simplify engine-out procedures. A starboard engine that was a mirror image of the port engine equalized single-engine performance of both powerplants. Piper also claimed improved flight characteristics due to a balanced airflow over each wing.

PIPER PA-44 "SEMINOLE"/ "TURBO SEMINOLE" 1978–82

STANDARD DATA: Seats 4. Gross wt. 3,800. Empty wt. 2,354. Fuel capacity 110. Engines two 180-hp Lycomings. **PERFORMANCE:** Top mph 193. Cruise mph 191. Stall mph 63. Initial climb rate 1,340. Ceiling 17,100. Range 898. Take-off distance (50') 1,400. Landing distance (50') 1,190. **STANDARD DATA:** (Turbo) Seats 4. Gross wt. 3,925. Empty wt. 2,430. Fuel capacity 110. Engines two 180-hp turbocharged Lycomings. **PERFORMANCE:** Top mph 224. Cruise mph 211. Stall mph 64. Initial climb rate 1,290. Ceiling 20,000+. Range 903. Takeoff distance (50') 1,500. Landing distance (50') 1,190.

In the light-twin field, Piper has always dominated the industry with the Apache, Twin Comanche, and Senecas. While the Seminole was more than a simple homogenization of existing Piper components, it did borrow most of its fuselage from the Arrow III, from what would be the forward firewall to the aft cabin bulkhead. The T-tail was actually developed on the Seminole first, but introduced on the Lance II. The wings are basically beefed-up versions of the semitapered Arrow III to within four feet of the tip. Like the Seneca II and the Navajo C/R, the Seminole uses counterrotating propellers for balanced thrust, and optional three-blade propellers in 1979 provided a quieter ride. Also in the same year, a propeller synchrophaser further reduced cabin noise levels.

Two 54-gallon fuel tanks are fitted in the engine nacelles. At 75 percent power and 7,000 feet, the Seminole cruises at 191 mph. When leaned to 65 percent, best-economy power cruise speed is 181 mph, and range is 898 miles with a 45-minute reserve. At 3,800 pounds gross, the Seminole weighs the same as Gulfstream American's Cougar, which flies between a pair of 160-hp engines; thus, each Seminole horsepower must heft only 10.6 pounds compared to the Cougar's 11.9 pounds/hp loading. From the beginning, Piper intended the Seminole as a relatively inexpensive alternative to high-performance singles.

In the middle of 1980, Piper introduced a turbocharged version of the Seminole powered by twin Lycoming TO-360 counterrotating engines. At 65-percent power economy cruise, the Turbo Seminole can travel at 194 mph over a distance of 920 miles burning fuel at a rate of 19 gph. Standard equipment includes a built-in oxygen system that consists of a rear-mounted bottle with easy-to-reach overhead outlets, night-lighted pressure gauge, oxygen masks, and a control-wheel mike button.

PIPER SENECA /II/III
1972–94

STANDARD DATA: Seats 6. Gross wt. 4,570. Empty wt. 2,839. Fuel capacity 98–128. Engines two 200-hp turbocharged counterrotating Continentals. **PERFORMANCE:** Top mph 226. Cruise mph 219. Stall mph 70. Initial climb rate 1,340. Ceiling 25,000. Range 627–903. Takeoff distance (50') 1,240. Landing distance (50') 1,860.

The Piper Seneca was first produced in 1972 and was sold alongside the Twin Comanche until 1973 when the latter was discontinued. More Senecas are powered by twin Teledyne Continental counterrotating engines with full-time turbocharging. The engines are rated at 200 hp at sea level and develop 215 hp at 12,000 feet, which allows for a 75-percent cruise speed of 218 mph. With the extended-range tanks, it's possible to travel 900 miles and arrive with a 45-minute fuel reserve. At economy power it's possible for the Seneca to get 55 seat miles per gallon with a load of six. Full-time turbocharging helps increase the Seneca's gross weight and climb performance. With turbocharging, power output is actually increased as the airplane gains altitude. Piper did away with the costly hydraulic wastegate system often found on other turbochargers and uses a low-cost fixed-bypass instead.

The ailerons were also lengthened to improve handling and slow-speed characteristics. A large utility door was located aft of the rear passenger door. The Seneca III added positive slow-speed characteristics. A new bobweight in the stabilator control system has heightened dynamic stability and reduced downspring forces. In the rudder, an antiservo tab helps increase directional stability and rudder effectiveness. The ailerons are long and aerodynamically balanced. Senecas also offered conference seating in a wide-ride cabin, measuring four feet in width. Five standard and four optional interior packages were available with several new aerodynamic speed enhancers.

Major additions in 1979 included optional three-blade propellers and a propeller synchrophaser. The three-blade props reduced cabin noise and vibration. The synchrophaser electronically seeks and maintains synchronization of the propellers to further reduce cabin noise levels. The Seneca II and III are certified for flight into known icing conditions when

equipped with the appropriate optional deice package, which was available for both two- and three-blade models. A heavy-duty brake option reduced landing distance over a 50-foot obstacle from a standard 2,110 feet to 1,860 feet.

PIPER AZTEC
1960–81

STANDARD DATA: (Aztec) Seats 6. Gross wt. 5,200. Empty wt. 3,183. Fuel capacity 137–177. Engines two 250-hp Lycomings. **PERFORMANCE:** Top mph 216. Cruise mph 206. Stall mph 62. Initial climb rate 1,400. Range 909–1,219. Ceiling 17,600. Takeoff distance (50') 1,980. Landing distance (50') 1,585.
STANDARD DATA: (Turbo) Seats 6. Gross wt. 5,200. Empty wt. 3,322. Fuel capacity 137–177. Engines two 250-hp turbocharged Lycomings. **PERFORMANCE:** Top mph 256. Cruise mph 247. Stall mph 62. Initial climb rate 1,470. Ceiling 24,000. Range 800–1,090. Takeoff distance (50') 1,980: Landing distance (50') 1,585.

The Piper Aztec grew from the Piper Apache design, and the two aircraft share the same model numerical designation of PA-23 established during the original Apache certification. The earliest versions of the Aztec differed only slightly in appearance from the Apache, although early Aztecs featured higher performance obtained from 150-hp engines. In 1964, these differences became greater with the Aztec C featuring fuel injection, a new configuration, and improved landing gear. The 1966 Aztec C was also the first model to offer turbocharging as an option.

The Aztec F is equipped with flap-to-stabilator trim interconnect to automatically retrim to neutral pitch-control pressures when the flaps are extended or retracted. Also, improved slow-flight characteristics give a more positive climb/approach control. The Aztec probably ranks as one of the most docile of the conventional low-wing light twins. While its maximum and cruise speeds compare favorably with the swiftest competitor, the short, thick wing permits slow and safe airspeeds. This means excellent short-field capabilities for critical situations. Both Aztecs can clear the equivalent of a five-story building in just 1,700 feet from brake release. The normally aspirated Aztec's 75-percent best-power cruise is 206 mph with a range of 1,134 miles and 45-minute reserve. Optional tanks stretch that range to 1,519 miles. The Turbo model has a cruise speed of 242 mph at 22,000 feet, 961 miles with standard fuel, or 1,318 miles with optional fuel.

PIPER AEROSTAR 600/601
1969–84

STANDARD DATA: (600A) Seats 6. Gross wt. 5,500. Empty wt. 3,735. Fuel capacity 165. Engines two 290-hp Lycomings. **PERFORMANCE:** Top mph 260. Cruise mph 253. Stall mph 85. Initial climb rate 1,800. Range 1,131. Ceiling 21,200. Takeoff distance (50') 1,950. Landing distance (50') 1,840.

STANDARD DATA: (601 B) Seats 6. Gross wt. 6,000. Empty wt. 3,958. Fuel capacity 165. Engines two 290-hp turbo-charged Lycomings. **PERFORMANCE:** Top mph 302. Cruise mph 296. Stall mph 89. Initial climb rate 1,460. Ceiling 30,000. Range 1,178. Takeoff distance (50') 2,490. Landing distance (50') 2,030.

STANDARD DATA: (601 P) Seats 6. Gross wt. 6,000. Empty wt. 4,056. Fuel capacity 165. Engines two 290-hp Lycomings. **PERFORMANCE:** Top mph 290. Cruise mph 296. Stall mph 89. Initial climb rate 1,460. Ceiling 25,000. Range 1,178. Takeoff distance (50') 2,490. Landing distance (50') 2,030.

PIPER "AEROSTAR" 600A

PIPER "AEROSTAR" 601B

The Aerostar is another outstanding design by Ted Smith. Originally built by the Ted Smith Aircraft Co. (a subsidiary of the American Cement Corp.), production began in 1967 on a limited basis. In 1969, the assets of the company were purchased by Butler Aviation International, which also acquired Mooney Aircraft Corp. one year later. The Aerostars built under this management were referred to as Aerostar Mooneys, but the project was soon suspended. In 1972 Ted R. Smith and Associates Inc. was formed, and production of the Aerostar executive transport resumed.

The Model 600 is powered by two 290-hp six-cylinder normally aspirated engines. Its basic structure consists of innovations to reduce weight and improve strength. The airframe contains only half as many components as that of many other comparable aircraft. Also, the Aerostar components are interchangeable with those of other sister ships. The Model 601 is the turbocharged version, and the 601P features pressurization. A slightly larger and more powerful development is designated the Aerostar 700 and is powered by two 350-hp Lycomings. Its speed is increased to 275 mph at sea level and its gross weight is boosted to 6,300 pounds. The latest 601B features wings extended 15 inches on each side to result in an increased gross weight, which has, in turn, boosted useful load by about 270 pounds.

Piper took over production of the Aerostars in 1979. The fastest Aerostar also has the distinction of being the fastest six-place general aviation piston twin in the world: the 601B. All three Piper Aerostars can attribute their performance to a sleek aerodynamically advanced design that features a radically aft-swept horizontal stabilizer, reduced and swept vertical stabilizer, midfuselage wings with trailing-edge taper, and an elongated pointed nose. Purchasing the Aerostars was a quick way for Piper to expand its twin lineup and fill the gap between the 250-hp Aztec and the 310- to 425-hp Navajos. For 1981, the Aerostar 601B and 601P were approved for flight into icing conditions to enhance their usefulness to corporate, commuter, and air-taxi operations.

PIPER PA-31 "NAVAJO"
1967–84

STANDARD DATA: (C) Seats 54. Gross wt. 6,500. Empty wt. 4,003. Fuel capacity 187. Engines two 310-hp turbocharged Lycomings. **PERFORMANCE:** Top mph 261. Cruise mph 248. Stall mph 81. Initial climb rate 1,220. Range 1,125. Ceiling 24,000. Takeoff distance (50') 2,290. Landing distance (50') 1,818.

STANDARD DATA: (CR) Seats 5–8. Gross wt. 6,500. Empty wt. 4,099. Fuel capacity 183–237. Engines two 325-hp turbocharged Lycomings, counterrotating. **PERFORMANCE:** Top mph 265. Cruise mph 253. Stall mph 80. Initial climb rate 1,220. Range 1,082–1,485. Ceiling 24,000+. Takeoff distance (50') 2,440. Landing distance (50') 1,818.

STANDARD DATA: (Chieftain) Seats 5–10. Gross wt. 7,000. Empty wt. 4,221. Fuel capacity 182–236. Engines two 350-hp turbocharged Lycomings, counterrotating. **PERFORMANCE:** Top mph 267. Cruise mph 254. Stall mph 85. Initial climb rate 1,120. Range 1,018–1,392. Ceiling 27,200. Takeoff distance (50') 2,780. Landing distance (50') 1,880.

STANDARD DATA: (Pressurized) Seats 6–8. Gross wt. 7,800. Empty wt. 4,842. Fuel capacity 192–242. Engines two 425-hp turbocharged Lycomings. **PERFORMANCE:** Top mph 280. Cruise mph 272. Stall mph 83. Initial climb rate 1,740. Range 995. Ceiling 29,000. Takeoff distance (50') 2,200. Landing distance (50') 2,700.

Taking to the air for the first time in 1964, the Piper Navajo was the first of a series of large executive airplanes to be produced by Piper. The Navajo is known for its excellent performance, easy-to-fly characteristics, and dependable systems. It was the first in its class to offer factory air-conditioning and the longest cabin interior available: 16 feet. Piper's exclusive engine nacelle was designed to house an extended shaft that put the prop blades well ahead of the cowling. This allowed the blades to bite into undisturbed air for greater propulsion efficiency.

Another feature of the Navajo was Altimatic V F/D, a truly automatic flight control at an economical price. To simplify flight operations, the Navajo's full-time turbochargers have no special controls, and safety devices prevent overboost or turbine overspeeding. The early Navajos were powered by 310-hp turbocharged Lycoming engines.

At one time, the Navajo family of aircraft included four models. The Navajo C, powered by 310-hp Lycomings, has accommodations for five passengers plus pilot in a standard or executive arrangement and up to eight persons with its optional commuter interior. The Navajo CR, introduced in 1975, offers stepped-up performance during takeoff, climb, and cruise, due to the increase in power brought about by its 325-hp Lycomings. Counterrotating three-blade props neutralize torque and eliminate the "critical engine." With either engine feathered, equal rate of climb and ceiling are assured. The Pressurized Navajo is powered by twin 425-hp Lycomings and provides executive class travel for six to eight. Optional pressurization was first offered in 1970.

The Chieftain's super-stretched 18-foot cabin allows it to perform as either an executive transport or light airliner. Powered by 350-hp Lycomings, it offers seating for six in an executive configuration or up to 10 in a commuter configuration. This latter aircraft was initially introduced as simply the PA-31-350 in 1973. The Navajo line was recertified for flight into icing conditions under newer more stringent standards in 1980. The Navajo family of aircraft was eventually trimmed to three models: basic Navajo, CR, and the Chieftain. Optional nacelle tanks on the Navajo CR and Chieftain in 1981 offered 54 gallons of extra fuel capacity, increasing the range of the Chieftain by 391 miles to a maximum range of 1,485 miles and boosting the range of the Navajo CR by 432 miles for a maximum range of 1,628 miles. The system incorporates two bladder tanks with nonicing fuel vents. The fuel simply gravity-feeds into main inboard tanks.

PIPER PA-31T "CHEYENNE" I/II/III/IA/XL 1975–85

STANDARD DATA: (I) Seats 6. Gross wt. 8,700. Empty wt. 4,907. Fuel capacity 300–382. Engines two 500-shp Pratt &

Whitney turboprops. **PERFORMANCE:** Top mph 290. Stall mph 83. Initial climb rate 1,750. Ceiling 28,020. Range 1,248–1,548. Takeoff distance (50') 2,444. Landing distance (50') 2,263.

STANDARD DATA: (II) Seats 6. Gross wt. 9,000. Empty wt. 4,983. Fuel capacity 382. Engines two 620-shp Pratt & Whitney turboprops. **PERFORMANCE:** Top mph 325. Stall mph 86. Initial climb rate 2,710. Ceiling 31,600. Range 1,588. Takeoff distance (50') 1,980. Landing distance (50') 2,480.

STANDARD DATA: (III) Seats 6. Gross wt. 10,500. Empty wt. 5,621. Fuel capacity 392. Engines two 680-shp Pratt & Whitney turboprops. **PERFORMANCE:** Top mph 330. Stall mph 92. Initial climb rate 2,450. Ceiling 30,500. Range 1,973–2,071. Takeoff distance (50') 2,320. Landing distance (50') 2,610.

STANDARD DATA: (1981 III) Seats 8–11. Gross wt. 11,000. Empty wt. 6,389. Fuel capacity 390–540. Engines two 720-shp Pratt & Whitney turboprops. **PERFORMANCE:** Top mph 336. Cruise mph 332. Stall mph 96. Initial climb rate 2,300. Ceiling 32,800. Range 1,415–2,106. Takeoff distance (50') 3,100. Landing distance (50') 2,650.

PIPER CHEYENNE I

PIPER CHEYENNE II XL

PIPER CHEYENNE III

Piper's first turboprop, the Cheyenne was based upon the Navajo airframe but powered by twin Pratt & Whitney turbines flat-rated at 620-shp and certified up to 680 shp. Flat-rating these free (as opposed to fixed-shaft) turboprops has the advantage of lowering gas temperature, prolonging engine life, lowering operating costs, and simplifying operation. Inside the cabin, six can sit in the comfort of a fully air-conditioned and pressurized atmosphere. The cabin can be maintained at sea-level pressure up to 12,300 feet. Further, the Cheyenne offers an extraordinary ratio between useful load and weight of the aircraft (a ratio of almost 1-to-1.2).

Piper expanded the Cheyenne line in 1978 to include three versions: the Cheyenne I, II, and III. The I and II models are powered by smaller engines than the original Cheyenne. The Model III retained the original 680-shp powerplant but was equipped with a new T-tail for improved stability by keeping the horizontal control surfaces clear of propwash. The Cheyenne III was introduced in late 1979 and was five feet longer than the Cheyenne II. The Cheyenne III is powered by twin flat-rated 720-shp Pratt & Whitney turboprops. It's the first turboprop to incorporate nacelle baggage lockers and the first to use Q-tip propellers that provide a quieter cabin and increased ground clearance.

Maximum range of the Cheyenne III is in excess of 2,300 miles, and maximum certificated altitude is 33,000 feet. A 6.3 psi differential will give the Cheyenne III a 10,000-foot cabin at 33,000 feet. Also in 1980, the Cheyenne I and II received a higher and 20-percent larger windshield. Headlining the 1981 changes among Piper turboprops were the addition of the Cheyenne II XL, introduced in late 1980, and extended range for the Cheyenne III. The Model II XL is a stretched version of the Model II and provides an additional two feet of cabin room for maximum passenger and pilot comfort. The Cheyenne III benefits from extended range as a result of an increase in gross takeoff weight. The increased rate allowance for Model IIIs equipped with optional nacelle tanks makes it possible to carry 30 extra gallons of fuel for a six-percent improvement in range.

PIPER PA-35 "POCONO"
1968–71

STANDARD DATA: Seats 11–18. Gross wt. 9,500. Empty wt. 4,900. Fuel capacity 200. Engines two 500-hp turbocharged Lycomings. **PERFORMANCE:** Top mph 242. Cruise mph 230. Stall mph 74. Initial climb rate 1,630. Range 650.

The Piper Pocono PA-35 was designed to serve as a high-capacity commuter airline, an unusually spacious executive aircraft, or a versatile cargo carrier. Its airframe incorporates a large circular hull measuring 88 inches in diameter. This large-capacity hull makes it possible to install a variety of seating configurations or handle bulky cargo loads. Passenger accommodations include seating for 17 plus pilot or 14 with toilet facilities. With a gross weight of 9,000 pounds, the Pocono has a useful load of 4,100 to 4,300 pounds. Its turbocharged 470-hp engines allow it to operate at cruising speeds in the 200- to 230-mph range, depending upon altitude. The Pocono is easily identified by a fuselage shape that retains a large diameter for a substantial distance aft of the wing trailing edge. There is minimal fuselage taper toward the tail.

RILEY "TURBO-ROCKET"
1962–69

STANDARD DATA: (Turbo-Rocket) Seats 6. Gross wt. 4,830. Empty wt. 3,000. Fuel capacity 140–170. Engines two 298-hp turbocharged Lycomings. **PERFORMANCE:** Cruise mph 302. Stall mph 65. Initial climb rate 2,200. Range 1,700. Ceiling 35,000. Takeoff distance (50') 985. Landing distance (50') 1,720.

STANDARD DATA: (Super 310 same as Cessna 310, except) Empty wt. 3,375. Optional fuel capacity 243. Engines two 310-hp turbocharged Continentals. **PERFORMANCE:** Top mph 311. Cruise mph 294. Initial climb rate 2,200. Ceiling 36,000. Range 1,700. Takeoff distance (50') 1,550. Landing distance (50') 1,790.

STANDARD DATA: (Super 340 same as Cessna 340, except) Empty wt. 3,868. Fuel capacity 243. Engines two 310-hp turbocharged Continentals. **PERFORMANCE:** Top mph 290. Cruise mph 270. Initial climb rate 1,800. Ceiling 32,000. Range 1,500. Takeoff distance (50') 1,950. Landing distance (50') 1,840.

STANDARD DATA: (Rocket 340 same as Cessna 340, except) Gross wt. 6290. Engines two 340-hp turbocharged Lycomings. **PERFORMANCE:** Top mph 300. Cruise mph 276. Initial climb rate 2,150. Ceiling 30,000. Range 1,451. Minimum field length 1,840.

STANDARD DATA: (Jet Prop 340 same as Cessna 340, except) Gross wt. 5,990. Engines two 620-ehp Lycoming turboprops. **PERFORMANCE:** Max cruise mph 345. Econ cruise mph 276. Initial climb rate 2,500. Ceiling 30,000. Range 1,382. Minimum field length 1,850.

STANDARD DATA: (Rocket Power 414 same as Cessna 414, except) Gross wt. 6,825. Engines two 400-hp fuel-injected Lycomings. **PERFORMANCE:** Top mph 300. Cruise mph 280. Initial climb rate 2,250. Ceiling 30,000. Range 1,308.

The Riley Turbo-Rocket and its two sister ships, the Riley 65 and the Riley Rocket, were all designed by the same Jack Riley who was the creative force behind the Riley Twin Navion in 1952. All aircraft are conversions of Cessna's popular 310, but in actuality, the modifications are extensive enough to warrant consideration as a completely new aircraft. The Turbo-Rocket was powered by twin 290-hp Lycoming engines equipped with the patented Riley dual turbo super-charger system for increased acceleration and power efficiency. No engine power is required to drive the turbocharger; no back pressure is imposed upon the engine. The maximum rated turbocharged operation does not exceed sea-level rated horsepower. Also added are airfoil nacelles for increased stability and "Free-flow" underwing exhausts.

The Riley 65 is powered by either twin 240-hp or 260-hp Continental engines. The Rocket houses twin 290-hp normally aspirated Lycoming engines. All aircraft are similar in structure and design. Other Riley conversions include:

- The Turbostream utilizing the 310-hp turbocharged Lycoming.
- The Super 310, a later version of the Turbostream.
- The Super 340, a Cessna 340 also powered by 310-hp turbocharged Lycomings.
- The Rocket 340, which has counterrotating 340-hp Lycomings to replace the standard Continentals.
- The Jet Prop 340 powered by two Lycoming turboprops flat rated at 620 ehp.
- The Jet Prop 421, a turboprop conversion of the Cessna 421 powered by the same Lycomings used in the Jet Prop 340.
- The Rocket Power 414 with power supplied by two 400-hp Lycomings.

ROCKWELL COMMANDER "SHRIKE" (AERO COMMANDER 500)
1958–80

STANDARD DATA: (Shrike) Seats 4–7. Gross wt. 6,750. Empty wt. 4,635. Fuel capacity 156. Engines two 290-hp Lycomings. PERFORMANCE: Top mph 215. Cruise mph 203. Stall mph 68. Initial climb rate 1,340. Range 950. Ceiling 17,500. Takeoff distance (50') 1,915. Landing distance (50') 2,235.
STANDARD DATA: (500U) Seats 4–7. Gross wt. 6,750. Empty wt. 4,635. Fuel capacity 156. Engines two 290-hp Lycomings. PERFORMANCE: Top mph 230. Cruise mph 215. Stall mph 68. Initial climb rate 1,340. Range 1,230. Takeoff distance (50') 1,375. Landing distance (50') 1,235.
STANDARD DATA: (500A) Seats 5–7. Gross wt. 6,250. Empty wt. 4,255. Fuel capacity 156. Engines two 260-hp Lycomings. PERFORMANCE: Top mph 228. Cruise mph 218. Stall mph 62. Initial climb rate 1,400. Ceiling 22,500. Range 1,225. Takeoff distance (50') 1,210. Landing distance (50') 1,150.
STANDARD DATA: (500) Seats 5–7. Gross wt. 6,000. Empty wt. 3,850. Fuel capacity 156. Engines two 250-hp Lycomings. PERFORMANCE: Top mph 218. Cruise mph 205. Stall mph 63. Initial climb rate 1,400. Ceiling 22,500. Range 1,100. Takeoff distance (50') 1,250. Landing distance (50') 1,350.

The Shrike Commander is the latest version of the well-known Aero Commander 500 with an extended nose and other features that deal mainly with styling and extras. The 500 is unsurpassed in many ways and enjoys pilot respect. The profusion of controls and gauges makes the Shrike appear complicated to operate when it is actually very easy by light-twin standards. Engines can be run at full throttle without restriction. All fuel tanks are interconnected, so no tank selection or crossfeeding is required. One-engine flight is managed without any particular fuss. The cabin is spacious, and there is freedom of movement almost on a par with an airliner.

The Shrike is a big plane with a span of about 50 feet, which makes it a handful on narrow taxiways and in tie-down areas for a pilot accustomed to small aircraft. Aero Commander was eventually bought by Rockwell International. One distinguishing feature of the Rockwell Shrike is its eyebrow windows for improved cockpit visibility. This business twin was certified in the utility category partly because the landing gear was designed for use on aircraft nearly twice the Shrike's gross weight. Such steady legs make landings on unimproved airstrips easy.

ROCKWELL COMMANDER 685
1972–74

STANDARD DATA: Seats 9. Gross wt. 9,000. Empty wt. 6,021. Fuel capacity 250–322. Engines two 435-hp Continentals. PERFORMANCE: Top mph 279. Cruise mph 256. Stall mph 86. Initial climb rate 1,490. Range 976–1284. Ceiling 27,500. Takeoff distance (50') 1,943. Landing distance (50') 2,312.

The Rockwell Commander 685 is a turbocharged high-performance piston-powered airplane designed to meet the business requirements of room and speed normally found in propjet aircraft. The seven- to nine-place 685 is powered by twin turbocharged 435-hp Continental engines with Hartzell constant-speed full-feathering three-blade props. It can cruise at speeds of 255 mph at 24,000 feet. Its cabin can be arranged in no less than 12 different ways and can maintain sea-level cabin pressure at altitudes up to 9,000 feet. The Commander's high wing, sturdy landing gear, and 75-knot stall speed allow it to operate from short unimproved strips. With 322 gallons of fuel, the 685 has a range of 1,731 miles with a 45-minute reserve. Its simple fuel system requires no crossfeeding. All fuel feeds into a central fuselage tank.

ROCKWELL TURBO COMMANDER 690A
1966–79

STANDARD DATA: (690B) Seats 7–10. Gross wt. 10,250. Empty wt. 6,195. Fuel capacity 389. Engines 700-shp Garrett AiResearch turboprops. PERFORMANCE: Top mph 330.

Cruise mph 321. Stall mph 89. Initial climb rate 2,849. Range 1,458. Ceiling 33,000. Takeoff distance (50') 1,666. Landing distance (50') 2,084.

STANDARD DATA: (681B) Seats 8–9. Gross wt. 9,400. Empty wt. 5,647. Fuel capacity 286–337. Engines two 605-shp AiResearch turboprops. **PERFORMANCE:** Top mph 290. Cruise mph 278. Stall mph 94. Initial climb rate 2,007. Ceiling 25,600. Range 1,062–1,315. Takeoff distance (50') 2,016. Landing distance (50') 1,200.

STANDARD DATA: (Hawk) Seats 8–10. Gross wt. 9,400. Empty wt. 5,783. Fuel capacity 286–337. Engines two 605-shp AiResearch turboprops. **PERFORMANCE:** Top mph 290. Cruise mph 280. Stall mph 94. Initial climb rate 2,025. Ceiling 25,000. Range 1,094. Takeoff distance (50') 1,975. Landing distance (50') 1,200.

The Turbo Commander first appeared in 1965 as a pressurized version of the Grand Commander. Power was supplied by twin 605-shp AiResearch turboprop engines, each driving a three-blade constant-speed reversible-pitch propeller. This model became known as the Turbo Hawk and was built until 1971 when it was replaced by the Turbo Commander 681B, another pressurized version similar to the Shrike Commander. A pair of 605-shp turboprops were still used until the 690 was introduced in 1972 with 717-shp powerplants.

The Turbo Commander cabin can be pressurized to 5.2 psi. the operational ceiling is 31,000 feet. Interior temperature is controlled by a high-volume climate system, and heated windshields provide maximum visibility in all weather conditions. The Turbo Commander is also certified for flight into known-icing conditions, and all deicing equipment is standard. While the 690A is just minutes slower that most business jets on a 900- to 1,000-mile business trip, fuel consumption is about 50 percent less.

The combination of reversible props, tough landing gear, high-wing, and 14-inch prop clearance are custom-tailored for short, rough landing strips. Engines that are flat-rated from 840 shp to a nominal 700 shp help the 690A climb directly to the best cruise altitude without lengthy step climbing. The 690B was offered in the Executive I and Executive II models. Many features that are usually considered optional are standard equipment in the Executive I, including avionics and cabin accommodations. The Executive II was for owners who wanted to select their own avionics and interior appointments.

ROCKWELL COMMANDER 700
1977–80

STANDARD DATA: Seats 6. Gross wt. 6,947. Empty wt. 4,704. Fuel capacity 210. Engine two 340-hp turbocharged Ly-

comings. **PERFORMANCE:** Top mph 254. Cruise mph 244. Stall mph 79. Initial climb rate 1,578. Ceiling 25,000. Range 1,214. Takeoff distance (50') 2,264. Landing distance (50') 2,154.

The pressurized 700 was designed and produced under a joint development agreement between Fuji Heavy Industries and Rockwell. The Model 700 was powered by two 340-hp Lycoming engines and was to be the first in a series of wide-bodied twin-engine aircraft to be produced by the two companies. The airframe subassemblies and major assemblies were to be manufactured by Fuji, and the aircraft were to be assembled by Rockwell using avionics, powerplants, brakes, wheels, and tires manufactured in the United States. The Rockwell 700 provides sea-level comfort up to 12,500 feet with a useful load of up to 2,283 pounds. Rockwell and Fuji Jet Industries terminated their agreement on the Commander 700 in December 1979.

ROCKWELL COMMANDER 840/980
1980–85

STANDARD DATA: (840) Seats 8. Gross wt. 10,325. Empty wt. 6,120. Fuel capacity 425. Engines two 717-shp Garrett AiResearch jetprops. **PERFORMANCE:** Cruise mph 335. Stall mph 86. Initial climb rate 1,000. Ceiling 31,000. Range 2,047. Takeoff distance (50') 1,830. Landing distance (50') 2,050.

STANDARD DATA: (980) Seats 8. Gross wt. 10,325. Empty wt. 6,271. Fuel capacity 425. Engines two 733-shp Garrett AiResearch jetprops. **PERFORMANCE:** Cruise mph 364. Stall mph 86. Initial climb rate 1,010. Ceiling 31,000. Range 2,079. Takeoff distance (50') 1,830. Landing distance (50') 2,150.

COMMANDER "JETPROP 840"

COMMANDER "JETPROP 980"

In 1980, Rockwell experienced an unprecedented increase in turboprop sales led by the Jetprop 980 and Jetprop 840. The former carries up to eight persons and is powered by Garrett TPE-10501K turboprops. It is characterized by a 309-

knot cruise, a 3,176-pound useful load, 5.2 psi pressurization, and enough fuel for a mission-efficient range of 2,040 nm with reserves.

The 840, powered by twin Garrett TPE-331-5-254K turboprops, boasts speeds up to 290 knots and a maximum range of 1,780 nm with reserves. Rockwell-developed high-technology sound control permits an easy conversation level in the cabins of both aircraft. Standard and custom cabin appointments permit the owner to outfit the interiors with hideaway tables, beverage servers, reclining chairs, telephones, and stereo systems.

ROCKWELL COMMANDER "JETPROP 1000" 1981

The 10-passenger Jetprop 1000 is the third in the series of winglet-tipped fuel-efficient models from Rockwell's General Aviation Division. This Commander represented the company's entry into the larger turboprop market because the 1000 has an 11,250-pound gross ramp weight. The 1000's 6.7 psi pressurization provides a 10,000-foot altitude cabin at flight altitudes up to an operation ceiling of 35,000 feet. In terms of fuel and mission efficiency, it is equal to Rockwell's 10,375-pound models.

Upon its announcement, the Commander 1000 was expected to cruise at 307 knots at 22,000 feet. Climb with both Garrett-AiResearch TPE 331-10 powerplants operating was supposed to exceed 2,800 fpm: single-engine climb 1,000 fpm. Range with normal reserves was predicted to be about 2,000 nm.

Rockwell claimed that the aerodynamic wing treatment, including winglets, supercritical propellers from Dowty Rotol, and new nacelle configurations, would reduce high-speed induced drag at altitude by as much as 17 percent over earlier models. The Model 1000's interior has separate crew, passenger, and lavatory compartments with additional space for refreshment consoles and a pressurized baggage area convenient to the passenger cabin.

SWEARINGEN MERLIN III 1969–81

STANDARD DATA: (III) Seats 8–11. Gross wt. 12,500. Empty wt. 7,400. Fuel capacity 648. Engines two 840-shp AiResearch turboprops. **PERFORMANCE:** Top mph 325. Cruise mph 288. Stall mph 96. Initial climb rate 2,530. Range 2,860. Ceiling 28,900. Takeoff distance (50') 2,150. Landing distance (50') 1,570.
STANDARD DATA: (IIIB) Seats 8–11. Gross wt. 12,500. Empty wt. 7,800. Fuel capacity 648. Engines two 900-shp

AiResearch turboprops. **PERFORMANCE:** Top mph 355. Cruise mph 345. Stall mph 95. Initial climb rate 2,825. Ceiling 32,500. Range 2,790. Takeoff distance (50') 2,790. Landing distance (50') 2,874.

In 1971, a Swearingen Merlin III placed first in the 5,851-mile transatlantic and transcontinental London to Victoria (British Columbia) air race. The Merlin III is an eight to 11 seat executive transport that offers near-jet speed while consuming less than half the fuel. It also claims the longest range (2,860 miles) of any business propjet with cruising speeds up to 325 mph. The luxury interior in the Merlin is one of the most lavish of any business airplane, and the cabin is a spacious 5 feet wide with 23 feet of usable length. Sea-level pressurization can be maintained up to 16,800 feet, and at 31,000 feet, the cabin atmosphere is still equivalent to that at 7,400. Power is provided by two AiResearch turboprops rated at 840 shp and equipped with single shafts, a negative torque sensing system, and full beta control reversing. Complete deicing gear is also provided.

Swearingen introduced the Merlin IIIB in September 1978 with new AiResearch powerplants producing 900-shp each and turning four-blade propellers equipped with synchrophasers. The IIIB has a 2,425-nm IFR range and a service ceiling of 32,500 feet. To the typical business user, this range capability permits a number of average 300- to 500-mile trips during one day without the need to refuel at out-of-the way places. Subsequent models featured a reshaped fairing between the wing root and fuselage for better aerodynamic flow and a new horizontal stabilizer leading edge contour for more efficient trim capability.

SWEARINGEN MERLIN IVA/"METRO II" 1971–81

STANDARD DATA: (Merlin IVA) Seats 12–15. Gross wt. 12,500. Empty wt. 8,200. Fuel capacity 554. Engines two 840-shp AiResearch turboprops. **PERFORMANCE:** Top mph 310. Cruise 276. Stall mph 99. Initial climb rate 2,400. Range 2,095. Ceiling 27,000. Takeoff distance (50') 2,050. Landing distance (50') 1,970.
STANDARD DATA: (Metro II) Seats 19. Gross wt. 12,500. Empty wt. 7,450. Fuel capacity 648. Engines two 940-hp AiResearch turboprops. **PERFORMANCE:** Top mph 294. Cruise 278. Stall mph 99. Initial climb rate 2,400. Range 2,150. Ceiling 27,000. Takeoff distance (50') 2,050. Landing distance (50') 1,970.

The Merlin IVA is an executive version of the Metro with 689 cu. ft. of pressurized cabin area and a large baggage

SWEARINGEN MERLIN IVA

compartment. It can carry up to 15 people in smooth over-the-weather flight with 7.0-psi pressurization. As an executive aircraft, it can be equipped with bar, galley, cabinets, and couch. Baggage capacity is 30 cu. ft. in the nose and 113 cu. ft. in the cabin. The Metro, introduced in 1974, is a 19-passenger turboprop airliner designed specifically for commuter service. It combines 300-mph cruise with a roomy air-conditioned pressurized cabin. A rear cargo door and optional movable cargo bulkhead provide passenger/cargo flexibility. Power is supplied by twin 940-shp turboprops.

WING "DERRINGER"
1965/1976/1981

STANDARD DATA: Seats 2. Gross wt. 3,050. Empty wt. 2,070. Fuel capacity 88. Engines two 160-hp Lycomings. **PERFORMANCE:** Top mph 232. Cruise mph 219. Stall mph 72.

Initial climb rate 1,700. Range 1,160. Ceiling 19,600. Takeoff distance (50') 1,180. Landing distance (50') 2,100.

The Wing Derringer was powered by twin 160-hp engines driving Hartzell constant-speed full-feathering propellers. The Derringer made use of unique manufacturing techniques with a patented wing construction utilizing a stretch-formed chemically milled exterior skin. All exterior surfaces were aerodynamically smooth. The Derringer's wings featured integral fuel tanks. After a delay of many years, it appeared as though the Derringer would reenter production in the early 1980s. The airplane's target was to be travelers who usually commuted in pairs. If the Model 1 had been a success, designer George Wing planned to add turbocharging and then possibly go to a four-place turbofan. Unfortunately, the Derringer never found its way into further production.

Section 3

Jet-engine aircraft

Since the airplane's inception, development of lighter, smaller, and more powerful propulsion has been a major focal point. During the 1930s, jet-engine technology really began to take shape with English and German scientists leading the way. With the advent of World War II, development was kicked into high gear in an effort to gain the upper hand against the respective foe. By that time, it had been well established that the secret to winning warfare was in air power. The side that controlled the skies would be the eventual victor. Unfortunately, usable jet-engine technology evolved too late during the war to be of any consequence.

As jet-engine research gained momentum, the power that was unleashed in these compact powerplants pushed aviation and aircraft into realms that were never even dreamed of when the Wrights first made that initial flight in 1903. Load-carrying capabilities have jumped to staggering levels and have effectively shrunk the size of our planet by making travel to faraway places commonplace. Speeds have escalated, thrusting aircraft faster than bullets travel, which allows us to truly chase the sun. In the following pages, we have attempted to show the end result of how the jet engine has developed into the aircraft power source of tomorrow and perhaps has made aviation's tomorrow come a little faster.

AEROSPATIALE SE 210 "CARAVELLE-12" 1959–81

STANDARD DATA: Seats 104–140. Gross wt. 127,870. Empty wt. 70,100. Fuel capacity 5,808. Engines two 14,500-lb. s.t. Pratt & Whitney turbofans. **PERFORMANCE:** Top cruise mph 505. Range 2,367. Takeoff run 8,070. Landing roll 4,985.

As one of the first jet airliners, the French-built twin-jet Caravelle has provided short- to medium-range service to more than 30 airlines since 1959. The first Model 1 Caravelles carry 61–80 passengers. Nine models later, the last produced, the Caravelle 12 carries 104–140 passengers and is almost 14 feet longer than the original design. Turbojet and turbofan powerplants have been provided by Rolls-Royce, General Electric, and Pratt & Whitney. Thrust increased from approximately 10,600 pounds to 14,500 pounds. As the Caravelle's capacities increased, not only was there the usual increase in fuselage strength and wing and tail surface areas, but the windshield area also expanded for greater cockpit visibility. An auxiliary power unit (APU) was added to provide for self-contained air-conditioning and other power needs while on the ground. Many Caravelles were equipped with the Aerospatiale/Lear-Seigler all-weather landing system.

AEROSPATIALE/HAC "CONCORDE" 1969–95

STANDARD DATA: Seats 128–144. Gross wt. 385,000. Empty wt. 169,000. Fuel capacity 30,985. Engines four 38,050-lb. s.t. Olympus 593 turbojets. **PERFORMANCE:** Top cruise mph 1,450. Initial climb rate 5,000. Range 4,020. Ceiling 65,000.

As a joint venture between the French company Aerospatiale and British Aircraft Corporation, the Concorde Super Sonic Transport (SST) took the lead in sales orders over its rival, the Russian TU-144. With costs, responsibility, and work on the Concorde divided fairly between the two partners, de-

liveries of the four-engine airliner started in 1974. Production finally got underway after extensive testing on prototypes over the first four years of development.

With the very look of speed, the shark-nosed giant was designed to cruise at Mach 2.05 for a maximum range of 4,020 miles. Accommodation for 128 economy-class passengers was available, although most airlines reduced seating and included a first-class section.

Construction of the Concorde prototypes began in 1965 with the first flight on March 2, 1969. Aerospatiale was responsible for the following Concorde items: rear cabin section, wings and wing control surfaces, hydraulic system, flight controls, navigation systems, and radio and air-conditioning systems. BAC was responsible for the rest of the airliner except engines and the autopilot. The Olympus engines were produced jointly by Rolls-Royce and SNECMA; the autopilot was designed jointly by Elliott in the UK and SFENA in France. Due to noise restrictions and environmental activist groups, flights into U.S. airspace were restricted during its transcontinental flight career.

AIRBUS A300 1974–94

STANDARD DATA: Seats 281–331. Gross wt. 302,000. Empty wt. 168,259. Fuel capacity 11,361–15,324. Engines two 51,008-lb. s.t. General Electric turbofans. **PERFORMANCE:** Top mph 582. Cruise mph 570. Approach mph 154. Range 1,000–2,190. Ceiling 35,000. Takeoff run 6,150. Landing roll 5,600.
STANDARD DATA: (A310) Seats 236. Gross wt. 330,690. Empty wt. 169,842. Fuel capacity 13,746. Engines two 50,000-lb. s.t. Pratt & Whitney JT9D-7R4E turbofans. **PERFORMANCE:** Top mph 557. Cruise mph 532. Ceiling 41,000+. Range 5,240. Takeoff distance 7,575. Landing distance 5,000.
STANDARD DATA: (A320) Seats 179. Gross wt. 158,730. Empty wt. 84,171. Fuel capacity 3,380. Engines two 25,000-lb. s.t. CFM CFM56-5 turbofans. **PERFORMANCE:** Top mph 560. Cruise mph 522. Ceiling 31,000+. Range 2,640. Takeoff distance 5,630. Landing distance 4,750.
STANDARD DATA: (A330) Seats 300. Gross wt. 450,000. Empty wt. 145,000. Fuel capacity 24,500. Engines two 64,000-lb. s.t. General Electric CF6-80C2 turbofans. **PERFORMANCE:** Top mph n/a. Cruise mph n/a. Ceiling n/a. Range 5,000+.

AIRBUS A300

AIRBUS A320

Production of the A300 Airbus is truly an international effort. Aerospatiale is responsible for building the nose section, flight deck, lower center fuselage, and engine pylons. Deutsche Airbus of Germany, made up of MBB and VFW-Fokker, manufactures the forward fuselage from the flight deck to the wings, the upper center fuselage, the rear fuselage and the vertical tail. Hawker Siddely makes the wings, while VFW-Fokker of the Netherlands manufactures the moving wing surfaces. CASA of Spain is responsible for the horizontal tail surfaces, landing gear doors, and the main doors. The General Electric turbofans are built under license by SNECMA and MTU. The A3OOB1 was the initial version powered by 49,000-lb. s.t. engines. The B2 is the first production model and the B4 is the long-range version of the wide-bodied transport. Standard all-tourist seating accommodations are for 281 passengers, and a high-density arrangement allows for 331 passengers.

BAC VC-10
1964–70

STANDARD DATA: (Super VC-10) Seats 131–174. Gross wt. 335,000. Empty wt. 155,380. Fuel capacity 23,257. Engines four 22,500-lb. s.t. Rolls-Royce turbofans. PERFORMANCE: Top mph 581. Cruise mph 550. Initial climb rate 2,300. Range 4,720. Ceiling 42,000. Takeoff distance (35') 8,300. Landing distance (50') 7,000.

The British Aircraft Corp. VC-10 is a long-range high-payload jetliner. With all four of its turbofan engines mounted in two sets below the tail and its horizontal stabilizer mounted on top of the rudder, the airliner presents a picture of strength and speed. First flown in June 1962, four years after the introduction of the DC-8 in America, the airliners initially went into commercial service on a route to West Africa from London. The airliner was built in Weybridge, England, by the former Vickers of Rome Aircraft. The four powerful Rolls-Royce engines, with a total of 18,000 pounds more than the International 707, permit a maximum takeoff weight of 312,000 pounds for the standard VC-10 and over one-third of a million pounds for the later Super VC-10. The Super VC-10 is 13 feet longer than standard and has an increased range and payload. Both the VC-10 and the Super VC-10 will cruise at 86 percent of the speed of sound.

BAC ONE-ELEVEN
1965–81

STANDARD DATA: (Series 500) Seats 97–119. Gross wt. 104,500. Empty wt. 54,582. Fuel capacity 3,705. Engines two 12,550-lb. s.t. Rolls-Royce turbofans. PERFORMANCE:

Top mph 541. Cruise mph 461. Stall mph 121. Initial climb rate 2,280. Range 1,705. Ceiling 35,000. Takeoff distance (35') 7,300. Landing distance (50') 4,720.

The BAC 111, built by the British Aircraft Corp., was designed for both short- and medium-range operation. This twin-engine airliner was first certified for United States operation in April 1964, and orders were placed by Mohawk, Braniff, and American Airlines. The first production model, the Series 200, flew for the first time in December 1963 and was powered by the smaller Rolls-Royce 10,330-lb. s.t. engines. The 300 Series were fitted with larger engines, greater fuel capacity, and a stronger landing gear. The 400 Series came equipped with a fuel dump system and was the first model certified for United States operation. The 475 series is fitted with low-pressure tires to permit operation on low-strength runways with surfaces of poorer grade. The final series, the 500, is a stretched version that can carry up to 119 passengers. Executive and freighter versions of the BAC 111 are also available. National Aircraft Leasing Ltd. offers a modified version for executive use; it features a redesigned interior.

BEECHCRAFT "BEECHJET 400"
1985–95

STANDARD DATA: Seats 8–10. Gross wt. 16,300. Empty wt. 10,620. Fuel capacity 732. Engines two 2,900-lb. s.t. Pratt & Whitney JT 15D-5 fanjets. PERFORMANCE: Top mph 530. Cruise mph 512. Initial climb rate 3,793. Ceiling 45,000. Range 2,044. Takeoff distance (50') 4,075. Landing distance (50') 2,830.

Formerly the Mitsubishi "Diamond" jet series, the manufacturing rights were bought up by Beechcraft in 1985 to actively oversee the production and marketing of the newly named "Beechjet" to fill out the Beechcraft line in the bizjet category. The aircraft remained largely the same through the merger and is a very formidable contender in its respective niche. With seating arrangements to accommodate up to eight passengers, all models contain lavatory facilities and substantial storage for charts and carry-on baggage. The Beechjet is capable of a maximum cruise of 530 mph at 29,000 ft. powered by two Pratt & Whitney JT 15D-5 engines flat rated at 2,900 lbs. of thrust each.

BOEING 707
1954–81

STANDARD DATA: (707-320C) Seats 219. Gross wt. 333,680. Empty wt. 146,000. Fuel capacity 23,855. Engines four 19,000-lb. s.t. Pratt & Whitneys. **PERFORMANCE:** Top mph 627. Cruise mph 600. Stall mph 121. Initial climb rate 3,550. Range 7,475. Ceiling 38,500. Takeoff distance (35') 10,900. Landing distance (50') 6,250.

The prototype of the Boeing 707 was the first jet transport to be completed and flown in the United States. Its first run was on July 15, 1954, and was known as the Model 367-80. Under the designation of KC-135, it was used by the U.S. Air Force for air-to-air refueling. In 1955, the Air Force permitted Boeing to produce commercial versions of the transport. These became known as the 707 and 720. The 707-120 was the first production version and was primarily designed for domestic use, though capable of over-ocean operations. Power was provided by four 13,000-lb. s.t. turbojets. The 707-220 followed with its 15,800-lb. s.t. Pratt & Whitneys. The 707-320 was the first intercontinental version and featured increased fuselage length and was powered by either 15,800- or 16,800-lb. s.t. turbofans. Accommodations provided for 195 to 219 economy class passengers. The usual arrangement was 14 first-class seats with 133 coach seats.

BOEING 720
1960–69

STANDARD DATA: (720B) Seats 153. Gross wt. 234,000. Empty wt. 112,883. Fuel capacity 14,880. Engines four 17,000-lb. s.t. Pratt & Whitneys. **PERFORMANCE:** Top mph 627. Cruise mph 611. Stall mph 116. Initial climb rate 4,080. Range 4,155. Ceiling 42,000. Takeoff distance (35') 6,450. Landing distance (50') 6,350.

Produced in two models, the 720 and the 720B, this intermediate-range Boeing transport looks very much like the Boeing 707. The first model, the 720, uses four Pratt & Whitney JT3D-7 turbojet engines rated at 12,500 pounds of thrust each. The 720B is powered by JT3D-3 turbofan engines with a thrust rating of 18,000 pounds each. The difference in thrust allows the 720B to carry almost 15,000 pounds more payload than the 720. One way to tell the difference between the 720 and its big brother the 707 is to count the over-wing emer-

gency-exit doors. The 707 has two doors over each wing, but the 720's smaller passenger capacity allows for only one over-wing door on each side. Another way to distinguish the two jetliners is to look at the engine housings. A large hump on top of the engine indicates the presence of a turbocompressor, or "TC," used for cabin pressurization and air conditioning. The 720 is equipped with two TCs; the 707 has three.

BOEING 727
1963–84

STANDARD DATA: (727-200) Seats 163–189. Gross wt. 184,800. Empty wt. 99,398. Fuel capacity 8,186–10,666. Engines three 14,500-lb. s.t. Pratt & Whitney turbofans. **PERFORMANCE:** Top mph 632. Cruise mph 592. Stall mph 122. Initial climb rate 2,500. Range 1,670. Ceiling 33,000. Takeoff distance (35') 9,340. Landing distance (50') 4,690.

The Boeing 727 was built with the intention of producing a short- to medium-range jet transport. It was flown for the first time in February 1963. A major innovation, compared with the company's earlier designs, was the choice of a rear-engine layout. The 727 is powered by three Pratt & Whitney turbofans; one is mounted at the base of the T-tail assembly. In all other respects, the 727 resembles the 707 and 720 series. Not only are the upper fuselages identical, but many parts are interchangeable. The 727-200 is the stretched version and was announced in 1965. It had a maximum capacity of 189 passengers compared to the earlier model's seating for 114. Optional turbofans rated at 15,000 lbs. s.t., 15,500 lbs. s.t., and 16,000 pounds s.t. can be installed. Since 1972, Hawker-de Havilland of Australia has been the sole supplier of rudders and main wing ribs for the 200 series.

BOEING 737
200/300/400/500
1967–95

STANDARD DATA: (737-200) Seats 115–130. Gross wt. 115,500–150,000. Empty wt. 60,210–138,500. Fuel capacity 5,151–5,311. Engines two 14,500-lb. s.t. Pratt & Whitney turbofans. **PERFORMANCE:** Top mph 586. Cruise mph 576. Stall mph 111. Initial climb rate 3,760. Range 1,545–2,370. Takeoff distance (35') 6,150–7,760. Landing distance (50') 4,300.

STANDARD DATA: (737-300) Seats 149. Gross wt. 135,000. Empty wt. 69,580. Fuel capacity 5,096. Engines two 20,000-lb. s.t. CFM CFM56-3b1 turbofans. **PERFORMANCE:** Top mph 565. Cruise mph 493. Ceiling 35,000+. Range 2,350. Takeoff distance 6,360. Landing distance 4,580.

The Boeing 737 is designed as a short-range twin-jet transport. Since its introduction in 1967, the 737 family has become the best-selling commercial jetliner in history with orders totalling more than 3,044 by 1993 from 159 customers in 81 countries. It differs in appearance from the 727 in that its two engines are mounted on the wings. The decision to build the 737 was announced in February 1965, and seven versions have been produced. The basic model 737-100 provides accommodations for 81–101 passengers plus baggage. The 737-200 has a lengthened fuselage and accommodates up to 130 passengers with standard seating for 115. In addition to the basic JT8D9 turbofan rated at 14,500 lbs. s.t., other available turbofans are the JT8D-15 (15,500 lbs. s.t.) and J18D-17 (16,000 lbs. st.). The 737 was offered in a business-jet version with a custom-styled luxury interior and a boosted fuel load.

BOEING 747
1969–95

STANDARD DATA: (747-200) Seats 385–500. Gross wt. 785,000. Empty wt. 363,068. Fuel capacity 51,000. Engines four 48,570-lb. s.t. Pratt & Whitney turbofans. **PERFORMANCE:** Top mph 608. Cruise mph 595. Stall mph 115. Initial climb rate 2,000. Range 6,218. Ceiling 45,000. Takeoff distance (35') 10,500. Landing distance (50') 6,170.
STANDARD DATA: (747-300) Seats 400+. Gross wt. 833,000. Empty wt. 384,480. Fuel capacity 44,953. Engines four 54,750-lb. s.t. Pratt & Whitney JT9D-7R4G2 turbofans. **PERFORMANCE:** Top mph 583. Cruise mph 564. Ceiling 45,000+. Range 5,650. Takeoff distance 10,450. Landing distance 6,920.

BOEING 747

BOEING 747-400

The Boeing 747, commonly known as the "Jumbo Jet," was designed to carry large numbers of passengers at low cost. The basic passenger design, designated 747-200 B, is capable of carrying up to 500 passengers in a 10-abreast seating arrangement. Basic accommodations are for 385 passengers made up of 48 first-class and 337 economy-class. The aircraft is powered by four Pratt & Whitney turbofan engines in pods and pylon-mounted to the underside of the wings. All current 747s can be outfitted with either 43,500-, 45,000-, 46,950-, 48,570-, or 49,000-lb. s.t. engines. A General Electric turbofan rated at 52,500 lbs. s.t. can also be used.

The first 747s to be delivered were received by Pan American in 1969. The 747-100 was the first model with a maximum takeoff weight of 713,000 pounds. Later, the 747-200 was introduced with a maximum takeoff weight of 775,000 pounds. The latest version, the 400, is the world's largest commercial jetliner and offers greater range, better fuel economy, and lower operating costs than previous 747 models. The 400's range is boosted 1,150 statute miles over the 300, giving a maximum range of 8,290 miles.

BOEING 757
1982–95

STANDARD DATA: Seats 239. Gross wt. 240,000. Empty wt. 126,250. Fuel capacity 9,370. Engines two 40,100-lb. s.t. Pratt & Whitney PW2037 turbofans. **PERFORMANCE:** Top mph 581. Cruise mph 528. Ceiling 40,000+. Range 4,570. Takeoff distance 10,450. Landing distance 4,600.

The Boeing 757-200 is a medium-sized, twin-engine jetliner designed for medium-to-long-range service and takes advantage of advanced technology for exceptional fuel economy, increased passenger comfort, lower noise levels, and elevated operating performance. The 757 also offers great versatility with a wide weight range (220,000–255,500 pounds) for greater payload capability. A freighter version is also available. The 757 is designed to carry 194 passengers in a typical mixed-class configuration and can carry an additional 45 passengers for charter service, which brings the 757's overall capacity between that of the 737-400 and the 767.

BOEING 767
1982–95

STANDARD DATA: Seats 290. Gross wt. 300,000. Empty wt. 176,200. Fuel capacity 13,900. Engines two 48,000-lb. s.t. Pratt & Whitney JT9D-7R4D. **PERFORMANCE:** Top mph 557. Cruise mph 528. Ceiling 40,000+. Range 6,210. Takeoff distance 5,650. Landing distance 4,750.

The 767 makes use of advanced technology to offer exceptional efficiency to help offset rising operational costs while bringing twin-aisle passenger-cabin convenience to routes that were never served by wide-bodied aircraft in the past. Because of its twin-aisle design, the 767 offers 87 percent of available seating to either be at a window or on an aisle. The 767ER is a freighter version scheduled for delivery to United Parcel Service in the fourth quarter of 1995. The freighter version has a basic maximum takeoff weight of 408,000 pounds. Future design studies have considered growth up to 412,000 pounds.

BOEING 777
1995

STANDARD DATA: Seats 375–400. Gross wt. 506,000–580,000. Empty wt. n/a. Fuel capacity 31,000. Engines two 77,000-lb. s.t. Pratt & Whitney PW4000 turbofans. **PERFORMANCE:** Top mph n/a. Cruise mph n/a. Ceiling 40,000+. Range 4,560–8,490. Takeoff distance n/a. Landing distance n/a.

The 777 is the newest advanced-technology jetliner to be offered by Boeing. The four-year development effort culminated on October 29, 1990, with the announcement that the 777 would indeed see production. Flight testing began in June 1994. Orders and options for more than 250 aircraft were tallied within a year. Boeing sees the 777 leading the way in jetliner technology well into the next century. The 777 is the largest twin fanjet yet to be brought into production. Different versions planned for production include engine options as well as a long-range version with 8,490-mile capability.

CANADAIR CL-600 "CHALLENGER"
1977–95

STANDARD DATA: Seats 8–13. Gross wt. 32,650. Empty wt. 13,567. Fuel capacity 14,610 lbs. Engines two 7,500-lb. s.t. Avco Lycoming ALF 502L turbofans. **PERFORMANCE:** Top mph 575. Cruise mph 554. Initial climb rate 2,412. Ceiling 49,000. Range 4,020. Takeoff distance (50') 5,000. Landing distance (50') 5,000.

In 1977, Canadair unleashed its Challenger series of business jets to go head to head with the Gulfstream II, Dassault Falcon 50, and the Lockheed JetStar II. Canadair's goal was to make a competitive aircraft that would fly faster, farther, more economically, and with greater comfort than its competitors. The end result would live up to all expectations except for the eventual upfront price tag, the belief being that operating costs were significantly less and would therefore offset any additional cost within time. The Challenger series is a highly luxurious jet that will accommodate most all business transportation needs. It has found its way into smaller airline and charter services. Most versions utilize the most advanced in avionics technology by offering an all-CRT display on the panel, commonly called a "glass cockpit."

CESSNA "CITATION"
1971–95

STANDARD DATA: (500 series) Seats 6–8. Gross wt. 11,500. Empty wt. 6,458. Fuel capacity 564. Engines two 2,200-lb. s.t. Pratt & Whitney JT15D-1 turbofans. **PERFORMANCE:** Cruise mph 400. Stall mph 98. Initial climb rate 2,900. Range 1,505. Ceiling 41,000. Takeoff distance (50') 3,275. Landing distance (50') 2,300.

STANDARD DATA: (I) Seats 7–8. Gross wt. 11,850. Empty wt. 6,464. Fuel capacity 564. Engines two upgraded 2,200-lb. s.t. Pratt & Whitney JT15D-1A turbofans. **PERFORMANCE:** Cruise mph 405. Stall mph 94. Initial climb rate 2,680. Ceiling 41,000. Range 1,535. Takeoff distance (35') 2,750. Landing distance (35') 2,300.

STANDARD DATA: (II) Seats 8–12. Gross wt. 12,500. Empty wt. 6,960. Fuel capacity 714. Engines two 2,508-lb. s.t. Pratt & Whitney JT15D-4 fanjets. **PERFORMANCE:** Cruise mph 443. Stall mph 93. Initial climb rate 3,500. Ceiling 43,000. Range 2,190. Takeoff distance (35') 2,400. Landing distance (35') 2,290.

STANDARD DATA: (III Transcontinental) Seats 10–15. Gross wt. 17,150. Empty wt. 9,441. Fuel capacity 990. Engines two 731 series Garrett AiResearch fanjets. **PERFORMANCE:** Cruise mph 540. Stall mph 107. Initial climb rate 5,325. Ceiling 45,000. Range 2,760. Takeoff run 3,990. Landing roll 3,400.

STANDARD DATA: (III Intercontinental) Seats 8–13. Gross wt. 19,100. Empty wt. 9,621. Fuel capacity 1,252. Engines two 731-series Garrett AiResearch fanjets. **PERFORMANCE:** Cruise mph 540. Stall mph 107. Initial climb rate 4,690. Ceiling 45,000. Range 3,450. Takeoff run 4,810. Landing roll 3,400.

CESSNA CITATION

CESSNA "CITATION" II

CESSNA "CITATION" III

CESSNA "CITATION" V

CESSNA "CITATION" VI

CESSNA "CITATION" VII

CESSNA "CITATION" X

The Cessna Citation was the first civilian jet produced by the giant of United States general aviation. Cessna had long experience with military-jet building under contracts for the T-37 (Tweety Bird) jet trainer. Deliveries of the Citation began in late 1971, and it became the best-selling business jet in the world. The first Citation's special features were a base price lower than most other executive jets and the capability of operating in and out of smaller airports. The Citation is powered by twin rear-fuselage-mounted Pratt & Whitney turbofans that produce 2,200 lbs. s.t. at takeoff and 2,090 lbs. s.t. maximum continuous at sea level. The main baggage compartment is located aft of the rear seats with additional storage in the nose. Entry is by a door and integral-step stairway at the left-hand forward end of the cabin.

The Citation I is similar in appearance to the original Citation but features an extended higher-aspect-ratio wing and upgraded JT15D1A engines. The result is that performance at operating altitudes is 11 percent faster, and the aircraft can reach those altitudes much quicker. For example, the Citation I can climb to 41,000 feet in about half the time required by the earlier Citation and is 38 mph faster at that altitude; range is boosted by about 100 miles.

Second in the lineup was the Citation II, a larger, faster, higher cruising, quicker climbing, and farther ranging version. It was intended for the company that sought the same Citation economy with a more spacious cabin and higher levels of fanjet performance. With different engines, fuel tankage, and a higher-aspect-ratio wing, the Citation II is not merely a "stretched" Citation I.

Third in the lineup is the Citation III with a new NASA-proven super-critical wing. It can climb to 41,000 feet in just 18 minutes and is available in two versions; the transcontinental has a range of 2,760 miles and the intercontinental has a range of 3,450 miles. The former is sufficient to fly nonstop across the United States. With double club seating, the Citation III can accommodate up to 10 passengers or up to 13 with forward-facing seats.

The most recent addition to the Cessna jet line for the 1990s and beyond is the Citation X.

CONVAIR 880
1960–64

STANDARD DATA: Seats 88–110. Gross wt. 184,500. Empty wt. 88,615. Fuel capacity 12,534. Engines four 11,650-lb. s.t. General Electric turbojets. **PERFORMANCE:** Top mph 615. Cruise mph 501. Stall mph 121. Initial climb rate 3,565. Range 3,995. Ceiling 41,000. Takeoff run 8,050. Landing roll 6,150.

First of General Dynamics jet passenger airplanes, the Convair 880 began to set speed records soon after its introduction into airline service. Still considered one of the fastest jetliners, the medium-range transport achieves much of its speed through the use of a comparatively thin wing swept back at 35 degrees. Powered by four General Electric engines, an advanced version of the engine used on the supersonic B-58 "Hustler" bomber, the 880 cruises at 615 mph. The combined power of the engines permits an airline operation at 89 percent of the speed of sound.

The FAA certified the 880 for airline use on May 1, 1960, and 15 days later Delta Airlines put the liner into commercial service. TWA began 880 service in January 1961. Airplane spotters can differentiate the Convair 880 from other transports with four engines mounted on the wings by its nose, engines, air scoops, and tail. The tip of the empennage is formed with a right angle, giving the appearance of being sharply cut off, unlike the smooth flare to a point as seen on other airliners. The engines of the 880 are narrow compared to those on Boeing or Douglas aircraft, and the long sleek nose comes almost to a point. Other features of the 880 not seen on the 707 or DC-8 are two air scoops located underneath the wing root on each side. These scoops collect air that is compressed and conditioned for cabin use.

CONVAIR 990
1962–64

STANDARD DATA: Seats 96–121. Gross wt. 244,200. Empty wt. 113,000. Fuel capacity 15,119–15,675. Engines four 16,100-

lb. s.t. General Electric turbofans. **PERFORMANCE:** Top mph 640. Cruise mph 610. Stall mph 105. Initial climb rate 3,250. Range 4,300–5,445. Ceiling 41,000. Takeoff run 5,350. Landing roll 4,770.

Nicknamed the "San Diego Anteater," the Convair 990 does look a bit like it's searching for ants on the runway. Its nose has a high slope from the cockpit window to the tip, which, aided by a short nose gear strut, gives the aircraft a rakish appearance. Easily identified in the air and on the ground by four large pods mounted on the top of the wing, the 990 was not widely accepted by United States airlines. Four General Electric aft-fan engines, each with a thrust of over 16,000 lbs., provide the push to cruise at 621 mph, the fastest airliner made when the FAA certification was awarded in 1962. But the G.E. engines were one reason for the small number of 990s purchased. Most airlines felt it was uneconomical to have an airplane that didn't use the almost-standard Pratt & Whitney engines.

The aircraft's long range came about by using the four wing pods as fuel tanks. The 24-foot-long pods, known as "antishock bodies," reduce the intensity of shock waves generated when an airplane reaches the speed of sound. In essence, they control the air flowing over the wing and therefore reduce drag. Although passengers enjoy the quiet and luxurious 990, the economics of having an oddball plane in the fleet has caused the disappearance of the airliner from the lucrative routes. Convair stopped producing passenger liners after making the 990, leaving that specialized business to Douglas and Boeing.

DASSAULT FALCON MYSTERE 10/20/30/40
1963–94

STANDARD DATA: (Falcon 20) Seats 8–14. Gross wt. 28,660. Empty wt. 15,970. Fuel capacity 1,385. Engines two 4,315-lb. s.t. General Electric turbofans. **PERFORMANCE:** Top mph 465. Cruise mph 405. Stall mph 95. Range 2,200. Ceiling 42,000. Takeoff distance (35') 3,790. Landing distance (50') 1,930.

The Dassault Mystere 20/Falcon is a lightweight, pressurized, twin-engine business jet that took to the air for the first time in 1963. Developed as a joint effort between Dassault and Aerospatiale, the aircraft was powered by two Pratt & Whitney turbojets rated at 3,300 lbs. s.t.; however, it was soon reengined with General Electric turbofans. Deliveries began in 1965, and Pan American placed the first orders. Several versions were built, differing by more powerful engines. The Series F featured high-lift devices (to improve takeoff and landing performance), more powerful engines, and increased fuel capacity. Standard passenger accommodations provide seating for 8 to 10, while a maximum of 12 to 14 is optional.

The Falcon 10 is merely a scaled down version of the Falcon 20F, and the model 10 seats four to seven in executive-like accommodations. Power is supplied by two 3,230-lb. s.t. Garrett AiResearch turbofans. The Falcon 30 and Mystere 40-100 are both further developments of the original airframe and provide for 30 to 40 passengers, respectively. The prototype for these aircraft first flew in 1973 and was fitted with 6,070-lb. s.t. Lycoming turbofans fed by a 1,400-gallon fuel supply.

DASSAULT-BREGUET FALCON 50
1977–94

STANDARD DATA: Seats 8–10. Gross wt. 36,600. Empty wt. 19,840. Engines three 3,708-lb. s.t. Garrett AiResearch turbofans. **PERFORMANCE:** Cruise mph 540. Range 3,450. Takeoff run 5,415. Landing roll 3,280.

Development of the new Falcon 50 began in May 1974. Some of the components of the Falcon 50 are modeled after those of the earlier Falcon 20, such as the front and center fuselage sections. The Falcon 50 makes use of advanced high-lift devices such as double-slotted trailing-edge flaps; the wings are designed to perform well at high Mach numbers. This luxurious jet is powered by three Garrett AiResearch turbofan engines, each flat-rated at 3,700 lbs. s.t. for takeoff. Two are mounted separately in pods on each side of the rear fuselage; the third is located in the tailcone with its intake just forward of the base of the vertical stabilizer. In order to make room for this third engine, the fuselage was lengthened and the fin was enlarged over that of the Falcon 20.

Accommodations are for up to 10 passengers in a spaciously appointed cabin, similar to other Falcons. The Falcon 20H was certified in May 1981 and made its first appearance as a certified aircraft at the Paris Airshow in 1981. Powered by Garrett ATF-3 engines, the Falcon 20H with its faster long-range cruise speed has a substantial increase in range.

DOUGLAS DC-8
1959–81

STANDARD DATA: (Super 61) Seats 259. Gross wt. 325,000. Empty wt. 148,897. Fuel capacity 23,390. Engines four 18,000-lb. s.t. Pratt & Whitney turbofans. **PERFORMANCE:** Top mph 600. Landing mph 153. Initial climb rate 2,270. Range 3,750. Takeoff run 9,980. Landing roll 6,140.

The DC-8 has been produced in eight versions that can be divided into two groups: the first five standard versions and the Super Sixty line. The Series 10, introduced in 1958, was powered by 13,500-lb. s.t. turbojets and had a 17,600-gallon fuel capacity. In the same year, the Series 20 flew with its 15,800-lb. s.t. turbojets and similar fuel tankage. The long-range Series 30 flew in 1959 and was outfitted with 16,800- or 17,500-lb. s.t. turbojets and 23,079 gallons of fuel. The long-range Series 40 was introduced in the same year and differed from the Series 30 by utilizing Rolls-Royce engines. The Series 50 was the first to employ turbofans: either 17,000 or 18,000 lbs. s.t.

The Series 61 was the first of the Super Sixties. It and the Series 62 were introduced in 1966 and were powered by 18,000-lb. s.t. turbofans. The 61 was the extended-fuselage version, and the 62 was designed for long-range routes. The Series 63 used 19,000-lb. s.t engines and combined the features of the 61 and 62.

DOUGLAS DC-9
1965–86

STANDARD DATA: (Series 50) Seats 139. Gross wt. 121,000. Empty wt. 55,700. Fuel capacity 3,700. Engines two 15,500- or 16,000-lb. s.t. Pratt & Whitney turbofans. **PERFORMANCE:** Top mph 576. Cruise mph 561. Initial climb rate 2,850. Range 932. Takeoff distance (35') 7,750. Landing distance (50') 4,720.

The DC-9 is the McDonnell Douglas short-to-medium-range rear-engine jet transport. It was designed to operate on shorter routes in and out of smaller airports. It stands lower to the ground than its larger brother, the DC-8. This facilitates passenger and baggage access at airports where there are no large terminal complexes with built-in loading and unloading ramps. The DC-8 Series 10 was the initial version powered by 12,250-lb. s.t. turbofans. The Series 20 was designed for operation in hot climates or high-altitude conditions with a longer wingspan similar to the Series 30 but with a shorter body similar to the Series 10. The Series 30 increased in size with 14,000-lb. s.t. turbofans and larger 150-passenger load. The Series 40 with still larger engines, 14,500 lbs. s.t., had increased fuel capacity and accommodations for up to 125 passengers.

DOUGLAS DC-10
1971–91

STANDARD DATA: (Series 30) Seats 225–380. Gross wt. 555,000. Empty wt. 263,500. Fuel capacity 35,800. Engines 49,008-lb. s.t. General Electric turbofans. **PERFORMANCE:** Top mph 610. Cruise mph 578. Landing mph 167. Initial climb rate 3,000. Range 4,375. Ceiling 34,000. Takeoff distance (35') 11,670. Landing distance (50') 5,960.

The Douglas DC-10 is designed to carry more passengers for less cost while still retaining a capability for utilizing airports with shorter runways. It is capable of operating economically over ranges from 300 to 3,200 miles. Standard seating accommodations are for 270 mixed-class passengers or for a maximum of 380. The DC-10 is powered by three turbofan engines; two are mounted on pylons beneath the wings and the third is installed above the aft fuselage at the base of the rudder. Four versions were built. The initial Series 10 had 40,000-lb. s.t. General Electric turbofans. The extended-range Series 20 had Pratt & Whitneys rated at 47,000 or 50,000 lbs. s.t. wet. The Series 30 was the same as the Series 20 but with General Electric engines. The Series 40 was a convertible freighter with Pratt & Whitney engines.

FOKKER F28
"FELLOWSHIP"
1980–90

STANDARD DATA: (4000) Seats 55–85. Gross wt. 73,000. Empty wt. 38,269. Fuel capacity 2,558–3,430. Engines two 9,908-lb. s.t. Rolls-Royce turbofans. **PERFORMANCE:** Top mph 380. Cruise mph 523. Threshold mph 127. Ceiling 35,000. Range 1,036–1,611. Takeoff distance 5,217. Landing distance 3,166.

In 1980, Empire Airlines, based in Utica, New York, entered into an agreement to purchase F28 Mk 4000s to put into commuter service. The F28 Fellowship short/medium-haul transport was originally developed by Fokker in collaboration

with other European aircraft manufacturers. Production is shared by Fokker-VFW of the Netherlands in association with MBB and VFW-Fokker in Germany and Short Brothers in Great Britain. The first flight of the prototype occurred in May 1967. The Mk 300 is similar to the Mk 400 with a short fuselage and seating for 65. The Mk 4000 is a long-fuselage version with high-density seating for up to 85. The Mk 6000 is a long version with slatted wings and seating for up to 79 passengers.

GATES LEARJET
1964–95

STANDARD DATA: (24E) Seats 6–8. Gross wt. 12,499. Empty wt. 7,025. Fuel capacity 715. Engines two 2,950-lb. s.t. General Electric turbojets. **PERFORMANCE:** Top mph 534. Cruise mph 507. Stall mph 101. Initial climb rate 7,220. Ceiling 45,000. Range 1,455. Balanced field length 3,000.

STANDARD DATA: (24F) Seats 6–8. Gross wt. 13,500. Empty wt. 7,130. Fuel capacity 840. Engines two 2,950-lb. s.t. General Electric turbojets. **PERFORMANCE:** Top mph 534. Cruise mph 507. Stall mph 101. Initial climb rate 7,100. Ceiling 51,000. Range 1,695. Balanced field length 3,297.

STANDARD DATA: (25D) Seats 8–10. Gross wt. 15,000. Empty wt. 7,640. Fuel capacity 910. Engines 2,950-lb. s.t. General electric turbojets. **PERFORMANCE:** Top mph 534. Cruise mph 507. Stall mph 107. Initial climb rate 6,300. Ceiling 51,000. Range 1,765. Balanced field length 3,937.

STANDARD DATA: (25F) Seats 6–8. Gross wt. 15,000. Empty wt. 7,575. Fuel capacity 1,103. Engines two 2,958-lb. s.t. General Electric turbojets. **PERFORMANCE:** Top mph 534. Cruise mph 507. Stall mph 107. Initial climb rate 6,300. Ceiling 51,000. Range 1,910. Balanced field length 3,937.

STANDARD DATA: (35A) Seats 6. Gross wt. 17,300. Empty wt. 9,110. Fuel capacity 931. Engines two 3,500-lb. s.t. AiResearch turbofans. **PERFORMANCE:** Top mph 534. Cruise mph 507. Stall mph 110. Initial climb rate 4,900. Ceiling 45,000. Range 2,785. Balanced field length 4,224.

STANDARD DATA: (36A) Seats 6. Gross wt. 18,300. Empty wt. 9,154. Fuel capacity 1,110. Engines two 3,500-lb. s.t. AiResearch turbofans. **PERFORMANCE:** Top mph 534. Cruise mph 507. Stall mph 110. Initial climb rate 4,525. Ceiling 45,000. Range 3,285. Balanced field length 4,784.

LEARJET 25D

LEARJET 36A

The Learjet is probably the most popular of all business jets. Indeed, the name is almost synonymous with executive jet aircraft. The first model 23 was delivered in 1964 with seating for eight. Two years later, the improved model 24 with airline transport category certification was introduced, and in 1968, a stretched 10-seat model 25 was offered. This aircraft has the most exceptional climb rate in its class. The model 23 at gross weight will climb at 6,900 fpm. All Learjets are approved for operation at 45,000 feet, and they have much better short-field performance than is common in this category of aircraft. One reason for the climb and takeoff advantage is weight: The model 23, which needs only 2,300 feet to clear a 50-foot obstacle at gross-weight takeoff, weighs only 6,500 pounds empty and grosses at 12,500 pounds. It can fly at 26,000 feet with one engine inoperable.

Models include the 24E with seats for six to eight and featuring a short balanced field length of 2,590 feet. The 24F has the same accommodations as the 24E but with a larger gross weight by 1,001 pounds. The 25D offers seating for eight to 10 and a 15,000-pound gross weight. The 25F with the same 15,000 gross weight has provisions for fewer passengers to allow for a greater fuel load. The 35A is a transcontinental version with a 17,000-pound maximum takeoff weight and a 2,858-mile range. The transoceanic 36A features a farther than 2,000-mile range and an 18,000-pound weight when fully loaded.

The 24- and 25-series models are powered by General Electric turbojets with 2,950 lbs. s.t. for takeoff. The 35A and 36A are outfitted with 3,500-lb. s.t. Garrett AiResearch turbofan engines; the 55, 55ER, and 55LR are all powered by two 3,700-lb. s.t. Garrett AiResearch turbofans and can carry 1,001 gallons of fuel for ranges up to 3,003 miles.

All models feature a new modified wing design to reduce approach speeds and balanced field length without sacrificing Mach cruise and range. In conjunction with the Dee Howard Co., Gates Learjet developed a new 20-series model with extended-range capabilities, the Century III 25G. The 30-series has its takeoff weight increased by 300 pounds and its landing weight boosted by 1,000 pounds. The TBO for the 20-series General Electric engine was increased from 4,000 to 5,000 hours.

GATES LEARJET
LONGHORN 54/55/56
1978–94

STANDARD DATA: (54) Seats 12. Gross wt. 10,216. Fuel capacity 825. Engines two 3,650-lb. s.t. Garrett AiResearch fanjets. **PERFORMANCE:** Top mph 550. Stall mph 100. Initial climb rate 5,380. Ceiling 51,000. Range 2,300. Balanced field length 3,190.

STANDARD DATA: (55) Seats 12. Gross wt. 18,500. Empty wt. 10,216. Fuel capacity 985. Engines two 3,650-lb.

s.t. Garrett AiResearch fanjets. **PERFORMANCE:** Top mph 550. Stall mph 100. Initial climb rate 5,020. Ceiling 51,000. Range 2,825. Balanced field length 3,900.

STANDARD DATA: (56) Seats 12. Gross wt. 20,000. Empty wt. 10,257. Fuel capacity 1,194. Engines two 3,650-lb. s.t. Garrett AiResearch fanjets. **PERFORMANCE:** Top mph 550. Stall mph 100. Initial climb rate 4,700. Ceiling 51,000. Range 3,380. Balanced field length 4,160.

STANDARD DATA: (28) Seats 12. Gross wt. 15,000. Empty wt. 7,895. Fuel capacity 697. Engines two 2,950-lb. s.t. General Electric turbojets. **PERFORMANCE:** Top mph 550. Stall mph 91. Initial climb rate 6,350. Ceiling 51,000. Range 1,525. Balanced field length 2,520.

STANDARD DATA: (29) Seats 10. Gross wt. 15,000. Empty wt. 7,824. Fuel capacity 786. Engines two 2,950-lb. s.t. General Electric turbojets. **PERFORMANCE:** Top mph 550. Stall mph 91. Initial climb rate 6,110. Ceiling 51,000. Range 1,780. Balanced field length 2,700.

Learjet's Longhorn series combines a revolutionary wing design, two of the most advanced engines introduced to the market, and 51,000-foot performance. The line of five aircraft has been designated the Learjet 28 and Learjet 29, both powered by General Electric turbojets, and the Learjet 54/55/56, and those three are powered by twin Garrett AiResearch fanjets. All the models are designed with a larger wing incorporating near-vertical winglets that have replaced the traditional Learjet tiptanks.

The wing's increased aspect ratio and super-critical winglets provide substantial aerodynamic improvements that in turn produce greater fuel efficiency and improved flight performance at high and low altitudes. The wing also has been responsible for significantly improved short-field performance. The balanced field length for the 28/29 series is only 2,520 feet and 3,520 feet for the 54/55/56 series. In addition, the 28/29 is able to climb from takeoff directly to 51,000 feet, something no other business jet can do.

GRUMMAN AMERICAN
GULFSTREAM II/III/IV
1967–94

STANDARD DATA: (II) Seats 19. Gross wt. 62,000. Empty wt. 29,000. Fuel capacity 3,478. Engines two 11,440-lb. s.t. Rolls-Royce Spey turbofans. **PERFORMANCE:** Top mph 588. Cruise mph 526. Stall mph 116. Initial climb rate 4,350. Range 3,886. Ceiling 43,000. Takeoff run 5,000. Landing roll 3,100.

STANDARD DATA: (III) Seats 19. Gross wt. 68,200. Empty wt. 38,300. Fuel capacity 4,400. Engines two 11,400-lb. s.t.

Rolls-Royce Spey turbofans. **PERFORMANCE:** Top speed
Mach 0.85. Cruise speed Mach 0.77. Stall mph 121. Ceiling
45,000. Range 4,330. Takeoff run 5,850. Landing roll 3,400.
STANDARD DATA: (IV) Seats 14–24. Gross wt. 70,200.
Empty wt. 33,400. Fuel capacity 4,340. Engines two 12,420-lb.
s.t. Rolls-Royce Tay turbofans. **PERFORMANCE:** Top mph
564. Economy cruise mph 528. Stall mph 121. Ceiling 45,000.
Range 4,952. Takeoff run 5,100. Landing roll 3,200.

The Grumman Gulfstream II was originally designed as
a business jet, but an enlarged version would eventually serve
in feeder airline use. This aircraft evolved from the Gulfstream
I turboprop, which was introduced in 1958. Production of the
swept-wing Model II version with turbofan engines started in
1965, and the first delivery was in 1967. It is one of the larger
business jets, with a gross weight of 58,000 pounds. It is also
one of the fastest, with a top speed of 589 mph, and it has a
long-range capability of up to 3,600 miles.

The Gulfstream II is at the upper limit of size for business jets. The next step upward is into the Boeing 737 or the
Douglas DC-9. It ranks as the fastest of the jets in this class by
a margin of nearly 10 mph. Engines are by Rolls-Royce. The
single-engine ceiling is 37,000 feet. The Gulfstream at gross
weight has a range of slightly fewer than 3,000 miles.

The Gulfstream III was certified in September 1980. Using a supercritical-wing design and powered by Rolls-Royce engines, the Model III has a long-range cruising speed of 555 mph.

The Gulfstream IV has seating for 24. Set at economy
cruise of 528 mph and at 45,000 feet, the G-IV is capable of
flying nonstop almost 5,000 miles.

HAWKER SIDDELEY
DH 125
1964–81

STANDARD DATA: Seats 9. Gross wt. 25,000. Empty wt.
12,700. Fuel capacity 1,416. Engines two 3,750-lb. s.t. Rolls-
Royce Viper 601 turbofans. **PERFORMANCE:** Top mph
524. Stall mph 94. Initial climb rate 4,500. Range 1,959. Ceiling 41,000. Takeoff distance (50') 5,350. Landing distance
(50') 2,550.

Beech Aircraft Corp. began to market the Hawker Siddeley DH 125 corporate jet in the United States in 1970. Desig-

nated the Beech Hawker, it featured a center cabin aisle re-
cessed below the level of the floor supporting the seats on either side. This gave sufficient cabin height to allow a passenger
stand-up headroom. Such an arrangement was made possible
by a wing attachment technique opposite to that used in the
Japanese-built Mitsubishi MU-2—the wing spar crosses the
fuselage above the cabin on the MU-2 and below the fuselage
on the Beech Hawker 125. On later models, a faired auxiliary
fuel tank is tucked up below the fuselage and behind the wing,
simultaneously improving streamlining and increasing range.

The DH 125 met with considerable success as a corporate executive transport because of its cruising range beyond
2,000 miles, its ability to operate above 41,000 feet, and its
ability to operate from runways that are fewer than 4,000 feet
long. The DH 125 was selected for production as a standard
Royal Air Force machine under the name "Dominie." Hawker
Siddeley continued to build the jet in Great Britain, but its
agreement with Beech was terminated in middle of 1975. Development of the DH 125 included a "700" series powered by
Garrett AiResearch TFE-731-3-1H engines.

HAWKER SIDDELEY
COMET 4
1956–64

STANDARD DATA: Seats 68–81. Gross wt. 162,000. Empty
wt. 74,900. Fuel capacity 10,686. Engines four 10,509-lb. s.t.
Rolls-Royce Avon turbojets. **PERFORMANCE:** Top mph
526. Cruise mph 500. Range 4,030. Takeoff run 6,750. Landing
distance (50') 6,880.

A BOAC Comet 4 was put into service Oct. 4, 1958, on
the world's first transatlantic jet service. It was a long-range
version of the basic Comet design and was easily recognized
by the projection of the two-pod fuel tanks on the leading edge
of each wing. Most of the flight tests for the Comet 4 were con-
ducted on the one and only Comet 3 built by Hawker. A great
deal of structural knowledge was gained through the unfortu-
nate accidents of four of the original nine Comet 1 models.
This knowledge was later tested on the model 3 and applied to
the model 4. Following the model 4, the Comet 4B was produced for intermediate-range flights carrying a high-density
passenger load. The model C-2 was a military cargo airplane
and was structurally far superior to the original Comet 1.

HAWKER SIDDELEY TRIDENT
1964–81

STANDARD DATA: Seats 97–180. Gross wt. 150,000. Empty wt. 81,778. Fuel capacity 6,750. Engines three 11,960-lb. s.t. turbofans and one 5,250-lb. s.t Rolls-Royce Spey turbojet. **PERFORMANCE:** Top mph 601. Cruise mph 533. Stall mph 129. Range 1,785. Takeoff distance (35') 8,900. Landing distance (30') 5,680.

The British triengine short- to medium-range jet first flew in airline service in 1964. It has been produced in four models. The 1E featured accommodations for a maximum of 115 passengers and was powered by 11,400-lb. s.t. turbofans. The 2F featured increased fuel capacity and takeoff weight and was fitted with 11,960-lb. s.t. turbofans. The 3B was a high-capacity short-haul transport with a lengthened fuselage and the addition of a 5,250-lb. s.t. turbojet in the tail for better takeoff performance. The Super 3B was an upgraded version of the 3B. The first automatic landing at London Airport was made with a Trident in 1965.

ILYUSHIN IL-62
1967–81

STANDARD DATA: Seats 168–186. Gross wt. 357,000. Empty wt. 146,390. Fuel capacity 26,420. Engines four 23,150-lb. s.t. Kuznetsov turbofans. **PERFORMANCE:** Top mph 560. Cruise mph 510. Landing mph 137. Range 4,160. Takeoff run 10,660. Landing roll 9,185.

Produced in Kazan, Russia (formally U.S.S.R.), the 174-foot airliner first flew to North America on September 15, 1967, on a maiden flight from Moscow to Montreal. It replaced the older TU-114, the giant turboprop transport, on Aeroflot's intercontinental routes. In July 1968, the IL-62 began service from Moscow to New York and would subsequently fly on all of Aeroflot's long-range flights, such as Moscow to Tokyo. The airliner is capable of carrying more than 150 passengers and reserve fuel on a flight of more than 4,800 miles. The basic IL-62 was announced in September 1962 during Khruschev's regime; the aircraft will carry up to 186 passengers, but other seating arrangements provide more leg room with 114 or 168 passengers.

Shown first at the Paris Air Show in 1971, the IL-62M-200 is a high-density version of the IL-62 that seats a maximum 198 economy-class passengers or 161 in a mixed-class configuration. The newer deluxe model has the same outer dimensions as those found on the basic model, but an additional fuel tank in the tail of the plane plus improved turbofan engines give the airplane greater range and payload.

Looking very much like the British VC-10, the IL-62 has its four engines horizontally mounted on the fuselage at the tail. Aside from airline markings, the easiest way to tell the two aircraft apart is by the two tail wheels mounted on a tall spindly strut just aft of the engine exhaust on the IL-62. The Russian airliner has two airflow guide vanes on the forward section of the fuselage, while the VC-10 builders placed air-guide vanes on the top wing surface.

ISRAEL COMMODORE/ WESTWIND JET
1968–81

STANDARD DATA: (Westwind) Seats 10. Gross wt. 20,700. Empty wt. 9,370. Fuel capacity 1,330. Engines two 3,109-lb. s.t. General Electric turbojets. **PERFORMANCE:** Top mph 428. Cruise mph 420. Stall mph 112. Initial climb rate 4,040. Range 1,600. Ceiling 45,000. Takeoff distance (35') 4,100. Landing distance (50') 3,400.

The Jet Commander originated with Aero Commander in 1967 when the Rockwell Company, then making Aero Commanders, was merged with North American. One of the conditions imposed by the government on approval of the merger was Aero Commander disposing of its jet. The purchaser turned out to be the State of Israel. Manufacturing in Israel began in 1969. The Jet Commander is one of the most frequently seen of the business jets along with the Lear. The Commander's appearance is also unique with a long, slim fuselage and short wings set far back. It is also one of the smaller of the business jets and one of the most economical to operate, consuming only about 225 gallons per hour.

The Jet Commander is so easy to control that flight controls are not boosted hydraulically and there is no artificial stall-warning device. In a deliberate stall, the Jet Commander will not fall off either wing. When Israel Aircraft industries began production of the Commodore Jet, several improvements were added: increased takeoff weight, strengthened landing gear, greater fuel capacity, and improved performance.

The 1123 Westwind features a longer cabin, auxiliary wingtip fuel tanks, more powerful engines, two additional cabin windows, and modified wing leading edges. The 1124 Westwind is the long-range version utilizing two 3,700-lb. s.t. Garrett turbofans with an 8,620-gallon fuel capacity.

LOCKHEED "JETSTAR"
1961–81

STANDARD DATA: Seats 10. Gross wt. 43,750. Empty wt. 24,178. Fuel capacity 2,660. Engines four 3,700-lb. s.t. Garrett AiResearch turbofans. **PERFORMANCE:** Top mph 552. Cruise mph 508. Stall mph 142. Initial climb rate 2,450. Range 3,189. Ceiling 38,000. Takeoff distance (50') 5,250. Landing distance (50') 3,900.

The Lockheed Georgia JetStar was the first of the executive jets and was uniquely the the only four-engine jet of its type in the class. In its time, the JetStar had many features that were normally found only on larger jet commercial airliners such as dual landing gear, thrust reversers, standing headroom throughout the cabin, backup systems, a complete lavatory, galley, and superior pressurization. This jet is rated as having a cruise speed of 550 mph. It can carry a maximum of 10 persons plus a crew of two. The Lockheed JetStar is capable of taking off on runways as short as 5,000 feet.

The JetStar II was introduced in 1974. The main difference between the two being the use of Garrett AiResearch turbofans flat rated at 3,700 lbs. s.t. instead of the previous 3,300-lb. s.t. Pratt & Whitney turbojets.

LOCKHEED L-1011 "TRISTAR"
1972–83

STANDARD DATA: Seats 250–400. Gross wt. 430,000. Empty wt. 222,941. Fuel capacity 23,814. Engines three 42,000-lb. s.t. Rolls-Royce three-shaft turbofans. **PERFORMANCE:** Top mph 500. Cruise mph 474. Stall mph 144. Initial climb rate 2,800. Range 2,677. Ceiling 42,000. Takeoff run 7,590. Landing roll 5,660.

Early in 1966 Lockheed became interested in the short- to medium-haul airliner market. The Model L-1011 was designed to enter this category with optimum payload-range performance and short-field characteristics. The Model L-1011 is powered by three 42,000-lb. s.t. turbofan engines, two of which are mounted in pods underneath each wing, and the third is located in the rear of the fuselage at the base of the tail unit. Fuel is carried in two integral wing tanks and an inboard tank. With a full load, the TriStar can travel a maximum of 4,467 miles. Accommodations provide for 256 passengers in a mixed coach and first-class arrangement or a maximum of 400 passengers in a high-density all-economy configuration.

MCDONNELL DOUGLAS MD80

STANDARD DATA: Seats 172. Gross wt. 140,000. Empty wt. 78,420. Fuel capacity 4,812. Engines two 18,550-lb. s.t. Pratt & Whitney JT8D turbofans. **PERFORMANCE:** Top mph 574. Cruise mph 505. Ceiling 35,000+. Range 1,563. Takeoff distance 7,250. Landing distance 4,860.

MCDONNELL DOUGLAS MD11

STANDARD DATA: Seats 315–400. Gross wt. 602,500. Empty wt. 277,000. Fuel capacity 32,185. Engines three 58,000-lb. s.t. Pratt & Whitney PW4358 turbofans. **PERFORMANCE:** Top mph 644. Cruise mph 588. Ceiling 45,000+. Range 5,010. Takeoff distance 10,100. Landing distance 6,470.

MITSUBISHI DIAMOND I/II/III
1979–94

STANDARD DATA: Seats 9–11. Gross wt. 13,890. Empty wt. 8,050. Fuel capacity 662. Engines two 2,500-lb. s.t. Pratt & Whitney Aircraft of Canada JT-15D-4 turbofans. **PERFORMANCE:** Top speed 0.78 Mach. Cruise mph 322. Minimum control mph 103. Range 1,800. Takeoff run 4,100. Landing roll 2,700.

The Diamond I was introduced in 1979 as Mitsubishi's example of a 500-mph-plus executive fanjet. Its twin turbofans are rated at 2,500 lbs. s.t. for takeoff and 2,375 lbs. s.t. for maximum continuous operation. The two Diamond I prototypes underwent 350 hours of test flying in Japan before their arrival in the United States for FAA certification. A Diamond offers the performance characteristics, cabin size, and comfort level of the medium-class swept-wing jets plus the low cost and economy associated with light jets and some turboprops. The Diamond I wing design, with its advanced flight control system of full-span flaps, wing spoilers, and T-tail empennage, is built for optimum performance.

MESSERSCHMITT MBB HFB 320 "HANSA"
1966–74

STANDARD DATA: Seats 15. Gross wt. 20,280. Empty wt. 11,960. Fuel capacity 1,099. Engines two 3,108-lb. s.t. General Electric turbojets. **PERFORMANCE:** Top mph 513. Cruise mph 420. Stall mph 111. Initial climb rate 4,250. Range 1,472. Ceiling 40,000. Takeoff distance (50') 2,740. Landing distance (50') 4,429.

The first production Hansa Jet flew on February 2, 1966, and received FAA certification on April 7, 1967. The Hansa 320 is one of the most distinctive commercial jet designs and is easily identified by the 15-degree forward sweep of the wings. Aerodynamically, the forward sweep of the wings performs the same function as the rearward sweep. The forward sweep forestalls the undesirable control problems that occur as the upper-wing airflow reaches transsonic speed by directing the airflow spanwise. The Hansa can be used as an executive transport or as a 15-passenger feeder liner. Production of the Hansa was initiated by Hamburger Flugzeugbau and carried the name of Messerschmitt-Bolkow-Blohm (MBB) when the two large German aircraft companies merged in 1969.

PIAGGIO-DOUGLAS PD408 VESPA-JET
1964–81

STANDARD DATA: Seats 5–9. Gross wt. 18,000. Empty wt. 10,650. Fuel capacity 984. Engines two 3,368-lb. s.t. Rolls-Royce Bristol Viper turbojets. **PERFORMANCE:** Top mph 529. Cruise mph 497. Stall mph 104. Initial climb rate 5,400. Range 1,332. Ceiling 45,000. Takeoff distance (35') 3,180. Landing distance (50') 2,990.

Under an agreement signed in 1961, Piaggio and Douglas Aircraft developed the PD-808 for military and commercial use. The aircraft was designed at Douglas and constructed by Piaggio. Taking to the air for the first time in 1964, the PD808 was powered by Bristol Siddeley Viper turbojets mounted on the sides of the rear fuselage. Accommodations provided for a crew of one or two, five passengers in individual seats, bar, toilet, and baggage space.

Power increased in 1966 to 3,300 lbs. s.t. The PD-808 differed from the original model by having larger tip tanks, a longer dorsal fin, and a forward-sliding nose fairing. By 1972, the aircraft was available in several versions: a five-seat executive version, a seven-seat executive transport, a six-seat version for the Italian Air Force, and one powered by 3,500-lb. s.t. AiResearch turbofans. Other PD-808s are powered by twin 3,360-lb. s.t. turbojets drawing from two integrated tanks of 511 gallons total capacity and wingtip tanks with 473 gallons total capacity.

ROCKWELL 75A "SABRE"
1963–83

STANDARD DATA: Seats 10. Gross wt. 23,000. Empty wt. 13,000. Fuel capacity 1,102. Engines two 4,315-lb. s.t. General Electric turbofans. **PERFORMANCE:** Top mph 563. Cruise mph 527. Stall mph 99. Initial climb rate 4,500. Range 1,938. Ceiling 45,000. Takeoff run (balanced) 4,900. Landing roll 2,525.

As the North American Sabreliner, this executive jet bore a famous name. It actually began as a military utility transport aircraft and dates back to 1958. The commercial version emerged in 1963 as the Sabreliner. In its civilian form as an airliner and business jet, the Sabreliner ranks as medium sized. Its speed by jet standards is modest with a cruise of 489 knots. Because the Sabreliner was originally designed as a military T-39 and was designed to meet military specifications, it shows unmistakable signs of its origin. It is larger and more rugged and powerful than jets that have been designed solely for civilian use. The Sabreliner has excellent climb performance and a ceiling of 45,000 feet. Rockwell also built a Sabre 60 jet equipped with 3,300-lb.-thrust engines. Both the 74 and 60 models were fitted with thrust reversers to aid in shorter landings and assist in braking on icy or wet runways.

TUPOLEV TU-144
1972–81

STANDARD DATA: Seats 140. Gross wt. 396,830. Empty wt. 187,400. Fuel capacity 209,440 lbs. Engines four 44,090-lb. s.t. Kuznetsov turbofans. **PERFORMANCE:** Top mph 1,550. Cruise mph 1,430. Operating altitude 59,000. Range 4,030. Takeoff distance (balanced) 9,845. Landing roll 8,530.

First shown at the 1965 Paris Air Show in model form, the TU-144 supersonic transport was the Soviet Union's ri-

val for the British-French Concorde. The TU-144 was reported to be in production with design changes incorporated following the tragic crash of a prototype aircraft at the 1973 Paris Show. With a configuration similar to the Concorde, the Russian jetliner also featured a nose that is lowered hydraulically 12 degrees to improve cockpit vision during takeoff and landing. The wings are of double-delta design with a sweep-back of 70–75 degrees on the inboard portions and about 40 degrees on the outboard sections. The main landing gear had 12 tires each (three rows of four). The tall, spindly nose gear had just two wheels. A maximum 130 passengers could be accommodated in an all-economy version, but the initial model seated 98 in mixed classes (18 in first class and 80 in tourist). On May 26, 1970, the Russian aircraft became the first commercial transport to exceed Mach 2.

Section 4

Homebuilt/kitbuilt aircraft

The inventor's spirit has long lived in the heart of the aviation enthusiast. The dream has been alive since perhaps the dawn of man, but building a flying machine that can carry man into the skies to fly with the birds has only recently become a reality. It is this spirit that drives certain individuals to plan and build their own aircraft regardless of the availability of production aircraft. There has never really been a lull in the experimental movement. As time and technology marches on, the movement continues to gain in popularity and numbers. Design innovation and the availability and use of the most technologically advanced materials has kept the fire burning while opening up doors to efficient structural and aerodynamic design.

During the energy crunch of the early 1970s, homebuilders began to focus strongly on efficiency aspects of design. Developing aircraft that could go farther, faster, and more economically than before. This led to the use of more innovative building materials and design. During the past decade, as product liability litigation clasped its icy grip around general aviation aircraft manufacturers, the inventive spirit was brought to new levels. In order for general aviation to survive, it needed to supply pilots with craft they could fly. The next generation of aircraft manufacturers was beginning to emerge. Innovative, efficient, state-of-the-art, and complex have become commonplace as new materials borrowed from the aerospace industry became the next fold in the evolution of the lightplane. As experimental aircraft became more specialized and complex, many the processes for the construction of homebuilt aircraft were simply out of reach for the average do-it-yourself type of aviation. The necessity for kits became apparent and a new industry was born. Now the more exotic is affordably common as the availability of these fine aircraft becomes greater.

Homebuilt/kitbuilt aircraft have kept general aviation alive during these trying times. The aircraft product has blossomed into new technology and persevered and again is enjoying new-found popularity as the sport aviator now has a multitude of avenues to choose from.

ACE MODEL D
"BABY ACE"

STANDARD DATA: Gross wt. 950. Empty wt. 575. Fuel capacity 17. Wingspan 26'5". Length 17'9". **PERFORMANCE:** Top mph 110. Cruise mph 100. Stall mph 34. Climb rate 1,200. Takeoff run 200. Landing roll 250. Range 350.

The Baby Ace is an ultralight monoplane specially designed for the amateur builder. It is the successor to the original Corben Baby Ace, which first flew in 1931 and was extensively redesigned in 1955 as the Model D. Baby Aces usually carry Continental engines rated from 65 to 85 hp and their performance is considered excellent by owners. Construction consists of a steel-tube fuselage, all-wood wings, and fabric covering.

ACE MODEL E
"JUNIOR ACE"

STANDARD DATA: Gross wt. 1,335. Empty wt. 809. Fuel capacity 22. Wingspan 26'. Length 18'. **PERFORMANCE:** Top mph 130. Cruise mph 105. Stall mph 65. Climb rate 500. Ceiling 10,000. Takeoff run 400. Landing roll 600. Range 350.

The Junior Ace is the successor to the Baby Ace. This side-by-side two-seater version is powered by a Continental 85-hp engine. Construction is the same, consisting of a steel-tube fuselage structure, all-wood wings, and fabric covering.

AERO DESIGN DG-1

STANDARD DATA: Gross wt. 2,300. Empty wt. 1,700. Fuel capacity 55–90. Wingspan 19'7". Length 20'4". Engines two 330-hp Mazda rotaries (automotive). **PERFORMANCE:** Top mph 400. Cruise 345. Stall mph 98. Climb rate (estimated) 3,000. Ceiling (estimated) 24,000.

The DC-1 holds the distinction of being the first custom-built Unlimited Class racer to be built in the United States after the 1930s. It is intended for competition in that category as recognized by the United States Air Racing Association of the National Aeronautic Association. The prototype flew in 1978, and in addition to racing, the design is adaptable for follow-on production of two-place, tandem seating models. It can be modified easily to a remotely piloted vehicle, and design studies examined the use of a J-85 series GE turbojet propulsion unit. The wings are the cantilevered midwing type with a fiberglass reinforced plastic spar, and the wings are foam-filled internally. The fuselage is a steel-tube frame covered by plywood and is fiberglass reinforced. Power is supplied by fore and aft Mazda rotary auto engines modified to produce in excess of 330 hp each. Both are fuel injected and turbocharged by custom AiResearch units and turn 68-inch three-blade propellers.

AERO DESIGNS
"PULSAR"

STANDARD DATA: Seats 2. Gross wt. 1,000. Empty wt. 460. Fuel capacity 17. Engine Rotax 582. **PERFORMANCE:** Top mph 160. Cruise mph 130. Initial climb rate 1,000. Ceiling 15,000. Range 500. Takeoff distance (50') 800. Landing distance (50') 800.

The Pulsar is a popular aircraft in the kitbuilding world for many of the right reasons. It's sleek, fast, economical, docile, and relatively inexpensive to build. The majority of the Pulsar kit is made of "prepreg" fiberglass, which enables the Pulsar to maintain its very high strength.

AEROSPORT "QUAIL"

STANDARD DATA: Gross wt. 792. Empty wt. 534. Fuel capacity 10. Wingspan 24'. Length 15'11". Engine 1600 cc Volkswagen. **PERFORMANCE:** Top mph 130. Cruise mph 115. Stall mph 48. Climb rate 850. Ceiling 12,000. Takeoff run 300. Landing roll 400. Range 230.

The Quail is a stubby little single-seater with an enclosed cabin that can be powered by a variety of engines, the KAM525 Kiekhaefer, the Volkswagen 1600, 1700, or a two-cylinder Franklin. This high-wing plane is constructed of all metal and stands on tricycle landing gear. The Quail's wing is similar to that of the Rail, and its tricycle gear can be equipped with optional wheel fairings.

AEROSPORT "RAIL"

STANDARD DATA: Gross wt. 730. Empty wt. 446. Fuel capacity 10. Wingspan 23'4". Length 15'9". Engine modified Volkswagen. **PERFORMANCE:** Top mph 90. Cruise mph 80. Stall mph 45. Ceiling 12,000. Range 220.

The original open-air pusher was powered by twin Aerosport 600 engines rated at 25 hp each. Top speed was about 80 mph, while standard cruise was cited at 66 mph. The Mk II Rail has been changed to take a modified Volkswagen powerplant mounted behind the pilot's head. The all-metal Rail seats only one, stands on a tricycle gear, and makes use of a T-tail assembly. The Rail has always emphasized easy construction, simplified tools, and economy of operation.

AEROSPORT "SCAMP"

STANDARD DATA: Gross wt. 768. Empty wt. 520. Fuel capacity 30. Wingspan 17'6". Length 14'. **PERFORMANCE:** Top mph 95. Cruise mph 85. Stall mph 45. Ceiling 12,000. Takeoff run 300. Landing roll 400. Range 150.

The Scamp can be used for limited aerobatics and is stressed to +3G and –3G. The single-seat biplane is powered by a modified Volkswagen engine (1,600 to 2,100cc) turning a fixed-blade prop. Standing on tricycle landing gear, it utilizes a T-tail, a lightweight-metal two-spar wing structure, and a semi-monocoque lightweight-alloy fuselage. First flown in 1973, the Scamp can be built from either plans or a kit.

AEROSPORT "WOODY'S PUSHER"

STANDARD DATA: Gross wt. 1,150. Empty wt. 630. Fuel capacity 12. Wingspan 29'. Length 20'5". **PERFORMANCE:** Top mph 98. Cruise mph 87. Stall mph 45. Climb rate 600. Takeoff run 300. Landing roll 400. Range 190.

The Woody's Pusher was designed by H.L. Woods, a former engineer at Bensen Aircraft Corp. He later founded Aerosport, Inc. to continue to market his plans and kits. The Woody's Pusher is a tandem two-seater with a parasol-mounted wing. The engine, which may range in power from 65 to 85 hp, is carried on top of the wing in a pusher fashion and turns a wooden fixed-blade prop. Originally the Pusher was designed with a fuselage of wood covered with plywood and fabric. Later models of the lightweight open-cockpit plane feature a steel-tube fabric-covered fuselage and metal leading edges on its wood-and-fabric wing assemblies. The landing gear is conventional.

AERO-SYSTEMS "CADET STF"

STANDARD DATA: Seats 2. Gross wt. 1,350. Empty wt. 785. Fuel capacity 25. Engine 85–115-hp Teledyne Continental. **PERFORMANCE:** Top mph 175. Cruise mph 130. Initial climb rate 800. Ceiling 15,000. Range 520. Takeoff distance (50') 800. Landing distance (50') 800.

The Cadet STF is a replica of the very popular Culver Cadet of the early 1940s; however, this new version of the Cadet has done away with some of the inherent long-term frailties that were found to affect the original. The most notable improvement is the steel-tube fuselage (STF) structure. Steel-tube construction has done away with the dreaded wood rotting problem that plagued the original all-wood fuselage and in turn has significantly increased strength and structural integrity without altering the racy lines of the aircraft. Overall weight has been reduced, increasing overall performance figures and providing more versatility within the finished product.

AIRCRAFT DESIGNS, INC. "STALLION"

STANDARD DATA: Seats 4. Gross wt. 3,200. Empty wt. 1,920. Fuel capacity 90. Engine 230-hp continental IO-520-G. **PERFORMANCE:** Top mph 239. Cruise mph 228. Initial climb rate 1,119. Ceiling 28,000. Range 1,540. Takeoff distance (50') 600. Landing distance (50') 500.

The Stallion is one of the newest in a string of composite kit aircraft that makes available advanced-technology building techniques to the kitbuilder. What makes the Stallion stand out among the other aircraft in its class is its method of construction, configuration, and multipurpose focus. Although the construction is largely composite, the Stallion utilizes a steel-tube inner fuselage cage that surrounds the cabin providing an integral high-strength central structure. The Stallion utilizes the same basic wing assembly as the Lancair IV and also uses the same retractable-gear mechanism. The configuration of the Stallion differs from the norm in its class by featuring a high-wing design that looks a lot like a Cessna 210 Centurion. The Stallion possesses a large payload capacity with quick-disconnect seats and features a large 72-×-36-inch rightside fuselage panel that removes for bulky cargo loading.

AIRCRAFT SPRUCE & SPECIALTY IAC "ONE DESIGN"

STANDARD DATA: Seats 1. Gross wt. 1,140. Empty wt. 740. Fuel capacity 18. Engine 160-hp Lycoming IO-320. **PERFORMANCE:** Top mph 184. Cruise mph 160. Initial climb rate 2,000. Ceiling n/a. Range 350. Takeoff distance n/a. Landing distance n/a.

One Design was designed by Dan Rihn to develop a single-class of affordable aerobatic competition for the sportsman pilot. The development of such a class would allow pilots to compete in a more controlled environment thus virtually eliminating the "have and the have nots" that seem to have infiltrated all competitions. This class will bring aerobatic competition back to the pilot's ability to perform well by providing a very capable aircraft—the same aircraft type—as an office to do his or her work. Construction is standard, mixed with steel-tube fuselage, wood wing, all fabric covered with aluminum forward of the cockpit, and fiberglass to cowl the engine.

ANDERSON "KINGFISHER"

STANDARD DATA: Gross wt. 1,500. Empty wt. 1,032. Fuel capacity 20. Wingspan 36'1". Length 24'. **PERFORMANCE:** Top mph 122. Cruise mph 90. Stall mph 42. Climb rate 550. Takeoff time 16 sec. Range 275.

Designer Anderson credits the highly popular VJ-22

Sportsman as the inspiration behind his own creation, the Kingfisher. There are many similarities between the two. Both use wings from production airplanes, the J-3 Cub in the case of the Kingfisher. Both use 100-hp Continental engines. General structural technique is similar with the fuselage built of spruce longerons and braces with mahogany plywood skin and an overall lightweight covering of fiberglass. The biggest difference is Anderson's choice of a tractor engine mounting rather than a pusher. In this way the engine mounts on its proper pads, the cooling, induction, and exhaust systems are standard, and there is no necessity to have the propeller custom made.

ARISTOCRAFT III

STANDARD DATA: Gross wt. 2,650–3,300. Empty wt. 1,600–1,800. Wingspan 36'10". Length 25'10". **PERFORMANCE:** Top mph 135. Cruise mph 120. Stall mph 55. Climb rate 500. Takeoff run 1,000. Landing roll 1,000. Range 800.

The Aristocraft was originally the last plane designed and built by the Waco Airplane Company. It was aimed at the cabin-class ultrasafe market. Terence O'Neil bought the rights, simplified its design, and increased its payload. The all-metal high-wing ship is one of the largest homebuilts and can seat up to six persons. Its speed and range make it excellent for cross-country travel.

AVIATION ADVENTURES "MUSTANG"

This ⅝-scale Mustang is fully aerobatic, seats two, and is powered by a Geschwender 351 CID Ford engine producing 300 to 350 hp. Because the original fighter had a liquid-cooled Rolls-Royce Merlin engine with an external radiator affixed to the underside of its fuselage, Aviation AdVentures chose to go the liquid-cooled route with the same automobile engine/reduction gear system by Geschwender Aeromotive that has been flying successfully on cropdusters. The conventional automobile distributor has been replaced with a dual magneto system that is more reliable and efficient during high engine RPMs. Likewise, the automobile carburetor has been exchanged for a Bendix PS SC pressure carburetor to meet the in-flight requirements of changing altitudes.

AVID AIRCRAFT, INC. MARK IV AEROBATIC SPEEDWING

STANDARD DATA: Seats 2. Gross wt. 1,150. Empty wt. 510. Fuel capacity 18. Engine 65-hp Rotax 582. **PERFOR-**

MANCE: Top mph 130. Cruise mph 120. Initial climb rate 850. Ceiling 12,500. Range 566. Takeoff distance 300. Landing distance 600.

Avid Aircraft's answer to a low-cost, lightweight, and high-performance lightplane for the sportsman pilot is the Mark IV series of aircraft. The Mark IV features quick-folding wings to allow towing to and from landing fields and makes for easy storage. Kits for this steel-tube and fabric aerobatic design come complete with the Rotax 582 engine.

AVID AIRCRAFT, INC. MARK IV HIGH-GROSS STOL

STANDARD DATA: Seats 2. Gross wt. 1,150. Empty wt. 510. Fuel capacity 14. Engine 65-hp Rotax 582. **PERFORMANCE:** Top mph 100. Cruise mph 90. Initial climb rate 1,000. Ceiling 12,500. Range 340. Takeoff distance 140. Landing distance 200.

Designed as a low-cost utility kit aircraft, the Mark IV High-Gross STOL has a longer wingspan and less fuel capacity in order to give the craft exceptional short-field capability with decent load-carrying capability. The Mark IV STOL kit includes the Rotax 582 engine.

AVID AIRCRAFT, INC. MAGNUM

STANDARD DATA: Seats 2+1. Gross wt. 1,750. Empty wt. 1,000. Fuel capacity 28. Engine 160-hp O-320 Lycoming. **PERFORMANCE:** Top mph 150. Cruise mph 130. Initial climb rate 1,800. Ceiling 12,500. Range 450. Takeoff distance 150. Landing distance 200.

The Magnum has the highest performance of all Avid Aircraft. The Magnum has the longest wingspan and uses a 160-hp O-320 Lycoming for its powerplant, which gives performance that far exceeds the rest of the Avid line. Construction is conventional standard of steel-tube and fabric.

BAKENG "DUCE"

STANDARD DATA: Gross wt. 1,500. Empty wt. 898. Fuel capacity 28. Wingspan 30'4". Length 20'9". Engine 120-hp Lycoming. **PERFORMANCE:** Top mph 145. Cruise mph 105. Stall mph 36. Climb rate 2,000. Ceiling 17,000. Takeoff run 150. Landing roll 150. Range 300.

The high-performance parasol-wing homebuilt received the "Outstanding New Design" and "Design Improvement" awards from the EAA in 1971. The V-strut braced wing utilizes both metal and spruce construction and is covered with fabric. The fuselage is also fabric covered but is built from steel tubes. The landing gear is the conventional tailwheel type, and the two seats are arranged in tandem fashion. Bakeng has also designed a biplane version of the Duce, called the Double Duce. Horizontally opposed and radial engines can be used.

"BANTAM"

STANDARD DATA: Gross wt. 790. Empty wt. 535. Fuel capacity 11.5. Wingspan 18'5". Length 13'9". **PERFORMANCE:** Top mph 140. Cruise mph 115. Stall mph 52. Climb rate 1,000. Takeoff run 550. Landing roll 500.

"BANTAM"

Designed for simple fabrication, Bill Warwick's Bantam uses no compound curves and very few simple ones. The cockpit area is a steel-tube structure taking all the wing, gear, and engine-mount loads. The remaining is wood construction with a plywood cover. The Bantam is a single-seat, low-wing plane that can use any engine from 65 to 100 hp.

BARNETT J-4B GYROPLANE

STANDARD DATA: Gross wt. 750. Empty wt. 441. Fuel capacity 15. Main rotor length 24'. Length 12'2". Engine 65-hp Continental. **PERFORMANCE:** Top mph 115. Cruise mph 90. Climb rate 700. Ceiling 14,000. Takeoff run 200. Landing roll 0–20. Range 250.

The Barnett Gyroplane is a single-place craft constructed of tubular steel, fiberglass, and aluminum. Its pusher prop is powered by a 65-hp Continental engine. The pilot sits inside an enclosed cabin shell. The J3-M differs from the J-4B by replacing the molded fiberglass cockpit nacelle with a flat-sided fabric-covered structure. Both models are fitted with tricycle gear and disc brakes.

BEDE BD-4

STANDARD DATA: Gross wt. 2,000. Empty wt. 1,080. Fuel capacity 57.6. Wingspan 25'7". Length 21'4". **PERFORMANCE:** Top mph 183. Cruise mph 174. Stall mph 63. Climb rate 1,400. Takeoff run 600. Landing roll 600. Range 750.

The BD-4 was designed to be built by homebuilders who have only simple shop tools and no previous experience; how-ever, the finished product is a high-performance, low-cost, all-metal aircraft capable of carrying two to four persons. Only the wings are constructed of fiberglass. The BD-4 can use any Lycoming engine from 108 to 200 hp. It is a high-wing enclosed-cabin design.

BEDE BD-5 "MICRO"

STANDARD DATA: Gross wt. 850. Empty wt. 410. Fuel capacity 35. Wingspan 17'. Length 13'3". Engine 70-hp Xenoah. **PERFORMANCE:** Top mph 230. Cruise mph 210. Stall mph 69. Climb rate 1,750. Ceiling 18,800. Takeoff run 820. Range 1,130.

The Bede Aircraft Co. did not compromise high performance and aerodynamic design for simple tooling and ease of construction in its snappy little single-seater BD-5. Originally it was powered by a 40-hp Hirth snowmobile engine and was fitted with a wingspan of 14 feet. The wingspan was stretched to 17 feet, and the more powerful Xenoah three-cylinder two-stroke engine was installed. The pilot is seated under a transparent canopy forward of the engine in a heated cockpit. The landing gear is fully retractable, and the entire fuselage/wing structure is constructed of lightweight alloy materials. The BD-5 was also designed in a jet version; the BD-5J became a regular airshow performer and appeared in a James Bond movie. BD Micro-Technologies, Inc. developed a support group to help builders of the BD-5s complete their projects.

BEDE BD-6

STANDARD DATA: Gross wt. 605. Empty wt. 375. Fuel capacity 21. Wingspan 21'6". Length 16'9". Engine 55-hp Hirth. **PERFORMANCE:** Top mph 140. Cruise mph 130. Stall mph 50. Climb rate 900. Ceiling 14,000. Takeoff run 600. Landing roll 400. Range 450.

The BD-6 was another in the line of "build-it-yourself" airplanes from Bede Aircraft. Essentially a single-seat version of the BD-4, it incorporated the same ease of construction aimed at the novice builder while utilizing the same German-made Hirth engine originally used in the BD-5. This high-wing all-metal ship seats one person in an enclosed cockpit and stands on nonretractable tricycle gear.

BEDE JET CORP. "BD-10"

STANDARD DATA: Seats 2. Gross wt. 4,140. Empty wt. 1,580. Fuel capacity 263. Engine 2,950-lb. s.t. GE CJ-610 fanjet. **PERFORMANCE:** Top mph 926. Cruise mph 620. Initial climb rate 30,000. Ceiling 45,000. Range 1,840. Takeoff distance (50') 600. Landing distance (50') 1,500.

One of the most significant developments in homebuilt aircraft, the BD-10 Jet has brought the fantasy almost within reach for most pilots: streaking around the sky in your own pocket-sized jet at Mach speeds and being the fastest kid on the block . . .. The aircraft is "almost within reach" because along with being the hottest kit on wings it also carries the highest price tag (approximately $250,000 less engine, avionics, and finishing products). As fast as this bird is, it still remains very docile at slow speeds and is simple enough for most competent prop pilots to fly. Construction of the BD-10 is made largely of state-of-the-art honeycomb-sandwich aluminum and is designed with all the seriousness of today's frontline fighter aircraft. The aircraft is complex in structure but not beyond the means of competent builders exhibiting the proper building skills. Build time is around 6,000 hours, and it does take a large amount of change, but in the grand scheme it is a lot less expensive to build and operate than most military-surplus jets available to the serious gen-av pilot.

BEETS G/B SPECIAL

STANDARD DATA: Gross wt. 925. Empty wt. 603. Fuel capacity n/a. Wingspan 25'. Length 16'4". Engine 70-hp Volkswagen. **PERFORMANCE:** Top mph 156. Cruise mph 120. Stall mph 35. Climb rate 2,000. Takeoff run 200. Landing roll 300. Range 600.

The G/B is a single-seat open-cockpit sporting plane featuring a high parasol-braced wing and conventional landing gear. While the fuselage is a fabric-covered steel-tube struc-ture, the wing is built with spruce spars and ribs, also fabric covered. All plans, kits, and components are sold through the Stolp Starduster Corp.

BENSEN GYROCOPTER

STANDARD DATA: Gross wt. 500. Empty wt. 247. Fuel capacity 6. Main rotor length 21'. Length 11'3". **PERFORMANCE:** Top mph 85. Cruise mph 60. Maximum climb rate 1,000. Range 100.

There are more than 20,000 active rotorcraft fans in the United States. Originator of the sport is Bensen Aircraft Corp. With purchase of the plans and component kits, it is possible to build a machine in a few weeks of spare time with only a drill press and a few wrenches. Bensen Gyrocopters can be towed behind a car or boat or flown under their own power. Float models are also available. The simple glider models are available as one- or two-seaters. The powered gyrocopters are available only with a single seater. Bensen's Gyrocopter is capable of climbing to 12,500 feet. (It is said that "for each 500 feet in altitude, the seat gets two inches narrower.") The powerplant is a 72- to 90-hp McCulloch.

"BIG COOTIE"

STANDARD DATA: Gross wt. 750. Empty wt. 467. Fuel capacity 12. Wingspan 18'9". Length 14'. **PERFORMANCE:** Top mph 140. Cruise mph 120. Stall mph 63. Takeoff run 500. Landing roll 500. Range 300.

The single-place "Powell Racer" is a tail-dragging biplane design constructed of wood, fabric, and tubular metal. Stressed for an engine up to 80 hp, the Big Cootie is usually pulled by a 65- to 80-hp Lycoming engine.

BIRDMAN TL-1

STANDARD DATA: Gross wt. 350. Empty wt. 100. Fuel capacity 4. Wingspan 34'. Length 20'. Engine 15-hp Tally Aircraft M.C.101 DT. **PERFORMANCE:** Top mph 60. Cruise mph 54. Stall mph 19. Climb rate 350. Ceiling 12,500. Take-off run 75. Landing roll 25. Range 200.

Because it is a mere 100 pounds, there is no debate that the Birdman TL-1 is an ultralight craft. In an effort to emphasize ease of construction and light weight, an unusual heat-shrink-to-fit synthetic mylar skin, Monokote, is used to cover the wood and foam-reinforced wings. The fuselage is a standard plywood monocoque, and the tail section is a V-type. While the main gear is attached underneath the wing, the pilot's legs and feet take the place of a nosewheel.

BOWERS "FLY BABY"

STANDARD DATA: Gross wt. 924. Empty wt. 605. Fuel capacity 16. Wingspan 28'. Length 18'10". **PERFORMANCE:** Top mph 120. Cruise mph 110. Stall mph 45. Climb rate 1,100. Takeoff run 200. Landing roll 300. Range 300.

For novice wooden-plane builders, the Fly Baby is one of the best. This single-place monoplane won the 1962 EAA competition for the best amateur plane with a C-85 engine. The Fly Baby has the distinction of being one of the most enduring designs in the homebuilt field. It has been tested with floats and in 1968 was fitted with biplane wings that were interchangeable with the single wings. The wings are a wooden structure covered with Dacron fabric, and the fuselage is a conventional plywood-covered wooden structure with a single open-cockpit seat. The 85-hp engine drives a two-blade fixed-pitch propeller. Options include a two-seat version and an enclosed canopy for additional comfort.

BOWERS "FLY BI-BABY"

STANDARD DATA: Gross wt. 970. Empty wt. 652. Fuel capacity 16. Wingspan 22'. Length 18'10". **PERFORMANCE:** Top mph 100. Cruise mph 90. Stall mph 40. Climb rate 900. Takeoff run 150. Landing roll 250. Range 275.

The Fly Baby is also distinguished by the fact that it can be flown as a monoplane or biplane, the biplane being named the Bi-Baby. The switch from monoplane to biplane wings takes only one hour.

BOWERS "NAMU II"

STANDARD DATA: Gross wt. 1,850. Empty wt. 1,200. Fuel capacity 32. Wingspan 33'. Length 21'6". Engine 125-hp Lycoming. **PERFORMANCE:** Top mph 140. Cruise mph 126. Stall mph 50. Climb rate 950. Ceiling 15,000. Range 500.

The Namu, named after the famous whale, first flew in 1975. The side-by-side two-seater features an enclosed canopy, dual controls, and conventional tail-wheel type gear. Its low-wing configuration is constructed from wood. Dacron fabric covers the wings and tail section. Plywood covers the fuselage except for the rear decking. Fuel is carried in one main tank just aft of the firewall.

BROKAW "BULLET"

STANDARD DATA: (Equipped with the 380-hp Lycoming.) Gross wt. 3,142. Empty wt. 2,033. Fuel capacity 47–92. Wingspan 24'4". Length 23'10". **PERFORMANCE:** Top mph 322. Cruise mph 293. Stall mph 86. Climb rate 2,100. Ceiling 28,000. Takeoff run (50') 2,000. Landing run (50') 1,300. Range 1,323.

Dr. D.F. Brokaw, with the aeronautical engineering help of Dr. Ernest R. Jones, developed a high-speed homebuilt with good cross-country capability, comfortable seating for two in tandem fashion, retractable gear, full-IFR capability, and the ability to perform aerobatics. The prototype took Brokaw seven years to build, but offspring can be built in about three years working from plans. The original powerplant was a 285-hp Continental, but the most common options are a 310-hp Continental or the 380-hp Lycoming turning a Sensenich three-blade propeller. Standard fuel capacity is 47 gallons with 45 auxiliary gallons, and all fuel is carried in the wings. The fuselage, wings, tail, and all control surfaces are built from lightweight alloy. The tricycle landing gear is retractable. The Bullet ranks as one the highest performance homebuilts in the skies because it is stressed to 6G for aerobatics with a 322-mph top speed and a service ceiling of 28,000 feet.

BUSHBY "MIDGET MUSTANG"

STANDARD DATA: Gross wt. 900. Empty wt. 580. Fuel capacity 15. Engine 125-hp Lycoming. **PERFORMANCE:** Top mph 225. Cruise mph 215. Stall mph 60. Climb rate 2,200. Takeoff run 400. Landing roll 750. Range 400.

Another sport plane inspired by the famous North American Mustang is the Bushby Midget Mustang. This little single-seater attains incredible speeds propelled by a Lycoming 125-hp powerplant. Its sleek appearance is due to its all-metal construction. Fabrication is simple. Only two simple wooden jigs are required, but Bushby can supply components or full kits that eliminate virtually all metal bending.

BUSHBY "MUSTANG II"

STANDARD DATA: Gross wt. 1,500. Empty wt. 975. Fuel capacity 25. Wingspan 24'4". Length 19'5". Engine 180-hp Lycoming. **PERFORMANCE:** Top mph 245. Cruise mph 220. Stall mph 63. Climb rate 1,800. Takeoff run 500. Takeoff run (50') 800. Range 650.

Kin to the Midget Mustang, this frisky tail-dragger seats two in side-by-side fashion and was developed as a cross-

country/sport plane. There is enough panel to accommodate full IFR gear. The Mustang II is a slightly slower ship using a 150-hp Lycoming engine. Construction is all metal with stressed skin. There are no complicated fittings or parts that require special skills or tools. The Mustang II can be equipped with the 180-hp Lycoming and Ray-Jay Ri 0325 turbocharger to offer 250-mph cruise with 30-gph economy.

CASSUTT SPECIAL II

STANDARD DATA: Gross wt. 800. Empty wt. 500. Fuel capacity 15. Wingspan 15'0". Length 16'. Engine 85-hp Continental. **PERFORMANCE:** Top mph 235. Cruise mph 180. Stall mph 62. Climb rate 2,000. Takeoff run 600. Landing roll 525. Range 600.

The Cassutt Formula I racer and sport plane is a little midwing flash that commonly wrings 200-plus mph out of 85-hp engines. This speedy ship performs well using either Continental, Lycoming, or Volkswagen engines. Its construction uses a welded steel-tube fuselage, wood wings, and flat spring-steel landing gear. Professionally designed for racing, aerobatics, and sport use, the Cassutt is stressed to positive 12 Gs.

CAVALIER

STANDARD DATA: Gross wt. 1,500. Empty wt. 900. Fuel capacity 34. Wingspan 26'10". Length 18'4". **PERFORMANCE:** Top mph 2,200. Cruise mph 155. Stall mph 50. Climb rate 1,500. Range 850. Landing roll 800.

The Cavalier is a sporty side-by-side two-seater of all wood-and-fabric construction. It can use any four-cylinder Continental, Lycoming, or Franklin engine up to 235 pounds in weight and rated in the 85- to 135-hp range. The ship can be switched from tricycle to conventional gear in a few minutes. Other options include wingtip fuel tanks and a third jump seat.

CHRISTEN "EAGLE II"

STANDARD DATA: Gross wt. 1,578. Empty wt. 1,025. Fuel capacity 26. Wingspan 19'11". Length 18'6". Engine 200-hp Lycoming. **PERFORMANCE:** Top mph 184. Cruise mph 165. Stall mph 58. Climb rate 2,100. Ceiling 17,000. Takeoff distance (50') 1,250. Landing distance (50') 1,575. Range 380.

The Eagle II is a two-seat sporting biplane that can be used for unlimited-class aerobatics as well as for advanced training. The Eagle II and II-F have a full electrical system (starter-alternator-battery). The Eagle II uses a 200-hp engine with constant-speed propeller. The Eagle II-F uses a 260-hp engine with fixed-pitch propeller. Characterized by their startling paint scheme, the Eagles feature swept symmetrical wings, a

CHRISTEN "EAGLE II"

strong fuselage, and a blown canopy that covers both cockpits. With a roll rate of 187 degrees/second and a power loading of 7.89 lbs/hp, the Eagle is a strong performer. The fuselage is built from welded steel tube and covered with metal back to the rear cockpit, then fabric is the rest of the way aft. The fabric-covered wings are built with aluminum ribbing over spruce spars. The amateur builder has the option of buying 25 kits in sequence, starting with the ailerons, to test his or her dexterity. The intention of the Eagle is to provide the homebuilder with an easy-to-build unlimited-aerobatic airplane.

CONDOR K-10 "SHOESTRING"

STANDARD DATA: Gross wt. 800. Empty wt. 525. Fuel capacity 10. Wingspan 19'. Length 17'8". **PERFORMANCE:** Top mph 225. Cruise mph 180. Stall mph 65. Climb rate 3,000. Takeoff run 500. Range 360.

One of the more successful Formula I racers is the Shoestring. Constructed from the conventional combination of steel tubing, wood, and fabric, the tiny racer houses a 100-hp O-200 Continental engine. The aircraft first flew in 1949 and entered its first competition in 1950. By 1974, the Shoestring racer had accumulated 14 first places in major air race competitions. Other recommended engines are the Continental 85- and 90-hp versions.

CORBY CJ-1 "STARLET"

STANDARD DATA: Gross wt. 650. Empty wt. 420. Fuel capacity 11. Wingspan 18'6". Length 14'9". **PERFORMANCE:** Top mph 160. Cruise mph 123. Stall mph 34. Climb rate 775. Takeoff run 1,100. Landing roll 1,100. Range 370.

The Starlet is a single-place semiaerobatic monoplane of wood, fabric, and tubular steel construction. It is designed to handle any Volkswagen or Continental engine up to 75 hp.

CVJETKOVIC CA-61 "MINI ACE"

STANDARD DATA: (Single-seater) Gross wt. 950. Empty wt. 606. Fuel capacity 17. Wingspan 27'6". Length 18'11". Engine 65-hp Continental. **PERFORMANCE:** Top mph 120. Cruise mph 100. Stall mph 42. Climb rate 1,200. Takeoff run 200. Landing roll 300. Range 425.

The CA-61 can be built as either a single-seat or side-by-side low-wing monoplane. It is designed for amateur builders with little or no previous experience in building light airplanes. With a minimum of tools, the plane can be assembled in less than 1,000 working hours. The structure is light with reduced wing loading, so in addition to the standard Continental powerplant, a VW conversion can be substituted. Another option is the availability of either fixed tricycle landing gear or retractable tailwheel type. Construction is all wood, and the wing is made in one piece with a main and auxiliary spar.

CVJETKOVIC CA-65

STANDARD DATA: Gross wt. 1,500. Empty wt. 900. Fuel capacity 28. Wingspan 25'. Length 19'. Engine 125-hp Lycoming. **PERFORMANCE:** Top mph 180. Cruise mph 155. Stall mph 55. Climb rate 1,000. Ceiling 15,000. Takeoff run 450. Landing roll 600. Range 500.

This airplane represents a further development of the CA-61 Mini Ace. The CA-65 is a low-wing monoplane with retractable landing gear and dual controls. The high degree of efficiency produced by its design yields economic performance at all speeds. It features a streamlined canopy, enclosed engine, tapered wing, and fully retractable gear. Its wood construction cuts requirements for tooling and special jigs to a minimum. For easy storage the wings fold up in an "aircraft carrier" style.

D'APUZZO "JUNIOR AERO SPORT"

STANDARD DATA: Gross wt. 1,275. Empty wt. 840. Fuel capacity 20. Wingspan 21'8", Length 18'3". Engine 180-hp Lycoming. **PERFORMANCE:** Top mph 160. Cruise mph 140. Stall mph 55. Climb rate 2,500. Ceiling 20,000. Takeoff run 400. Landing roll 550 Range 300.

This single-seat sporting biplane is a smaller version of the Senior Aero Sport and is built from the standard combination of a fabric-covered wooden wing and a fabric-covered steel-tube fuselage. The powerplant drives a constant-speed metal propeller to produce a maximum speed of 160 mph.

D'APUZZO "SENIOR AERO SPORT"

STANDARD DATA: Gross wt. 2,050. Empty wt. 1,450. Fuel capacity 36–62. Wingspan 27'0". Length 21'0". Engine 260-hp Lycoming. **PERFORMANCE:** Top mph 155. Cruise mph 140. Stall mph 52. Climb rate 2,000. Takeoff distance (50') 700. Landing distance (50') 900. Range 400.

The aerobatic Senior Aero Sport is available as either a single- or two-seater. One example is the grand champion homebuilt at the 1968 EAA Fly-In at Rockford, Illinois. This sport biplane has a wood-faired steel-tube fuselage and wire-braced steel-tube tail section. Fabric covers the entire airplane. The fuel supply and the front seat passenger are very close to the center of gravity, so trim is little affected by expending fuel or by the presence or absence of a passenger. A variety of engines can be used from 190 to 260 hp.

D'APUZZO "SPORTWING"

STANDARD DATA: Gross wt. 1,845. Empty wt. 1,185. Fuel capacity 30. Wingspan 27'0". Length 21'7". Engine 160-hp Lycoming. **PERFORMANCE:** Top mph 142. Cruise mph 127. Stall mph 47. Climb rate 1,500. Takeoff distance (50') 790. Landing distance (50') 850. Range 380.

The D-201 Sportwing is a completely redesigned ver-

sion of the Senior Aero Sport. Of special interest is the attention that was given to reducing the cost and complexity of building the airplane without sacrificing the safety aspects of the previous models. The fuselage is a conventional steel-tube structure with aluminum-alloy panels used for covering forward of the cockpit and fabric used aft of the cockpit. The wings are the conventionally braced biplane type with long-span ailerons on the lower wings. Power is supplied by Lycoming engines ranging from 150 to 200 hp; the most common powerplant is the 160-hp Lycoming. Seating is in tandem fashion with a canopy as an option.

DAVIS DA-2A

STANDARD DATA: Gross wt. 1,125. Empty wt. 610. Fuel capacity 20. Wingspan 19'3". Length 17'10". **PERFORMANCE:** Top mph 120. Cruise mph 115. Stall mph 62. Climb rate 400. Takeoff run 800. Landing roll 700. Range 450.

In 1966, the Davis all-metal design was voted the most popular at the Rockford EAA Fly-In. It requires little work on the part of the builder because of its simple construction with no compound curves or expensive fittings. The Davis design uses a 100-hp Continental and is one of the few do-it-yourself planes with a V-tail.

DAVIS DA-5A

STANDARD DATA: Gross wt. 775. Empty wt. 460. Fuel capacity 17. Wingspan 15'7". Length 15'9". Engine 65-hp Continental. **PERFORMANCE:** Top mph 160. Cruise mph 140. Stall mph 60. Climb rate 800. Ceiling 14,500. Takeoff run 600. Landing roll 600. Range 450.

This single-seat low-wing monoplane makes use of the same V-type tail as the DA-2A. The pilot sits inside an enclosed canopy behind a 65-hp Continental turning a fixed-pitch prop. Both the wings and fuselage are a lightweight alloy structure with stressed skins, and the landing gear is the non-retractable tricycle type.

DIAMANT C.P. 60

STANDARD DATA: Gross wt. 1,880. Empty wt. 1,100. Fuel capacity 45. Wingspan 31'6". Length 22'. **PERFORMANCE:** Top mph 134. Cruise mph 118. Stall mph 51. Climb rate. 492. Takeoff run 850. Landing roll 900. Range 450.

The Diamant is a three- or four-seat version of the Emeraude. This low-wing high-performance monoplane is powered by a 100-hp Continental engine. It is also available in a four-place model propelled by a 150-hp Lycoming designated the Super Diamant. Both were created by designer Claude Piel.

DOODLE BUG

STANDARD DATA: Gross wt. 970. Empty wt. 616. Fuel capacity 25. Wingspan 18'. Length 16'6". **PERFORMANCE:** Top mph 196. Cruise mph 170. Stall mph 70. Climb rate 2,000. Takeoff run 1,000. Landing roll 800. Range 700.

This fast single-seater picked up three trophies when it flew to the 1955 EAA Fly-In at Oshkosh, Wisconsin. With its 12" gallon main fuel tank and a pair of 6½-gallon fiberglass tip tanks, the Doodle Bug boasts an amazing 700-mile range. It is built from welded steel tube. The fuselage and tail group is fabric covered. The wings are all metal. It is powered by a 90-hp Continental.

DSK-1 "HAWK"

STANDARD DATA: Gross wt. 893. Empty wt. 525. Fuel capacity 9–14. Wingspan 20'4". Length 15'. Engine 65-hp Lycoming. **PERFORMANCE:** Top mph 156. Cruise mph 141. Stall mph 50. Climb rate 1,500. Ceiling 12,000. Takeoff run 600. Landing roll 550. Range (14 gals) 480.

The Hawk is a single-seat low-wing monoplane stressed to 9Gs. Originally it was designed to be built around a surplus 200-gallon drop-tank, but plans also provide for a bulkhead and stressed-skin structure. The wings are built with twin light-alloy spars, and the landing gear is the nonretractable tricycle type. Fuel is carried in a forward tank with the capacity of nine gallons, but an optional 14-gallon tank can be added in the aft section.

DURAND MARK V

STANDARD DATA: Gross wt. 1,840. Empty wt. 1,210. Fuel capacity 24.5. Wingspan 24'6". Length 20'3". Engine 150-hp Lycoming. **PERFORMANCE:** Top mph 170. Cruise mph 135. Stall mph n/a. Climb rate 1,200. Ceiling 15,000. Range 520. Takeoff run 550. Landing roll 450.

The Durand biplane features a negative-stagger configuration so that it does not produce a full stall, only a very short period of "nibbling" with little loss of altitude. The structure is rated at +3.8Gs and −1.5Gs. Roll is produced by a combination of effects when a spoiler is activated, instead of by use of ailerons. According to its designer, a spoiler for roll control actually helps an airplane turn in the direction of the bank, while ailerons do not. The trailing edges of the wings are taken up by full-span flaps. With a standard 150-hp Lycoming, the Durand can carry two people with 128 pounds of baggage at 135 mph over a range of 520 miles. Cockpit controls are basic, with dual sticks in lieu of standard control wheels. The cabin features exceptional visibility by using a forward sliding canopy instead of side doors normally associated with high-wing and biplane cabin aircraft.

DYKE DELTA

STANDARD DATA: Gross wt. 1,750. Empty wt. 1,000. Fuel capacity 41. Wingspan 22'. Length 19'. **PERFORMANCE:** Top mph 190. Cruise mph 170. Stall mph (no stall). Climb rate 2,000. Takeoff run 700. Landing roll 1,500. Range 700.

John Dyke wanted a high-speed airplane with folding wings that would be compact enough to tow home for garage storage—thus the unique delta design. The basic fuselage skeleton, vertical stabilizer, and wing spars are of welded steel tube. The wings have an all-metal frame and have been tried with either fiberglass or aluminum covering. Virtually the entire planform surface of the Delta provides lift at cruise speeds. A 180-hp Lycoming provides the power.

EAA "ACRO-SPORT"

STANDARD DATA: Gross wt. 1,178. Empty wt. 739. Fuel capacity 20. Wingspan 19'7". Length 17'6". Engine 100 to 200 hp. **PERFORMANCE:** Top mph 180. Cruise mph 130. Stall mph 50. Climb rate 3,500. Ceiling 14,000. Takeoff run 350. Landing roll 800. Range 350.

The Acro-Sport is a hot little aerobatic ship that is also delightful to handle. Some say that it flies similarly to the two-place Pitts, but since the Acro-Sport is a single-seater and much lighter, it is easier to land, has a shorter roll at takeoff, and has an improved glide ratio. This bipe was designed by EAA President Paul Poberezny, who wanted to come up with a plane that could be used in high school industrial arts programs and Civil Air Patrol groups as an educational tool. The Acro-Sport can be fabricated with tools normally found in a high-school shop. It is built with steel tube covered by fabric and 100- to 200-hp engines.

EAA "ACRO-SPORT II"

STANDARD DATA: Gross wt. 1,520. Empty wt. 875. Fuel capacity 25. Wingspan 21'8". Length 18'11". Engine 180-hp Lycoming. **PERFORMANCE:** Cruise mph 123. Range 400.

The Acro II, a two-place larger version of the single-place Acro Sport, can be constructed for little more than its single-place siblings. With its larger wheels, wide landing gear, and light gross weight, the Acro II is a fun, docile sport airplane designed for engines ranging in power from 115 to 200 hp. When fitted with a 180-hp Lycoming, its empty weight of 875 pounds makes it one of the lightest custom-built airplanes. Like all Acro Sports, its cockpit is designed to be comfortable for pilots up to 6'6" and 240 pounds. The airframe is somewhat larger than the really "midget" biplanes to avoid "touchy" flight characteristics and allow for more baggage. Designed by Paul Poberezny, the Acro II features an M-6 airfoil with a 43-inch chord.

EAA "SUPER ACRO-SPORT"

STANDARD DATA: Gross wt. 1,350. Empty wt. 884. Fuel capacity 20. Wingspan 19'7". Length 17'6". Engine 200-hp Ly-

coming. **PERFORMANCE:** Top mph 156. Cruise mph 135. Stall mph 50. Climb rate 3,700. Ceiling 15,000. Takeoff run 1,025. Landing roll 800. Range 300.

This further development of the Acro-Sport is intended for unlimited international-class aerobatic competition. Though basically similar in appearance to its counterpart, the Super Acro-Sport takes advantage of a more powerful engine turning a fixed-pitch prop, an improved roll rate, and inverted flight capabilities. Its two wings have almost symmetrical airfoil sections. Also added was a trim tab on the starboard elevator and a servo tab on the port side.

EAA BIPLANE

STANDARD DATA: Gross wt. 1,023. Empty wt. 640. Fuel capacity 12. Wingspan 20'. Length 17'. **PERFORMANCE:** Top mph 125. Cruise mph 110. Stall mph 55. Climb rate 1,000. Takeoff run 500. Landing roll 550. Range 200.

The EAA decided in 1955 to develop a single-seat sport biplane as a service to its members. The prototype was built as a classroom project by students of St. Rita's High School in Chicago. It flew for the first time in 1960. The plane is, in a sense, the predecessor to the Acro-Sport, the difference being that the A-1 Biplane is lighter and uses a smaller engine, an 85-hp Continental. Construction is the same.

EAA HEATH PARASOL

STANDARD DATA: Gross wt. 700. Empty wt. 450. Fuel capacity 9. Wingspan 31'3". Length 17'3". **PERFORMANCE:** Top mph 73. Cruise mph 62. Stall mph 30. Climb rate 500. Takeoff run 400. Landing roll 400. Range 350.

The Heath Parasol was one of the more distinctive light-weight homebuilt aircraft designs in the late 1920s and early 1930s. That makes it one of the oldest designs still being built. This single-seater is powered by either a Volkswagen conversion or a 65-hp Continental and is constructed of wood, fabric, and tubular steel. At present, the plans for the Parasol are no longer marketed by EAA.

EAA NESMITH "COUGAR"

STANDARD DATA: Gross wt. 1,250. Empty wt. 624. Fuel capacity 25. Wingspan 20'6". Length 18'11". Engine 115-hp Lycoming. **PERFORMANCE:** Top mph 195. Cruise mph 166. Stall mph 53. Climb rate 1,300. Ceiling 13,000. Takeoff run 450. Landing roll 350. Range 750.

Plans for the Cougar were first handled by its designer, Robert Nesmith, and subsequently by EAA. First flown in 1957, the Cougar is a high-wing, enclosed-cabin, sporting monoplane that resembles the Whitman Tailwind to a small degree. The wing's all-wood two-spar structure is covered with plywood and fabric. The fuselage is a fabric-covered steel-tube framework. The conventional landing gear can be fitted with optional main-gear fairings. Inside the cabin, seating is for two in a side-by-side fashion with dual controls.

EAA "POBER PIXIE"

STANDARD DATA: Gross wt. 900. Empty wt. 543. Fuel capacity 12.3. Wingspan 29'10". Length 17'3". Engine 50-hp VW conversion. **PERFORMANCE:** Top mph 130. Cruise mph 85. Stall mph 30. Climb rate 500. Ceiling 13,000. Takeoff run 300. Landing roll 300.

The single-seat Pober Pixie is another homebuilt designed by Paul Poberezny. It originally started as an effort to help pilots beat high operational costs and was designated "Project Econoplane" in 1974. Inspired by a Heath Parasol LN, the Pixie is a parasol monoplane powered by a Limbach VW engine rated at 50 to 75 hp. Full-span ailerons give excellent roll with little yaw on entry and recovery.

EDI "EXPRESS 90"

STANDARD DATA: Seats 4. Gross wt. 2,895. Empty wt. 1,700. Fuel capacity 92. Engine 260-hp Lycoming IO-540. **PERFORMANCE:** Top mph 240. Cruise mph 210. Initial climb rate 1,300. Ceiling 22,000. Range 1,450. Takeoff distance (50') 650. Landing distance (50') 1,100.

Originally designed and built as the Wheeler Express by Ken Wheeler, Wheeler Technology, the Express 90 is a four to six-place, all composite, low-wing, fixed-gear monoplane that subscribes to the high-tech school of kitbuilt aircraft. Express Design, Inc., acquired the rights to manufacture the Express 90 and is one of the more popular multipurpose cross-country aircraft. Two major features of the Express are its load-carrying capabilities and the versatile seating options available to the owner/builder.

EOS

STANDARD DATA: Gross wt. 1,000. Empty wt. 670. Fuel capacity 15. Wingspan 26'. Length 16'8". Engine 55-hp Volkswagen. **PERFORMANCE:** Top mph 180. Cruise mph 175. Stall mph 55. Climb rate 1,100. Takeoff run 1,000. Landing roll 800.

The EOS/SFA is a single-seater with retractable gear and a tractor-thrust configuration. The fuselage is built from lightweight alloy pop-riveted and epoxy-resin bonded with a fiberglass engine cowling. It is not intended to be the simplest aircraft to build but rather to provide a mix between maximum design efficiency and minimum construction complexity. No compound forming is necessary. There's a castering nose gear, and the tricycle landing gear are manually retracted. Steering is via rudder and differential braking. The 1,834cc VW drives a 50-inch diameter ground-adjustable wooden propeller with three blades.

EVANS VP-I "VOLKSPLANE"

STANDARD DATA: Gross wt. 700. Empty wt. 480. Fuel capacity 8. Wingspan 24'. Length 18'. **PERFORMANCE:** Top mph 95. Cruise mph 75. Stall mph 45. Climb rate 600. Takeoff run 500. Landing roll 400. Range 200.

Ultrasimple wooden construction and the familiar VW engine mean low-cost flying fun and ease of construction. The fuselage of the VP-1 is little more than a plywood box. The wings use a spruce frame covered with fabric. Any stock VW engine from 1,500cc to 2,100cc can be used; only small changes need to be made. The VP-1 is available as a single-seater and as a side-by-side two-seater. It has been said that the VP-1 handles similarly to the Piper Cub. Minimal welding is in the control-stick assembly, the flying struts, and the stabilator horn. The VP-1 and VP-2 can be stowed at home and require no trailer for highway towing.

EVANS VP-2

STANDARD DATA: Gross wt. 1,040. Empty wt. 640. Fuel capacity 14. Wingspan 27'. Length 19'. Engine 60-hp Volkswagen. **PERFORMANCE:** Top mph 100. Cruise mph 75. Stall mph 45. Climb rate 500. Ceiling 10,000. Takeoff run 700. Landing roll 400. Range 200.

The VP-2 is generally similar to its smaller brother, the VP-1, except for an increased span and chord measurement, and the fuselage width is 12 inches wider to make room for the extra passenger. Any stock VW engine from 1,834cc to 2,100cc can be used. The VP-2 with a passenger aboard is designed for "normal category" use, which allows nonaerobatic operation and all maneuvers incident to normal flying. Without a passenger, "utility category" use is permitted, which includes stalls, lazy eights, chandelles, and steep turns with a bank angle of more than 60 degrees. Aerobatics are not approved in either the VP-1 or VP-2.

EXPERIMENTAL AVIATION "BERKUT"

STANDARD DATA: Seats 2. Gross wt. 2,000. Empty wt. 1,035. Fuel capacity 55. Engine 205-hp IO-36-B1A Lycoming. **PERFORMANCE:** Top mph 250. Cruise mph 220. Initial climb rate 2,000. Ceiling 29,500. Range 1,228. Takeoff distance 1,000. Landing distance 1,000.

Since Burt Rutan made the advantages of a canard design configuration so apparent with his line of composite aircraft, builders have been taking the ball and running with it in order to improve a good thing. The Berkut is perhaps the epitome of the design evolution. The structure has evolved from the carved, foam-core with applied wet-lay-up fiberglass into vacuum-formed wet-lay-up composite sandwich construction. This method of component construction greatly increases part integrity and strength, and it significantly reduces weight of the finished product. The Berkut utilizes a fully retractable landing gear and many other significant changes that have improved the original concept. The Berkut is available as a kit.

FALCONAR AMF S-14

STANDARD DATA: Gross wt. 1,500. Empty wt. 1,000. Fuel capacity 18. Wingspan 32'. Length 23'. **PERFORMANCE:** Top mph 150. Cruise mph 115. Stall mph 35. Climb rate 1,200. Takeoff run 100. Landing roll 250. Range 400.

The AMF S-14 is a two-place taildragger modeled after the Adam RA-14. The S-14 was first flown in 1961. It is pow-

ered by 85- to 150-hp engines. Its fuselage is a conventional wooden box-girder structure covered with plastic-coated fabric. The 514's wings are a braced high-wing design of all-wood and fabric with STOL characteristics.

FALCONAR "FLYING FLEA"

STANDARD DATA: Gross wt. 700. Empty wt. 410. Fuel capacity 12. Wingspan 20'. Length 14'. **PERFORMANCE:** Top mph 105. Cruise mph 8,085. Stall mph 35. Climb rate 500–600. Ceiling 16,400. Range 275.

The first Flying Flea took to the air back in 1933 and quickly earned a reputation for being temperamental. The version pictured here is an authentic copy of the original biplane built by Mignet except for installation of a McCulloch 72-hp engine and two minor rigging changes. Mignet was a furniture manufacturer, and he impishly named his creation "LePou de Ciel," or "Louse of the Sky." It started out to be "Everyman's Airplane" that could be built for $500 (complete) in the Great Depression years. Mignet's Flea carried a 17-hp engine and had a speed range from 25 to 62 mph.

F.E.W. "P-51D/TF"

STANDARD DATA: Seats 1–2. Gross wt. 2,000. Empty wt. 1,100. Fuel capacity 58. Engine 300-hp automotive conversion V8. **PERFORMANCE:** Top mph 250. Cruise mph 210. Initial climb rate 2,000. Ceiling 16,000. Range 750. Takeoff distance (50') 900. Landing distance (50') 1,000.

For years, many experimental aircraft builders have strived to re-create their favorite World War II fighters in miniature. For most, many hurdles had to be negotiated to get the right look, feel, sound, and of course, performance all at the right cost of ownership. Until the advent of composite building techniques, forming all those compound curves of a fighter in metal just wasn't within the means of your average builder. Then, getting the proper powerplant to look and sound like "the real thing" was next to impossible with the technology and funds at hand. Now with automotive/aviation V-8 conversions attaining a respectable degree of reliability, cost, and power coupled with these modern, prepreg, composite techniques, the right combination has been reached. F.E.W.'s P-51D is a 67-percent scale version of the most famous fighter of World War II, and it looks the part, sounds the part, and flies the part. The P-51D is stressed to ±6Gs for aerobatics and is available in a dual-control version, the P-51TF.

FIKE MODEL E

STANDARD DATA: Gross wt. 1,150. Empty wt. 690. Fuel capacity 15. Wingspan 22'5". Length 19'2". Engine 80-hp Continental. **PERFORMANCE:** Top mph 110. Cruise mph 100. Stall mph 37. Climb rate 800. Ceiling 10,000+. Takeoff run 400. Landing roll 600. Range 280.

William Fike, designer and Alaska airline pilot, created this two-place cabin monoplane. The Model E's airframe structure includes a Piper J-3 tail assembly, a welded steel-tube fuselage, and an all-wood fabric-covered wing. Power is supplied by an 85-hp Continental engine. The wing can be removed within 10 minutes to enable the plane to be towed.

FLAGLOR "SCOOTER"

STANDARD DATA: Gross wt. 650. Empty wt. 390. Fuel capacity 5. Wingspan 28'. Length 15'8". Engine 40-hp Volkswagen. **PERFORMANCE:** Top mph 90. Cruise mph 80. Stall mph 34. Climb rate 600. Takeoff run 250. Landing roll 250. Range 175.

The Scooter was originally powered by a Cushman golf cart engine, which was ultimately replaced by a 1,500cc VW engine rated at 40 hp. At the 1967 EAA meet, this tiny, high-wing, enclosed-cabin taildragger received both "Outstanding Ultralight" and "Outstanding Volkswagen Powered" awards. Construction is of wood with a plywood covering, except for the aft section of the fuselage, which is fabric covered. The VW engine is mounted over the cabin and turns a two-blade propeller.

FLIGHT DYNAMICS "FLIGHTSAIL VII"

STANDARD DATA: Gross wt. 1,600. Empty wt. 1,100. Fuel capacity 12. Wingspan 39'. Length 29'. **PERFORMANCE:** Top mph 95. Cruise mph 80. Stall mph 35. Climb rate 500. Takeoff time 20 sec. Range 200.

What makes this bird truly different is that it can either be towed behind a 70-hp ski boat or it can have a 90-hp Conti-

nental pylon mounted above the fuselage to fly the Flightsail under its own power. The structure is built from bolted aluminum, foam, and epoxy. This two-seater amphibian features twin booms and twin tails.

GARRISON OM-1 "MELMOTH"

STANDARD DATA: Gross wt. 2,950. Empty wt. 1,500. Fuel capacity 154. Wingspan 23'0". Length 21'6". Engine 195-hp Continental. **PERFORMANCE:** Top mph 209. Cruise mph 201. Stall mph 80. Climb rate 1,800. Takeoff distance (50') 2,500. Landing distance (50') 2,500. Range 3,400.

The Melmoth first flew in 1973 and was developed by Peter Garrison from the British Practavia Sprite (also partly a Garrison project). The Melmoth represented considerably more work than the average homebuilder would like to tackle. In fact, it was more of a research prototype than a backyard project. The Melmoth was conceived and designed as an exercise in extreme efficiency in all aspects of flight. It carried an unusually large amount of fuel for an aircraft of its size with a 41-gallon main tank and two 35-gallon tiptanks on each wing, which yielded the exceptional range. Some of the Melmoth's extras included double-slotted flaps, adjustable incidence ailerons, autopilot, and retractable landing gear. Unfortunately, the aircraft was destroyed in a highly unusual accident in which a landing aircraft struck Melmoth while waiting on the ground at the end of a runway. Garrison survived the accident and proceeded to design and construct a replacement.

HARMON "DER DONNERSCHLAG"

STANDARD DATA: Gross wt. 600. Empty wt. 350. Fuel capacity 10. Wingspan 19'6". Length 14'6". Engine 75-hp Volkswagen. **PERFORMANCE:** Top mph 120. Cruise mph 110. Stall mph 55. Climb rate 800. Ceiling 10,000. Takeoff run 150. Landing roll 250. Range 500.

The language translation of this open-cockpit sport plane's name is "The Thunderclap." The airframe of this plane was used as the foundation for "Mr. America." Both share similar wings, fuselage, tail unit, and landing gear. The wings are a wire-braced shoulder type with two simple beam spars. As with the Mr. America, seating is for one behind a modified Volkswagen engine turning a two-blade wooden prop.

HARMON "MR. AMERICA"

STANDARD DATA: Gross wt. 650. Empty wt. 430. Fuel capacity 9. Wingspan 19'8". Length 15'2". Engine 60- to 70-hp Volkswagen. **PERFORMANCE:** Top mph 125. Cruise mph 110. Stall mph 48. Climb rate 800. Ceiling 12,000. Takeoff run 200. Landing roll 300. Range 400.

Harmon chose the long-established combination of a welded steel-tube fuselage and tail surfaces with a wooden spar and rib wings. In addition, the wings can be easily removed for storage and towing. The entire aircraft can be built with hand tools, except for the use of a welding rig. Mr. America's powerplant is a nearly stock 1,600cc Volkswagen engine bored to 1,650cc. The engine develops an honest 60 hp to produce what is said to be rapid acceleration on takeoff to about 800 fpm at 90 mph during initial climb.

HARRIS GEODETIC LW 108

STANDARD DATA: Gross wt. 1,000. Empty wt. 585. Fuel capacity 16. Wingspan 28'1". Length 19'4". Engine 80-hp Continental. **PERFORMANCE:** Top mph 150. Cruise mph 130. Stall mph 40. Climb rate 1,500. Takeoff run 500. Range 400.

The LW-108 offers the comfort of side-by-side seating underneath an enclosed canopy. Possibly the most outstanding feature of this low-wing tail-dragger is its unique geodetically-constructed fuselage. It is said to be both lightweight and economical to build while providing exceptional strength without sacrificing a low-drag fuselage shape. The framework is all spruce and plywood.

HATZ CB-1 BIPLANE

STANDARD DATA: Gross wt. 1,400. Empty wt. 850. Fuel capacity 18. Wingspan 25'4". Length 19'. Engine 100-hp Lycoming. **PERFORMANCE:** Top mph 100. Cruise mph 80. Stall mph 40. Climb rate 600. Takeoff run 400. Landing roll 300. Range 200.

The first flight of this tandem, two-seat, and open-cockpit biplane took place in 1968. The wings are a fabric-covered wooden structure, while the fuselage is built from welded-steel

tubing. The design weight of the Hatz (850 pounds) makes it the lightest two-place biplane available. It performs well with the 85-hp Continental and is stressed to take engines up to 150 hp. The Hatz can be trimmed to fly hands off (more or less), which helps out when trying to read a map in an open cockpit. Control response is slow enough to give a feeling of a much larger aircraft, and it is capable of all aerobatic maneuvers in its power range.

HILLMAN "HORNET"

STANDARD DATA: Gross wt. 1,400. Empty wt. 800. Fuel capacity 22. Rotor span 25'5". Length 21'2". Engine 150-hp Lycoming. **PERFORMANCE:** Top mph 100. Cruise mph 90. Climb rate 1,000. Ceiling 12,000. Range 200.

The Hornet was the 1978 "Overall Award" winner at Oshkosh and received the "Best Helicopter Design Award" at the Popular Rotorcraft Convention in Rockford, Illinois. Standard features include a comfortable cockpit for two, excellent visibility, room for a variety of avionics, and dual controls. Flight performance has been favorably compared with that of the Hughes 300.

HOLLMAN HA-2M "SPORTSTER"

STANDARD DATA: Gross wt. 1,050. Empty wt. 620. Fuel capacity 12. Rotor diameter 28'. Length 13'. Engine 135-hp Lycoming. **PERFORMANCE:** Top mph 90. Cruise mph 75. Minimum mph 28. Climb rate 500. Ceiling 7,000. Takeoff run 350. Landing roll 0. Range 90.

The Sportster is the world's first two-place gyroplane designed for the homebuilder who has limited access to power

HOLLMAN HA-2M "SPORTSTER"

tools. Ninety percent of the structure is bolted or riveted together, and a minimum of machined parts are used. For convenience, the Sportster is designed to be towed behind a car. Two average people, 350 pounds combined, can fly comfortably inside its nearly enclosed cockpit for up to 90 miles on a cross-country trip. A 130-hp Franklin, 135-hp Lycoming, or 150-hp Lycoming engine can be used. With the engine cut, the Sportster has a 1,000-fpm sink rate.

HOVEY "BETA BIRD"

STANDARD DATA: Gross wt. 650. Empty wt. 405. Fuel capacity 7.5. Wingspan 25'6". Length 16'11". **PERFORMANCE:** Top mph 85. Cruise mph 80. Stall mph 40. Climb rate 500. Takeoff run (50') 400. Landing run (50') 400. Range 180.

The single-seat "Beta Bird" was first flown at Mojave, California, in April 1979. It is powered by a 1,385cc converted VW engine and offers the homebuilder simplified methods of construction. The wings fold for transport or storage. The fuselage pod is plywood and spruce construction with a stiffened aluminum tailboom to support the tail. The wings are spruce in a two-spar configuration, and the ribs are single-piece aluminum tubes. The tail group is fabricated from aluminum tubing, pop-riveted together with gussets, and covered with Dacron. Only 250 feet are needed for takeoff and landing, and the 7½-gallons of fuel yield 180 miles.

HOVEY "WHING-DING II"

STANDARD DATA: Gross wt. 310. Empty wt. 122. Fuel capacity ½. Wingspan 16'4". Length 12'11". **PERFORMANCE:** Top mph 45. Cruise mph 45. Stall mph 26. Climb rate 200. Takeoff run (50') 300. Landing run (50') 300. Range 22.

This 15-hp, 300-pound gross-weight biplane is the ultimate in lightness and simplicity. The tail surfaces are constructed from ½-inch-thick styrofoam artboard faced with high-strength craft paper on both sides; the critical areas are reinforced with ⅛-inch plywood gussets. The tail boom is a 3-inch aluminum pipe filled with foam to resist buckling. The fuselage is basically a 6-inch wide box of plywood filled with foam that serves as an engine mount and a mast support for the wings. The prop is chain driven from a 15-hp McCulloch, two-cycle, go-kart engine. The wings have two spars and are fabric covered.

HU-GO CRAFT

STANDARD DATA: Gross wt. 848. Empty wt. 558. Fuel capacity 12. Wingspan 17'. Length 14'8". **PERFORMANCE:** Top mph 115. Cruise mph 105. Stall mph 55. Climb rate 1,000. Takeoff run 500. Landing roll 500. Range 250.

With a lot of lift for its small size and light weight, the HU-GO Craft wrings a 105-mph cruise speed out of a mere 65-hp Continental. This single-seater bipe is largely conventional in construction with fuselage and tail group of welded-steel tubing and wings of wood. All surfaces are fabric covered.

INTERNATIONAL COMMUTER IIA

STANDARD DATA: Gross wt. 1,300. Empty wt. 700. Fuel capacity 22. Rotor span 25'. Length 29'. Engine 150-hp Lycoming. **PERFORMANCE:** Top mph 100. Cruise mph 90. Climb rate 1,071. Ceiling 13,000. Range 200.

The Commuter was designed by Harold "Pop" Emigh who includes among his accomplishments the Navajo and Polaris ballistic missile systems and the Emigh Trojan, which is listed in the single-engine section. He stressed safety and reliability in every component of this two-seater to assure the safest helicopter possible. The main rotor and tail rotor are gear driven, so there are no rubber belts or chains to readjust or fail. It is powered by the proven 150-hp Lycoming aircraft engine with a dual ignition. Such complicated parts as the main rotor transmission, tail rotor gear box, rotor blades, and the like are assembled at the factory. The airframe is Chrome-Moly steel tubing and can be constructed with a minimum of common tools. The Commuter will autorotate better than most helicopters; with engine off, it descends at a rate of only 1,200 to 1,400 fpm.

JANOWSKI "DON QUIXOTE"

STANDARD DATA: Gross wt. 600. Empty wt. 291. Wingspan 24.93'. Length 16'. Engine 25–50-hp Volkswagen. **PERFORMANCE:** (23 hp). Top mph 84. Cruise mph 77. Stall mph 39. Climb rate 244. Ceiling 6,820. Range 310. Takeoff run 761. Landing run (50') 1,256.

The prototype Don Quixote designed and built by M.R. Janowski was powered by a 230-hp two-stroke Saturn engine, also designed by Janowski; however, several problems were inherent in the two-stroke engine, and so the more readily available Volkswagen engine was settled upon. A heavier engine called for strengthening the airplane's structure. To cover the widest range of homebuilders in various countries, it was decided that the Don Quixote would make use of conventional wood and fabric along with more modern polyurethane foam and epoxy/fiberglass. The J-1B can withstand loading of +4G and –2G, but in the foam/fiberglass version of the plane, +6G and –3G are possible. Construction of the plane follows conventional building rules with spruce wood, birch plywood, and flat sheets of plexiglass as basic materials.

JAVELIN "WICHAWK"

STANDARD DATA: Gross wt. 2,000. Empty wt. 1,280. Fuel capacity 39. Wingspan 24'. Length 19'3". Engine 180-hp Lycoming. **PERFORMANCE:** Top mph 140. Cruise mph 127. Stall mph 45. Climb rate 1,700. Takeoff run 150.

The Wichawk is structurally similar to the Boeing Stearman biplane and is stressed for up to 12Gs positive and six Gs negative. Standard seating is for two in a side-by-side config-

uration, which is rather unusual for a sport biplane of its type. Optional tandem seating is also available. While the 180-hp Lycoming is most often used, the ship can be adapted to house various horizontally opposed or radial engines. The wings make use of wooden spars with lightweight alloy ribs, and the fuselage is constructed from welded steel tubes.

JEFFAIR "BARRACUDA"

STANDARD DATA: Gross wt. 2,200. Empty wt. 1,495. Fuel capacity 44. Wingspan 24'9". Length 21'6". Engine 220-hp Lycoming. **PERFORMANCE:** Top mph 218. Cruise mph 200. Stall mph 62. Climb rate 2,200.

The Barracuda is a sophisticated enclosed-cabin two-seater in the image of the Thorp T-18 but with tricycle landing gear, all-wood construction, and a three-blade controllable-pitch propeller. It was designed by former RAF fighter pilot Geoffrey Siers. The landing gear features electrohydraulic retraction. The cabin is fitted with dual controls, gull-wing doors, and two armchair-type seats.

JODEL D-11 "BEBE"

STANDARD DATA: Gross wt. 1,290. Fuel capacity 10. Wingspan 26'11". Length 20'6". **PERFORMANCE:** Top mph 124. Cruise mph 114. Stall mph 35. Climb rate 800. Ceiling 16,000. Takeoff run 500. Landing roll 800. Range 300.

This low-wing taildragger of all-wood construction comes from France where homebuilding was flourishing long before the movement took hold in the United States. The distinguishing feature of the Jodel is the bent wing with a straight center section and dihedral in the outer panels only. It is powered by Continental engines of 65 to 90 hp and seats two in side-by-side fashion.

"JUNGSTER I"

STANDARD DATA: Gross wt. 1,000. Empty wt. 605. Fuel capacity 16. Wingspan 16'8". Length 16'. **PERFORMANCE:** Top mph 200. Cruise mph 150. Stall mph 52. Climb rate 2,500+. Takeoff run 300. Landing roll 800. Range 300.

The Jungster I was developed as an ⁵⁄₁₀ scale version of the famous Jungmeister aerobatic airplane. The intention was to capture many of the flying qualities of the Jungmeister in a smaller size. This all-wood and fabric-covered biplane has a sweptback wing design of about 11 degrees to keep the center of lift close to the center of gravity. It can handle engines rated from 85 to 150 hp and is a frisky single-place aerobatic plane.

"JUNGSTER II"

STANDARD DATA: Gross wt. 1,375. Empty wt. 739. Fuel capacity 16. Wingspan 22'4". Length 16'11". **PERFORMANCE:** Top mph 170. Cruise mph 148. Stall mph 5. Climb rate 3,500. Takeoff run 200. Landing roll 800.

The Jungster II is a follow-up design that grew out of experience with the Jungster I. The intent was to create a plane with the same open-cockpit concept, but to increase speed and capacity so that it would be an acceptable cross-country airplane. The Jungster II uses the same design and construction concepts, except that it is just a little bit bigger, has a single extended parasol-type wing, and uses a welded steel-tube center section. Engines rated from 85 to 180 hp are used.

JURCA MJ-2 "TEMPETE"

STANDARD DATA: Gross wt. 950. Empty wt. 639. Fuel capacity 16. Wingspan 19'6". Length 18'6". **PERFORMANCE:** Top mph 120. Cruise mph 102. Stall mph 41. Climb rate 555. Takeoff run 820. Range 375.

Marcel Jurca incorporated many Jodel components in the design of the MJ-2 Tempete. The Tempete is a cantilevered low-wing monoplane that can be fitted with engines ranging in horsepower from 65 to 125. The standard version is powered by a 65-hp engine. Another common version powered by a 90-hp engine cruises at 120 mph and climbs to 3,280 in three minutes. It can perform aerobatics without loss of altitude.

JURCA MJ-5 "SIROCCO"

STANDARD DATA: Gross wt. 1,300. Empty wt. 726. Fuel capacity 36. Wingspan 21'6". Length 20'6". **PERFORMANCE:** Top mph 190. Cruise mph 162. Stall mph 60. Climb rate 2,500. Takeoff run 820. Landing roll 750. Range 570.

The Sirocco is an all-wood, fiberglass- or fabric-covered, and low-wing aircraft that can give the homebuilding enthusiast the wild performance of a small fighter ship. Identified by its "rooster tail," the Sirocco seats two in tandem fashion and sports retractable landing gear for adding speed. Any 85- to 150-hp engine can be used.

JURCA MJ-7 "BABY MUSTANG"

STANDARD DATA: Gross wt. 2,000. Empty wt. 1,175. Fuel capacity 30. Wingspan 25'10". Length 22'4". **PERFORMANCE:** Top mph 225. Cruise mph 175. Stall mph 65. Takeoff run 900. Landing roll 800. Range 570.

Sportplane enthusiasts have always shown an interest in building replicas of fighter planes. Unlike planes from World War I, World War II ships have been difficult to re-create due to their massive engines, complex metal structure, and sheer size. To facilitate homebuilding, designer Marcel Jurca created scaled-down versions of the P-51 Mustang, the Supermarine Spitfire, and the Focke-Wulf FW-190. The Mustang was designed in ⅔ or ¾ scale. Only the relative size of a pilot's head identifies the baby P-51 from its bigger ancestor. The ship first flew with a 200-hp Ranger inline engine. Other engines that can be used include: any of the six-cylinder Rangers, the 125-hp Menasco, the 130-hp Gipsy Major, the 125- to 160-hp Canadian Rambler, or the General Motors Buick F-58. Materials used are wood and fabric.

JURCA MJ-8 "BABY FOCKE-WULF"

STANDARD DATA: Gross wt. 2,400. Empty wt. 400. Fuel capacity 32. Wingspan 25'10". Length 21'8". **PERFORMANCE:** Top mph 225. Cruise mph 150. Stall mph 50. Climb rate 2,000. Takeoff run 380. Landing roll 800. Range 575.

The replica of the German Focke-Wulf 190, the finest piston-engine fighter developed for the Luftwaffe, is available in ¾ scale only. Engines from 220 to 350 hp can be used.

JURCA MJ-10 "BABY SPITFIRE"

STANDARD DATA: Gross wt. 2,000. Empty wt. 900. Fuel capacity 34. Wingspan 27'8". Length 23'4". **PERFORMANCE:** Top mph 225. Cruise mph 140. Stall mph 60. Climb rate 1,650. Takeoff run 740. Landing roll 700. Range 630.

This scaled-down version of the hero of the Battle of Britain is available in ¾ scale only. As with all Jurca World War II fighters, the materials used are wood and fabric. Retractable landing gear is also a common feature. Engines for the Spitfire range from 220 to 350 hp.

KELEHER IK-1 "LARK"

STANDARD DATA: Gross wt. 855. Empty wt. 555. Fuel capacity 12. Wingspan 23'. Length 17'. **PERFORMANCE:** Top mph 135. Cruise mph 122. Stall mph 55. Climb rate 1,000. Takeoff run 550. Landing roll 700. Range 300.

The Lark is an enclosed-cockpit midwing monoplane. This single-seat taildragger is relatively unusual with its strut-braced midwing configuration. The fuselage is of steel-tube construction, and the wing uses wooden spars and ribs. The whole aircraft is fabric covered. Engines vary from 65 to 100 hp.

"KITTIWAKE"

STANDARD DATA: Gross wt. 1,350. Empty wt. 925. Fuel capacity 26. Wingspan 24'. Length 19'8". **PERFORMANCE:** Top mph 135. Cruise mph 115. Stall mph 48. Climb rate 950. Range 500.

The Kittiwake single-seat low-wing monoplane was designed to make full use of all-metal materials and modern construction while retaining a simplicity of design that lends itself to homebuilding. The wings attach directly to the sides of the fuselage so that the Kittiwake can be constructed or stored in a garage. The Kittiwake stands on tricycle landing gear and is used as a sporting light aircraft and a glider towplane. Power is supplied by a 100-hp Continental.

KRAFT "SUPER FLI"

STANDARD DATA: Gross wt. 1,450. Empty wt. 1,060. Fuel capacity 23. Wingspan 24'6". Length 20'. Engine 200-hp Lycoming. **PERFORMANCE:** Top mph 185. Cruise mph 135. Stall mph 48. Climb rate 1,800. Ceiling 12,000. Takeoff run 800. Landing roll 1,000. Range 400.

World-champion model builder and radio-control-system manufacturer Phil Kraft used his know-how to design and construct the Super Fli. This unlimited aerobatic low-winger has seating for one under a transparent canopy. Fuselage construction is a steel-tube frame covered by aluminum, while the wings are a spruce and plywood structure covered with plywood.

LACEY M-10

STANDARD DATA: Gross wt. 1,118. Empty wt. 638. Fuel capacity 20. Wingspan 20'. Length 20'. **PERFORMANCE:** Top mph 140. Cruise mph 120. Stall mph 55. Climb rate 1,000. Takeoff run 600. Landing roll 600. Range 440.

The Lacey is one of the simplest designs for the homebuilder to construct. In the words of its designer, "There are no compound curves and very few simple ones. The wing has no washin, no washout, no dihedral, and no incidence angle; the wing's bottom is flat and fits flat on top of the fuselage. It has no taper, no slots, no flaps, no spoilers, no wingtips, no struts, no wires, no braces, and no spars." The two-place towable Lacey is propelled by a 90-hp Continental.

LACO-125

STANDARD DATA: Gross wt. 1,400. Empty wt. 860. Fuel capacity 24. Wingspan 22'9". Length 19'6". Engine 125-hp Continental. **PERFORMANCE:** Top mph 124. Cruise mph 113. Stall mph 50. Climb rate 900. Range 300.

The Laco-25 is a sturdy two-seat biplane that is easy to fly yet very agile. To aid the builder, there are no castings, forgings, or other difficult-to-build-or-obtain parts. The fuselage is a Warren truss type of chrome moly tubing with wooden formers and stringers. The wings are conventional two-spar construction with wooden ribs and chrome moly fittings for strength. This homebuilt derives its designation from the use of a 125-hp Continental in the prototype, which is interchangeable with the 145-hp engine. The weight distribution of the Laco-125 is such that larger four-cylinder powerplants can be substituted.

LANCAIR "320/360"

STANDARD DATA: Seats 2. Gross wt. 1,685. Empty wt. 1,190. Fuel capacity 42. Engine 160–180-hp Lycoming IO-320/IO-360. **PERFORMANCE:** Top mph 260. Cruise mph 240. Initial climb rate 2,700. Ceiling 22,000. Range 1,140. Takeoff distance (50') 390. Landing distance (50') 900.

The Lancair line of kitbuilt aircraft began back in 1985 when Lance Neibauer designed the retractable-gear Lancair 235. The 235 was designed to go as fast as possible and provide economical operation in cross-country comfort for two full-size adults. As if this wasn't enough, Neibauer wanted the slippery-looking craft to have very docile flight characteristics and do it all powered by the Lycoming O-235 which put out only 100–115 hp. Results of the finished product were astounding. Not only did the 235 stand up to its expectations, it also cruised at better than 200 mph and burned something in the neighborhood of six gph. The basic look of the 320/360 has remained the same with improvements being made as the line developed. Higher horsepower and refinements in structure and aerodynamics helped make the 320/360 one of the most popular kits on the market with more than 800 units sold in 1993 alone. Standard kits and "fast-build" kits are available.

LANCAIR "IV"

STANDARD DATA: Seats 4. Gross wt. 3,200. Empty wt. 1,750. Fuel capacity 82. Engine 350-hp Continental TSIO-550. **PERFORMANCE:** Top mph 361. Cruise mph 341. Initial climb rate 2,600. Ceiling 35,000. Range 1,450. Takeoff distance (50') 1,200. Landing distance (50') 1,400.

The Lancair IV was a natural progression from the 235 and the 320. Lance Neibauer wanted to build a four-place re-

tractable that would give him and the kitbuilder the most bang for the buck. The IV is essentially a scaled-up version of the 320 with a 30-ft. wingspan and a twin-turbo 350-hp Continental swinging a three-blade constant-speed prop. The aircraft is faster, lighter, roomier, has more useful load, and is less expensive than any production aircraft in its class. Since its introduction in 1991, the Lancair IV has broken many speed and altitude records for its class type and at altitude has reached sustained speeds in excess of 395 mph with no tailwind. The entire airframe is constructed of vacuum-formed, oven-cured, prepreg carbon fiber. Building time is approximately 2,500 hrs. A pressurized version is also available.

LANCAIR "ES"

STANDARD DATA: Seats 4. Gross wt. 2,800. Empty wt. 1,600. Fuel capacity 76. Engine 200-hp Continental IO-360-ES. **PERFORMANCE:** Top mph n/a. Cruise mph 192. Initial climb rate 1,200. Ceiling 18,000. Range 1,360. Takeoff distance (50') 800. Landing distance (50') 800.

The Lancair ES is essentially a fixed gear, lesser horse-power version of the Lancair IV. Although the appearance is basically the same for both aircraft, they are really quite different from one another. The concept of the ES was to give the kitbuilder a fast, economical, and roomy four-seater without the complexity and expense of a retractable. The ES provides exceptional performance and flight characteristics with its 35-ft. wingspan and 200-hp engine. Construction is advanced composite prepreg that has been vacuum-formed and auto-claved to give unparalleled uniformity and component integrity throughout the airframe. The ES will accommodate four full-sized adults comfortably and contains 20 cubic feet of baggage space and a load limit of 175 pounds. Kits are sold less engine, avionics, and finishing products.

LARKIN "SKYLARK"

STANDARD DATA: Gross wt. 1,246. Empty wt. 790. Fuel capacity 17. Wingspan 26'6". Length 19'6". Engine 100-hp Volkswagen. **PERFORMANCE:** Top mph 115. Cruise mph 105. Stall mph 42. Climb rate 550. Ceiling 12,000. Takeoff run 600. Landing roll 400. Range 525.

The Skylark is a beautifully designed two-seater that looks more like it was intended to land on water than return to Earth. Its configuration includes an enclosed cabin with a pusher engine and prop mounted overhead and centered between twin booms. The booms are attached to the wings and connected by one single elevator surface at the rear between twin vertical stabilizers. One unique feature of the airplane's structure is the use of a square tubular aluminum keel that is responsible for the loads from the landing gear and the main fuselage. An optional V-shaped lower hull of fiberglass can be added for amphibious operations.

LEVI RL3 "MONSOON"

STANDARD DATA: Gross wt. 1,500. Empty wt. 870. Fuel capacity 28. Wingspan 25'10". Length 20'3". **PERFORMANCE:** Top mph 130. Cruise mph 115. Stall mph 45. Climb rate 800. Takeoff run 500. Landing roll 700. Range 600.

This two-place low-wing taildragger was first built in India by an Italian engineer who studied in England and France. A Canadian company brought it to the United States. The Monsoon is of conventional all-wood construction and covered with fabric. The prototype was powered by a Continental 85-hp engine, and other versions have a 125-hp Lycoming.

LOVING'S "LOVE"

STANDARD DATA: Gross wt. 885. Empty wt. 613. Fuel capacity 15. Wingspan 20'. Length 17'2". **PERFORMANCE:** Top mph 215. Cruise mph 142. Stall mph 58. Climb rate 2,100. Takeoff run 500. Landing roll 1,200. Range 450.

The Love racer features reverse gull wings and full wheel covers. It is built from fabric around a wooden frame. With an 85-hp Continental powerplant, it is capable of speeds in excess of 200 mph.

LUTON "MAJOR"

STANDARD DATA: Gross wt. 1,030. Empty wt. 600. Fuel capacity 13. Wingspan 35'2". Length 23'9". **PERFORMANCE:** Top mph 120. Cruise mph 105. Stall mph 35. Climb rate 750. Takeoff run 250. Landing roll 150. Range 300.

The Luton Major was first flown in 1939. This two-seat high-wing monoplane features an airframe that is similar to the Luton Minor. Its wings are vee-bracing struts and fold back along the fuselage for towing. The fuselage is an all-wood structure covered with plywood. Power is provided by a 55- to 65-hp Lycoming or 65- to 85-hp Continental.

LUTON "MINOR"

STANDARD DATA: Gross wt. 750. Empty wt. 450. Fuel capacity 7.5. Wingspan 25'. Length 20'9". **PERFORMANCE:** Top mph 85. Cruise mph 75. Stall mph 28. Climb rate 450. Takeoff run 250. Landing roll 120. Range 180.

This single-seat strut-braced parasol monoplane carries Volkswagen air-cooled engines rated from 30 to 65 hp. First flown in 1936, the design was upgraded in 1960 to handle 55-hp engines and up. The Luton Minor's wings are built around

a wooden two-spar structure in two halves and supported by a tubular center-section pylon structure. The wings are removable for transporting and storage. The fuselage is an all-wood plywood-covered structure.

MACDONALD S-20

STANDARD DATA: Gross wt. 720. Empty wt. 456. Fuel capacity 10. Wingspan 25'. Length 18'6". Engine 53-hp Volkswagen. **PERFORMANCE:** Top mph 110. Cruise mph 90. Stall mph 38. Climb rate 850. Takeoff run 300. Landing roll 300. Range 250.

The S-20 utilizes all-metal construction but keeps it simple by the extensive use of pop rivets. It features open-cockpit seating for one, low wings, and conventional landing gear. The fuselage is of steel-tube truss construction with a lightweight alloy skin. The constant-chord wings are also covered with the same lightweight alloy skin.

MEAD "ADVENTURE"

STANDARD DATA: Gross wt. 800. Empty wt. 460. Fuel capacity 20. Wingspan 20'. Length 13'. Engine 65- to 85-hp Continental. **PERFORMANCE:** Top mph 188. Cruise mph 180. Stall mph 57. Climb rate 1,600. Takeoff run 800. Landing roll 700. Range 650.

The Model 100 Adventure's simplicity of operation is equaled only by its simplicity in construction: a modern high-performance sandwich-composite structure. The materials and working techniques are descendants of Rutan's VariEze technology. The Adventure is a stunning performer with a combination of high-speed cruise, slow stall speeds, and good climb performance. The general configuration is a single-seat, low midwing, tractor-monoplane with fixed tricycle landing gear. The aircraft can be powered by any of the Continental Motors A- or C-series engines of 65 to 85 hp driving a fixed-pitch wooden propeller. The wing is a two-piece assembly to minimize the space required to build and to facilitate its removal from the fuselage. The fuselage is built from flat sheets of half-inch-thick polystyrene foam and is constructed from the inside out. The canopy is a single-piece freeblown unit.

MERKEL MARK II

STANDARD DATA: Gross wt. 1,540. Empty wt. 1,200. Fuel capacity 18. Wingspan 25'6". Length 22'9". Engine 220-hp Franklin. **PERFORMANCE:** Top mph 206. Cruise mph 160.

Stall mph 55. Climb rate 2,500. Takeoff run 300. Landing roll 300. Range 250.

This two-seat aerobatic biplane is stressed to a +6Gs and –3Gs limit, and +9Gs to –4.5Gs ultimate. It was first flown in 1973, and its designer, Edwin Merkel, planned to produce the biplane in a two-seater trainer version and a single-place competition model. The Mark II has a lightweight alloy skin on a welded-steel tube fuselage; the wings feature a single-spar torsional structure. Other extras include an antiservo tab, ground-adjustable trim tab, and optional cockpit canopy.

MEYER'S "LITTLE TOOT"

STANDARD DATA: Gross wt. 1,230. Empty wt. 914. Fuel capacity 18. Wingspan 19'. Length 16'6". Engine 160 hp. **PERFORMANCE:** Top mph 200. Cruise mph 125. Stall mph 55. Climb rate 2,500. Takeoff run 300. Landing roll 300. Range 250.

George Meyer's "Little Toot" has long been one of the nation's most popular homebuilt sport biplanes. It is constructed with a sheet-metal-covered steel-tube cockpit section and monocoque sheet-metal rear fuselage. The Little Toot uses two-spar wooden wings covered with fabric. The original was fitted with a Continental 90-hp engine, but the airplane is capable of housing engines up to 200 hp. The Little Toot has an eight-degree sweepback on the upper wing. The straight lower wing carries wide, almost full-span ailerons that give the ship an unusually high roll rate. A fiberglass engine cowling is available.

MILLER JM-2

STANDARD DATA: Gross wt. 1,100. Empty wt. 630. Fuel capacity 12. Wingspan 15'. Length 19'. Engine 100-hp Continental. **PERFORMANCE:** Top mph 235. Cruise mph 190. Stall mph 70. Climb rate 1,600. Takeoff run 1,500. Landing roll 2,000. Range 300.

Designed by J.W. Miller, the JM-2 took a different approach to Formula I airplane racing. Both the engine and main wings are set aft of the pilot's enclosed cockpit. A Continental drove a pusher prop; the spinner took the place of the tailcone. Two sections of the vertical propeller shroud act as the vertical stabilizer, and the elevators are placed in T-tail fashion. The wings are covered with honeycomb material reinforced by fiberglass and resin. The fuselage is constructed from four fiberglass panels.

MILLER "LIL' RASCAL"

STANDARD DATA: Gross wt. 1,100. Empty wt. 600. Fuel capacity 12. Wingspan 20'8". Length 15'3". Engine 85-hp Continental. **PERFORMANCE:** (estimated) Top mph 110. Cruise mph 90. Stall mph 58.

The "Lil' Rascal" by Merle B. Miller began flight testing in early 1978. This biplane makes use of a steel-tube fuselage and tail section covered with Stits Poly-Fibre Dacron. The wings are constructed of spruce and plywood and are covered with the same fabric. The landing gear is the nonretractable tailwheel type, and seating is for two persons in a side-by-side open cockpit. The standard 85-hp engine turns a fixed-pitch prop.

MINI COUPE

STANDARD DATA: Gross wt. 850. Empty wt. 497. Fuel capacity 13. Wingspan 22'4". Length 16'4". **PERFORMANCE:** Top mph 145. Cruise mph 119. Stall mph 400. Climb rate 850. Ceiling 12,500. Takeoff run 300. Landing roll 400. Range 300.

The Mini Coupe made its first flight in 1971 and was certified in 1972. By late 1975, approximately 150 sets of plans had been sold. The Mini Coupe is a lightweight all-metal single-seat sporting aircraft powered by a 65-hp modified Volkswagen 1,600cc engine. Its wings are of constant-chord design with all-metal stressed-skin construction, metal ailerons, and no flaps or trim tabs. Its landing gear is the nonretractable tricycle type with oversize tires. The single-seat can be either covered by a canopy or open.

MINI-HAWK "TIGER HAWK"

STANDARD DATA: Gross wt. 800. Empty wt. 525. Fuel capacity 12. Wingspan 18'. Length 13'3". Engine 72-hp Revmaster Volkswagen. **PERFORMANCE:** Top mph 175. Cruise mph 160. Stall mph 50. Climb rate 1,000. Ceiling 10,000. Takeoff run 400. Landing roll 400. Range 700.

The Mini-Hawk combines the economy of the Volkswagen engine with that of detachable wings for towing or storage. Standard VW engines up to 67 hp are applicable. The wings can be removed in under 10 minutes. Its all-metal construction is built around a configuration that includes low wings with trailing-edge flaps and seating for one under an enclosed canopy. The tricycle landing gear includes a steerable nosewheel with disc brakes and wheel fairings all around.

MONNETT "MONEX"

STANDARD DATA: Gross wt. 650. Empty wt. 380. Wingspan 16'8". Length 15'2". Fuel capacity 10. Engine Monnett "AeroVee" VW 2,180cc. **PERFORMANCE:** Top mph 230. Climb rate 2,000+. Range 400+.

MONNETT "MONEX"

MONNETT "MONI"

The Monex made its maiden flight on September 30, 1980, to begin the testing program. It is a very high-performance single-place conventionally geared aircraft designed for amateur builders with limited building experience. Design limits are +6Gs and –4Gs. The Moni is a tricycle version.

MONNETT "SONERAI"

STANDARD DATA: Gross wt. 750. Empty wt. 440. Fuel capacity 11. Wingspan 16'8". Length 16'8". **PERFORMANCE:** Cruise mph 150. Stall mph 40. Climb rate 1,200. Takeoff run 500. Landing roll 500. Range 300.

The 150-mph Sonerai is a real "spark plug" in the VW/racing picture. This midwing sport plane/racer was de-

signed to meet all PRPA Formula VEE requirements for 1,600cc VW-powered aircraft. Its wings are aluminum, built with folding panels so the aircraft can be towed tail-first on its own gear. Fuselage and tail are of standard chrome moly tubing. Cowling is fiberglass, and fuselage and tail surfaces are fabric covered.

MONNETT "SONERAI II"

STANDARD DATA: Gross wt. 925. Empty wt. 506. Fuel capacity 10. Wingspan 18'8". Length 18'10". Engine 65- to 70-hp Volkswagen. **PERFORMANCE:** Top mph 165. Cruise mph 140. Stall mph 45. Climb rate 750. Takeoff run 900. Landing roll 500. Range 420.

After enjoying success with his original VW-powered Sonerai, John Monett decided to develop the Sonerai II, a tandem-seated version. Both pilot and passenger sit under a bubble canopy that is hinged on the right side. The Sonerai II differs mainly by being slightly larger, making use of a somewhat more powerful engine, and by being stressed for aerobatics when flown by the pilot alone.

MOONEY "MITE"

STANDARD DATA: Gross wt. 780. Empty wt. 500. Fuel capacity 11–17. Wingspan 26'10". Length 17'8". **PERFORMANCE:** Top mph 143. Cruise mph 130. Stall mph 43. Climb rate 1,000+. Takeoff run 300. Landing roll 275. Range 600.

The Mooney Mite, first flown in 1947, was constructed by Mooney Aircraft, a company formed by the executives of the Culver Aircraft Corp. This single-seat monoplane was originally powered by a 25-hp Crosley converted automobile engine. The Mooney Mite is built with a combination of steel-tube, wood, and fabric materials. The most common engine is the 65-hp Continental.

OLDFIELD "BABY LAKES"

STANDARD DATA: Gross wt. 850. Empty wt. 475. Fuel capacity 12. Wingspan 16'8". Length 13'9". Engine 80-hp Continental. **PERFORMANCE:** Top mph 135. Cruise mph 118. Stall mph 50. Climb rate 2,000. Takeoff run 300. Landing roll 400. Ceiling 17,000. Range 250.

Barney Oldfield's Baby Great Lakes flies much like its big brother, the Great Lakes Sport Trainer. The "Baby Lakes" was designed to get the same sort of flying ease and performance at lower cost. It uses a steel-tube fuselage, wooden wings, and fabric cover, and it offers unusually lively aerobatic performance when powered by an 80-hp Continental engine. The "Baby Lakes" can also be fitted with a 50- to 100-hp Continental, a 108-hp Lycoming, or a 125-hp Lycoming. Its makers say it will outfly aircraft with twice the horsepower, and it is the least-expensive high-performance biplane available to the homebuilder.

OSPREY

STANDARD DATA: Gross wt. 900. Empty wt. 600. Fuel capacity 16. Wingspan 24'9". Length 17'9". **PERFORMANCE:** Top mph 120. Cruise mph 105. Stall mph 55. Climb rate 2,000. Takeoff run 200. Range 350.

The Osprey is a tiny single-place flying boat. It is built from fir and pine; the vertical fin is an integral part of the structure. The hull is skinned with mahogany plywood and fiberglassed. The steel-tube pylon mount for the engine is bolted to the wing center section. A simple wing-folding mechanism holds the wings in position with the same steel pin that locks them in the extended position. Power is provided by a 90-hp Continental.

OSPREY II

STANDARD DATA: Gross wt. 1,570. Empty wt. 960. Fuel capacity 38. Wingspan 26'. Length 21'. Engine 150-hp Lycoming. **PERFORMANCE:** Top mph 145. Cruise mph 130. Stall mph 60. Climb rate 1,100. Takeoff run (land) 300. Takeoff run (water) 520. Landing roll 600. Range 550.

The Osprey II is a considerably improved enclosed-cockpit version of the original Osprey. It boasts one of the most streamlined designs in the homebuilt amphibian class. George Pereira achieves the necessary aqua-dynamics of the hull in a rather unique way. After the fuselage is complete, urethane foam is attached to the bottom and then sculptured into shape before several layers of fiberglass are added. The wings are an all-wood structure with a single box-spar. The hull or fuselage is also an all-wood structure of marine plywood. The engine is mounted in a pusher fashion atop a steel-tube pylon. The landing gear is a retractable tricycle type.

PAYNE "KNIGHT TWISTER IMPERIAL"

STANDARD DATA: Gross wt. 900–1,100. Empty wt. 694. Fuel capacity 35. Wingspan 17'. Length 16'1". Engine 140-hp Lycoming. **PERFORMANCE:** Top mph 170. Cruise mph 120. Stall mph 50. Climb rate 1,000. Takeoff run 475. Landing roll 800. Range 680.

The Knight Twister Imperial is actually a Knight Twister upgraded to race in the Sport Biplane class. Piloted by Don Fairbanks, it won the Silver Biplane Race at Reno in 1971. The differences in the Imperial version were a redesigned wing section and an increase in wingspan, tailplane span, and fuel capacity. The fuel is carried in two tanks, a 21-gallon upper and a 15-gallon bottom. The wings are fabric-covered wood structures, and the fuselage is a fabric-covered steel-tube truss structure with wood stringers.

PAZMANY PL-1

STANDARD DATA: Gross wt. 1,326. Empty wt. 800. Fuel capacity 25. Wingspan 28'. Length 18'11". Engine 95-hp Continental. **PERFORMANCE:** Top mph 120. Cruise mph 115. Stall mph 51. Climb rate 1,000. Ceiling 18,000. Takeoff run 550. Landing roll 175. Range 600.

The prototype PL-1 was stressed to 9Gs for aerobatics and featured a low-wing tricycle-gear configuration with a sliding canopy. In 1968, the Chinese Nationalist Air Force in Taiwan presented a PL-1, which they built, to Generalissimo Chiang Kai-Shek. Nearly 400 sets of plans were sold for the PL-1 before sales were discontinued. The fuselage of the plane is all-metal with only flat or single-curvature skins. The wings are built around a single all-metal spar with a leading edge torsion box. In the cabin, seating is side-by-side with dual controls, and there is room for 40 pounds of baggage.

PAZMANY PL-2

STANDARD DATA: Gross wt. 1,416. Empty wt. 875. Fuel capacity 25. Wingspan 28'. Length 19'4". Engine 100-hp Lycoming. **PERFORMANCE:** Top mph 138. Cruise mph 119. Stall mph 52. Climb rate 1,280. Takeoff run 700. Landing roll 700. Range 492.

Along with the PL-1, the PL-2 is the only design for amateur builders that is also used for military trainers. The PL-2 is simply an advanced version of the PL-1. The external shape and flight characteristics are almost identical, but the construction has been simplified. The PL-2 offers a wider cockpit, better canopy and fuselage lines, simplified dihedral, and the possibility of using engines from 90 to 150 hp. Despite its aerodynamically clean lines, there are no compound curves anywhere in the skin. This is partly the result of the use of a fiberglass cowl to streamline the nose. Pilots who have flown

the PL-2 say it is an airplane flown with the fingers and not the fist. And, like the PL-1, it is stressed for aerobatics.

PAZMANY PL-4A

STANDARD DATA: Gross wt. 850. Empty wt. 578. Fuel capacity 12. Wingspan 26'8". Length 16'6". **PERFORMANCE:** Top mph 120. Cruise mph 98. Stall mph 48. Climb rate 650. Takeoff run 485. Landing roll 435. Range 375.

When designer Ladislao Pazmany was encouraged to come up with an easy-to-build, simple, safe, and inexpensive metal plane that could carry a Volkswagen 1,500cc engine, he came up with the PL-4A. Not the least part of its attractiveness is economy of operation and roadability; folding wings make it a cinch to trail home and park in the family garage. Pazmany supplied the fiberglass pieces, plexiglass windscreen and canopy, landing gear, welded engine mount, and control stick.

PIETENPOL "AIR CAMPER"

STANDARD DATA: Gross wt. 1,150. Empty wt. 622. Fuel capacity 15. Wingspan 29'. Length 18'5". **PERFORMANCE:** Top mph 100. Cruise mph 80. Stall mph 40. Climb rate 500. Takeoff run 400. Landing roll 600. Range 320.

The do-it-yourself craze was just getting started as a Depression-born phenomenon when the Air Camper replaced the earlier primary glider as aviation's favorite backyard building project. In 1930, *Modern Mechanics* magazine featured the Ford Model A engine as the perfect powerplant for the little homebuilt. The two-seat open-cockpit monoplane is said to land like a Luscombe and handle like a J-3 Cub. Modern Air Campers are powered by Corvair, Lycoming, or Continental engines.

PITTS S-1S "SPECIAL"

STANDARD DATA: Gross wt. 1,950. Empty wt. 710. Fuel capacity 19. Wingspan 17'4". Length 14'3". **PERFORMANCE:** Top mph 156. Cruise mph 140. Stall mph 57. Climb rate 2,600. Takeoff run 450. Landing roll 1,000. Range 350.

Originally designed and designated "Lil' Stinker" by aircraft-design legend Curtis Pitts, the Pitts Special is one of the world's most outstanding aerobatic aircraft. It was no mere coincidence that the U.S. Aerobatic Team members, which outflew all competition in the 1972 world aerobatic meet and established themselves as virtually unbeatable champions, flew only Pitts biplanes. While there are a number of fine aerobatic ships around the sky, there's got to be a reason why so many of the top performers fly the Pitts. The plans called for installation of a 180-hp engine, but it is not uncommon to find aircraft powered by a 200-hp engine.

POLLIWAGEN

STANDARD DATA: Gross wt. 1,250. Empty wt. 600. Fuel capacity 19. Wingspan 26'. Length 16'. Engine 78-hp Revmaster VW. **PERFORMANCE:** (designer figures) Top mph 200+. Cruise mph 180. Stall mph 38. Climb rate 700. Ceiling 28,000. Range 1,000. Takeoff run 450. Landing roll 550.

Designed by Argentine-born Joseph Alvarez, the Polliwagen derives its name from its appearance and its engine type. It is powered by a Revmaster R-2100 turbocharged Volkswagen conversion. The Revmaster powers a two-position constant-speed Maloof metal propeller of 59 inches diameter. The Polliwagen's exceptionally clean lines give it an excellent speed-to-power ratio as well as fine aerodynamic handling characteristics. The wings are Wortmann FX-67-K-150 wing section with full-span trailing-edge flaps and ailerons. The wings and fuselage make use of foam/epoxy composite construction. Kits included prefabricated parts: molded windshield and canopy, landing gear, disc brakes, complete panels, composite-structure wingtip fuel tanks, outward-breaking cabin structure, T-tail, and the like.

POWELL "ACEY DEUCY"

STANDARD DATA: Gross wt. 1,275. Empty wt. 750. Fuel capacity 14. Wingspan 32'6". Length 20'9". **PERFORMANCE:** Top mph 104. Cruise mph 87. Stall mph 27. Climb rate 650–700. Takeoff run 250. Landing roll 250. Range 250.

This parasol-type tandem-seat monoplane was designed by John Powell, formerly a commander in the U.S. Navy. It is powered by a Continental A65 four-banger and features a combination of wood, fabric, and tubular-steel construction.

PROWLER AVIATION "PROWLER/JAGUAR"

STANDARD DATA: Seats 2. Gross wt. 2,500. Empty wt. 1,560. Fuel capacity 72. Engine 350-hp Rodeck V-8. **PERFORMANCE:** Top mph 300. Cruise mph 250. Initial climb rate 2,500. Ceiling n/a. Range 1,200. Takeoff distance (50') 1,100. Landing distance (50') 1,200.

Back in 1973, George Morse, the founder of Prowler Aviation, saw the need for an alternative aircraft powerplant that was economical, lightweight, powerful, efficient, and wouldn't break the bank at overhaul time. Morse settled on the Rodeck automotive racing engine. This customized, all-aluminum, and liquid-cooled V-8 develops 350 hp and burns 13 gallons of 100-octane avgas per hour. Prowler Aviation became a reality in 1985, and after three years of development, the Prowler I prototype took to the skies. The World War II fighteresque homebuilt aircraft began to receive its share of notice and the first kit was sold in 1988. The beautiful lines of the Prowler/Jaguar are very reminiscent of the Spitfire from World War II, and the combination airframe/powerplant gives the airplane fighterlike flight characteristics. The aircraft cruises at 250 mph and is fully aerobatic.

QUESTAIR "SPIRIT"

STANDARD DATA: Seats 2–3. Gross wt. 1,700. Empty wt. 1,025. Fuel capacity 40. Engine 210-hp Continental IO-360. **PERFORMANCE:** Top mph 287. Cruise mph 228. Initial climb rate 2,000. Ceiling n/a. Range 1,180. Takeoff distance (50') n/a. Landing distance (50') n/a.

The Spirit is actually the second of two extremely fast aircraft from Questair. The Spirit is a toned-down fixed-gear version of the record-setting Venture design. The Spirit's unusually stubby design is very reminiscent of an egg with wings. Nonetheless, the Spirit and the Venture are very popular with kitbuilders primarily for their exceptional performance and relatively forgiving flight characteristics. The airframe structure is all-aluminum with all of the compound-curve components provided in the kit to ease the building process. Approximate building time is 2,000 hours.

QUESTAIR "VENTURE"

STANDARD DATA: Seats 2. Gross wt. 2,000. Empty wt. 1,240. Fuel capacity 56. Engine 280-hp Continental IO-550. **PERFORMANCE:** Top mph 345. Cruise mph 276. Initial climb rate 2,600. Ceiling 25,000. Range 1,150. Takeoff distance (50') 1,000. Landing distance (50') 1,600.

When the Venture was introduced, few could believe the performance figures that were being claimed by this stubby little plane. But seeing is believing, and as the records fell, more and more people started taking Questair's Venture as an aircraft to be reckoned with. The basic formula is really quite simple and is one that has held fast since the airplane was invented: largest engine + smallest practical airframe = speed. Of course, the trick is to simultaneously keep it safely flyable and easy to build. This speedy little two-seater is of all-aluminum construction with a retractable tricycle landing gear. There's ample room in the cockpit for two full-sized adults and about 50 pounds of baggage.

"QUICKIE"

STANDARD DATA: Gross wt. 480. Empty wt. 240. Fuel capacity 8. Wingspan 16'8". Length 17'4". Engine 18-hp Onan two-cylinder. **PERFORMANCE:** Top mph 126. Cruise mph 121. Stall mph 49. Climb rate 425. Ceiling 12,300. Takeoff run 660. Landing roll 835. Range 550.

The "Quickie" is an unusual design that can cruise at 121 mph and actually fly for 100 miles on a single gallon of avgas. The design work was accomplished by Burt Rutan of VariEze and VariViggen fame. The project was masterminded by Tom Jewett and Gene Sheehan. Basic to the Quickie's economy is the 18-hp Onan horizontally opposed flat four-stroke engine commonly used to power lawnmowers and RV generators. The wide canard of the Quickie carries the main landing wheels at each end, and a tiny tailwheel at the rear end is covered with a small rudder. Complete kits include engine, pre-

fabricated cowling, canopy, all the machined parts, all the welded parts, and some of the tools in an effort to save construction time for the inexperienced builder. Construction is from composite materials. The cockpit is suitable for one pilot up to 210 pounds.

"QUICKIE Q2"

STANDARD DATA: Gross wt. 960. Empty wt. 537. Wingspan 16'8". Engine 63-64 Revmaster Volkswagen. **PERFORMANCE:** Top mph 180. Climb rate 1,000. Range 750. Takeoff run 500.

The Q2 is a newer two-place side-by-side version of the composite-construction Quickie canard-platform aircraft. It is designed for high performance on low horsepower with high efficiency. The proven Revmaster 2,100-D was detuned to just under 65 hp by removing the blower and running the engine RPM back down to 3,200. Typical cruise for the Q2 is 155 mph at a 12,000-foot density altitude burning 3.6 gph for 45 mpg. According to its designers, the Q2's equivalent flatplate area is 1.37, cleaner than the Glasair or the original VW-powered VariEze prototype. Like the Quickie, the Q2 is built from basic foam and epoxy/fiberglass composite construction and is similar in configuration.

RAND KR-1

STANDARD DATA: Gross wt. 600. Empty wt. 310. Fuel capacity 7.5. Wingspan 17'2". Length 12'6". **PERFORMANCE:** Top mph 140. Cruise mph 130. Stall mph 42. Climb rate 700 fpm. Takeoff run 300. Landing roll 800. Range 500.

The Taylor Monoplane with a wingspan of almost 22 feet prompted Rand's original concept. Rand ended up with a wing that had a wider chord but spanned only 17 feet, and the airplane weighed 150 pounds less than the Monoplane. Powered by a Volkswagen engine, it can squeeze 32 miles out of a gallon of automotive gas. The structure of the KR-1 combines both conventional and unconventional materials. The ship is basically a wooden box with polystyrene foam to round out the aerodynamic shape; it is covered with 4-ounce Dynel fabric and epoxy resins. The wings are modeled after the airfoil of the British Spitfire. Retractable gear adds to its performance.

RAND KR-2

STANDARD DATA: Gross wt. 900. Empty wt. 480. Fuel capacity 12–60. Wingspan 20'8". Length 14'6". Engine 2,100cc VW. **PERFORMANCE:** Top mph 200. Cruise mph 180. Stall mph 45. Climb rate 1,200. Takeoff run 350. Landing run 500. Range 2,000.

The KR-2 is a two-place version of the KR-I and is generally similar in construction. The low wings are removable, the main gear is retractable, and the tailwheel is steerable. With a stock 1,600cc engine, cruise speed is 140 mph. With a 2,100cc turbocharged VW conversion, cruise is 180 mph at 3,200 RPM. To achieve simplicity of construction, the airplane is designed so that no machining or welding is required in building the airframe. The cost and construction time is minimized by using a combination of wood, polyurethane foam, Dynel fabric, and epoxy resin. The result is a structurally strong, clean, and hard surface to make the airplane exceptionally fast for the power used.

REDFERN FOKKER DRI

STANDARD DATA: Gross wt. 1,485. Empty wt. 1,100. Fuel capacity 30. Wingspan 23'5". Length 19'. Engine 160- to 145-hp Warner radial. **PERFORMANCE:** Top mph 115. Cruise mph 105. Stall mph 50. Climb rate 2,500. Takeoff run 150. Landing roll 300. Range 350.

This replica of the Red Baron's famed fighter is not one of the easier-to-build homebuilts. The cost of materials, a good deal of skill in using hand tools and a torch, several years of spare time, and a lot of scrounging for props, wheels, and the like are necessary to end up with a show-stopper like the Fokker. The fuselage is built from steel tube and plywood, then fabric covered. The all-wood wings are fabric covered. The 145-hp Warner Radial is usually the recommended engine.

REDFERN NIEUPORT 21

STANDARD DATA: Gross wt. 1,391. Empty wt. 1,006. Fuel capacity 30. Wingspan 27'5". Length 19'. Engine 145- to 165-hp Warner. **PERFORMANCE:** Top mph 120. Cruise mph 110. Stall mph 45. Climb rate 1,500. Takeoff run 100. Landing roll 300. Range 350.

This replica of the famous World War I Nieuport 21 is powered by a seven-cylinder Warner radial engine in the 145- to 165-hp range. A single open cockpit is situated close under the trailing edge of the upper wing.

RENEGADE

STANDARD DATA: Gross wt. 652. Empty wt. 400. Fuel capacity 7.5. Wingspan 16'. Length 14'. **PERFORMANCE:** (40 hp) Top mph 130. Cruise mph 120. Stall mph 49. Climb rate 1,000. Takeoff run 560. Landing roll 400. Range 375.

This Formula-V sport racer features a straightline mid-wing design. Its designer, Charles Lasher, chose steel-tube construction for the fuselage and tail because of its ability to withstand the shock of a crash better than other materials. The wings are a wooden-frame structure with fabric covering. The ship is made to handle any Volkswagen engine from 35 to 65 hp.

RICHARD COMMUTER

STANDARD DATA: Gross wt. 1,500. Empty wt. 805. Fuel capacity 50. Wingspan 25'. Length 19'9". **PERFORMANCE:**

Top mph 150. Cruise mph 140. Stall mph 40. Climb rate 900. Takeoff run 1,200. Landing roll 1,500. Range 900.

The Commuter is a high-wing cabin monoplane that features all-metal construction with no complicated compound-curve skin panels. The two-place taildragger carries 125- to 150-hp Lycoming powerplants. Occupants sit side-by-side.

RLU-1 "BREEZY"

STANDARD DATA: Gross wt. 1,200. Empty wt. 700. Fuel capacity 18. Wingspan 33'. Length 22'6" **PERFORMANCE:** Top mph 105. Cruise mph 75. Stall mph 25. Climb rate 500. Takeoff run 450. Landing roll 450. Range 250.

Minimum structure and maximum open-air fun are the formula for the Breezy. It is a three-place airplane with two seated abreast on the second seat, but it can easily be adapted as a single-seater or tandem two-seater. Apart from the welding, nothing much about the construction of the Breezy would trouble the average craftsman. The original design utilizes a Piper Super Cruiser wing. The ship is pushed by a 90-hp Continental.

ROTORWAY "SCORPION 133"

STANDARD DATA: Gross wt. 1,250. Empty wt. 800. Fuel capacity 10. Rotor diameter 25'. Length 27'. Engine 133-hp RotorWay. **PERFORMANCE:** Top mph 95. Cruise mph 80–90. Stall mph 125. Climb rate 800. Range 120. Ceiling 10,000. Hover I.G.E. 6,500.

An economical personal helicopter was made possible by simplifying the otherwise complex rotor mechanism. When introduced to the public, it was an open-cabin single-seater. In 1970, a two-cycle powerplant rated at 125 hp became available, and the single-place helicopter became the Scorpion Too, a two-place craft with a gross weight of 1,125 pounds. In 1975, RotorWay developed its own four-cylinder engine to better meet the helicopter's requirements for a two-person load and an empty-vehicle weight of less than 700 pounds. The Scorpion rotor system incorporates an elliptical hub plate designed to withstand stresses many times those encountered during operation. Its enclosed cabin is constructed of lightweight fiberglass.

RUTAN "DEFIANT"

STANDARD DATA: Gross wt. 2,900. Empty wt. 1,610. Fuel capacity 90. Wingspan 29'2". Engines two 160-hp Lycomings. **PERFORMANCE:** Top mph 214. Cruise mph 210. Stall mph 75. Climb rate 1,600. Range 1,128. (No plans available.)

The Rutan Defiant is a four-seat twin-engine proof-of-concept offshoot of the other Rutan canard designs. The Defiant was intended for eventual mass production. It made use of the VariEze rear-mounted swept cantilever wings with winglet surfaces, canard foreplane, and a retractable nosewheel with a fixed main landing gear. The two engines were mounted in tractor and pusher positions feeding off a 45-gallon tank for each. The Defiant was intended to be a simple aircraft with no flaps, fixed-pitch propellers, and few complex systems. Its designers claimed that the Defiant had no minimum controllable airspeed.

RUTAN "LONG-EZ"

STANDARD DATA: Gross wt. 1,325. Empty wt. 700. Fuel capacity 52. Wingspan 26'3". Length 100". Engine 108- to 115-hp Lycoming. **PERFORMANCE:** Top mph 220. Cruise mph 185. Stall mph 66. Climb rate 1,150. Ceiling 26,900. Range 1,298. Takeoff run 775. Landing roll 780.

Rutan's Long-EZ is a larger and heavier version of the VariEze built around the 115-hp Lycoming engine. It has over four feet more wingspan and nearly half again the wing area of the VariEze. It takes off in 100 feet less distance and lands in only slightly more than half the distance of the original VariEze. While identical in length—100 inches—the long version is two inches wider. During one record flight, Dick Rutan logged 52.2 hours on a two-week round-trip to Florida from Mojave, averaging a 183-mph airspeed.

RUTAN "VARIEZE"

STANDARD DATA: Gross wt. 1,050. Empty wt. 570. Fuel capacity 26. Wingspan 22'2". Length 15'. Engine 100-hp Continental. **PERFORMANCE:** Top mph 195. Cruise mph 190. Stall mph 65. Climb rate 1,600. Takeoff run 900. Landing roll 900. Range 700.

This sleek, fast, and lightweight homebuilt is capable of achieving a top speed of 175 mph with a 1,600cc VW conversion or 210 mph with Continental's 100-hp engine. The unusual aircraft combines the use of a NASA GA(W)-1 airfoil with Whitcomb winglets and was actually the first aircraft to fly with the latter. The wing is a nonlaminar flow airfoil optimized for good lift and stall qualities. The ship's low induced drag lets the pilot negotiate steep, 90-degree banks with strong spiral stability.

RUTAN "VARIVIGGEN"

STANDARD DATA: Gross wt. 1,700. Empty wt. 950. Fuel capacity 25. Wingspan 19'. Length 19'. Engine 150-hp Lycoming. **PERFORMANCE:** Top mph 160. Cruise mph 152. Stall mph. 53. Climb rate 800. Takeoff run 800. Landing roll 500. Range 450.

One of the most unusual homebuilts ever designed also has an unusual name. Despite the unique appearance of the VariViggen, its basic design was actually the first shape that ever managed powered flight. The tail-first pusher configuration was also employed by the Wright brothers. This two-seat tandem pusher is named after the Swedish Saab 37 Viggen, a faster-than-Mach 2 delta-wing fighter with a canard surface. The airframe is all wood and fabric with the exception of a tubular-steel engine mount.

SAPPHIRE C.P. 80

STANDARD DATA: Gross wt. 770. Empty wt. 525. Fuel capacity 10. Wingspan 23'8". Length 20'10". Engine 90 hp. **PERFORMANCE:** Top mph 190. Cruise mph 150. Stall mph 67. Climb rate 2,300. Ceiling 19,000+. Takeoff run 650. Landing roll 650. Range 300.

The Sapphire is a single-seat racing airplane of all-wood construction designed by Claude Piel, who is famous for his Emeraude Diamant and Beryl designs. The airplane is stressed for the load factors of +12Gs and –9Gs at the maximum takeoff weight of 770 pounds. The Sapphire can accommodate any engine from 50 to 100 hp. Its wing is fully cantilevered and tapered for minimum drag and has a tip-to-tip laminated box spar to avoid heavy root fittings and wing alignment problems. The fuselage consists of three bulkheads and is entirely plywood covered. The cockpit offers plenty of room for any pilot.

SAWYER "SKYJACKER II"

STANDARD DATA: Gross wt. 2,250. Empty wt. 1,650. Fuel capacity 50. Wingspan 18'. Length 18'. Engine 200-hp Lycoming. **PERFORMANCE:** Top mph 130. Cruise mph 105.

Stall mph 45. Climb rate 400. Takeoff run 1,200. Landing roll 1,000. Range 525.

Sawyer's objective for constructing this vehicle was to prove the stability, controllability, and capability of such a radical low-aspect-ratio aircraft. The size for this type of aircraft is unlimited due to the nature of its lifting-body design. The Skyjacker is cheap to build because there are no compound curves, highly stressed areas, or complex control systems. The design will not stall or spin and has no rudders. The Skyjacker is not yet marketed as a sporting aircraft, but is a two-seat research vehicle of all-metal construction.

UAC-200 "SCRAPPY"

STANDARD DATA: Gross wt. 1,428. Empty wt. 981. Fuel capacity 28. Wingspan 20'8". Length 16'8". **PERFORMANCE:** Top mph 188. Cruise mph 151. Stall mph 55. Climb rate 3,700. Takeoff run 950. Landing roll 1,250. Range 500.

The Scrappy is a single-place sport biplane constructed of steel tubing, wood, and fabric. A 200-hp Lycoming engine provides the power.

S.E.5A. REPLICA

STANDARD DATA: Gross wt. 1,100. Empty wt. 900. Fuel capacity 24. Wingspan 22'. Length 18'. **PERFORMANCE:** Top mph 95. Cruise mph 85. Stall mph 50. Climb rate 600. Takeoff run 200. Range 250.

This little single-seat biplane is a ⅝-scale model of the famous British S.E.5A fighter of World War I. Designed by William Wienberg of Kansas City, Missouri, it is constructed of wood and fabric. The wing structure consists of conventional wooden spars and ribs with center-section bracing struts and fabric covering. The fuselage is an all-wooden box structure covered with plywood. The tail assembly is a wire-braced steel-tube structure also covered with Ceconite fabric. Accommodations include a single-seat cockpit and a small baggage compartment behind the headrest.

SEQUOIA F.8L "FALCO"

STANDARD DATA: Gross wt. 1,808. Empty wt. 1,212. Fuel capacity 31. Wingspan 26'3". Length 21'4". Engine 160-hp Lycoming. **PERFORMANCE:** Top mph 212. Cruise mph 190. Stall mph 62. Climb rate 1,140. Ceiling 19,000. Takeoff run (50') 1,150. Landing roll (50') 1,150. Range 870.

The Falco is a two-place aircraft—with an optional third seat for a child—that offers an unbeatable combination of high-speed cross-country travel with complete aerobatic capability. Designed by an Italian, Stelio Frati, a Falco equipped with an optional Christen inverted fuel and oil system is capable of unlimited inverted flight and the full range of aerobatic maneuvers. Landing gear are fully retractable, activated by a simple mechanical system. Designer Frati has been responsible for such airplanes as the Waco Meteor/SF 260 and the F20 Pegaso. Between 1956 and 1968, 101 Falcos were built as production aircraft. Earmarked for homebuilt construction in the United States through Sequoia Aircraft Corp., the Falco is made of wood, except for the firewall forward, the landing gear, and the sliding canopy. Fuselage and wing skins are Dacron. Power is supplied by either a 150- or 160-hp Lycoming behind a fixed-pitch or constant-speed prop. Gear and flaps are operated electrically.

SHEFFIELD "SKEETER X-1"

STANDARD DATA: Gross wt. 730. Empty wt. 500. Fuel capacity 5.5. Wingspan 22'. Length 13'6". **PERFORMANCE:** Top mph 85. Cruise mph 75. Stall mph 42. Climb rate 600. Takeoff run 600. Landing 600. Range 160.

The Skeeter is a lightweight sporting plane featuring a single seat and a single strut-braced wing mounted in parasol fashion. The wing is constructed from wooden spars and fabric covering with the exception of the leading edge, which is covered with metal. The fuselage is constructed from a steel-tube frame that is paneled with either wood or metal in the cockpit area only. The airframe is not covered aft of the cockpit. Power is supplied by Volkswagen engines rated from 50 to 72 hp.

SINDLINGER "HAWKER HURRICANE"

STANDARD DATA: Gross wt. 1,375. Empty wt. 984. Fuel capacity 32. Wingspan 25'. Length 19'8". Engine 180-hp Lycoming. **PERFORMANCE:** Top mph 200. Cruise mph 170. Stall mph 62. Climb rate 1,850. Ceiling 21,000. Takeoff run 490. Landing roll 550. Range 575.

Sindlinger's ⅝-scale version of the British Hawker Hurricane first flew in 1972. The wings and fuselage are constructed of wood with a fabric covering. The powerplant turns a metal constant-speed prop. A 14-gallon fuel tank is located just aft of the firewall; optional 10-gallon tanks can be built into the wing root. The landing gear is a steerable tailwheel type with the main gear retracting into the wings. The pilot sits under a sliding canopy.

"SIZZLER"

STANDARD DATA: Gross wt. 1,350. Empty wt. 950. Fuel capacity 33. Wingspan 18'4". Length 20'7". **PERFORMANCE:** Top mph 180. Cruise mph 160. Stall mph 70. Climb rate 900. Takeoff run 1,200. Landing roll 700. Range 600.

The two-place Sizzler features a T-tail arrangement and gets a fair amount of lift from its fuselage. The low-wing monoplane is built entirely of metal and is flush-riveted throughout. Compound curves are no problem on the Sizzler, which uses flat panels. It stands on tricycle landing gear and carries a 125-hp Continental engine.

SKYSTAR "KITFOX"

STANDARD DATA: Seats 2. Gross wt. 1,200–1,400. Empty wt. 495–705. Fuel capacity 21–25. Engine 50- to 80-hp Rotax 503, 582, or 912. **PERFORMANCE:** Top mph 95–135. Cruise mph 85–125. Initial climb rate 880–1,200. Ceiling n/a. Range 170–640. Takeoff distance (50') 200. Landing distance (50') 200–240.

The SkyStar Kitfox series became one of the most popular kitplane lines of the 1980s and 1990s. The popularity is largely due to the fact that the Kitfox Classic IV or Speedster can be bought for comparatively reasonable prices in the kit-building marketplace. This enables the builder/pilot to construct and own an honest sportplane that can double as a light-utility aircraft on a budget. Kitfoxes have been optioned with floats and skis and can operate well in tight confines with good short-field capabilities.

SKYSTAR "VIXEN"

STANDARD DATA: Seats 2. Gross wt. 1,400. Empty wt. 725. Fuel capacity 26. Engine 80-hp Rotax 912. **PERFORMANCE:** Top mph 123. Cruise mph 112. Initial climb rate 1,200. Ceiling n/a. Range 618. Takeoff distance (50') 230. Landing distance (50') 220.

The SkyStar Vixen is a two-place fixed-trigear sportplane designed to give the sport flier a newer and more up-to-date look as well as good performance with STOL capabilities. Construction is conventional steel-tube, wood, and fabric covering. A 32-foot wing is available as an option. Two adults and more than 150 pounds of baggage can be accommodated.

SMITH "MINIPLANE"

STANDARD DATA: Gross wt. 1,000. Empty wt. 616. Fuel capacity 17. Wingspan 17'. Length 15'3". Engine 65- to 85-hp

SKYSTAR "VIXEN"

Continental or 100- to 125-hp Lycoming. **PERFORMANCE:** Top mph 130. Cruise mph 122. Stall mph 56. Climb rate 1,600. Ceiling 13,000. Takeoff run 375. Landing roll 500. Range 275.

The primary appeals of the Smith Miniplane are its small-size construction simplicity and open-cockpit romance, which is a combination that not all homebuilt biplanes can offer. The fuselage framework is a conventional truss structure of welded steel tubing, faired to shape with wooden stringers. As on most similar designs, the vertical stabilizer is welded up as part of the rear fuselage structure. The wings are made from spruce spars and ribs. Several engines can provide the power: 65- to 85-hp Continentals or 100- to 125-hp Lycomings.

SMYTH "SIDEWINDER"

STANDARD DATA: Gross wt. 1,450. Empty wt. 867. Fuel capacity 17. Wingspan 24'10". Length 19'4". Engine 125-hp Lycoming. **PERFORMANCE:** Top mph 185. Cruise mph 160. Stall mph 55. Climb rate 900. Ceiling 15,000. Takeoff run 800. Landing roll 1,500. Range 425.

In order to simplify construction of the Sidewinder, several standard components are borrowed from other established aircraft. The bubble canopy is from a Thorp T-18. The landing gear is taken from a Wittman. This fully enclosed two-seater has all-metal wings with aluminum skin and an all-metal steel-tube fuselage also covered with aluminum skin. Though the prototype was fitted with a 125-hp powerplant, engines from 65 to 125 hp can be used.

SORRELL "HIPERBIPE"

STANDARD DATA: Gross wt. 1,911. Empty wt. 1,236. Fuel capacity 39. Wingspan 22'10". Length 20'10". Engine 180-hp Lycoming. **PERFORMANCE:** Top mph 170. Cruise mph 160. Stall mph 49. Climb rate 1,500. Ceiling 20,000. Takeoff run 400. Landing roll 595. Range 502.

Even the most advanced aerobatic maneuvers are possible in the Hiperbipe, such as vertical eight-point rolls or inside/outside vertical eights, and the like. But the Hiperbipe doesn't sacrifice the comforts usually missing with open-cockpit aerobatic models, such as complete carpeting, full electrical system, lights, and radio. Welded steel tubes are used for the fuselage, tail group, engine and landing gear mounts, interplane struts, and flight control systems. Wing construction is all-wood with a stressed skin. Landing gear is the Wittman type. The engine cowling and wheel fairings are fiberglass. The entire airframe is covered with fabric, including the plywood-covered wings.

SPENCER "AIR CAR"

STANDARD DATA: Gross wt. 3,200. Empty wt. 2,190. Fuel capacity 94. Wingspan 37'4". Length 26'5". Engine 285-hp Continental. **PERFORMANCE:** Top mph 147. Cruise mph 135. Stall mph 43. Climb rate 1,000. Takeoff time 16 sec. Range 700.

The Air Car is a four-place retractable with a strong family resemblance to the old Republic Seabee. The resemblance is no accident because the Air Car was designed by the same man, P.H. Spencer. The Seabee was designed in metal, but Spencer has gone back to wood covered with fiberglass for the basic Air Car hull structure. Extensive use is made of molded fiberglass for the fuselage, cabin section, engine cowl, wing root fairings, tips, floats, and miscellaneous parts. The heart of the Air Car design is a single steel-tube weldment combining the engine mount, wing-spar carry-throughs, and lift strut attach points. This steel skeleton attaches to the hull and carries all major flight loads. The all-wooden wings have a mahogany three-ply skin. The original powerplant was a 260-hp Lycoming; a 210- or 285-hp Continental may also be mounted on the airframe.

SPEZIO "TUHOLER"

STANDARD DATA: Gross wt. 1,400. Empty wt. 810. Fuel capacity 23. Wingspan 24'9". Length 18'3". **PERFORMANCE:** Top mph 160. Cruise mph 128. Stall mph 45. Climb rate 2,000. Takeoff run 160. Landing roll 300. Range 400.

After a day of flying, you can take the folding Spezio Tuholer home behind your car. Offering the thrill of open-cockpit flying, this two-seat monoplane is powered by a 125-hp Lycoming. (The name Tuholer means "two holer," for two cockpits). The ship should not be built by anyone who is afraid to weld. The fuselage and tail structure call for the use of steel tubing. Its large center section, supporting the folding-wing mechanism, is fashioned from a trio of one-inch .049 tubing with end plates, fittings, and large bolts that allow the wings to fold for storage.

"SPORTAIRE"

STANDARD DATA: Gross wt. 1,600. Empty wt. 984. Fuel capacity 22. Wingspan 26'4". Length 20'6". **PERFORMANCE:** Top mph 160. Cruise mph 150. Stall mph 55. Climb rate 1,000. Takeoff run 750. Landing roll 500. Range 400.

This two-place low-wing monoplane stands on tricycle gear and is propelled by a Lycoming 125-hp engine. Building materials include tubular steel, wood, and fabric.

"SPRITE"

STANDARD DATA: Gross wt. 1,400. Empty wt. 850. Fuel capacity 12. Wingspan 24'. Length 20'. Engine 130-hp Continental. **PERFORMANCE:** Top mph 138. Cruise mph 128. Stall mph 55. Climb rate 800. Takeoff roll 750. Landing roll 800.

The Sprite was designed to the United Kingdom's semi-aerobatic certification category with a positive load factor of 4.5Gs and allowing legal spins and maneuvers past 60 degrees of banking. To go fully aerobatic would be self-defeating, adding extra weight not needed for training, touring, or sport flying. Metal was selected instead of wood because it offered a better potential for mass-production kits. Sprite builders start off making the wings based upon a strong main spar of thick webbing, capped on the top and bottom with standard-size ex-

trusion and backing plates. Wing ribs come from a single jig. The fuselage sides are bowed to prevent drumming of flat panels. Many parts of Sprites can be borrowed from other types of commercial aircraft: gear legs, brakes, wheels, fuel tanks, and the like. The standard powerplant is the Rolls-Royce 130-hp Continental driving a fixed-pitch two-blade prop.

"STARDUST II"

STANDARD DATA: Gross wt. 790. Empty wt. 520. Fuel capacity 15. Wingspan 16'. Length 18'. **PERFORMANCE:** Top mph 258. Cruise mph 178. Stall mph 58. Takeoff run 900. Landing roll 1,800. Range 500.

The Stardust is a single-seat homebuilt Formula 1 racer designed by John Scoville. It accommodates engines rated from 65 to 100 hp. The fuselage is built from molybdenum steel tube with lightweight alloy and fabric covering. Its wings feature a composite structure of steel and wood, with a wood-and-fabric covering.

"STARDUST JS-2"

STANDARD DATA: Gross wt. 790. Empty wt. 520. Fuel capacity 15. Wingspan 16'. Length 18'. **PERFORMANCE:** Top mph 250. Cruise mph 178. Stall mph 58. Takeoff run 1,500. Landing roll 1,800. Range 500.

The Stardust is a single-place Formula I sportracer constructed from conventional wood, fabric, and tubular steel. It is propelled by the regulation 85- or 100-hp Continental.

STEEN "SKYBOLT"

STANDARD DATA: Gross wt. 1,680. Empty wt. 1,080. Fuel capacity 340. Wingspan 24'. Length 19'. Engine 180-hp Lycoming. **PERFORMANCE:** Top mph 145. Cruise mph 130. Stall mph 50. Climb rate 2,500. Ceiling 18,000. Takeoff run 400. Range 450.

The Skybolt is a two-seat aerobatic biplane designed by Lamar Steen. It first flew in 1970 and received the EAA award for "Best School Project." The Skybolt is stressed to +12Gs and −10Gs. The fabric-covered wings are built around two spruce spars. The fuselage is a fabric-covered welded steel-tube structure. The aircraft can be fitted with engines ranging in size from 125 to 260 hp.

STEPHENS "AKRO"

STANDARD DATA: Gross wt. 1,100. Empty wt. 830. Fuel capacity 21. Wingspan 24'4". Length 19'. Engine 180-hp Lycoming. **PERFORMANCE:** Top mph 192. Cruise mph 175. Stall mph 54. Climb rate 2,100. Ceiling 22,000. Takeoff run 400. Landing roll 900. Range 375. Plans for the Akro are no longer available.

The Akro was designed to meet the requirements of unlimited aerobatic competition. It is stressed to +12Gs and –11Gs. The Akro's wing is a one-piece all-wood structure with two spars, and its fuselage is a fabric-covered steel-tube frame. Seating is for one under a sliding bubble canopy. The Model B fuel and oil systems are designed for inverted flight. The Akro is one of the most popular aerobatic ships in the monoplane class. All control surfaces are fully static balanced.

STEWART "FOO FIGHTER"

STANDARD DATA: Gross wt. 1,100. Empty wt. 720. Fuel capacity 19. Wingspan 20'8". Length 18'9". **PERFORMANCE:** Top mph 145. Cruise mph 115. Stall mph 45. Climb rate 1,200. Takeoff run 450. Landing roll 550. Range 345.

It's not difficult to mistake the Foo Fighter for a Pfalz, a Spad, or an Albatross, but the plane that actually inspired this design was the Alcock A-1, a World War I warbird that resembles the Sopwith Pup. One distinguishing feature of the Foo Fighter is its lower wing that crosses below the fuselage, aft of the gear, and attaches on the centerline. The airframe is built from steel tubing and covered with fabric. A Ford Falcon auto engine was installed first, but a 130-hp Franklin Sport Four also can be used.

STEWART "HEADWIND"

STANDARD DATA: Gross wt. 750. Empty wt. 450. Fuel capacity 6. Wingspan 28'3". Length 17'. **PERFORMANCE:**

Top mph 110. Cruise mph 80. Stall mph 35. Climb rate 600. Takeoff run 300. Landing roll 400. Range 195.

The virtue of the Headwind is not high speed or altitude performance but utter simplicity of design and construction and ease of handling. In the words of the designer, Don Stewart, "It's not quick and skittish like a lot of homebuilts, but in fact flies a lot like a J-3 or Champ with a very docile stall." The Headwind is described as an extremely simple airplane of steel tubing construction for the fuselage and tail. The wings are two wooden spars with either sawed plywood or formed aluminum ribs. All the fittings are flat, and only two of them require any preassembly. The engine bolts directly to the front of the fuselage, saving a separate engine mount. A 36- to 65-hp VW engine is used.

STEWART "S-51D"

STANDARD DATA: Seats 2. Gross wt. 2,960. Empty wt. 2,200. Fuel capacity 70. Engine 400-c.i.d. 300–600-hp liquid-cooled automotive V-8. **PERFORMANCE:** Top mph 265. Cruise mph 235. Initial climb rate 2,380. Ceiling 23,600. Range 660. Takeoff distance (50') 1,370. Landing distance (50') 2,080.

The S-51D is the culmination of over 25 years in development. Jim Stewart's dream was to develop the most accurate reduced-scale P-51D to hit the homebuilt circuit. Many times the project was put on hold due to many obstacles that producing an aircraft of this type can throw at you. Stewart, an aeronautical engineer by trade, made great strides to make the S-51 as close to the real thing in looks, structure, and performance as possible. Stewart chose aluminum for the entire airframe. Stewart also quickly realized that a kit was required to market the aircraft because very few homebuilders had the tools or the talent to form all of the compound-curved panels. All of the panels in the kit are hydro-formed to obtain the distortion-free curves that make this kit a successful endeavor. Kits are available in a variety of packages to save time and/or money for the builder. The basic kit requires about 3,500 hours of work, and a fast-build kit reduces the required time by about 1,200 hours.

STITS "PLAYBOY"

STANDARD DATA: Gross wt. 902. Empty wt. 600. Wingspan 22'2". Length 17'4". **PERFORMANCE:** Top mph 145. Cruise mph 130. Climb rate 1,050. Range 400.

One of the more popular designs by Ray Stits, the Playboy was designed for backyard builders to construct from easy-to-follow plans or simple-to-do work kits. The Playboy can handle any one of several four-cylinder engines with 85 to 160 hp. Probably the most common is the 85-hp Continental. Construction is mixed: wooden wings and a steel-tube fuselage. All surfaces are fabric covered. The Playboy is easily recognizable because of its sliding canopy and strut-braced low-wing design.

STODDARD-HAMILTON "GLASAIR SUPER II TD"

STANDARD DATA: Gross wt. 2,100. Empty wt. 1,200. Fuel capacity 59. Wingspan 23'4". Length 20'6". Engine 150- to 180-hp Lycoming. **PERFORMANCE:** Top mph 232. Cruise mph 224. Stall mph 59. Climb rate 2,700. Takeoff run 350.

The Glasair Super II TD (taildragger) is a high-tech all-composite side-by-side two-place airplane. The Glasair is constructed from prepreg composite shells provided by Stoddard Hamilton Aircraft. Such a technique offers structural integrity without the use of steel tubes or aluminum. A one-piece wing was designed to take advantage of skin strength without joints. A one-piece spar is made in a mold at the factory out of unidirectional glass for spar caps and bidirectional glass on a 45-degree bias for the shear webs. This is then bonded into the lower wing shell to save an amateur the builder's time. The engine for the Glasair is a Lycoming IO-320 that turns a fixed-pitch propeller. Also recommended are 150 hp or 180 hp powerplants. The fuselage is built from three main pieces and requires no jigging but only three bulkheads, the firewall, seatback, and a small aft bulkhead. The landing gear legs are pressure-molded unidirectional glass. The Glasair II is also available with a fixed tricycle gear and a retractable tricycle gear.

STODDARD-HAMILTON "GLASAIR III"

STANDARD DATA: Seats 2. Gross wt. 2,500. Empty wt. 1,625. Fuel capacity 72. Engine 250- to 300-hp Lycoming. **PERFORMANCE:** Top mph 284. Cruise mph 294. Initial climb rate 3,750. Ceiling 24,000. Range 1,500. Takeoff distance (50') 700. Landing distance (50') 900.

The big brother of the Glasair line takes advantage of the same high-tech construction processes of its siblings but with a little more length in the fuselage and a bit more juice in the nose. The III flies 40–60 mph faster than the other Glasairs. The III is a two-place tricycle-gear retractable.

STODDARD-HAMILTON "GLASAIR III"

STODDARD-HAMILTON "GLASTAR"

STANDARD DATA: Seats 2. Gross wt. 1,650. Empty wt. 900. Fuel capacity 34. Engine 125-hp Continental IO-240. **PERFORMANCE:** Top mph n/a. Cruise mph 140. Initial climb rate n/a. Ceiling n/a. Range n/a. Takeoff distance (50') n/a. Landing distance (50') n/a.

The new GlaStar was signed off for flight by the FAA on November 28, 1994, and made its first flight on November 29, 1994. The aircraft responded well and predictably throughout the entire test flight. Takeoff and landing were uneventful and very easy to execute. The two-place, side-by-side kitplane introduces a special blend of construction media, utilizing a steel-tube frame, a composite shell fuselage and an all-aluminum wing, rudder, and stabilizer. The GlaStar does look like a smoothed-out Cessna 150 with a much larger cockpit and baggage area; however, a GlaStar has a higher gross weight capacity and gets off the ground much quicker, climbs and cruises faster, and utilizes high-tech improvements. Options are expected to include IFR panels, skis, floats, and tundra tires. The GlaStar can be converted to conventional gear for greater utility and will carry up to 250 pounds of baggage.

STODDARD-HAMILTON "TURBINE 250/III"

STANDARD DATA: Seats 2. Gross wt. 2,500. Empty wt. 1,650. Fuel capacity 86. Engine 450-shp Allison turbine. **PERFORMANCE:** Top mph 330. Cruise mph 280. Initial climb rate 4,200. Ceiling 25,000. Range 1,200. Takeoff distance (50') 600. Landing distance (50') 1,000.

In 1994, Stoddard-Hamilton decided to take the airframe of its Glasair III and strap on 450 shp of an Allison 250 turbine. The combination gave the ship exceptional performance with regards to straight-and-level flight speeds and rate of climb. Speeds in excess of 340 mph have been recorded and the climb to ceiling can be accomplished in under eight minutes.

STOLP "ACRODUSTER 1"

STANDARD DATA: Gross wt. 1,190. Empty wt. 750. Fuel capacity 25. Wingspan 19'. Length 15'9". **PERFORMANCE:** Top mph 180. Cruise mph 165. Stall mph 70. Climb rate 3,000. Takeoff run 300. Landing roll 800. Range 360.

First introduced in 1973, the SA-700 Acroduster 1 is a single-seat fully aerobatic biplane suitable for engines in the 125- to 200-hp range. Its fuselage is an all-metal structure constructed from lightweight alloy, and the wings are conventional two-spar structures with spruce spars, plywood ribs, and fabric covering. A unique feature of the Acroduster 1 is that when the

STOLP "ACRODUSTER 1"

stick is pulled back, all four ailerons are raised slightly to help maintain aileron control when the airplane is stalled in a normal attitude. The opposite happens when the stick is pushed forward to aid control when the airplane is in an inverted stall.

STOLP "ACRODUSTER TOO"

STANDARD DATA: Gross wt. 1,800. Empty wt. 1,100. Fuel capacity 37. Wingspan 21'5". Length 18'6". Engine 200-hp Lycoming. **PERFORMANCE:** Top mph 210. Cruise mph 150. Stall mph 55. Climb rate 2,400. Takeoff run (50') 1,200. Landing run (50') 1,800. Range 450.

The Acroduster Too, originally called the Schrack-Stolp Super Starduster Too, is a scaled-down ⅞-scale version of the highly successful Starduster Too, which was designed by Lou Stolp. The Acroduster's designer, Morgan Schrack, beefed up the little ship to withstand up to 9Gs. He made it possible to remove the front windscreen, cover the front cockpit with a hatch cover, and add a sliding bubble canopy over the rear hole. The fuselage was also metalized back to the rear of the cockpit. Lycoming engines from 180 to 200 hp provide the power.

STOLP SA-100 "STARDUSTER"

STANDARD DATA: Gross wt. 1,080. Empty wt. 700. Fuel capacity 24. Wingspan 19'. Length 16'6". **PERFORMANCE:**

Top mph 147. Cruise mph 132. Stall mph 50. Climb rate 2,000. Takeoff run 200. Landing roll 300. Range 450.

This single-place member of the Stolp family is the younger brother to the two-place Starduster Too. The Starduster is intended for the 125-hp Lycoming engine, but it has been built with engines ranging from 85 to 170 hp with a constant-speed prop. Good visibility, very tame stall and landing characteristics, and something called "charisma" are all traits of the Starduster.

STOLP "STARDUSTER TOO"

STANDARD DATA: Gross wt. 1,704. Empty wt. 1,200. Fuel capacity 42. Wingspan 24'. Length 19'8". Engine 180-hp Lycoming. **PERFORMANCE:** Top mph 180. Cruise mph 130. Stall mph 56. Climb rate 1,800. Takeoff run (50') 450. Landing run (50') 900. Range 500.

The Starduster Too is the two-place member of the Stolp family. Though not specifically designed or offered as an aerobatic airplane, this graceful flyer can handle the stunts when in competent hands. Stolp recommends the 180-hp Lycoming with a constant-speed prop as the optimum powerplant. The fuselage is welded-steel tubing with wooden fairings and a fabric covering. The wings use two spruce spars, ribs of quarter-inch plywood, and a fabric cover. All four wings carry ailerons.

STOLP SA500 "STARLET"

STANDARD DATA: Gross wt. 1,000. Empty wt. 630. Fuel capacity 20. Wingspan 25'. Length 17'. Engine 100-hp Continental. **PERFORMANCE:** Top mph 150. Cruise mph 130. Stall mph 55. Climb rate 1,500. Takeoff run (50') 500. Landing run (50') 900. Range 500.

The little sister of the Stolp family is the Starlet, a single-place parasol-winged monoplane. This ship was originally designed to handle a Volkswagen engine (1,500cc) but was subsequently modified to house small aircraft engines such as a 108-hp Lycoming.

STOLP "V-STAR"

STANDARD DATA: Gross wt. 1,000. Empty wt. 650. Fuel capacity 20. Wingspan 23'. Length 17'2". Engine 100-hp Continental. **PERFORMANCE:** Top mph 150. Cruise mph 90. Stall mph 35. Climb rate 1,800. Takeoff run (50') 300. Landing run (50') 500. Range 359.

In response to demand for a low-cost and low-horsepower aerobatic homebuilt, Stolp designed the V-Star, which is basically a biplane version of the parasol-winged Starlet. Stressed to 9Gs, the V-Star was originally powered by a 65-hp Continental turning a fixed-pitch propeller; however, the airplane is certified to be outfitted with engines from 60 to 125 hp.

STUKA JU 87-82

STANDARD DATA: Gross wt. 2,260. Engine 220-hp Lycoming. **PERFORMANCE:** Top mph 132. Cruise mph 124. Stall mph 64. Climb rate 1,000. Takeoff roll 750.

The original Junkers became synonymous with the abbreviation "Stuka," from the word *Sturzkampfflugzeug*, which is a term applicable to all dive bombers. Like the original, the Langhurst replica Stuka is a two-place aircraft with a single control from the front seat. The rear seat faces the tail, which makes flying in that location quite an experience. The replica is completely of metal construction with an inner steel-tube frame and an aluminum skin. Because the original rib type was unknown, Langhurst utilized the NACA 2415, which looks very much like the original. The 7/10 Stuka is actually a full-sized airplane by most homebuilt standards. It has a full electrical system, full hydraulic system, and complete fuel management system. The landing gear and tailwheel unit are standard from a PT-19.

SUPER EMERAUDE
C.P. 328

STANDARD DATA: Gross wt. 1,540. Empty wt. 850. Fuel capacity 232. Wingspan 26'6". Length 21'. Engine 100-hp Continental. **PERFORMANCE:** Top mph 172. Cruise mph 120. Stall mph 52. Climb rate 700. Ceiling 14,000. Takeoff run 600. Landing roll 850. Range 620.

Besides designing the Super Emeraude, Claude Piel has

also created the Diamant and Beryl. The Emeraude is a low-wing monoplane that achieves excellent performance from a 100-hp Continental with a fixed-pitch prop. It features an enclosed cockpit for two in side-by-side fashion. Construction materials consist of wood and fabric. The most significant improvement in the Super Emeraude is a reinforced structure to allow the use of engines up to 150 hp and to be fully aerobatic when flown solo. It is distinguished by a larger and swept-back vertical tail, which improves directional stability. The airplane has all modern features including slotted flaps, slotted ailerons, single-leg landing gear, steerable tailwheel, and sliding canopy. The Super Emeraude is approved for categories N, U, and A.

"SYLKIE"

STANDARD DATA: Gross wt. 1,650. Empty wt. 1,020. Fuel capacity 28. Wingspan 24'11". Length 20'7". Engine 150-hp Lycoming. **PERFORMANCE:** Top mph 234. Cruise mph 182. Stall mph 48. Climb rate 1,800. Ceiling 19,000. Range 960. Takeoff run 1,850. Landing run 1,200.

Designer Wayne Barton used a beefed-up Emeraude fuselage and a Minicab wing of 24'11" span and 110 sq.ft. area (fully cantilevered with 15-percent rib chord at the root) for the Sylkie. In building the fuselage, the standard rightside and leftside frame construction method was used. In building the Minicab wing, the spar center sections were strengthened to provide a 9+G ultimate load factor for a 1,200-pound frame. Landing gear retracts, and dual controls are called for with brakes on the left side only. Three fuel tanks are located inside the fuselage with a 28-gallon fiberglass main tank aft of the passenger seats below the baggage compartment. The stabilator was designed with a 12-degree rotation capability around its single spar, which is built in two units. The engine is enclosed in a conventional fiberglass cowling with the nosegear door hinged to the aft part of the cowl. Dacron covering and Randolph's fabric dope finish everything off.

TAYLOR MODEL A
"COOT" (AMPHIBIAN)

STANDARD DATA: Gross wt. 1,950. Empty wt. 1,200. Fuel capacity 24–50. Wingspan 36'–37'. Length 20'–22'. **PERFORMANCE:** Cruise mph 100–130. Stall mph 45–50. Climb rate 600–1,000. Takeoff run (land) 200. Takeoff time (water) 10–12 sec.

The Model A differs from the Model B in that it can be fitted with a fiberglass hull; the Model B has a twin-boom tail. The amphibian is basically of wood construction and can be built by anyone with basic manual training experience using

TAYLOR MODEL A "COOT" (AMPHIBIAN)

ordinary tools. Power can be supplied by any engine from 150 to 220 hp with a controllable propeller. The Coot is a comfortable two-place ship with side-by-side seating and dual controls. The folding wings make road towing and home storage possible. (Molt Taylor emphasizes with all his aircraft designs that performance and specification figures are greatly dependent on such variables as engine size, fuel capacity, etc.)

TAYLOR "MINI-IMP"

STANDARD DATA: (60 hp) Gross wt. 800. Empty wt. 500. Fuel capacity 12+. Wingspan 25'. Length 16'. **PERFORMANCE:** Cruise mph 150+. Stall mph 48. Climb rate 1,200. Takeoff run 800. Range 500.

The Mini-Imp is a single-seat version of the two-seat Imp. It features an unusual configuration with a pusher prop aft of an inverted V-type tail assembly and cantilevered high wing that folds back for towing and storage. The wing is the latest NASA design with a spoiler and flaps. The retractable gear is the tricycle spring-legged type. A controllable propeller is available. Power is provided by any engine from 60 to 115 hp. The most common engines are the 60-hp Franklin, 60-hp Limbach VW, 70-hp Turbo Revmaster VW, 80-hp Turbo Kawasaki (1,000cc), 100-hp Continental, and 115-hp Avco Lycoming Modification. The aluminum and fiberglass Mini-Imp requires a minimum of tools to construct, and all hard-to-build parts are available. It offers unequaled safe flyability and stability, positive spiral stability, limited aerobatic capability (stressed to 9Gs), and good fuel economy (3.5 gph).

TAYLOR "MONOPLANE"

STANDARD DATA: Gross wt. 620. Empty wt. 410. Fuel capacity 7.5. Wingspan 21'. Length 15'. **PERFORMANCE:** Top mph 105. Cruise mph 90. Stall mph 38. Climb rate 950. Takeoff run 200. Landing roll 150. Range 230.

The Monoplane single-place taildragger was designed to house low-powered engines in the 30- to 65-hp range, like the English JAP or the German VW (both air-cooled). Some say that the Taylor Monoplane bears a striking resemblance to the World War II Spitfire. It features all-wood construction and is

covered with a $\frac{1}{16}$-inch plywood stressed skin. The ribs are conventional built-up-truss type in a basic box design. The aircraft was designed especially for the amateur builder who does not have a comprehensive workshop at his or her disposal. The airfoil section was carefully chosen for its high-lift and gentle-stall characteristics. Since the first prototype flew in June 1960, no modifications of any kind have been incorporated.

TAYLOR "TITCH"

STANDARD DATA: Gross wt. 745. Empty wt. 500. Fuel capacity 10. Wingspan 18'9". Length 16'2". **PERFORMANCE:** Top mph 170. Cruise mph 155. Stall mph 53. Climb rate 1,100. Takeoff run 140. Landing roll 120. Range 380.

The Taylor Titch has a reputation as a pleasant-to-fly aerobatic plane. Stall occurs at a very high angle of attack, and the airplane recovers straight forward with no wing drop and a height loss of only 50 feet. This single-place monoplane features all-wood wings with plywood and fabric covering. Its fuselage is also an all-wood structure that includes a double-curvature plywood covering and aluminum cockpit side panels. When the low-powered Taylor Monoplane became known in the United States, requests were made for permission to fit larger engines than the design permitted. This led to the introduction of the Titch (English for anything small). The Titch is stressed for any engine from 40 to 90 hp, the only provision being a reposition of the engine bulkhead for engines with 65 hp or more. This allows for the use of VW, Lycoming, or Continental powerplants.

"TEENIE TWO"

STANDARD DATA: Gross wt. 585. Empty wt. 310. Fuel capacity 9. Wingspan 18'. Length 12'11". Engine 1,600cc Volkswagen. **PERFORMANCE:** Top mph 140. Cruise mph 110. Stall mph 50. Climb rate 1,000. Takeoff run 600. Landing roll 800. Range 400.

One of the smallest homebuilts around, the Teenie Two is an all-metal single-place monoplane that measures slightly under 13 feet in length. Built entirely from aluminum except for the landing gear and controls, it needs no bending brake nor is any metal or riveting experience required. Most of the sheet-metal bending to build the Teenie Two is done by hand, and the design is close to optimum simplicity. Power is provided by a Volkswagen conversion.

"TERMITE"

STANDARD DATA: Gross wt. 658. Empty wt. 432. Wingspan 23'6". Length 15'1". **PERFORMANCE:** Top mph 95. Cruise mph 83. Landing mph 38. Climb rate 450. Ceiling 6,000. Takeoff run 350. Landing roll 400. Range 150.

The original Termite, designed by Wilbur Smith, was powered by a 36-hp Aeronca engine, but since then other engines such as the 38-hp Continental and the 65-hp Lycoming have been used. The Termite is a single-seat sporting monoplane with a braced parasol-type wing. Its wing structure is built with two wooden spars, an aluminum leading edge, and fabric covering aft of the front spar. The fuselage is an all-wood structure with plywood covering from the rear of the cockpit forward and fabric covering aft. The tail section is also fabric covered. The Termite's landing gear is a Piper Cub type.

THORP T-18

STANDARD DATA: Gross wt. 1,500. Empty wt. 900. Fuel capacity 29. Wingspan 20'10". Length 18'. **PERFORMANCE:** Top mph 200. Cruise mph 175. Stall mph 65. Climb rate 2,000. Takeoff run 300. Landing roll 900. Range 500.

The Thorp T-18 is without a doubt one of the most popular homebuilts in existence. This two-place speedster can wring 160 mph out of a 125-hp engine. Its monoplane design with slightly upturned wings is clean and streamlined in appearance. A tight cowling, sleek canopy, very clean exterior metalwork, and light weight help explain its speed. John Thorp, designer of the T-18, has retired from his aircraft activities and has removed the plans from the market.

TINKER TOY

STANDARD DATA: Gross wt. 1,650. Empty wt. 1,188. Fuel capacity 20. Wingspan 28'3". Engine 140-hp Corsa. **PERFORMANCE:** Cruise mph 100. Stall mph 60. Range 300.

Powered by a 140-hp Corsa engine, the Tinker Toy was built around a Fly Baby wing and makes use of a pusher prop to keep the cabin quiet. The powerplant burns 4.5 gph at 3,500 RPM and turns a Warnke ground-adjustable prop. The Fly Baby wing was selected for Tinker Toy because it was a high-

lift wing. To get away from a long drive shaft running back to behind the tail, the engine was hung underneath the wing at CG position with the prop spinning right behind the trailing edge. A bottom spar and top member were then used to carry a large vertical fin, leaving clearance for the propeller blades. It took some engineering to design the top spar that attached the tail to the center point of the spinning propeller hub. Landing-gear legs were made from heat-treated truck leaf-spring stock with the wheels encased in fiberglass pants.

TOURBILLION YC-12

STANDARD DATA: Gross wt. 952. Empty wt. 628. Fuel capacity 16. Wingspan 22'. Length 19'. **PERFORMANCE:** Top mph 146. Cruise mph 127. Stall mph 47. Climb rate 900 fpm. Takeoff run 855. Landing roll 900. Range 500.

The Tourbillion (Whirlwind) is a single-seat, amateur-built, and lightweight low-wing plane that comes from France. It is available in several models that differ only in their engine size. Most common is the 65-hp Continental. Airframe construction includes wood and fabric wings and a plywood-covered fuselage structure.

TRI-R TECHNOLOGIES "KIS"

STANDARD DATA: Seats 2. Gross wt. 1,200. Empty wt. 680. Fuel capacity 20. Engine 80-hp Limbach L 2000. **PERFORMANCE:** Top mph 150. Cruise mph 135. Initial climb rate 1,000. Ceiling 14,000. Range 600. Takeoff distance (50') 1,000. Landing distance (50') 1,100.

The KIS (keep it simple) series of aircraft became a vision of designer Rich Trickel when he was commissioned by Lance Neibauer (Lancair) to design and develop the molds and structural techniques used in the building of the Lancair series of aircraft. Trickel designed the KIS as a high-performance entry- or training-level aircraft that could reap the benefits of the composite technology that he had accomplished with the Lancair. Using epoxy preimpregnated glass cloth (prepreg), combined with high-density foam core and honeycomb Nomex, the vacuum-formed components for the KIS could become reality. The extreme light weight and high strength from this type of composite construction allows for the use of smaller engines to get superior performance for an aircraft. The KIS series is available with a number of options for configuration and powerplants. The KIS TD is a taildragger; the KIS Super and TR-1 are higher horsepower versions of the KIS with 120 hp and 125 hp respectively. All four of the kits are sold less engine, upholstery, avionics, and paint.

TRI-R TECHNOLOGIES "KIS TR-4 CRUISER"

STANDARD DATA: Seats 4. Gross wt. 2,300. Empty wt. 1,200. Fuel capacity 50. Engine 180-hp Lycoming IO-360. **PERFORMANCE:** Top mph 185. Cruise mph 165. Initial climb rate 1,200. Ceiling 17,000. Range 800. Takeoff distance (50') 1,200. Landing distance (50') 1,500.

Rich Trickel's addition to the Tri-R Technologies family, the TR-4 Cruiser, is a four-place fixed-gear aircraft that follows the form of the previous KIS models. The Cruiser made its debut at Oshkosh 1994 and was well received as a practical, kitbuilt, family aircraft that was inexpensive to build and operate. The Cruiser can accommodate four full-sized adults, full fuel, carry 66 pounds of baggage, and cruise at 165 mph anywhere within an 800-mile range. Any way you slice it, this is one practical aircraft. The Cruiser requires around 1,500 hours to complete.

TROYER SPORTPLANE VX

STANDARD DATA: Gross wt. 456. Empty wt. 306. Fuel capacity 5. Wingspan 23'9". Length 15'9". **PERFORMANCE:** Top mph 95. Cruise mph 85. Stall mph 34. Climb rate 600. Takeoff run 195. Landing roll 150. Range 200.

Few homebuilts weigh less than this VW-powered mid-wing model. The Troyer Sportplane weighs only 306 pounds empty. Oddly enough, it has a welded steel-tube fuselage and tail assembly. Its wings use spruce spars and ribs built from ¼-inch square spruce, ply gusseted. Steel tubing also forms the flying struts for the wing, but a little balsa wood is used for fairing. Power is supplied by either the Heath B4 or a converted VW engine.

"TURBULENT"

STANDARD DATA: Gross wt. 620. Empty wt. 342. Fuel capacity 10.5. Wingspan 21'6". Length 17'. **PERFORMANCE:** Top mph 100. Cruise mph 85. Stall mph 29. Climb rate 500. Takeoff run 440. Landing roll 300. Range 350.

This brainchild of Roger Druine is so good that Rollason Aircraft in England and Flugzeubau in West Germany started manufacturing them. The Turbulent's airframe is an all-wood structure covered with fabric. It uses a box spar with a built-up rear spar, conventional ribs, and a plywood-skinned leading edge forming a rigid D section. A happy feature of the Turbulent wing is leading edge slots and Friese-type ailerons that bring the stall down to around 29 mph with full aileron control all the way. Volkswagen engines from 30 to 40 hp are commonly used.

TURNER T-40

STANDARD DATA: Gross wt. 1,050. Empty wt. 750. Fuel capacity 18. Wingspan 22'3". Length 19'5". **PERFORMANCE:** Top mph 170. Cruise mph 145. Stall mph 52. Climb rate 900. Takeoff run 850. Landing roll 750. Range 450.

The Turner airplane family got started in 1958. First aircraft in the series was the T-40, a sleek, hot little single-seater that won the 1961 "Outstanding Design" trophy at the Experimental Aircraft Association Fly-in. Of all-wood construction

and featuring a sliding-hood canopy, the T-40 was first powered by a 65-hp engine and did without all the frills associated with an electrical system. In this form, it cruised at 128 mph and blitzed along at 145 mph with the throttle firewalled. Later, an 85-hp package was added.

TURNER T-40A

STANDARD DATA: Gross wt. 1,500. Empty wt. 950. Fuel capacity 20. Wingspan 24'11". Length 19'5". **PERFORMANCE:** Top mph 170. Cruise mph 150. Stall mph 56. Climb rate 1,600. Takeoff run 865. Landing roll 760. Range 520.

The T-40 was so successsful that it collected 18 awards and convinced Turner that the only thing wrong with it was that nobody could ride along to enjoy the reading on the airspeed indicator; thus, he created the T-40A. It is a two-place version of the predecessor. Turner simply divided the entire fuselage of the T-40 down the middle and increased the cabin width from 24 to 40 inches. Flight tests showed that the 85-hp engine would still deliver 163 mph top speed with a fuselage nearly twice as wide as before and with considerably more airframe weight. Both Turners feature folding wings.

TURNER T-40B

STANDARD DATA: Gross wt. 1,600. Empty wt. 828. Fuel capacity 20. Wingspan 22'3". Length 19'9". **PERFORMANCE:** Top mph 175. Cruise mph 155. Stall mph 57. Climb rate 1,200. Takeoff run 850. Landing roll 500. Range 475.

The Turner T-40B is basically the same as the T-40A, but with tricycle landing gear and other improvements. Development of the prototype began in 1966 and the first flight was made in 1969. Originally an 85-hp engine was used, but it was replaced by a 125-hp Lycoming in order to improve high-altitude performance. Other refinements on the basic T-40A frame included a bubble canopy, hydraulically operated double-slotted flaps, and a fixed leading-edge droop.

VAN'S AIRCRAFT, INC.
"RV-3"

STANDARD DATA: Gross wt. 1,050. Empty wt. 695. Fuel capacity 24. Wingspan 19'11". Length 19'. Engine 125-hp Lycoming. **PERFORMANCE:** Top mph 195. Cruise mph 185. Stall mph 48. Climb rate 1,900. Ceiling 21,000. Takeoff run 200. Landing roll 300. Range 600.

Richard VanGrunsven's all-metal single-seat monoplane won the "Best Aerodynamic Detailing" award at the 1972 EAA Fly-in. The wings are built around a single I-beam spar and a lighter rear spar. The fuselage and tail unit are built of light alloy, and the engine is covered with a fiberglass cowling. The conventional landing gear has Cleveland brakes and fiberglass wheel fairings.

VAN'S AIRCRAFT, INC.
"RV-4/-6/-6A"

STANDARD DATA: (RV-4) Seats 2. Gross wt. 1,500. Empty wt. 905. Fuel capacity 32. Engine 160-hp O-320 Lycoming. **PERFORMANCE:** Top mph 205. Cruise mph 194. Initial climb rate 2,050. Ceiling 25,000. Range 650. Takeoff distance 300. Landing distance 300.

STANDARD DATA: (RV-6 and 6A) Seats 2. Gross wt. 1,600. Empty wt. 965. Fuel capacity 38. Engine 160-hp O-320 Lycoming. **PERFORMANCE:** Top mph 202. Cruise mph 191. Initial climb rate 1,900. Ceiling 21,500. Range 775. Takeoff distance 300. Landing distance 300.

Van's RV series of home and kitbuilt aircraft are among the most popular airplanes. The combination of performance, low cost, ease of construction, and overall good looks seems to be a winning one. Construction is conventional aluminum alloy riveted together without complex panels or compound curves. All of the RV aircraft are capable of sport aerobatics and have exceptional STOL capabilities. The RV-3 is an all-metal single-seat sportplane with a conventional gear. The RV-4 is the two-place tandem version of the RV-3 with a slightly longer wingspan. The RV-6 and RV-6A are side-by-side two-seat sportplanes that are designed for excellent touring and sport flying. The RV-6A has the exact airframe as the RV-6 but incorporates a tricycle rather than a conventional gear.

VCA-1

STANDARD DATA: Gross wt. 1,100. Empty wt. 710. Fuel capacity 24.5. Wingspan 20'. Length 18'. Engine 100-hp Continental. **PERFORMANCE:** Top mph 150. Cruise mph 130. Stall mph 57. Climb rate 1,100. Range 200.

The VCA-1 is a tiny single-seat low-wing monoplane of all-metal construction. The wing section is NASA GA(W)-1 with no sweepback. It has a constant chord with plain ailerons and electrically operated flaps. The fuselage uses 2024-T3 aluminum alloy. The tricycle landing gear is nonretractable. A Continental 0-200 flat-four engine drives a two-blade Sensenich fixed-pitch propeller. The cockpit is enclosed and sweeps back to a combination fuselage and T-tail empennage.

"VELOCITY"

STANDARD DATA: (Fixed gear) Seats 4. Gross wt. 2,250. Empty wt. 1,250. Fuel capacity 65. Engine 200-hp Lycoming IO-360. **PERFORMANCE:** Top mph 215. Cruise mph 200. Initial climb rate 1,400. Ceiling 20,000. Range 1,200. Takeoff distance (50') 850. Landing distance (50') 800.

STANDARD DATA: (Retractable gear) Seats 4. Gross wt. 2,250. Empty wt. 1,250. Fuel capacity 65. Engine 200-hp Lycoming IO-360. **PERFORMANCE:** Top mph 230. Cruise mph 220. Initial climb rate 1,500. Ceiling 20,000. Range 1,320. Takeoff distance (50') 850. Landing distance (50') 800.

The first Velocity took to the sky in 1985 and followed with its public debut at the Sun-N-Fun Fly-in at Lakeland, Florida, in early 1986. The Velocity made quite an impression, and kits for this four-place canard-design pusher were served up like hotcakes. Construction is all-composite, and the systems are simple with no complex jigs or advanced tooling necessary. With an available two-car garage and 1,200–1,500 hours, a Velocity could be in your future.

VIKING "DRAGONFLY"

STANDARD DATA: Gross wt. 1,075. Empty wt. 590. Wingspan 22'. Engine 1,600cc Volkswagen. **PERFORMANCE:**

Top mph 150. Climb rate 800. Range 500 (estimated). Takeoff run 450.

Winner of the "Outstanding New Design" award at Oshkosh 1980, the Dragonfly is another canard-configured composite homebuilt in the same vein as the Quickie and VariEze. With two-place side-by-side seating under a bubble canopy, the Draonfly is powered by a stock 1,600cc VW engine. The intention of the aircraft is to provide builders with a project that is inexpensive to build and also inexpensive to operate on a readily available engine. The wing and canard are built as a single piece in a jig, and the job can be accomplished in a normal two-car garage. The cockpit width is 43 inches, like that of a Cessna 172. A molded canopy was selected to avoid the soap-bubble effect of a free-blown canopy. A typical 140-mph cruise burns gas at the rate of 45 mpg. A Great American-brand propeller has a 4-inch pitch and 52-inch diameter. The designers have claimed that there will never be an authorization to use a 1,200cc VW, any certified aircraft engine, or any turbocharged powerplant.

VOLMER VJ-22 "SPORTSMAN"

STANDARD DATA: Gross wt. 1,500. Empty wt. 1,000. Fuel capacity 20. Wingspan 36'6". Length 24'. Engine 85- to 100-hp Continental. **PERFORMANCE:** Top mph 95. Cruise mph 85. Stall mph 45. Climb rate 600. Ceiling 13,000. Takeoff time 20 sec. Range 320.

Volmer Jensen's two-place Sportsman amphibian has to be called one of the more successful homebuilt designs around.

Building it costs about a tenth as much as buying a comparable airplane. Saltwater can't hurt its fiberglassed plywood hull, so corrosion is no problem. The Sportsman uses fabric-covered Aeronca Chief or Champion wings. It is essentially a small flying boat fitted with wheels that can be exchanged for skis. Power is supplied by a 100-hp Continental mounted in pusher fashion.

WAG-AERO "CUBy"

STANDARD DATA: Gross wt. 1,400. Empty wt. 720. Fuel capacity 12–26. Wingspan 35'2". Length 22'4". Engine 65- to 125-hp Continental. **PERFORMANCE:** Top mph 102. Cruise mph 94. Stall mph 39. Climb rate 490. Ceiling 11,200. Takeoff run 375. Range 220–455 (with auxiliary).

The CUBy is a replica of the ever-popular Piper J-3 Cub. It was designed by Dick Wagner, president of Wag-Aero, the nation's biggest homebuilder's supply house in Lyons, Wisconsin. Wagner was well aware of the demand for a kit version of the venerable puddle-jumper whose name has become a household word. Power is supplied by an 85-hp Continental. There is very little difference between the CUBy and the original J-3, except for a crank-operated elevator trim tab instead of the jackscrew adjustment that moved the stabilizer plane.

WAG-AERO "WAG-A-BOND"

STANDARD DATA: (Classic) Gross wt. 1,250. Empty wt. 640. Fuel capacity 26. Wingspan 29'4". Length 18'9". Engine 65- to 100-hp Continental. **PERFORMANCE:** Top mph 105. Cruise mph 95. Stall mph 45. Climb rate 625.

The Wag-A-Bond can be built in either of two versions, the Classic (performance figures above) or the Traveler. The Classic is a replica of the Piper PA-15 Vagabond, and the Traveler is a modified and updated version of the Vagabond with port and starboard doors, overhead skylight window, extended sleeping deck, extended baggage area, and provisions for engines up to 115 hp. The wings are strut-braced, high-wing, and all-wood structures covered with fabric. The spar and ribs are spruce with mahogany plywood gussets. The ailerons are fabric-covered aluminum. The fuselage is welded steel-tube. With a 108-hp Lycoming, the Traveler has a top speed of 122 mph, a cruise speed of 115 mph, and a climb rate of 850 fpm.

WAR "CORSAIR"

STANDARD DATA: Gross wt. 900. Empty wt. 600. Fuel capacity 12–15. Wingspan 20'. Length 16'6". Engine 100-hp Continental. **PERFORMANCE:** Top mph 170. Cruise mph 145. Stall mph 55. Climb rate 1,200. Range 400–500. Takeoff run 800–1,000.

The half-scale Corsair is built around a plywood box core and covered with styrofoam and fiberglass, in the manner of the KR-1 and KR-2 homebuilts. The fuselage is a standard four-longeron torsion box, while the tail and wings use conventional wooden structure. The wing is made from a laminated plywood-covered hollow front spar. The rear spar is laminated as a solid single-piece unit faced with plywood. Plywood ribs are used at the root, the center-section joints, and the tip sections. For landing gear, an air-oil oleo system is used, with either an electrical or manual ratchet system for retraction. Engines in the 65- to 125-hp range can be used, so performance varies greatly.

WAR "FOCKEWULF"

STANDARD DATA: Gross wt. 900. Empty wt. 610. Fuel capacity 12. Wingspan 20'. Length 16'7". **PERFORMANCE:** Top mph 165. Cruise mph 140. Stall mph 55. Climb rate 1,000. Ceiling 12,500. Takeoff run 1,000. Landing roll 1,200. Range 400.

WAR Aircraft Replicas is a company formed to market kits and plans for ½-scale World War II aircraft replicas. The FockeWulf 190 was singled out to be the first prototype, and development started in 1973. The first flight was made in

1974. Subsequent versions were to be the F4U Corsair, Hawker Sea Fury, and the Republic Thunderbolt. All were to use the same common wooden fuselage box and wing spar construction. In order to duplicate the various fighter aircraft, polyurethane foam is shaped and converted with high-strength laminating fabric and epoxy resin to form a rigid yet lightweight structure. Landing gear are electrically retractable tailwheel type with an emergency system. Power is supplied by a modified 70-hp 1,600cc Volkswagen engine turning a three-blade fixed-pitch prop.

WATSON "WINDWAGON"

STANDARD DATA: Gross wt. 485. Empty wt. 273. Fuel capacity 4. Wingspan 18'. Length 12'6". Engine 30-hp Watson ½ VW. **PERFORMANCE:** Top mph 110. Cruise mph 90. Stall mph 40. Climb rate 500. Ceiling 10,000. Range 300. Takeoff run 250. Landing roll 300.

The Windwagon measures 18 feet from wingtip to wingtip, and it features all-aluminum construction with pop rivets. The tricycle gear is nonretractable. Wings are removable for storage or transportation. The powerplant is a modified 900cc half-Volkswagen engine that drives a four-blade propeller. On just two cylinders, top speed is 110 mph, and climb rate is 450 to 500 fpm. The wing features a Clark Y wing section with constant chord. There are conventional ailerons and no flaps. The fuselage is a conventional semi-monocoque structure made from pop-riveted aluminum.

WELSH WR-3 "RABBIT"

STANDARD DATA: Gross wt. 1,050. Empty wt. 640. Fuel capacity 12. Wingspan 28'. Length 17'8". Engine 100-hp Continental. **PERFORMANCE:** Top mph 108. Cruise mph 98. Stall mph 48. Climb rate 500. Ceiling 10,500. Takeoff distance (50') 480. Landing roll 500. Range 290.

The Welsh Rabbit, designed by George Welsh, is a two-place trigeared homebuilt with a single high wing. Construction of the fuselage and tail group is welded-steel tube covered by Dacron. The wings have externally strut-braced metal spars and metal ribs covered by Dacron and fitted with corrugated-skin aluminum ailerons.

WENDT WH-1 "TRAVELER"

STANDARD DATA: Gross wt. 1,400. Empty wt. 900. Fuel capacity 22. Wingspan 30'. Length 19'6". Engine 65- to 85-hp Continental. **PERFORMANCE:** Top mph 131. Cruise mph 115. Stall mph 65. Climb rate 750. Range 580. Ceiling 13,000. Takeoff run 800. Landing roll 700.

The intention was that Wendt Traveler would be a high-performance cross-country ship with a max range of more than 500 miles, a sea-level rate of climb of 700 fpm, and a ceiling of 17,000 feet. The prototype was built largely of wood to make it simple for homebuilders. Seating was tandem style to reduce form drag. At 2,450 RPM, the WH-1 Traveler cruised at better than 120 mph at 300 feet MSL, stalled at 65 IAS, clean and climbed at 500 fpm with two onboard. The wings were detachable using NACA 643A-418 with an 18-percent thickness. Both the fuselage and wings were built of wood, the tailcone formed of ⅛-inch mahogany plywood over ⅞-inch spruce longerons. Wooden wing spars were used, and the forward 37 percent of chord covered with mahogany ply forming a D-box. The spring-steel landing gear is similar to the Wittman type, bolted to the wing carry-through structure. Wendt originally used a McCauley cruise prop of 71-inch diameter and 48-inch pitch.

WHITE "DER JAGER"

STANDARD DATA: Gross wt. 888. Empty wt. 534. Fuel capacity 24. Wingspan 20'. Length 17'. **PERFORMANCE:** Top mph 145. Cruise mph 133. Stall mph 54. Climb rate 2,000. Takeoff run 175. Landing roll 250. Range 532.

Though modeled after World War I fighters, the Der Jager is not a replica. Its builder, Marshall White, patterned the wing shape after that of the German Albatross. The tail assembly is patterned after that of the Fokker D-7, and the gear after that of the FockeWulf "Strosser." The frameworks of the fuselage and the tail group are of welded-steel tube that is fabric covered. The wings are wood with no flaps. The prototype was fitted with a 115-hp Lycoming, but the airplane is so light that anything down to the Volkswagen 1,600cc engine will fly it nicely.

"WHITE LIGHTNING"

STANDARD DATA: Seats 4. Gross wt. 2,400. Empty wt. 1,400. Fuel capacity 70. Engine 210-hp Continental IO-360. **PERFORMANCE:** Top mph 280. Cruise mph 265. Initial climb rate 1,900. Ceiling 20,000. Range 1,600. Takeoff distance (50') 1,300. Landing distance (50') 1,300.

During the past 15–20 years, composite construction of homebuilt aircraft has taken a firm hold of the technology and rewritten the rules regarding form and function. Now it is feasible to let the imagination fly and allow the most fluid and streamlined of aerodynamic shapes to become reality. One of

these products is the White Lightning. This craft falls into the sleek-and-speedy four-place-composite dream-machine group. The configuration is conventional, but frontal area and overall wetted area are greatly trimmed to the minimum thanks to composite technology. This makes for great performance and efficiency specs as well as being quite pleasing asthetically. Seating is for four with the two rear passengers facing aft with legs pointing to the tail. This seating arrangement allows for a less-critical C.G. Although the White Lightning is a tight package, there is ample room for any avionics complement a pilot should need.

WILLIAMS-CANGIE "SUNDANCER"

STANDARD DATA: Gross wt. 1,115. Empty wt. 835. Fuel capacity 16. Wingspan 19'9". Length 16'1". Engine 135-hp Lycoming. **PERFORMANCE:** Top mph 235. Stall mph 65.

The Sundancer is built around the basic fuselage and tail unit of the Bushby Midget Mustang. The single-seat racing biplane was codesigned by Art Williams and Carl Cangie, built by Ralph Thenhaus, and flown by Sidney White. It set a national class record of faster than 194 mph the first time that it was flown. It won the championship at Reno in 1973, then went on to victories in the five races in which it was entered in 1974. The fuselage of the Sundancer has a flush-riveted stressed skin. The wings are a conventional lightweight alloy structure with no flaps.

WILLIAMS "STINGER"

STANDARD DATA: Gross wt. 835. Empty wt. 385. Fuel capacity 8. Wingspan 19'. Length 15'10". Engine 100-hp Continental. **PERFORMANCE:** Top mph 260. Stall mph 65.

This single-seat Formula I racing monoplane was designed by Art Williams. The wings are an all-wood structure with laminated spruce spars. The fuselage is built from lightweight alloy and employs a monocoque structure. Flown by John Paul Jones, it captured second place at the 1973 Reno Air Races. In the same year it recorded the best single-lap speed of

234.7 mph. The craft was then sold to the late former astronaut Deke Slayton who continued racing Stinger for the next 20 years. Stinger, like its related ships Falcon and Sundancer, is a one-of-a-kind custom racing plane. Arthur Williams offers no plans or drawings for sale to the homebuilding public.

WITTMAN "TAILWIND"

STANDARD DATA: (100-hp version) Gross wt. 1,300. Empty wt. 700. Fuel capacity 25. Wingspan 22'6". Length 19'3". Engine 80-, 90-, and 100-hp Continental, or 100- to 135-hp Lycoming. **PERFORMANCE:** (100-hp version) Top mph 165. Cruise mph 150. Stall mph 55. Climb rate 900. Ceiling 16,000+. Takeoff run 800. Landing roll 600. Range 600+.

Aviation legend Steve Wittman's idea in 1953 was to create a fast and economical cross-country airplane that could tote two people and 60 pounds of baggage. Additionally, the airplane would fly with the greatest of ease and would have gentle stall characteristics at the low end of the speed spectrum. The first five airplanes built were loaded to gross weight and subjected to 4Gs. So successful did the Tailwind design turn out that for some years it stood alone in its class for its cruise speed as well as for its aerobatic-quality handling, though Wittman considers it to be a utility aircraft. Not until John Thorp came along with his low-wing T-18 could any two-place homebuilt match the Tailwind's performance. Improvements to the design include a modified airfoil, which is longer than the original wing by 19 inches. The modified airfoil slows landing and takeoff speeds, improves rate of climb, gives high ceilings, and boosts cruise speed at altitude. Also, revisions have been made to allow the use of a 150-hp Lycoming, a 145-hp Continental, and the Olds/Buick 215-cu. in. V-8s.

WITTMAN "WITT'S VEE"

STANDARD DATA: Gross wt. 700. Empty wt. 430. Fuel capacity 10. Wingspan 16'6". Length 18'2". **PERFORMANCE:**

Top mph 170. Cruise mph 150. Stall mph 48. Climb rate 1,000. Takeoff run 800. Range 400.

The real bomb in the Formula VEE circuit is Steve Wittman's Witt's V. The amazing thing about this racing ship is its speed. Wittman has had it up to 170 mph (not quite supersonic, but three miles a minute). Wittman made "Bonzo" a household word back in the Goodyear Racedays.

ZENAIR MONO-Z

STANDARD DATA: Gross wt. 960. Empty wt. 630. Fuel capacity 15. Wingspan 22'. Length 19'6". Engine 100-hp Continental. **PERFORMANCE:** Top mph 125. Cruise mph 110. Stall mph 48. Climb rate 820. Takeoff run (50') 1,000. Landing run (50') 1,000. Range 400.

The Mono-Z is a single-place scaled-down version of the original Zenith. It offers maximum operating economy with VW power at a 3-gph cruise. Detachable wings leave an 8-foot-wide section for easy road towing; only 20 minutes are required to install both wings. It is stressed for 9Gs, and it becomes a powerful aerobatic performer with a 100-hp engine. Powerplant possibilities range from the VW 1,600cc to 100-hp Continental.

ZENAIR "TRI-Z"

STANDARD DATA: Gross wt. 1,850. Empty wt. 1,100. Fuel capacity 34. Wingspan 26'6". Length 22'6". Engine 150 hp. **PERFORMANCE:** Top mph 160. Cruise mph 143. Stall mph 53. Climb rate 1,000. Takeoff run (50') 1,400. Landing run (50') 1,400. Range 530.

The natural step up from the Zenith is this three-passenger version. Designed primarily to satisfy the need for a good cross-country performer that falls into the sportplane category, the Tri-Z can be fitted with medium power engines in the 125- to 180-hp category. With only two persons in the front seats,

ZENAIR "TRI-Z"

the rear bench can be covered with 210 pounds of baggage. The Tri-Z easily adapts to floats or taildragger options and is easy to fly. It has docile handling characteristics.

ZENAIR "ZENITH"

STANDARD DATA: Gross wt. 1,500. Empty wt. 930. Fuel capacity 24. Wingspan 23'. Length 20'6". Engine 125 hp. **PERFORMANCE:** Top mph 151. Cruise mph 141. Stall mph 54. Climb rate 1,100. Takeoff run (50') 1,400. Landing run (50') 1,400. Range 450.

The French-born designer Chris Heintz graduated from

E.T.H. (engineering institute) in Zurich, Switzerland, worked on the Concorde at Aerospatiale, and joined Avion's Pierre Robin (famous for the Jodel series) as chief engineer before he started work on the Zenith. This homebuilt has a split personality in that with 100 hp it will cruise for four hours at 130 mph carrying two passengers and baggage. A 150-hp engine and an aerobatic option turns the Zenith into a powerful performer. The Zenith is stressed for engines from 85 to 160 hp. Two-place seating is under a sliding canopy in a fuselage formed by four longerons with stiffened skins blind riveted to longerons. Five bulkheads carry the top skin. The constant-chord wings have a single cantilevered spar with three sections and electronically operated flaps. One-piece all-moving horizontal and vertical control surfaces constitute the tail.

Section 5

Sailplane and motorglider aircraft

The pure flight. Soaring is likened by enthusiasts as birdlike without the aid of power to keep you aloft. Just you and your piloting skill to ride the rising currents of air. When a sailplane or glider is towed or winched to altitude, it is truly the skill of energy transfer and light touch, of being at one with your surroundings and making the most of what mother nature has donated to your cause. As with other form of aircraft, the sailplane has enjoyed marked improvement and development throughout history from the wood- and linen-craft built and flown by Otto Lilienthal to the modern, sleek composite craft that seem to capture the smallest of rising air currents with little effort.

Motorgliders gained prominence in Europe where rising columns of warm air and large expansive landing strips are less than the norm. The concept was to produce a glider or sailplane with a small air-cooled engine that could be utilized for takeoffs and for regaining lost altitude. This proved particularly handy on cool days or when there was no available tow-plane in the vicinity. Motorgliders are not as prominent in the United States, where weather is cooperative more often, but they can be spotted from time to time. The motorglider has proven to be a very efficient form of personal transport by only requiring miserly amounts of fuel to cover great distances.

AHRENS AR 124

Design of this single-seat sailplane began in 1974, and the first flight of the prototype was that same year. The cantilevered midwing has a constant chord with ailerons and upper-surface spoilers but no tabs or flaps. The fuselage is all-aluminum with a flush-riveted skin, and the swept T-tail has a one-piece elevator. One unsprung nosewheel with a disc brake and a tailwheel comprise the landing gear. Seating is for one pilot under a molded one-piece canopy.

AmEAGLE
"AMERICAN EAGLET"

The American Eaglet is a self-launching sailplane designed to eliminate the need for two planes, ground crews, and the requirement to operate out of a regular glider port. Its in-air-restartable engine reduces the need for off-field landings. The wings and inverted-V tailfeathers are built from spruce spars surrounded by urethane foam and covered with precured fiberglass skins. The fuselage is comprised of two preformed fiberglass shells pop-riveted to an aluminum-tube framework and tailboom. The Eaglet's powerplant is not designed for sustained powered flight. The MC 101 engine and folding propeller are provided for takeoff, in-flight restarts, and climbs only. Fuel tank capacity is five gallons and is generally sufficient for one takeoff and climb to 2,000 feet AGL and three airborne restarts and climbs from 500 feet back up to 2,000 feet.

BRIEGLEB BG-12

Gus Briegleb began designing and building sailplanes in the 1930s. In 1940, he came up with his sixth design, the BG-6, and initially sold it in kit form. As a utility-training glider, it had a lift-to-drag ratio of 16 and a minimum sink of about 3 fps. The BC-7 was an improved version using the same fuselage and tail but with a tapered wing 123 sq. ft. in area and 40 feet in span. Finally, the BC-12 was designed in 1956 with a 50-foot span and 141 sq. ft. of wing area. Empty weight was 525 pounds. Its full-cantilever wing was fitted with trailing-edge flaps. It was built entirely of wood, and its lift-to-drag ratio was an excellent 34 and minimum sink rate was 2.3 fps. The BG-12-16 used the same wing but has a low-profile fuselage of reduced cross-section dimensions. Its fin and rudder sweep forward (ala Mooney), and the BC-12 elevator/horizontal stabilizer is replaced with an all-flying stabilator fitted with antiservo tabs. The flaps are longer and the sailplane has a better lift-to-drag ratio.

BRYAN
(SCHREDER) RS-15

Designer R.E. Schreder built the RS-15 to OSTIV Standard Class specifications. Licensed in the amateur-built experimental category, its assembly is relatively simple with most major components premade to cut building time to about 500 hours. The shoulder-type wings are all-metal with the exception of polyurethane foam ribs. Provision for a 200-pound water ballast is inside the wing's box spars. Seating is for one pilot in a prefabricated fiberglass pod from which an aluminum-tube tailboom stretches back to an all-metal V tail. The tail and wings can be folded and removed for storage or travel.

BRYAN
(SCHREDER) HP-18

Intended to be an improved competition sailplane stressed to 12Gs, the HP-18 is basically a larger version of the RS-5. Its longer fuselage has been revamped to reduce drag. Refinements to the aircraft include improved gap seals, redesigned wingtips, a removable tailwheel, and overall better aerodynamics.

CAPRONI VIZZOLA
CALIF A-21S/A-21SJ

A quick glance at the gross weight or wingspan of the Calif motorglider or sailplane should tell the enthusiast that the pair are not ordinary aircraft. With over 80 feet of wingspan, the A-21 S/A is the only production turbojet-powered sailplane in the world. It offers side-by-side seating and all-metal construction. The engine retracts into the fuselage just aft of the cockpit. Cruise speed is 124 mph and climb is 945 fpm. On 36 gallons of fuel, range is about 217 miles, with a ceiling of 43,300 feet. Takeoff run requires only 1,181 feet. Up to 90 percent of the parts between the sailplane and the motorglider are common to both, so the glider can be transformed easily into a jet glider, even in retrofit. The landing gear for both aircraft features dual main gear that retract into the undercarriage. Two small wheels are built into the wingtips. The wing is all-metal with a single spar, stressed skin, and fiberglass tips; the wing is fitted with top-hinged, differentially operated ailerons plus lower-hinged, aerodynamically balanced flaps/spoilers. The fuselage has a monocoque forward section of fiberglass with a load-carrying lightweight alloy structure. The tailboom is an all-metal stressed-skin unit ending in an all-metal single-spar tailplane.

DSK "DUSTER"

The Duster is signed for amateur builders with an estimated construction time of 700 hours. Both plans and kit components are available. Its shoulder-type wings have a single wooden spar with plywood ribs and plywood covering. Wing features include washed-out tips, trailing-edge flaps, airbrakes, and ailerons. The fuselage is also built from plywood, with straight sides for simplified construction. Only the nose and fairings are fiberglass. Seating is for one pilot with the option of an open or closed cockpit. Also, optional power can be added without altering the design of the aircraft. A 26-hp powerplant is under development.

EXPLORER "AQUA GLIDER"

The Explorer Aircraft Aqua Glider can be towed behind any powerboat capable of speeds in excess of 35 mph. The biplane wings have a forward stagger and make use of a conventional

Manufacturer and model	Wingspan: ft. in.	Wing aspect ratio	Length overall: ft. in.	Empty: lbs.	Max. T-O: lbs.	Best glide ratio	at (speed): mph	Stalling speed: mph	Max. speed (still air)
USA									
Ahrens AR 124	42 7¾	13.5	20 0	350	640	26	69	34.5	150
AmEagle American Eaglet	36 0	18	16 0	160	360	27	52	38	115
Briegleb BG-12	50 0	17.9	21 11	525	750	34	NA	35	136
Bryan (Schreder) RS-15	49 2½	21.4	22 0	440	940	38	NA	46	150
Bryan (Schreder) HP-18	49 2½	21.1	23 6	420	920	40	NA	40	150
Caproni V1220LA Calif A-21S	80 3	25.7	30 6	961	1164	43	65	43	156
Caproni V1220LA Calif A-21SJ	80 3	25.7	30 6	1464	1781	43	75	43	156
DSK BJ-1b Duster	42 7¾	17.4	NA	390	620	NA	NA	NA	NA
Explorer PG-1 Aqua Glider	16 0	5	13 8	180	400	6.5	45	35	65
Flight Dynamics Seasprite	34 0	6.96	20 0	165	500	6	NA	NA	NA
Glaser-Dirks DG200	49 2½	22.5	23	570	990	44.6	68	41	168
Glasfugel Hornet C	49 2½	23	21	461	992	38.2	66.5	37.3	155
Glasfugel 304	49 2½	22.78	21 2	519	994	43	72	37	155
Marske Monarch C	42 0	9.5	11 6	220	450	19	40	24	70
Monnett Monerai	36 0	16.6	19 7	220	450	28	60	38	120
Oldershaw O-3	55 0	24.1	23 0	780	1000	37	68	50	125
PIK-20E	49 2½	22.5	21 5	660	1036	40	73	47	174
Rand KR-1B	27 0	NA	12 10	484	800	21.12	NA	38	144
Ryson ST-100 Cloudster	57 8	15.61	25 6.4	1212	1650	28	NA	NA	NA
Scheibe Flugzeugbau SF-H34	51 8	17	24 6	660	1100	35	59	40	156
Scheibe Flugzeugbau SF-25	59	17.8	24 7	970	1430	29	53	42.5	112
Scheibe Flugzeugbau SF-28	53 5	14.5	26 10	860	1300	27	53	40	112
Schweizer SGS 1-26	40 0	10	21 6½	430	700	23	NA	33	114
Schweizer SGS 2-32	57 1	18.05	26 9	850	1430	34	59	50	140
Schweizer SGS 2-33A	51 0	11.85	25 9	600	1040	22.25	NA	35	98
Schweizer SGS 1-34B	49 2½	16.04	25 9	550	800	34	52	NA	135
Schweizer SGS 1-35	49 2½	23.29	19 2	440	930	39	NA	32	139
Schweizer Sprite	46 2	15.2	20 7	475	710	31	53	36	125
Shempp-Hirth Nimbus 2C	66 7	28.6	23 11	770	1278	49	56	40	168
Shempp-Hirth Janus B	59 8	20.0	28 2	805	1370	39.5	68	40	137
Shempp-Hirth Janus C	65 4	23	28 3	783	1543	43.5	68	43	155
Shempp-Hirth Janus CM	65 4	23	28 3	1025	1543	42.5	68	43	155
Shempp-Hirth Ventus A	49 2	23.7	20 10	474	949	43.5	62	41	155
Shempp-Hirth Ventus B	49 2	23.7	21 5	486	949	43.5	62	41	155
Volpar-Spencer Drag-N-Fly	17 0	2.56	15 11	225	425	NA	NA	NA	75
Woodstock	39 0	14.5	NA	235	450	24	NA	35	NA

single wooden spar and balance floats on the tips of the lower wing. The hull is built from spruce and mahogany plywood, then covered with fiberglass up to the waterline. Standard twin jumper skis are attached to the bottom of the hull.

FLIGHT DYNAMICS "SEASPRITE"

Because the Flightsail (or unpowered Seasprite) can be fitted with a 90-hp engine as well as towed behind a 70-hp power-boat, it is listed in the homebuilt aircraft section of this book. Glider specifications are included in the specifications and performance chart in this section.

GLASER-DIRKS

Three models of the D-G single-seater glider—the standard-class DG-100 and DG-100G and the racing-class DG-200 sailplanes—combine superior flight performance and many common features. Very high and solid landing gear with a large 5-inch wheel, good rudder effectiveness, and docile stall characteristics make for safe landings in fields that would be difficult for others. The impact-resistant cockpit is designed to give maximum protection to the pilot in the event of a crash landing. The wings are a fiberglass-and-foam sandwich with flaps and carbon-fiber ailerons. The semimonocoque fuselage and T-tail are also of glass-and-foam structure.

GLASFLUGEL HORNET C/304

Two Glasflugel sailplanes are the Hornet C and the 304. The Hornet was the top standard-class sailplane at the 1979 nationals contest. The 304 is a 15-meter-class smaller version of the 604. The Hornet offers a retractable monowheel, water ballast, and a large flush-fitting canopy. It is a shoulder-wing cantilever monoplane with a T-tail and Wortmann wing section. The entire structure is a fiberglass monocoque and fiberglass/foam sandwich. Its carbon-fiber wing construction reduces the empty weight to 463 pounds compared to previous models. The Glasflugel 304 is a racing-class aircraft with a two-part double-tapered wing built with a fiberglass/hard-foam sandwich shell. The fuselage is a pure fiberglass shell with a one-piece canopy, and the empennage has a T-tail constructed of fiberglass and hard foam in a sandwich.

MARSKE "MONARCH C"

Plans and kits are available to the homebuilder for the Monarch C ultralight motorglider. Power is supplied by a 12-hp McCulloch engine located behind the pilot's seat; however, engines up to 20 hp can be used. The high wing makes use of a wooden rear spar with wood-and-foam ribs. Fiberglass covers the leading edge, and the remainder of the wing is covered with fabric. Despite its fragile appearance, the Monarch C is stressed to +8Gs and –4Gs. The fuselage pod is molded in two pieces then joined at the centerline; there are no horizontal tail surfaces. A single landing wheel is beneath pilot.

MONNETT "MONERAI"

The Monerai follows the precedents set by its VW-powered sportplane siblings Sonerai I and II by offering simplified construction and economy with high performance. Designed for the first-time builder or the expert, the Monerai can be either a true sailplane for the purist or, with the addition of a pod-mounted engine, a self-launching sailplane for those who wish to operate independent of towplanes. A chrome-moly-tubing primary-fuselage structure combines with a molded fuselage shell and extruded aluminum tail boom to make up a lightweight and ultrasmooth exterior with integral structural integrity for pilot safety. If any damage should be suffered by the fuselage structure, the molded shell can be easily removed to facilitate repairs. The preformed canopy, molded ABS components, sewn seat sling, and simplified control-system components are offered to make construction easier. The optional engine is designed to be removed easily so that the ship can be used as a pure sailplane at the pilot's whim. The wing uses a single-piece skin bonded to an extruded main spar and completely formed ribs.

OLDERSHAW 0-3

Vernon Oldershaw's motorglider features a retractable powerplant that can be used for takeoff and climb to soaring altitude. A 31-hp Yamaha snowmobile two-stroke flat-twin engine drives a wooden pusher propeller and feeds from a 2½-gallon fuel supply. The shoulder-type wings are built with a spruce spar, plywood ribs, and plywood skin; the wing does feature ailerons and airbrakes. The fuselage is all-wood except for fiberglass skin from the nose back to the wing.

PIK-20E

The PIK motorized glider has a manually retractable engine and propeller. The Rotax 503 500cc two-stroke two-cylinder engine produces 43 hp at 6,200 RPM. With double carburetors and resonance exhaust system, the whole snowmobile engine has been redesigned and built to aircraft requirements. The propeller is belt-driven giving a 1:2 reduction. When not in use, the powerplant is retracted into the fuselage by a manual crank and lever in the cockpit wall. The glider features fiberglass monocoque construction. Half of the fuselage/wing fairing has been taken to the wing so that the main rib and wing spar are 20mm higher in order to save weight. The wings, flaps, and complete tail are of sandwich construction with fiberglass skin and PVC-foam core. Wing spars are made of carbon fiber. The PIK boasts a maximum L/D ratio of 40 to 1. With power on, takeoff can be accomplished in less than 1,000 feet if a 50' obstacle has to be cleared and rate of climb is 787 fpm. Cruising speed is 84 mph at 75 percent power, burning 4.4 gph from the 8.7-gallon fuel tank.

RAND KR-1B

This sleek motorglider is essentially a stock KR-1 with longer wings and a bigger tail. For a wing curve, an RAF-48 standard KR-1 airfoil was used for the center section and the GA(W)-2 airfoil for the replacement outer panels. The outer wing section provides a clean and responsive curve for use with a spoiler/flap control, permitting deadstick landings at 70 mph IAS. Where the stock KR-1 wingspan is 17'2", the motorglider wingspan measures 27' from tip to tip, thereby increasing square footage from 64 to 91. Power is supplied by a 60-hp VW engine. Maximum cruise is 130 mph, and with 33 gallons of fuel, range is 950 miles while getting 29 mpg. At the standard 4-gph burn rate, 33 gallons should deliver 8.25 hours of flying at 120 mph for a range of 1,020 miles.

RYSON ST-100 "CLOUDSTER"

The Cloudster is a powered sailplane or an airplane that soars, whichever you prefer. The all-metal airplane is fitted with a 100-hp Continental and a Wortmann FX 67-170/17 airfoil. The flaps, which also serve as airbrakes, are electrically actuated, and the ailerons and flaps are interconnected to operate together from –12 degrees to +8 degrees. After that, the flaps continue down to any desired position. The two-wheel fixed landing gear is extremely clean and gives a gliding performance as good as if they were retractable. The tailwheel is steerable. Both seats are designed to accommodate parachutes, and the cockpit is heated and ventilated. A full-vision one-piece canopy hinges on the right side. As a touring airplane, it cruises at 135 mph (75-percent power) using just 6 gph to yield a range of 690 miles. At lower power settings, the range can be greatly increased. Only 20-percent power is required to keep the Cloudster in level flight.

SCHEIBE-FLUGZEUGBAU SF-H34/SF 25/SF 28

The two-place all-fiberglass SF-H34 has pleasant flight characteristics and a low construction weight. Schempp-Hirth airbrakes on the top surface of the wings are provided for glide-angle control. The nosewheel is fixed, and the main landing wheel is sprung. A disc brake is mounted with the main landing wheel. Visibility is excellent through the one-piece blown plexiglass canopy. Both seats offer adjustable rudder pedals and backrests. Due to the sailplane's low weight, small size, and rearward-placed mainwheel, it is quite easy to handle on the ground, an important consideration for training. Other motorgliders are the SF 25 and SF 28. The SF 25 is powered by a 65-hp Limbach engine, which is based upon well-proven Volkswagen components and is mounted forward of the cockpit in conventional tractor style. The gliding performance has been improved by an increased wingspan and modified fuselage. Seating is side by side. The SF 28 is powered by the same Limbach engine, but offers tandem seating; the front pilot is seated ahead of the wing, and the rear pilot sits over the main spar. The SF 25 cruises at 93 mph, climbs at 450 fpm, and takes off in 500–650 feet. The SF 28 cruises at 100 mph, climbs at 450 fpm, and takes off in 500–650 feet.

SCHEMPP-HIRTH

Schempp-Hirth sailplanes include the Ventus A, an advanced 15-meter-class plane with carbon-fiber technology, thin wings, and a low-profile fuselage. The Ventus B is a 15-meter-class craft with a larger cockpit for tall pilots. The Nimbus 2C (open class) has a 20.3-meter wingspan with either carbon or carbon/fiberglass construction. The Janus B has an 18.2-meter wingspan for high-performance tandem two-place flying. The Janus C has a 20-meter span with carbon wings, seating for two, and competition-type performance. The Janus CM, with a 20-meter span, is a two-place motorglider with carbon wings and fully retractable engine.

SCHWEIZER SGS 1-26

The single-seat SGS 1-26 was originally designed to be marketed in kit form to homebuilders. The later SGS 1-26E is the production version that introduced an all-metal fuselage. The all-metal midwing has fabric-covered ailerons and airbrakes. A nonretractable nosewheel with Schweizer brake is located behind the nose skid.

SCHWEIZER SGS 2-32

This high-performance sailplane has a cockpit that is large enough to carry a pilot and either one large or two smaller passengers. Production began in 1964, and national gliding records were established by pilots flying this aircraft. The wings and fuselage are all-metal structures. The wings have speed-limiting brakes; only the tail fin has a fabric-covered control surface. The nonretractable nosewheel is fitted with a hydraulic brake.

SCHWEIZER SGS 2-33A

Designed for training and family soaring, the SGS 2-33A flew for the first time in 1966 and entered production in 1967. The two-seater has a strut-braced high-wing built entirely from metal. The fuselage is constructed of welded steel tube, the nose covered with fiberglass, and the remainder is covered with fabric. In addition to the production model, a kit is available to homebuilders.

SCHWEIZER SGS 1-34B

This high-performance single-seat sailplane is designed to meet Standard Class specifications and is stressed to +8.33Gs and –5.33 Gs. The all-metal aluminum wings are the shoulder type with a Wortmann FX-61-163 at the root and Wortmann FX-60-126 at the tip. The fuselage is also built with aluminum alloy. The SGS 1-34B features double-flap speed-limiting airbrakes and an optional retractable nosewheel. The standard nonretractable nosewheel is fitted with a Cleveland brake and is balanced by a forward skid and tailwheel.

SCHWEIZER SGS 1-35A/1-35C

The SGS 1-35 is available in two models. The Model A is an unrestricted 15-meter-class sailplane with interconnected flaps and ailerons and an empty weight of 490 pounds. The Model C is a less expensive spin off intended for club use with no provision for water ballast. The C has a nonretractable nosewheel and a 425-pound empty weight. Its shoulder-type wings are covered with an aluminum-stressed skin and have no spoilers or airbrakes. The T-tail has a fabric-covered elevator. The landing gear consists of a nose skid and the choice of a tail skid or tailwheel. Instead of airbrakes, 80-degree flaps are used. G-force limits are 8.33 positive and 5.33 negative.

SCHWEIZER 1-36 "SPRITE"

The Sprite is an all-metal one-design sailplane that is compact, lightweight, and intended for clubs, schools, or individual owners who want Diamond "C" performance. With a 46-foot wingspan, it has an all-aluminum structure with standard effective dive brakes, T-tail, a large cockpit, and good visibility. Two landing gear positions are offered: a forward-wheel position, which makes the ship a "taildragger," or an aft-wheel position with a nonspring tailwheel and an aluminum nose skid. The latter is recommended for school and club operation. Standard equipment includes tip wheels, deluxe seat cushions, headrest, and rudder pedal adjusters.

VOLPAR-SPENCER "DRAG-N-FLY"

This single-seat water glider is built from plastic and foam materials and designed to be controlled easily by the nonpilot. The Drag-N-Fly is towed behind a ski boat and can be disconnected by the pilot. The fuselage is hinged to facilitate storage or travel. The cockpit is located forward of the biplane wings, and two floats are located underneath the lower wing. The airfoils are shaped from styrofoam blocks, reinforced by plywood spars, and covered with fiberglass. The fuselage and floats are made from plywood and are also covered with fiberglass.

"WOODSTOCK"

No special jigs or fixtures are needed to build the Woodstock. Every effort has been made to keep the hardware simple. The Woodstock weighs only 235 pounds empty and can be launched by auto tow, aero tow, winch tow, or bungee-launched off a hill. The wing is built around a single main spar formed as a hollow box and plywood ribs. The fuselage is also framed with plywood, and both wings (forward of the spar) and fuselage are covered with plywood. The wings pin to the fuselage with three ⁵⁄₁₆-inch pins and to each other with two ½-inch pins.

Appendix A

Aircraft prices

Aircraft listed in this appendix are grouped according to their price range. An actual market price will vary depending upon how the airplane is equipped and the age of the airplane.

UNDER $25,000
Single-engine aircraft

Aero Commander "Lark"
Aero Commander 200
Aeronca 65TC & L-3
Aeronca 7AC Champion
Aeronca 11AC/11CC
Aeronca 15AC "Sedan"
Beechcraft "Skipper"
Beechcraft Sport 150
Bellanca 7AC "Champ"
Bellanca "Junior"/"Cruisair"/"Cruisemaster"
Cessna 120/140
Cessna 150 "Commuter"/"Aerobat"
Cessna 152/152 "Aerobat"
Cessna 175 "Skylark"
Champion "Traveller"/"Challenger"
Champion 7FC "Tri-Traveller"
Ercoupe, Aircoupe
Fleet 80 "Canuck"
Funk Model B
Grumman American Trainer
Grumman American TR-2
Interstate S1B "Cadet"
Luscombe 8A-8F "Silvaire"
Luscombe 11-A "Sedan"
Maule M-4/M-5
Messerschmitt 209 "Monsun"
Mooney M-18 "Mite"
Piper J-3 "Cub"
Piper J-4 "Cub Coupe"
Piper PA-15 "Vagabond"/PA-16 "Clipper"/PA-17 "Pacer"
Piper J-5 "Cub Cruiser"/PA-12 "Super Cruiser"
Piper PA-20 "Pacer"
Piper PA-22 "Tri-Pacer"
Piper PA-22-108 "Colt"
Piper "Tomahawk"
Porterfield 65 "Collegiate"/"90 Flyabout"
Rearwin 8135 "Cloudster"
Rearwin 7000 "Sportster"
Rearwin 185 "Skyranger"
Stinson 76/L-5 "Sentinel"
Stinson 10A "Voyager"
Stinson 108 "Voyager"
Taylorcraft

Multiengine aircraft

Champion Lancer

$25,000–$75,000
Single-engine aircraft

American Champion "Scout"
American Champion "Citabria Explorer"

Beechcraft Custom 180 "Sundowner"
Beechcraft "Sierra"/"Super"/"Super 200"
Bellanca 8GCBC "Scout"
Bellanca "Citabria"
Bellanca 8KCAB "Decathlon"
Bellanca 300 "Viking"
Bucker BU131 "Jungmann"
Bucker "Jungmeister"
Cessna 170
Cessna 172 Skyhawk
Cessna Cutlass RG
Cessna Hawk XP
Cessna 177 "Cardinal Classic"
Cessna "Cardinal RG"
Cessna L-19 "Bird Dog"
Cessna 180 "Skywagon"
Cessna 182 "Skylane"
Cessna 185 "Skywagon"
Cessna AG "Carryall"
Cessna 190/195
Cessna "Ag Wagon"/"Ag Truck"/"Ag Husky"
Consolidated Vultee (Convair) L-1 3
de Havilland Canada DHC-1 "Chipmunk"
Diamona Aircraft DA-20 "Katana"
Fairchild PT-19/-23/-26
Fairchild F-24
Great Lakes Sport Trainer
Gulfstream American "Cheetah"
Gulfstream American "Tiger"
Gulfstream American "Super Ag-Cat"
Helio Courier H-295/395/391
Meyers OTW
Mooney Mark 22 "Mustang"
Navion "Rangemaster"
Piper PA-18 "Super Cub"
Piper "Cherokee"/"Cruiser"/"Warrior"
Piper PA 28-161 "Warrior II"
Piper Cherokee 180 "Archer"
Piper Cherokee "Arrow"/"Turbo Arrow"/"Arrow II"
Piper Cherokee 235 "Dakota/Pathfinder"
Piper Cherokee Six 260/300
Piper "Lance"/"Turbo Lance"
Piper "Comanche"
Piper "Pawnee"/"Brave"
PZL-104 Wilga "Thrush"
Republic "Seabee"
Rockwell Commander 112/112TC/114
Rockwell Commander "Thrush"
Ryan PT-22
Ryan "Navion"
Shinn 2150-A
Siai-Marchetti S.205 (WACO 5.220)/S.208
Socata "Rallye"
Sportavia Avion-Planeur RF4D
Stinson (Vultee) V-74/L-1 "Vigilant"
Stinson "Reliant"
Temco/Globe "Swift"
Arctic "Tern"
Varga Kachina
Waco open-cockpit biplanes
Zlin Z 526 L

Multiengine aircraft

Aero Commander 520
Aero Commander 560
Aero Commander 680/"Courser"
Beagle B.206 "Basset"
Beech 76 "Duchess"
Beech "Travel Air"
Beech "Twin Bonanza"
Beech "Queen Air"
Beech Model 18
Beech H18 "Super-Liner"
Camair "Twin Navion"
Cessna T-50 "Bobcat"
Cessna 310
Cessna 320 "Skyknight"
Cessna 337 "Skymaster"/"Pressurized Skymaster"
Gulfstream "Cougar"
Piper "Apache"
Piper PA-30/39 "Twin Comanche"
Piper PA-44 "Seminole"/"Turbo Seminole"
Piper Aztec
Wing "Derringer"

$75,000–$150,000
Single-engine aircraft

Aerospatiale "Tampico"
Aerospatiale "Tobago"/"Tobago XL"
Beagle "Pup"
Beechcraft Model 33 "Bonanza"/"Debonair"
Beechcraft Model 35 "Bonanza"
Boeing/Stearman "Kaydet" Series
Cessna "Skylane RG"
Cessna 205/206/"Stationair 6"
Cessna "Stationair 8"/7/"Skywagon" 207
Cessna 210 "Centurion"
Lake "Buccaneer"/"Renegade"
Mooney Mark 20 Series "201/231"/"Ranger"/"Chaparral"
Mooney M20J "MSE"
Mooney M20M "TLS"
Naval Aircraft Factory N3N-3
Noorduyn "Norseman" (C.C.F.)
Piper "Saratoga"/"Turbo"/"SP"/"Turbo SP"
Siai-Marchetti SF.260
Temco "Buckeroo"
Waco cabin biplanes

Multiengine aircraft

Beech "Baron"
Beech "Duke"

Cessna 335
Cessna 401/402
Cessna 411/414 Chancellor
Piper Aerostar 600/601
Riley "Turbo-Rocket"
Rockwell Commander "Shrike"
Rockwell Commander 685
Rockwell Commander 700

$150,000–$300,000
Single-engine aircraft

Aerospatiale "Trinidad/Trinidad TC"
Beechcraft "Staggerwing"
Beechcraft T-34 Mentor
Beechcraft A36/A36TC "Bonanza"
de Havilland Canada DHC-2 "Beaver"
de Havilland Canada DHC-3 "Otter"
Fairchild Hiller Turbo-Porter
Helio H-550A "Stallion"
Mooney M-20R "Ovation"

Multiengine aircraft

Cessna 303 "Crusader"
Cessna 340
Cessna 421 "Golden Eagle"
Cessna "Titan"
Grumman Goose/Widgeon
Piper Seneca/II/III
Piper PA-31 "Navajo"

OVER $300,000
Single-engine aircraft

AEROSPATIALE "TBM 700"

Multiengine aircraft

Beech 99 "Airliner"
Beech "King Air"
Beechcraft "Super King Air 300/350"
Beechcraft "Starship"
Cessna 441 "Conquest"
Cessna Corsair
Evangel 4500 STOL
Mitsubishi MU-2
Piper PA-31T "Cheyenne" I/II/III/IA/XL
Rockwell Turbo Commander 690A
Swearingen Merlin III
Swearingen Merlin IVA/"METRO II"

Appendix B

Addresses

PRODUCTION AIRCRAFT MANUFACTURERS

Aerospatiale
2701 Forum Drive
Grand Prairie, Texas 75053-4005

Raytheon (Beech Aircraft)
P.O. Box 85
Wichita, Kansas 67201-0085

Pinkney Aircraft (Bellanca)
3331 Summit Boulevard #27
Pensacola, Florida 32503

Cessna Aircraft Company
P.O. Box 7706
Wichita, Kansas 67277-7706

American Champion Aircraft
3202 Washington Avenue
Rochester, Wisconsin 53167

Gulfstream Aerospace
P.O. Box 22500
Oklahoma City, Oklahoma 73123

Lake Aircraft
606 Oyer Boulevard
Kissimee, Florida 32741

Lake Maule (Maule)
Route 5, Box 319
Moultrie, Georgia 31768

Mooney Aircraft Corporation
P.O. Box 72
Kerville, Texas 78028

Piper Aircraft Corporation
Vero Beach, Florida 32960

Commander Aircraft Company
Wiley Post Airport Hangar 8
Bethany, Oklahoma 73008

Siai-Marchetti
800-859-4757

Socata (see Aerospatiale)

HOMEBUILT/KITBUILT AIRCRAFT

ACE MODEL D "BABY ACE"
ACE MODEL E "JUNIOR ACE"
Ace Aircraft Co.
Chesapeake, WV 25315

AERO DESIGN DG-1
AERO DESIGNS "PULSAR"
Pulsar
11910 Radium Street
San Antonio, Texas 78216

AEROSPORT "QUAIL"
AEROSPORT "RAIL"
AEROSPORT "SCAMP"
AEROSPORT "WOODY'S PUSHER"
Aerosport Inc.
Box 278
Holly Springs, NC 27540

AERO-SYSTEMS "CADET STF"
Aero-Systems
9031 Suncrest St.
Wichita, KS 67212

AIRCRAFT DESIGNS, INC. "STALLION"
Aircraft Designs, Inc.
6 Harris Ct., Bldg. S
Monterey, CA 93940

AIRCRAFT SPRUCE & SPECIALTY IAC "ONE DESIGN"
Aircraft Spruce & Specialty
P.O. Box 424
Fullerton, CA 92632

ANDERSON "KINGFISHER"
Anderson Aircraft
40 Sunnyside Road
Mahwah, NJ 07430

ARISTOCRAFT III
O'Neil Airplane Co.
791 Livingston
Carlyle, IL 62231

AVID AIRCRAFT, INC. MARK IV AEROBATIC
  SPEEDWING
AVID AIRCRAFT, INC. MARK IV HIGH-GROSS STOL
AVID AIRCRAFT, INC. MAGNUM
Avid Aircraft
P.O. Box 728
Caldwell, Idaho 83606

BAKENG "DUCE"
Bakeng Aircraft
19025 92nd W.
Edmonds, WA 98020

BEDE BD-4
BEDE BD-6
Bede Aircraft Corp.
Spirit of St. Louis Airport
18421 Edison Ave.
Chesterfield, MO 63005

BEDE BD-5 "MICRO"
BD Micro-Technologies, Inc.
1260 Wade Rd.
Siletz, OR 97380

BEDE JET CORP. "BD-10"
Bede Jet Corp.
Spirit of St. Louis Airport
18421 Edison Ave.
Chesterfield, MO 63005

BEETS G/B SPECIAL
Stolp Starduster Corp.
4301 Twining
Riverside, CA 92509

BENSEN GYROCOPTER
Bensen Aircraft
RDU Airport
P.O. Box 2746
Raleigh, NC 27602

"BIG COOTIE"
Roy L. Shirlen
4713 Oakridge
Winston-Salem, NC 27105

BIRDMAN TL-1
Birdman Aircraft Inc.
480 Midway Airport
Daytona Beach, FL 32014

BOWERS "FLY BABY"
BOWERS "FLY BI-BABY"
BOWERS "NAMU II"
Peter M. Bowers
10458 16th Ave. South
Seattle, WA 98168

BROKAW "BULLET"
Brokaw Aviation Inc.
2625 Johnson Point
Leesburg, FL 32748

BUSHBY "MIDGET MUSTANG"
BUSHBY "MUSTANG II"
Bushby Aircraft Inc.
P.O. Box 13B
Minooka, IL 60447

CASSUTT SPECIAL II
Southern Aeronautical Corp.
14100 Lake Candlewood Ct.
Miami Lakes, FL 33014

CAVALIER
MacFam World Traders
4623 Fortune Road S.E.
Calgary, Alberta T2A 2A7

CHRISTEN "EAGLE II"
Aviat, Inc.
The Airport
Box 1149
Afton, WY 83110

CONDOR K-10 "SHOESTRING"
Condor Aero Inc.
Box 762
Vero Beach, FL 32960

CORBY CJ-1 "STARLET"
510 NW 46th Terrace
Plantation, FL 33317

CVJETKOVIC CA-61 "MINI ACE"
CVJETKOVIC CA-65
Anton Cvjetkovic
5324 W. 121 St.
Hawthorne, CA 90250

D'APUZZO "JUNIOR AERO SPORT"
D'APUZZO "SENIOR AERO SPORT"
D'APUZZO "SPORTWING"
Nick E. D'Apuzzo
1029 Blue Rock Lane
Blue Bell, PA 19422

DAVIS DA-2A
DAVIS DA-5A
Leeon D. Davis
Box 207
405 North St. Paul
Stanton, TX 79782

DIAMANT C.P. 60
E. Lifiner
P.O. Box 272
St. Laurent, Montreal, Canada

DOODLE BUG
L.K. Heuberger
10605 Whitehawk
Reno, NV 89508

DSK-1 "HAWK"
DSK Airmotive Inc.
Box 629
Fort Walton Beach, FL 32548

DURAND MARK V
Durand Assoc.
84th & McKinley
Omaha, NE 68122

DYKE DELTA
John W. Dyke
2840 Old Yellow Springs Road
Fairborn, OH 45324

EAA "ACRO-SPORT"
EAA "ACRO-SPORT II"
EAA "SUPER ACRO-SPORT"
EAA BIPLANE
EAA HEATH PARASOL
EAA NESMITH "COUGAR"
EAA "POBER PIXIE"
Acro Sport, Inc.
P.O. Box 462
Hales Corners, Wisconsin 53130

EDI "EXPRESS 90"
Express Design, Inc.
P.O. Box 609
Redmond, OR 97756

EOS
EOS/SFA of California
751 Fairway Lane
Anaheim, CA 92807

EVANS VP-I "VOLKSPLANE"
EVANS VP-2
Evans Aircraft
P.O. Box 744
La Jolla, CA 92037

EXPERIMENTAL AVIATION "BERKUT"
Experimental Aircraft Berkut
3025 Airport Avenue
Santa Monica, CA 90405

FALCONAR AMF S-14
FALCONAR "FLYING FLEA"
Falconar
11343 104 St.
Edmonton, Alberta T5G 2K7 CANADA

F.E.W. "P-51D/TF"
Fighter Escort Wings
Ardmore Airpark No. 206
Gene Autry, OK 73436-0206

FIKE MODEL E
William J. Fike
Box 683
Anchorage, AK 99501

FLAGLOR "SCOOTER"
Headberg Aviation
11620 SW 131 Avenue
Miami, FL 33186

FLIGHT DYNAMICS "FLIGHTSAIL VII"
Flight Dynamics
Box 5070
Raleigh, NC 27607

HARMON "DER DONNERSCHLAG"
HARMON "MR. AMERICA"
Harmon Engineering Co.
Rt. 1, Box 186
Howe, TX 75059

HARRIS GEODETIC LW 108
J. Warren Harris
283 East–500 North
Vernal, UT 84078

HATZ CB-1 BIPLANE
Dudley R. Kelly
Route 4
Versailles, KY 40383

HlLLMAN "HORNET"
Hillman Helicopters, Inc.
Box 1411
Scottsdale, AZ 85252

HOLLMAN HA-2M "SPORTSTER"
Hollman Aircraft
11082 Bel Aire Ct.
Cupertino, CA 95014

HOVEY "BETA BIRD"
HOVEY "WHING-DING II"
R.W. Hovey
Box 1074
Canyon Country, CA 91351

INTERNATIONAL COMMUTER IIA
International Helicopters
Box 107
Mayville, NV 14757

JANOWSKI "DON QUIXOTE"
Andrew Baracz
56 Signal Hill Trail
Sparta, NJ 07871

JAVELIN "WICHAWK"
Javelin Aircraft Co.
9175 East Douglas
Wichita, KS 67207

JEFFAIR "BARRACUDA"
Jeffair Corp.
Box 975
Renton, WA 98055

JODEL D-11 "BEBE"
Sturgeon Air Ltd.
36 Airport Road
Edmonton, Alberta, Canada

"JUNGSTER I"
"JUNGSTER II"
K & S Aircraft
4623 Fortune Road SE
Calgary, Alberta, Canada

JURCA MJ-2 "TEMPETE"
JURCA MJ-5 "SIROCCO"
JURCA MJ-7 "BABY MUSTANG"
JURCA MJ-8 "BABY FOCKE-WULF"
JURCA MJ-10 "BABY SPITFIRE"
Jurca Plans
581 Helen Street
Mt. Morris, MI 48458

KELEHER IK-1 "LARK"
James Keleher
2150 Chester Drive
Tracy, CA 95376

"KITTIWAKE"
Proctor Aircraft Association Ltd.
Greenball, Crawley Ridge
Camberley, Surrey, England

KRAFT "SUPER FLI"
Kraft Systems, Inc.
450 W. California Ave.
Box 1268
Vista, CA 92083

LACEY M-10
Joe Lacey
1600 McArthur
Irving, TX 75060

LACO-125
LACO
Banning Municipal Airport
P.O. Box 415
Desert Hot Springs, CA 92240

LANCAIR "320/360"
LANCAIR "IV"
LANCAIR "ES"
Lancair International
2244 Airport Way
Redmond, OR 97756

LARKIN "SKYLARK"
Larkin Aircraft Corp.
Box 66899
Scotts Valley, CA 95066

LEVI RL3 "MONSOON"
Western Aircraft Supplies
623 Markerville
Alberta, Canada

LOVING'S "LOVE"
Neal Loving
660 Wright St.
Yellow Springs, OH 45387

LUTON "MAJOR"
LUTON "MINOR"
Sturgeon Air Ltd.
36 Airport Road
Edmonton, Alberta, Canada

MacDONALD S-20
MacDonald Aircraft Co.
1282 Fowler Creek Rd.
Sonoma, CA 95476

MEAD "ADVENTURE"
Mead Engineering
Box 354
Colwich, KS 67030

MERKEL MARK II
Merkel Airplane Company
3920 North Charles Street
Wichita, KS 67204

MEYER'S "LITTLE TOOT"
Meyer Aircraft
576 Abby Drive
Corpus Christi, TX 78413

MILLER JM-2
J.W. Miller Aviation Inc.
Horseshoe Bay Airport
Box 757
Marble Falls, TX 78654

MILLER "LIL' RASCAL"
Aeroneering Inc.
Box 22064
Savannah, GA 31403

MINI COUPE
Bill Johnson
Box 1
Hillsboro, OR 97123

MINI-HAWK "TIGER HAWK"
Mini-Hawk International Inc.
1930 Stewart Street
Santa Monica, CA 90404

MONNETT "MONEX"
MONNETT "SONERAI"
MONNETT "SONERAI II"
Great Plains Aircraft Supply Co. Inc.
P.O. Box 545
Boys Town, NE 68010

MOONEY "MITE"
Mooney Mite Aircraft Corp.
Box 3999
Charlottesville, VA 22903

OLDFIELD "BABY LAKES"
Barney Oldfield Aircraft Company
P.O. Box 5974
Cleveland, OH 44101

OSPREY
OSPREY II
Osprey Aircraft
3741 El Ricon Way
Sacramento, CA 95825

PAYNE "KNIGHT TWISTER IMPERIAL"
Vernon W. Payne
Rt. 2, Box 319M
Escondido, CA 92025

PAZMANY PL-1
PAZMANY PL-2
PAZMANY PL-4A
Pazmany Aircraft Corp.
P.O. Box 80051
San Diego, CA 92138

PIETENPOL "AIR CAMPER"
Ron Pietenpol
1604 Meadow Circle S.E.
Rochester, MN 55904-5251

PITTS S-1S "SPECIAL"
Aviat, Inc.
The Airport
Box 1149
Afton, WY 83110

POLLIWAGEN
Polliwagen
8782 Hewitt Place
Garden Grove, CA 92644

POWELL "ACEY DEUCY"
John C. Powell
4 Donald Drive
Middletown, RI 02840

PROWLER AVIATION "PROWLER/JAGUAR"
Prowler Aviation, Inc.
3707 Meadow View Dr.
Redding, CA 96002

QUESTAIR "SPIRIT"
QUESTAIR "VENTURE"
Questair, Inc.
3800 McAree Rd.
Waukegan, IL 60087

"QUICKIE"
"QUICKIE Q2"
Quickie Aircraft Corp.
P.O. Box 786
Mojave, CA 93501

RAND KR-1
Rand-Robinson Engineering Co.
6171 Cornell Dr.
Huntington Beach, CA 92647

RAND KR-2
Rand-Robinson Engineering, Inc.
5842 K McFadden Ave.
Huntington Beach, CA 92649

REDFERN FOKKER DRI
REDFERN NIEUPORT 21
Redfern & Sons, Inc.
Route 1
Athol, ID 83801

RENEGADE
Southern Aeronautical Corp.
14100 Lake Candlewood Court
Miami Lakes, FL 33014

RICHARD COMMUTER
Charles K. Richard
2561 W. Avenue K
Lancaster, CA 93534

RLU-1 "BREEZY"
Charles B. Roloff
Breezy Aircraft
Box 358
Palos Park, IL 60464

ROTORWAY "SCORPION 133"
RotorWay
14805 S. Interstate 10
Tempe, AZ 85284

RUTAN "LONG-EZ"
RUTAN "VARIEZE"
RUTAN "VARIVIGGEN"
Rutan Aircraft Factory
Box 656
Mojave Airport, CA 93501

SAPPHIRE C.P. 80
E. Littner
Box 272
Saint-Laurent, Quebec
H4L 4V6, Canada

SAWYER "SKYJACKER II"
Ralph V. Sawyer
45432 Leatherwood
Lancaster, CA 93534

UAC-200 "SCRAPPY"
W.A. Skipper
1907 14th Avenue, Greeley, CO 80631

S.E. 5A Replica
Replica Plans
P.O. Box 346
Yarrow, British Columbia
VOX 2AO Canada

SEQUOIA F.8L "FALCO"
Sequoia Aircraft Corp.
900 West Franklin St.
Richmond, VA 23220

SHEFFIELD "SKEETER X-1"
Sheffield Aircraft
4750 S. Mead
Littleton, CO 80123

SINDLINGER "HAWKER HURRICANE"
Sindlinger Aircraft
37030 204th Avenue S.E.
Auburn, WA 98002

"SIZZLER"
L.K. Heuberger
10605 Whitehawk
Reno, NV 89508

SKYSTAR "KITFOX"
SKYSTAR "VIXEN"
SkyStar Aircraft Corp.
100K N. Kings Rd.
Nampa, ID 83687

SMITH "MINIPLANE"
Dorothy Smith
3502 Sunny Hills Dr.
Norco, CA 91760

SMYTH "SIDEWINDER"
George Blair
Box 185
Newbury Park, CA 91320

SORRELL "HIPERBIPE"
Sorrel Aviation
Rt. 1, Box 660
Tenino, WA 98589

SPENCER "AIR CAR"
Spencer Amphibian Air Car
12780 Pierce St.
Pacoima, CA 91331

SPEZIO "TUHOLER"
William Spezio
25 Madison Ave.
Northampton, MA 01060

"SPORTAIRE"
Rogers Aircraft
758 Libby Drive
Riverside, CA 92507

"SPRITE"
Practavia Ltd.
Wycombe Air Park
Booker, Buckinghamshire, U.K.

"STARDUST II"
"STARDUST JS-2"
J.R. Scoville
172 Cedarwood Terrace
Rochester, NV 14609

STEEN "SKYBOLT"
Steen Aero Lab
15623 De Gaulle Circle
Brighton, CO 80601

STEWART "FOO FIGHTER"
STEWART "HEADWIND"
Stewart Aircraft
11420 Route 165
Salem, OH 44460

STEWART "S-51D"
Stewart 51, Inc.
3120 Airport W. Dr.
Vero Beach, FL 32960

STODDARD-HAMILTON "GLASAIR SUPER II TD"
STODDARD-HAMILTON "GLASAIR III"
STODDARD-HAMILTON "GLASTAR"
STODDARD-HAMILTON "TURBINE 250/III"
Stoddard-Hamilton Aircraft, Inc.
18701 58th Ave. N.E.
Arlington, WA 98223

STOLP "ACRODUSTER 1"
STOLP "ACRODUSTER TOO"
STOLP SA-100 "STARDUSTER"
STOLP "STARDUSTER TOO"
STOLP SA500 "STARLET"
STOLP "V-STAR"
Stolp Starduster Corp.
4301 Twining Street
Riverside, CA 92509

STUKA JU 87-82
Louis Langhurst
Rt. 1, Box 315
Carriere, MS 39426

SUPER EMERAUDE C.P. 328
E. Littner
Box 272
Saint-Laurent, Quebec
H4L 4V6, Canada

"SYLKIE"
Wayne Barton
11145 Cherokee St.
Northglenn, CO 80234

TAYLOR MODEL A "COOT" (AMPHIBIAN)
TAYLOR "MINI-IMP"
M.B. (Molt) Taylor
P.O. Box 1171
Longview, WA 98632

TAYLOR "MONOPLANE"
TAYLOR "TITCH"
Mrs. John F. Taylor
25 Chesterfield Crescent
Leighon-Sea, Essex, England

"TEENIE TWO"
C.Y. Parker
Box 625
Coolidge, AZ 85228

TINKER TOY
Don Taylor
220 S. Frederick Ave.
Evansville, IN 47714

TOURBILLION YC-12
E. Liftner
P.O. Box 272
St. Laurent, Montreal, Canada

TRI-R TECHNOLOGIES "KIS"
TRI-R TECHNOLOGIES "KIS TR-4 CRUISER"
Tri-R Technologies
1114 E. 5th St.
Oxnard, CA 93030

TROYER SPORTPLANE VX
Troyer Boats
Route 4
White Cloud, Ml 49349

"TURBULENT"
Sturgeon Air Ltd.
36 Airport Road
Edmonton, Alberta, Canada

TURNER T-40
TEDDE
3717 Ruth Road
Ft. Worth, TX 76118

TURNER T-40A
TURNER T-40B
Turner Educational Ent.
Box 425
Stratford, CT 06497

VAN'S AIRCRAFT, INC. "RV-3"
Van's Aircraft
22730 SW Francis
Beaverton, OR 97005

VCA-1
Jame Dennis Enterprises
1601 North-West 29 St.
Miami, FL 33142

"VELOCITY"
Velocity Aircraft
200 W. Airport Dr.
Sebastian, FL 32958

VIKING "DRAGONFLY"
Viking Aircraft
P.O. Box 9000
Suite 234P
Carlsbad, CA 93008

VOLMER VJ-22 "SPORTSMAN"
Volmer Aircraft
Box 5222
Glendale, CA 91201

WAG-AERO "CUBy"
WAG-AERO "WAG-A-BOND"
Wag-Aero, Inc.
P.O. Box 181
1216 North Road
Lyons, WI 53148

WAR "CORSAIR"
WAR "FOCKE-WULF"
WAR Aircraft Replicas
348 South Eighth St.
Santa Paula, CA 93023

WATSON "WINDWAGON"
Gary Watson
Route 1
Newcastle, TX 76372

WENDT WH-1 "TRAVELER"
Fred Reynolds
3611 Waco St.
San Diego, CA 92117

WHITE "DER JAGER"
Marshall White
5141 Warner Ave.
Meadowlark Airport
Huntington Beach, CA 92647

"WHITE LIGHTNING"
White Lightning Aircraft Corp.
179 Aviation Ave.
P.O. Box 497
Walterboro, SC 29488

WITTMAN "TAILWIND"
WITTMAN "WITT'S VEE"
S.J. Wittman
P.O. Box 276
Oshkosh, WI 54901

ZENAIR MONO-Z
ZENAIR "TRI-Z"
ZENAIR "ZENITH"
Zenair Ltd.
236 Richmond St.
Richmond Hill, Ontario
Canada L4C 3Y8

SAILPLANES AND MOTORGLIDERS

AHRENS AR 124
Ahrens Aircraft Corp.
P.O. Box 432
Ramey, Puerto Rico 00604

AmEAGLE "AMERICAN EAGLET"
AmEagle Corp.
841 Winslow Court
Muskegon, MI 49441

BRIEGLEB BG-12
Sailplane Corp. of America
El Mirage Route, Box 101
Adelanto, CA 92301

BRYAN (SCHREDER) RS-15
BRYAN (SCHREDER) HP-18
Bryan Aircraft Inc.
Williams County Airport
P.O. Box 488
Bryan, OH 43506

CAPRONI VIZZOLA CALIF A-21S/A-21SJ
Distributed in the United States by Morris-Thomson Aviation
of Statesboro, Georgia.

DSK "DUSTER"
DSK Aircraft Corp.
13161 Sherman Way
North Hollywood, CA 91605

EXPLORER "AQUA GLIDER"
Explorer Aircraft Co.
P.O. Box 60036
Reno, NV 89506

FLIGHT DYNAMICS "SEASPRITE"
Flight Dynamics, Inc.
P.O. Box 5070
State University Station
Raleigh, NC 27607

GLASER-DIRKS
Distributed in the United States by Glaser-Dirks West of
Berkeley, California.

MARSKE "MONARCH C"
Marske Aircraft Corp.
130 Crestwood Dr.
Michigan City, IN 46360

MONNETT "MONERAI"
Great Plains Aircraft Supply Co. Inc.
P.O. Box 545
Boys Town, NE 68010

OLDERSHAW 0-3
Oldershaw
2508 Tailsman Dr.
Bakersfield, CA 93304

PIK-20E
The PIK motorized glider is distributed in this country by
PIK Pacific.

RAND KR-1B
Jeanette Rand
Rand-Robinson Engineering Inc.
6171 Cornell Drive
Huntington Beach, CA 92647

RYSON ST-100 "CLOUDSTER"
Ryson Aviation Corp.
548 San Fernando St.
San Diego, CA 92106

SCHEIBE-FLUGZEUGBAU SF-H34/SF 25/SF 28
Distributed in the United States by Morris-Thompson Aviation of Statesboro, Georgia.

SCHEMPP-HIRTH
Sold in the United States by Morris-Thomson Aviation.

SCHWEIZER SGS 1-26
SCHWEIZER SGS 2-32
SCHWEIZER SGS 2-33A
SCHWEIZER SGS 1-34B
SCHWEIZER SGS 1-35A/1-35C
SCHWEIZER 1-36 "SPRITE"
Schweizer Aircraft Corp.
Box 147
Elmira, NY 14902

"WOODSTOCK"
DSK Aircraft Corp.
13161 Sherman Way
North Hollywood, CA 91605

Index